n Vernon 25th

have had the pleasure
etters from you since
in France, and can
rquis de la Fayette
t an acknowledge:
altho' his doing it is
the same time am sur
Company —
have a little more
l ever should be) I
at the occurrences
that have come under

The Founding Fathers

His Excel: G: WASHINGTON Esq: LL.D. LATE COMMANDER IN CHIEF OF THE ARMIES OF THE U.S. OF AMERICA & PRESIDENT OF THE CONVENTION OF 1787

Painted & Engrav'd by C.W. Peale. 1787

The Founding Fathers

GEORGE WASHINGTON

A Biography in His Own Words

Edited by
RALPH K. ANDRIST

With an Introduction by
DONALD JACKSON
Editor, *The Papers of George Washington*

JOAN PATERSON KERR
Picture Editor

Published by NEWSWEEK, New York
Distributed by HARPER & ROW, PUBLISHERS, INC.

George Washington, A Biography in His Own Words,
has been produced by the Newsweek Book Division:

Joseph L. Gardner, Editor

Janet Czarnetzki, Art Director

S. Arthur Dembner, Publisher

This book is based on *The Papers of George Washington,*
edited by Donald Jackson and published by the University Press of Virginia.
The texts of Washington documents in this edition have been
supplied by Mr. Jackson, and permission to reproduce excerpts
from these documents has been obtained from their owners.

For information address Harper & Row, Publishers, Inc.
10 East 53rd Street, New York, N.Y. 10022
Published simultaneously in Canada by Fitzhenry & Whiteside Limited, Toronto.

Contents

Introduction

by Donald Jackson
Editor of The Papers of George Washington

Among the nation's finest historical treasures is the collection of letters, diaries, military records, and financial documents left to us by George Washington. The wonder is that so many have survived, considering how the ravages of time and the carelessness of human hands have dealt with them.

The Library of Congress now holds a large share of these papers, and they are treated with professional care. Hundreds of others are lodged in libraries and archives, and in private collections; these, too, are given the respectful custodianship they deserve. But it was not always so.

Washington himself was the first to realize that his lifetime of public service had generated a body of papers well worth preserving. He hired secretaries and copyists, took care to see that his correspondence was boxed in sturdy trunks and shipped to safety during the Revolution, and even planned to build a small library at Mount Vernon where the records of a young nation and its first President could be stored and organized. Although the library never was built, the attention that Washington paid to his papers was without doubt the greatest factor in their survival. He could not have predicted that his heirs and fellow countrymen would be less dedicated to keeping the collection intact and available to posterity.

When Washington died in 1799, he bequeathed most of his papers to his nephew Bushrod Washington, a justice of the Supreme Court, who also was to have the Mount Vernon mansion and some of the lands around it after the death of Martha Washington. There is no reason to believe that Bushrod was not fully devoted to the preservation of the papers—although he had a habit of giving away samples to autograph seekers. Perhaps he merely failed to appreciate how zealous a stewardship is required to prevent such a collection from eroding away at the hands of well-meaning persons.

Martha Washington had a widow's prerogative to destroy the letters she had exchanged with her husband, and destroy them she did. At least, her granddaughter said that Martha burned them, and no more than two letters from Washington to his wife are known to have survived.

Bushrod planned to write a biography of his uncle—was planning it, in fact, within two weeks after Washington's death—but somehow he never got to the writing stage. Instead, he agreed that the work should be written by John Marshall, who was then Secretary of State and later would become Chief Justice. By 1807 Marshall had completed the five volumes entitled *The Life of George Washington*, the first extensive biography of our first President. During his work on these volumes, he borrowed large quantities of the original papers and kept them in Richmond, some for more than twenty years. Improper storage caused heavy damage from rodents, dampness, and other enemies of paper and ink.

If Bushrod was too generous in giving away samples of Washington's letters to autograph collectors and souvenir hunters, he was far outdistanced in this endeavor by the next biographer of Washington. Jared Sparks, editor of the *North American Review*, had decided by 1826 that he wished to publish a large edition of Washington's writings. Bushrod hesitated to make the material available because he and Marshall had been working on a similar undertaking, but in 1827 he agreed to Sparks's proposal. Thus the precious archive fell into the temporary possession of a man who could not only rewrite Washington's words without a qualm but could also mutilate and give away pages, partial pages, and even single lines of text to anyone who asked.

Sparks's editorial method must be viewed against the background of his times, when strict procedures for the arrangement and publication of historical documents had not been well developed. Writing to Bushrod at the beginning of his editorial work in 1827, he said: "I believe it may be set down as a rule, that in every case it will be safe to print, even with the names, whatever reflects credit upon all persons concerned, but whenever the heat of party, or local causes, give an unfavorable tone to the writer's feelings and sentiments, and lead him into harsh reflections upon others, there will be room for deliberation, and perhaps a motive for passing by letters in other respects highly interesting." That is not the way in which valid history is written.

The willingness of Jared Sparks to distribute free samples is shown in this letter to Richard Henry Dana, Jr., in 1861, long years after his need to have access to the manuscripts was ended: "I regret that I cannot furnish you with an autograph letter of Washington. I have had many such, but the collectors have long ago exhausted my stock. The best I can do is to enclose a very small specimen of his handwriting." The specimen, of course, represented a letter mutilated and destroyed.

This literary carnage was made easier by the fact that Sparks was allowed to take great quantities of letters to his home in Boston. What the world gained from it all was a twelve-volume edition called *The Writings of George Washington* (Boston, 1834–37). Because Sparks was so selective, so prone to revise, and so eager not to publish anything that he thought might show Washington in an improper light, the edition is far less useful than it might have been.

Bushrod Washington died in 1829 and the papers passed into the hands of his nephew, George Corbin Washington. Because officers of the United States Government had long recognized the value of the manuscripts, the Secretary of State asked the new owner in 1833 if he would consider placing them on deposit with the Government. After some negotiation, which included getting Sparks to begin returning the papers in his possession, an actual sale, not a deposit, was arranged in 1834. George C. Washington spent two more years, and made a trip to Sparks's home in Boston, before he had convinced himself that he had rounded up all the public papers of the first President. A parcel of private papers was sold to the Government later.

Now the safety of the papers was assured. They might suffer a bit from the damp summers and the dry winter heat of government buildings in the District of Columbia, but they were at least protected from the snip-snip of Jared Sparks's scissors.

It is obvious that Washington's heirs could not have turned over all the manuscripts, including incoming and outgoing correspondence. Washington failed to retain copies of many letters that he wrote; those he received were subject to loss. Even after a substantial portion had been acquired by the Government, hundreds more remained unknown or unavailable.

Through the years these papers have slowly accumulated in collections large and small. Well-known institutions such as the New York Public Library, the Historical Society of Pennsylvania, the Massachusetts Historical Society, and the Huntington Library have acquired great collections. Autograph collectors still maintain a lively interest in Washington letters, and most of these are eventually donated or sold to public institutions, where they become available for study. Although it will be many years before copies of every extant Washington document are assembled in one place, it is now possible to estimate that 95 per cent of such papers are known.

Publication of Washingtoniana continued sporadically after the Jared Sparks edition. A formidable but selective edition was edited by Worthington C. Ford and published between 1889 and 1893. Today most students of Washington rely upon *The Writings of George Washington*, edited by John C. Fitzpatrick and published in thirty-nine volumes (1931–44) by the George Washington Bicentennial Commission. Fitzpatrick's labors were enormous, and performed under difficult circumstances, including a limited staff and considerable pressure to hold down costs during the Depression years. It was inevitable that he should miss many important documents. What is more significant, however, is the fact that he was able to publish only letters and other documents written by Washington. None of the incoming correspondence was reproduced. As someone has said, reading the volumes is a bit like listening to only one side of a conversation.

By 1966 the feeling was growing among historians, librarians, and archivists that a new edition of Washington papers was very much needed. Scholars no longer would settle for one side of a correspondence. The United States was looking forward to a series of Bicentennial observances in the 1970's, and no figure was more important than Washington in the forging of a new, young nation. It seemed regrettable that no intensive work was being done on Washington's papers, especially since the papers of other Founding Fathers—Franklin, Adams, Jefferson, Hamilton, and Madison—were the subject of vigorous publishing programs. Washington's home state of Virginia soon offered the most suitable combination of sponsors for such a new, comprehensive edition of Washington's papers. The Mount Vernon Ladies' Association of the Union, which has owned and preserved Washington's home along the Potomac for more than a century, volunteered financial support and expert guidance. The University of Virginia in Charlottesville offered office space, staff, additional financing, and the facilities of the famed Alderman Library. Federal agencies are participating. A statewide institution, the University Press of

Virginia, will begin publication of the edition in 1975, and the complete work will require more than sixty volumes.

Ever since John Marshall's day, books dealing with Washington have appeared regularly. These have ranged from the quaint fantasies of Mason Weems, who gave us the hatchet and the cherry tree, to serious studies by men such as Washington Irving, Woodrow Wilson, Douglas Southall Freeman, and James Thomas Flexner. The best of these have one thing in common: reliance on that priceless creation of Washington and the men of his times, the papers so miraculously preserved in the face of heavy odds.

In this biography prepared by the Newsweek Book Division, Ralph Andrist has chosen to let Washington speak mainly for himself. His letters are always wise, sometimes eloquent, and never dull to a generation that has taken renewed interest in one of the greatest historical figures of all time.

EDITORIAL NOTE

Most of the Washington writings reprinted in this biography have been excerpted from the longer original documents being published in their entirety by the University Press of Virginia. Omissions at the beginning or ending of a document are indicated by ellipses only if the extract begins or ends in the middle of a sentence; omissions within a quoted passage are also indicated by ellipses. The original spellings have been retained; editorial insertions are set within square brackets.

Chronology of Washington and His Times

George Washington born at Popes Creek, Virginia, February 22 (February 11, Old Style)	1732	Charter granted to Colony of Georgia
	1739	War of Jenkins' Ear, 1739–42
	1740	King George's War, 1740–48
Father dies	1743	
Travels west with surveying party	1748	
Helps lay out town of Alexandria	1749	
Sails to Barbados with brother Lawrence	1751	
Courts Elizabeth Fauntleroy; Lawrence Washington dies	1752	Iroquois cede land south of Ohio River to Virginia; French move to defend Ohio territory
Adjutant in provincial militia; leads mission to French in Ohio country	1753	Fort Duquesne erected by French; Albany Congress
Battle of Fort Necessity; resigns commission; leases Mount Vernon	1754	French and Indian War, 1754–63
Fort Duquesne expedition; commander of Virginia forces; Dagworthy dispute	1755	Braddock assumes British command in America
Visits Boston to appeal to Shirley	1756	Hostilities spread to Europe, Seven Years' War, 1756–63
Illness forces retirement from field	1757	
Proposes to Martha Custis; action in Ohio; resigns commission	1758	French abandon Fort Duquesne
Marries Martha Custis, January 6; enters House of Burgesses	1759	
	1760	Reign of George III of England, 1760–1820
Visits Dismal Swamp	1763	Proclamation of 1763
	1764	Sugar Act and Colonial Currency Act
	1765	Stamp Act
	1767	Townshend duties adopted
Wins Ohio land grant; signs Association	1769	Burgesses pass Virginia Resolutions and Association
Tours Ohio with James Craik	1770	Lord North's ministry, 1770–82; Boston Massacre
	1772	Revival of committees of correspondence
John Custis enters King's College; Martha Parke Custis dies	1773	Tea Act; Boston Tea Party
First Continental Congress	1774	Intolerable Acts; reign of Louis XVI of France, 1774–92
Second Continental Congress; named Commander in Chief of Army; siege of Boston	1775	Battles of Lexington and Concord; capture of Ticonderoga; Bunker Hill; Olive Branch petition; Howe succeeds Gage as British commander; Montgomery and Arnold attack Quebec
Seizes Dorchester Heights; British evacuate Boston; Battles of Long Island and Harlem Heights; retreat through New Jersey; attacks Trenton	1776	Charles Lee holds Charleston; Declaration of Independence
Battles of Princeton, Brandywine, and Germantown; winter at Valley Forge	1777	Howe moves on Philadelphia; Battle of Saratoga; Congress adopts Articles of Confederation

Disclosure of Conway Cabal; Battle of Monmouth	1778	Clinton named British commander; France enters war; Congress rejects North's peace plan; Savannah falls to British
Battle of Stony Point	1779	Spain joins war; *Bonhomme Richard* defeats *Serapis*; Franco-American forces fail to recapture Savannah
Connecticut troops mutiny; Lafayette returns from France; Rochambeau conference; Arnold's treason	1780	British occupy Charleston; Battle of Camden
Battle of Yorktown; John Custis dies	1781	Mutiny of Pennsylvania and New Jersey troops; Congress creates executive departments; Articles of Confederation ratified; America names peace mission
Carleton-Digby peace proposals; French troops sail to West Indies	1782	North ministry ends; Carleton replaces Howe; British evacuate Savannah; preliminary peace treaty signed
Newburgh Addresses; visits northern New York; New York City evacuated; farewell to officers; returns to Mount Vernon	1783	Cessation of hostilities; Pennsylvania militia march on Congress
Heads Potomac Company	1785	
	1786	Annapolis Convention; Shays' Rebellion
President of Philadelphia Convention	1787	Northwest Ordinance; *Federalist* papers published, 1787–88
	1788	Ratification of Constitution
First inaugural as President; tours New England and New York	1789	Organization of First Congress; opening of French Revolution
Assumption debate ends in compromise; capital moved to Philadelphia; Beckwith mission	1790	Hamilton's first Report on Public Credit; Harmar expedition; Hamilton's report on the Bank
Cabinet divides on constitutionality of Bank; travels through southern states	1791	Congress passes excise tax on whiskey; Report on Manufactures; Legislative Assembly governs France, 1791–92
Tries to end Jefferson-Hamilton feud; Madison drafts a farewell address; Washington re-elected	1792	Resistance to excise; presidential electors chosen; abolition of French monarchy and institution of National Convention, 1792–95; War of First Coalition against France, 1792–97; Lafayette is imprisoned
Second inaugural; Neutrality Proclamation; Genêt and the *Little Sarah* incident; Jefferson resigns	1793	Execution of Louis XVI; France declares war on Britain; Republican majority in Second Congress, 1793–95
Proclaims embargo; Jay mission to England; Monroe sent to Paris; Whisky Rebellion	1794	Neutrality Act; Battle of Fallen Timbers
Hamilton leaves Cabinet; Jay's Treaty controversy; Fauchet-Randolph incident; Lafayette's son reaches America	1795	Treaty of San Lorenzo; Directory rules France, 1795–99
Pinckney replaces Monroe; Washington issues Farewell Address	1796	Supreme Court first rules an act of Congress unconstitutional; presidential election; Directory refuses to receive Pinckney
Retires to Mount Vernon	1797	Inauguration of Adams and Jefferson; special mission to France; XYZ Affair
Accepts command of Army; dispute over Hamilton's rank; confers with generals in Philadelphia	1798	Quasi war with France, 1798–1800
Concern over McHenry's competence; troubled by dispatch of commissioners to France; George Washington dies at Mount Vernon, December 14	1799	France ruled by Consulate headed by Napoleon Bonaparte, 1799–1804

11

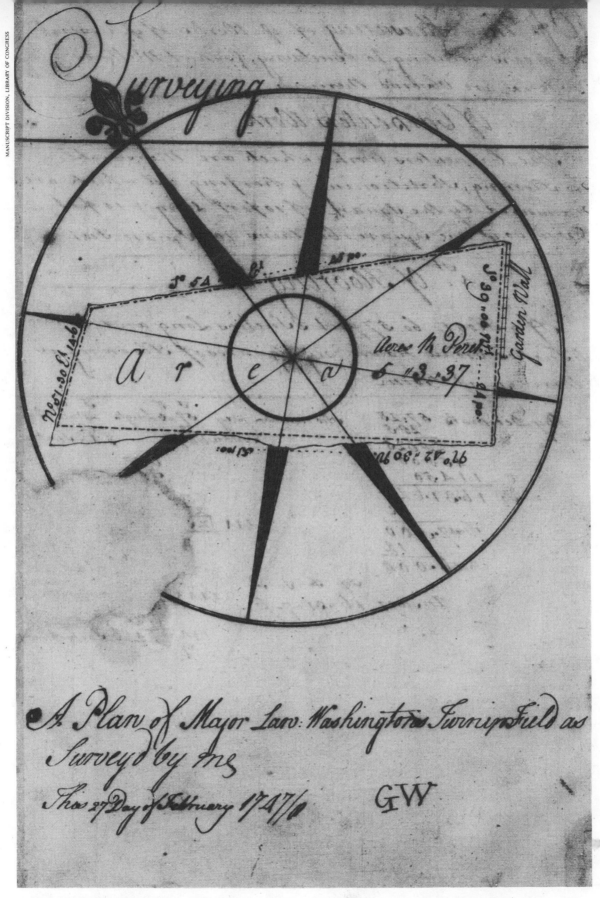

At sixteen George Washington made this survey drawing of his brother Lawrence's turnip field.

Chapter 1

Coming of Age in Virginia

George Washington gazes serenely upon us from portraits and stares empty-eyed from marble busts, as he has done upon many generations of Americans. Jaw firm in obvious resoluteness of purpose, the Washington of the portraits and statues does not smile. His life, one feels, is too dedicated to inspiring ragged troops so that they will fight one more day, too preoccupied with leading the nation through the shoals of early independence, to allow time for smiling. This Washington who has been bequeathed to us, however, is not only impossibly noble, he is not even a man of flesh and blood. All the warmth, the human foibles, the earthiness, have been excised, for in acclaiming a great man, America created a paragon that never existed. Facts that might detract from the image of a demigod were suppressed; particulars that would enhance the picture were magnified and even invented.

The George Washington of fable was coming into being even before the man himself was dead, and after his death the legend grew to absurd proportions. Even today the myth of the hatchet and the cherry tree refuses to die, although there is not the slightest doubt that it was stitched together out of whole cloth by Mason Weems, a book peddler and sometime preacher, in the 1806 edition of his life of Washington. Parson Weems is also responsible for other persistent items of folklore: the youthful Washington throwing a stone across the Rappahannock River (not a dollar across the Potomac); General Washington observed by a Quaker farmer as he knelt to pray in the snow at Valley Forge.

It is not easy to take the Father of his Country down from his pedestal and seek out what kind of human being he was. Even while he was alive, he wore a cloak of dignity that discouraged familiarity, and the blurring effects of time have made the search for the man more difficult. But once the obscuring layers are peeled away, an individual does stand revealed, a man of weaknesses as well as strengths, of enthusiasms, warmths, antagonisms. If such things as a love for dancing and the theater, and a weakness for cardplaying and fox hunting, were marks of frivolity, then George Washington was frivolous to that extent. He was frail enough to cherish a love for the wife of a close friend, but strong enough to keep his passion within circumspect bounds. He was not the military genius he is sometimes credited with having been, for some of his battles, especially the early ones, were not always models of strategic subtlety. In other words, he was a more interesting and more complex person than the one created by the mythmakers. If in time Washington occasionally did come to resemble the dedicated man of the portraits, it was largely because he accepted duty as his hard taskmaster and forced himself to surmount his frailties. As for his military abilities, he became immeasurably wiser with experience, while his foes were learning little; he discovered how to use his ragged Continentals on the half-wild American terrain, while the British and Hessians persisted in trying to fight as though they were on Europe's open fields and meadows. And as the nation's first President, he established major precedents that have endured for two centuries.

Biographers have found it difficult to obtain a revealing perspective on Washington. His contemporaries saw him in different lights; his towering presence and multiple accomplishments filled some with uncritical adoration, but to others they were cause for jealous denigration. Even those who strove to be impartial were hard put to get at the essence of the man, because Washington's reserve made him keep his thoughts and feelings largely to himself. When a friend asked him to set down his memoirs for future generations, he declined, saying he had no talent for that kind of writing. Fortunately he left a large body of other writings that provide material for a portrait of himself in his own words. It is not a portrait seen full face—for he is not addressing himself to us—but a composite made up of a hundred glimpses seen from many angles: Washington writing to a friend, instructing his farm manager, pleading with Congress, addressing his troops, occasionally putting private thoughts in his diary. His family genealogy and the record of his early years, however, must be given in conventional historical narrative.

Anyone who searches among Washington's forebears for the seeds of his greatness will be disappointed. By the time of his birth in 1732, the Washington family was well established on Virginia's Northern Neck, the long peninsula lying between the Rappahannock and Potomac rivers. But though they were good and respectable people, they were not outstanding; they were men of property, but their holdings were very modest compared to those of many Virginia landowners. The Washingtons were the kind of men who provided county justices, vestrymen for the parish churches, and, frequently, members for the House of Burgesses, the lower house of Virginia's General Assembly, but made little mark on the history of the Colony. The first Washington to settle on American soil—George's great-grandfather John—came to Virginia in 1657 as mate on a ship. John married well, prospered, and willed the bulk of his fifty-seven-hundred-acre estate to his eldest son, Lawrence. A good manager, a man who could extract money from what he had, Lawrence Washington increased his inheritance by only a few hundred acres and died at the young age of thirty-eight, leaving a widow and three children, John, Augustine, and Mildred. Augustine Washington would be the father of George.

Since he was a second son, Augustine Washington's bequest in his father's will was small. But soon after he came of age in 1715, he married Jane Butler, who added a modest inheritance to his, so that the young couple began their life together with some 1,740 acres. It was still small by Virginia standards, but Augustine began to add to it. His first purchase was a farm on the south bank of the Potomac between Bridges Creek and Popes Creek, which had once belonged to his grandfather John. There, on Popes Creek, Augustine built a home several years later. It must have been quite a small house, for it was described as having only four rooms, and the contractor agreed to build it for five thousand pounds of tobacco, a modest sum. Not much else is known about it, but this house would be the birthplace of George Washington. Augustine Washington also prospered, building a gristmill on Popes Creek near his home and becoming a justice of the peace, a church warden, and a sheriff. He acquired more land, including a twenty-five-hundred-acre tract farther up the Potomac where Little Hunting Creek emptied into the river. This he bought from his sister Mildred and her husband; it had been her inheritance and also had once belonged to John Washington. In time it would be known as Mount Vernon. Augustine became active in the development of iron ore and in iron smelting. He and his wife had three children, Lawrence, Augustine, and Jane. He was only thirty-five, and the future looked bright. Then in May, 1730, he returned from an extended trip to England on iron-furnace business to learn that his wife had died the previous November.

Augustine Washington's situation helps to explain why widowed men and women of the period usually remarried so quickly. Marriage was for practical as well as romantic reasons. It was a two-person job to manage a home and fields, watch over the slaves, take care of the children. Augustine's eye soon rested on Mary Ball, rather succinctly described as healthy, of moderate height, with a rounded figure and a pleasant voice. Mary was the sole offspring of the union of Joseph Ball, a widower nearing sixty, and Mary Johnson, a widow who could not even write her own name. Nor was the daughter to acquire much facility with the pen; the samples of Mary's orthography that survive are truly wonderful examples of how far phonic English can be stretched without snapping. Mary Ball's father had died when she was only three, leaving her four hundred acres of land, three slaves, cattle, and "all [the] feathers that are in the kitchen loft to be put into a bed for her." Her mother married again, was widowed, and herself departed this world when Mary was twelve, leaving her an orphan but bequeathing her more land and other property. Thus Mary brought a considerable amount of property to her union with Augustine Washington.

The couple was married in March of 1731. He was thirty-six, Mary was twenty-three. The following February 11 (Old Style, changed to February 22, when England adopted the Gregorian calendar in 1752), in the house on Popes Creek, was born a son whom they named George. The historian can only guess about the events of George Washington's childhood. At Popes Creek he would have become familiar with farm animals probably as soon as he was aware of the world around him, and he came to accept the enslavement of black human beings as part of the normal order of things. He undoubtedly was taken at some time to his father's nearby gristmill with its rumbling machinery, and there were certainly visits to neighbors with his parents. There was the birth of a new sister, Betty, when he was not quite a year and a half old, and before another year and a half there was Samuel, who had scarcely become part of the family when George—not yet three—had to try to comprehend that his half-sister Jane had died. His half-brothers Lawrence and Augustine, Jr., both much older than he, could have been no more than dim and unreal creatures, for they

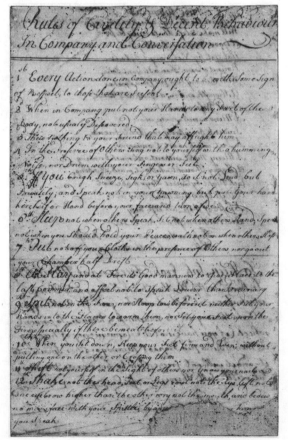

were in England at school. In 1735 Augustine Washington moved his family to the land he had bought along Little Hunting Creek on the Potomac. In the new home two more brothers were born: John Augustine, who would be known as Jack, and Charles.

In 1738 George's half-brother Lawrence returned from England. He was twenty—fourteen years older than George—urbane, educated, traveled; and the younger brother quickly idolized him. Despite the difference in age, they were to become close friends. Late that same year Augustine Washington bought a tract of land on the Rappahannock about two miles from the village of Fredericksburg, the first town George had ever seen. The place was called Ferry Farm because it was near a crossing of the river, and the family moved there on December 1, 1738. The following year Britain and Spain went to war, and Lawrence Washington became an officer in the volunteer "American Regiment" that took part in a disastrous assault on the Spanish stronghold of Cartagena on the northwest coast of what is now Colombia. Lawrence's war tales made him even more of a hero to his younger brother, and George's enthusiasm for things military apparently dated from this time.

From the age of about seven until he was eleven George received what schooling he got probably in part from a tutor and very likely for a time at a school in nearby Fredericksburg. He learned arithmetic, how to read, and how to spell after a fashion. His strong point was figures: he went on to study trigonometry, and then surveying. The very earliest specimens of Washington's handwriting that survive are his school copybooks. In them, in a firm, bold hand, he solved arithmetic problems; copied down forms for a typical will, a tobacco receipt, a land lease, and other legal papers; and wrote out tables for finding the date Easter will fall on in any given year and similar useful and useless information. Unhappily, most of these entries tell us little about the boy himself. The following exercises are among those written when George Washington was thirteen.

[August 13, 1745]

SURVEYING

Is the Art of Measuring Land and it consists of 3 Parts 1st. The going round and Measuring a Piece of Wood Land. 2d Plotting the Same and 3d To find the Content thereof and first how to Measure a Piece of Land....

SOLID MEASURE

Is that of Timber, Stone Digging, and Liquods, and the Rule for Working is

To Multiply the Length & Breadth together; & that Product by the Depth or thickness & the Last Product will be the Content in Cubick Inches which if Timber or Stone divide by 1728 (the Cubick Inches in a Foot

Two pages from Washington's school copybooks show his early interest in surveying and the first twelve of 110 maxims he copied out under the heading of "Rules of Civility and Decent Behavior in Company and Conversation." Ink from reverse pages makes them difficult to read.

17

Solid) & the Quotient gives the Content in Solid Feet....

Mount Vernon and its Associations BY BENSON J. LOSSING, 1883

Destroyed in 1779, Washington's birthplace, "a four-roomed house, with a chimney at each end," was described and depicted by Lossing in his book on Mount Vernon.

A DESCRIPTION OF THE LEAP YEAR, DOMINICAL LETTER, GOLDEN NUMBER, CYCLE OF THE SUN ROMON INDICTION EPACT &C. WITH MEMORIAL VERSES ON THE ECCLESIASTICAL AND CIVIL KALENDER

The Golden Number or Prime is a Circular Revolution of 19 years in which term of years it hath been anciently Supposed that the Sun & Moon do make all the Variety of Aspects one to another....

GEOGRAPHICAL DEFINITIONS

Defin. 1st. The Globe of the Earth is a Spherical Body Composed of Earth & Water &c. Divided into Contenants Islands & Seas.

2d. A Contenent is a great Quantity of Land not Divided nor Seperated by the Sea wherein are many Kingdoms & Principalities, as Europe, Asia & Africa is one Contenent & America is Another....

7 The Ocean is a general Collection of the Waters wch. environeth the Earth on every side....

The Provinces of North America are

New France	New Jersey	Carolina North & South
New England	Mary Land	Terra Florida
New York	Virginia	Mexico or New Spain
Pensylvania		

The Chief Islands are

Iselands	Hispaniola	Jamaica
Greenland	Cuba	Barbadoes & the rest of
Colofornia	Porto Rico	the Caribbee Iselands

Augustine Washington died on April 12, 1743, at the age of forty-eight. He left more than ten thousand acres, divided into at least seven tracts. Although all of his children were well remembered in his will, Lawrence, as the eldest son, got by far the largest share, including the plantation on Little Hunting Creek. George, the third son, received the Ferry Farm and, like the others, some slaves and personal property. His inheritance—neither especially large nor productive—made little difference, for his mother did not yield it to him when he became twenty-one; he had to wait another eighteen years after that before she would consent to move elsewhere. Mary Ball Washington did not remarry, was a poor manager, made frequent demands on her children, and later evinced not the slightest pride in her illustrious son's accomplishments.

Lawrence Washington renamed his Little Hunting Creek home Mount Vernon, in honor of Admiral Edward Vernon, who had led the Cartagena expedition against the Spanish. Not long after his father's death he married Anne Fairfax, the daughter of Colonel William Fairfax, whose impressive home, Belvoir, neighbored on Mount Vernon. And so, as young George came to visit at Mount Vernon, the doors of Belvoir were also opened to him. Belvoir was an important influence on the boy, who was rapidly growing into a young man, large of hands and feet, unusually strong, taller than those about him, and undoubtedly awkward and unsure of himself. At Belvoir and Mount Vernon he acquired the social graces so necessary to a member of Virginia's Northern Neck society.

In 1747 a notable event occurred at Belvoir: the arrival from England of Thomas, Lord Fairfax, cousin of Colonel Fairfax, a fox-hunting, woman-hating nobleman. He was proprietor of the Northern Neck, which meant that because of a royal grant to a forebear he was virtually feudal lord of all the expanse of land lying between the Potomac and the Rappahannock, to their most remote sources in the mountains, a huge domain of more than five million acres. When a surveying party was sent into his lordship's western land, George Washington, then sixteen, was permitted to go. Although he was qualified to run simple surveys, he did not go as a working member of the party but rather as a companion to George William, the son of Colonel Fairfax and a nephew of Lord Fairfax, who was with the party to represent his lordship's interests. George's diary account of the adventure is the earliest existing spontaneous writing from his hand.

A Journal of my Journey over the Mountains began Fryday the 11th. of March 1747/8

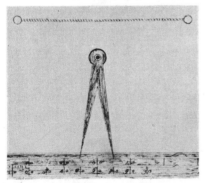

The George Washington Atlas, WASHINGTON, 1932; LIBRARY OF CONGRESS

A chain, dividers, and scale drawn by Washington when he was fourteen

Fryday March 11th. 1747/8. Began my Journey in Company with George Fairfax Esqr.; we travelld this day 40 Miles to Mr. George Neavels in Prince William County.

Saturday March 12th. This Morning Mr. James Genn the surveyor came to us. We traveld over the Blue Ridge to Capt. Ashbys on Shannondoah River. Nothing remarkable happen'd.

Sunday March 13th. Rode to Lordships Quarter about 4 Miles higher up the River. We went through most beautiful Groves of Sugar Trees & spent the best part of the Day in admiring the Trees & richness of the Land.

Monday 14th. We sent our Baggage to Capt. Hites (near Frederick Town). Went ourselves down the River about 16 Miles to Capt. Isaac Pennington (the Land exceeding Rich & Fertile all the way produces abun-

19

dance of Grain Hemp Tobacco &ca.) in order to Lay of some Lands on Cates Marsh & Long Marsh.

Tuesday 15th. We set out early with Intent to Run round the s[ai]d. Land but being taken in a Rain & it Increasing very fast obliged us to return it clearing about one oClock. Our time being too Precious to Loose we a second time ventured out & Worked hard till Night & Then returnd to Penningtons. We got our Suppers & was Lighted into a Room & I not being so good a Woodsman as the rest of my Company I striped my self very orderly & went into the Bed as they call'd it when to my Surprize I found it to be nothing but a Little Straw Matted together without Sheets or any thing else but only one Thread Bear blanket with double its Weight of Vermin such as Lice Fleas &c. I was glad to get up (as soon as the Light was carried from us) & put on my Cloths & Lay as my Companions. Had we not have been very tired I am sure we should not have slep'd much that night. I made a Promise not to sleep so from that time forward chusing rather to sleep in the open Air before a fire as will appear hereafter.

Wednesday 16th. We set out early & finish'd about one oClock & then Travell'd up to Frederick Town where our Baggage came to us. We cleaned ourselves (to get Rid of the Game we had catched the Night before) & took a Review of the Town & thence return'd to our Lodgings where we had a good Dinner prepar'd for us Wine & Rum Punch in Plenty & a good Feather Bed with clean Sheets which was a very agreeable regale.

Thursday 17th. Rain'd till Ten oClock & then clearing we reached as far as Major Campbells one of there Burgesses about 25 Miles from Town. Nothing Remarkable this day nor Night but that we had a Tolerable good Bed [to] lay on.

Fryday 18th. We Travell'd up about 35 Miles to Thomas Barwicks in Potomack where we found the River so excessively high by Reason of the Great Rains that had fallen up about the Allegany Mountains as they told us which was then bringing down the melt'd Snow & that it would not be fordable for severall Days it was then above Six foot Higher than usual & was Rising we agreed to stay till Monday. We this day calld to see the Fam'd Warm

Belvoir, home of the Fairfaxes, was destroyed in 1783 but looked much like this artist's rendering when Washington knew and loved it.

Thomas, Lord Fairfax

Springs. We camped out in the field this Night. Nothing Remarkable happen'd till sonday the 20th.

Sonday 20th. Finding the River not much abated we in the Evening Swam our horses over & carried them to Charles Polks in Maryland for Pasturage till the next Morning.

Monday 21st. We went over in a Canoe & Travell'd up Maryland side all the Day in a Continued Rain to Collo. Cresaps right against the Mouth of the South Bra[nch] about 40 Miles from Polks I believe the worst Road that ever was trod by Man or Beast.

Tuesday 22d. Continued Rain and the Freshes kept us at Cresaps.

Wednesday 23d. Rain'd till about two oClock & Clear'd when we were agreeably surprisd at the sight of thirty odd Indians coming from War with only one Scalp. We had some Liquor with us of which we gave them Part it elevating there Spirits put them in the Humour of Dauncing of whom we had a War Daunce. There Manner of Dauncing is as follows Viz. They clear a Large Circle & make a great Fire in the Middle then seats themselves around it the Speaker makes a grand Speech telling them in what Manner they are to Daunce. After he has finish'd the best Dauncer Jumps up as one awaked out of a Sleep & Runs & Jumps about the Ring in a most comicle Manner. He is followd by the Rest then begins there Musicians to Play. The Music is a Pot half [full] of Water with a Deerskin Streched over it as tight as it can & a Goard with some Shott in it to Rattle & a Piece of an horses Tail tied to it to make it look fine. The one keeps Rattling and the other Drumming all the While the other is Dauncing.

Fryday 25th. 1748. Nothing Remarkable on thursday but only being with the Indians all day so shall slip it. This day left Cresaps & went up to the Mouth of Patersons Creek & there swum our Horses over got over ourselves in a Canoe & traveld up the following Part of the Day to Abram Johnstones 15 Miles from the Mouth where we crossed.

Saterday 26. Travelld up the Creek to Solemon Hedges Esqr. one of his Majestys Justices of the Peace for the County of Frederick where we camped. When we came to Supper there was neither a Cloth upon the Table nor a Knife to eat with but as good luck would have it we had Knives of own. . . .

Fryday April the 1st. 1748. This Morning Shot twice at Wild Turkies but killd none. Run of three Lots & returnd to Camp.

Saterday April 2d. Last Night was a blowing Rainy night. Our Straw catch'd a Fire that we were laying upon & was luckily Preserv'd by one of our Mens awaking when it was in a [blaze]. We run of four Lots this day which Reached below Stumps.

Sunday 3d. Last Night was a much more blostering night than the former. We had our Tent Carried Quite of with the Wind and was obliged to Lie the Latter part of the Night without covering. There came several Persons to see us this day. One of our Men Shot a Wild Turkie.

[George was completely unsympathetic when German settlers from Pennsylvania followed the surveying party. He apparently did not understand that these people, squatters on the land, knew the surveyors were the fore-runners of trouble.]

Monday 4th. This morning Mr. Fairfax left us with Intent to go down to the Mouth of the Branch. We did two Lots & was attended by a great Company of People Men Women & Children that attended us through the Woods as we went shewing there Antick tricks. I really think they seem to be as Ignorant a Set of People as the Indians. They would never speak English but when spoken to they speak all Dutch. This day our Tent was blown down by the Violentness of the Wind. . . .

Wednesday 6th. Last Night was so Intolerably smoaky that we were obliged all hands to leave the Tent to the Mercy of the Wind and Fire. This day was attended by our afore[mentione]d. Company untill about 12 oClock when we finish'd we travelld down the Branch to Henry Vanmetriss on our Journey was catchd in a very heavy Rain. We got under a Straw House untill the Worst of it was over & then continued our Journey.

Relics of Washington's early surveying and military expeditions include his telescope (above), and his drawing instruments, pack saddle, and camp chest (right).

RIGHT: *Century Magazine*, MAY 1890
OTHERS: *Mount Vernon*, LOSSING

Thursday 7th. Rain'd Successively all Last night. This Morning one of our men Killed a Wild Turky that weight 20 Pounds. We went & Surveyd 15 Hundred Acres of Land & Returnd to Vanmetriss about 1 oClock. About two I heard that Mr. Fairfax was come up & at 1 Peter Casseys about 2 Miles of in the same Old Field. I then took my Horse & went up to see him. We eat our Dinners & Walked down to Vanmetriss. We stayed about two Hours & Walked back again and slept in Casseys House which was the first Night I had slept in a House since I came to the Branch.

Fryday 8th. We breakfasted at Casseys & Rode down to Vanmetriss to get all our Company together which when we had accomplished we Rode down below the Trough in order to Lay of Lots there. We laid of one this day. The Trough is [a] couple of Ledges of Mountain Impassable running side & side together for above 7 or 8 Miles & the River down between them. You must Ride Round the back of the Mountain for to get below them. We Camped this Night in the Woods near a Wild Meadow where was a Large Stack of Hay. After we had Pitched our Tent & made a very Large Fire we pull'd out our Knapsack in order to Recruit ourselves every [one] was his own Cook. Our Spits was forked sticks. Our Plates was a Large Chip. As for Dishes we had none.

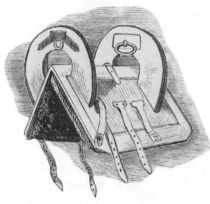

[Fairfax and Washington either tired of the adventure, or the former considered his duty done, for they left the surveyors to carry on by themselves and headed for home, becoming lost once on the way.]

Saterday 9th. Set the Surveyors to work whilst Mr. Fairfax & myself stayed at the Tent. Our Provision being all exhausted & the Person that was to bring us a Recruit disappointing us we were obliged to go without untill we could get some from the Neighbours which was not till about 4 or 5 oClock in the Evening. We then took our Leaves of the Rest of our Company. Road Down to John Colins in order to set off next Day homewards.

Sunday 10th. We took our farewell of the Branch & travelld over Hills and Mountains to 1 Coddys on Great Cacapehon about 40 Miles.

Monday 11th. We Travelld from Coddys down to

Frederick Town where we Reached about 12 oClock. We dined in Town and then went to Capt. Hites & Lodged.

Tuesday 12th.   We set of from Capt. Hites in order to go over Wms. Gap about 20 Miles and after Riding about 20 Miles we had 20 to go for we had lost ourselves & got up as High as Ashbys Bent. We did get over Wms. Gap that Night and as low as Wm. Wests in Fairfax County 18 Miles from the Top of the Ridge. This day see a Rattled Snake the first we had seen in all our Journey.

Wednesday the 13th. of April 1748. Mr. Fairfax got safe home and I myself safe to my Brothers which concludes my Journal.

Title page of a book of surveys started by Washington when he was seventeen and, at right, as a later artist imagined him at that age

Toward the end of that year, 1748, George William Fairfax married a charming young lady named Sarah Cary and brought her home to live at Belvoir. Sally, as she was known, was almost two years older than George; but from then, almost to the time of his death, George

Washington would hold the image of Sally Fairfax somewhere in his heart.

Other concerns in George's life were more worrisome or somber. His beloved brother Lawrence was suffering from a cough that worsened steadily and was ominously suggesting consumption. Mary Ball Washington was showing no disposition to make a home on her own land but was giving every sign of settling permanently on George's patrimony, the Ferry Farm. And by 1749 seventeen-year-old George was already occupied with earning a living, working as a surveyor and doing well. Through midsummer of that year he was helping to lay out the new town of Alexandria on the Potomac, and then he became the county surveyor of Culpeper County. In November he was on the frontier again, doing some work for Lord Fairfax, who had moved into the Shenandoah Valley. He wrote about it to a friend.

[November, 1749]

Dear Richard

The Receipt of your kind favor of the 2d. of this Instant afforded Me unspeakable pleasure as I am convinced I am still in the Memory of so Worthy a friend a friendship I shall ever be proud of Increasing. You gave me the more pleasure as I receiv'd it amongst a parcel of Barbarians and an uncooth set of People. The like favour often repeated would give me Pleasure altho I seem to be in a Place where no real Satis: be had. Since you receid my Letter on October Last I have not sleep'd above three Nights or four in a bed but after Walking a good deal all the Day lay down before the fire upon a Little Hay Straw Fodder or bairskin which ever is to be had with Man Wife and Children like a Parcel of Dogs or Catts & happy's he that gets the Birth nearest the fire. There's nothing would make it pass of tolerably but a good Reward. A Dubbleloon is my constant gain every Day that the Weather will permit my going out and some time Six Pistoles. The coldness of the Weather will not allow my making a long stay as the Lodging is rather too cold for the time of Year. I have never had my Cloths of but lay and sleep in them like a Negro except the few Nights I have lay'n in Frederick Town.

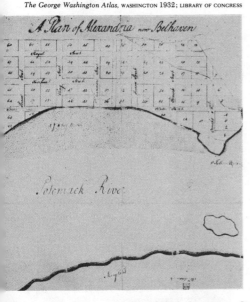

Washington's plan of the new town of Alexandria, Virginia, made in 1749 while he was helping to lay it out

During this same period George became acutely conscious of girls, and, like most young men on their first discovery of the fascinating subject, he tended to get a little purple and flowery in writing about it, as this somewhat rambling and obscure letter to a friend named Robin indicates. It was written from the frontier in late 1749 or the spring of 1750; the "Low Land Beauty" has never been identified.

*Photograph of a lost portrait of
Sally Cary, wife of Washington's
friend and neighbor, George William
Fairfax, and his first real love*

As its the greatest mark of friendship and esteem absent Friends can shew each other in Writing, and often communicating their thoughts to his fellow companions makes me endeavour to signalize myself in acquainting you from time to time and at all times my situation and employments of Life, and could Wish you would take half the Pain of contriving me a Letter by any oppertunity as you may be well assured of its meeting with a very welcome reception. My Place of Residence is at present at his Lordships where I might was my heart disengag'd pass my time very pleasantly as there's a very agreeable Young Lady Lives in the same house (Colo. George Fairfax's Wife's sister) but as thats only adding Fuel to fire it makes me the more uneasy for by often and unavoidably being in Company with her revives my former Passion for your Low Land Beauty whereas was I to live more retired from young Women I might in some measure eliviate my sorrows by burying that chast and troublesome Passion in the grave of oblivion or etarnall forgetfulness for as I am very well assured that's the only antidote or remedy that I ever shall be releivd by or only recess that can administer any cure or help to me as I am well convinced was I ever to attempt any thing I should only get a denial which would be only adding grief to uneasiness.

During this vulnerable time, Washington was guilty of writing nebulous and moonstruck love poems. One such, which celebrated the charms of a passing fancy named Frances Alexander, was written as an acrostic, but before he quite finished it, George wearied either of the poem or of Frances.

From your bright sparkling Eyes, I was undone;
Rays, you have more transparent than the Sun,
A midst its glory in the rising Day,
None can you equal in your bright array;
Constant in your calm and unspotted mind;
Equal to all, but will to none Prove kind,
So knowing, seldom one so Young, you'l Find.
Ah! woe's me, that I should love and conceil
Long have I wish'd, but never dare reveal
Even though severely Loves Pains I feel;
Xerxes that great, was't free from Cupids Dart,
And all the greatest Heroes, felt His mark.

26

The young surveyor's work was so profitable that in October, 1750, he was able to purchase two pieces of land on Bullskin Creek, a tributary of the Shenandoah, and before the year was over he bought another tract, totaling almost fifteen hundred acres. As soon as winter ended in 1751, George was at work again, on surveys that sometimes took him to the frontier but often enough occupied him near enough at home so that he could visit brothers, sister, mother, and friends. Meanwhile, Lawrence's worsening health was casting a shadow. He had gone to London in the summer of 1749 to consult doctors but without result. Twice George accompanied him to the warm springs at Berkeley up the Potomac, the same springs George had seen on his 1748 trip. The spring waters, though reputed to have curative powers, helped Lawrence little, and it was decided that he should go to Barbados in the West Indies, whose winter climate was believed to be beneficial for lung ailments. Once again his half-brother dropped his own activities to go along. The pair left Virginia near the end of September, 1751; the following excerpts are from the diary George kept during the only trip he was ever to make outside of what would become the continental United States.

Eighteenth-century map with the island of Barbados at lower right

7 October 1751. But Little Wind at S Wt. & So. with calm smooth Sea and fair Weather. Saw many fish swimming abt. us of which a Dalphin we catchd. at Noon but cou'd not intice with a baited hook two Baricoota's which played under our Stern for some Hours. The Dalpin being small we had it dressed for Supper....

19 October 1751. Hard Squals of Wind and Rain with a f[?]mented Sea jostling in heaps occasion[ed] by the Wavering wind which in 24 hours Veer'd the Compass not remaining 2 hours in any point. The Seamen seem'd disheartned confessing they never had seen such weather before. It was universally surmis'd there had been a violent hurricane not far distant. A prodigy in the West appear'd towards the suns setting abt. 6 [P.M.] remarkable for its extraordinary redness....

[2 November 1751.] We were grea[tly al]arm'd with the cry of Land at 4 A:M: we quitted our Beds with Surpprise and found the land plainly appearing at [a]bout 3 leagues distance wh[en] by our reckonings we shou'd have been near 150 Leauges to the Windward we to Leeward [abt.] the distance above mention[ed] and had we been but 3 or 4 leagues more we shoud have been [o]ut of sight of the Island run down the Latit[ude a]nd probably not have discove[red the] Error in time to have gaind [l]and for 3 Weeks or More.

The land so narrowly sighted was Barbados. Two days after they arrived, a physician examined Lawrence and announced that his tuberculosis could be cured, and for a time the brothers were happy. They were constantly asked out, though George accepted the invitations of one of their frequent hosts with qualms because there was smallpox in the household (Lawrence was immune). The inevitable happened; George came down with the disease. It left his face somewhat pockmarked, but one day in the future it would let him move unafraid in army camps where soldiers were dying from the dreaded disease. It soon became apparent, however, that Barbados was doing Lawrence's racking cough no good, and he decided as a last resort to try the climate of Bermuda. There was nothing George could do for him, and on December 21, 1751, the two parted and the younger brother left for home, where he arrived early in February.

George busied himself again with his surveying work. In March, 1752, he added another 552 acres to his holdings on Bullskin Creek. And for the first time he considered himself not only enough in love, but old enough—he was twenty—and with sufficiently promising prospects, to think about addressing himself seriously to a young lady, Elizabeth ("Betsy") Fauntleroy, daughter of a man of high position in the Colony; she previously had spurned him. Now young Washington wrote, through her father, asking for a second chance.

May 20th. 1752

Sir

I shoud have been down long before this but my business in Frederick detain'd me somewhat longer than I expected and imediately upon my return from thence I was taken with a Violent Pleurisie which has reduced me very low but purpose as soon as I recover my strength to wait on Miss Betsy, in hopes of a Revocation of the former, cruel sentence, and see if I can meet with [any alter]ation in my favor. I have inclos'd a letter to her which I shoud be much obligd to you for the delivery of it. I have nothing to add but my best Respects to your good Lady and Family and that I am Sir, Yr. most Obedient Hble. Servt.

G WASHINGTON

Betsy Fauntleroy

Whatever the enclosed letter said, it apparently left Betsy unmoved. So far as we know, George gave up the pursuit then and there; Betsy went on to marry another. In mid-June of 1752, Lawrence arrived home. During his months on Barbados and Bermuda he had grown worse. He bravely set about trying to put his affairs in order, and on July 26, 1752, at Mount Vernon, he came to the end of his young life.

Chapter 2

Wilderness Warrior

Lawrence Washington had been Adjutant General of Virginia, the commanding officer of the Colony's militia, and even before his brother's death George had begun a campaign to obtain the office for himself. It made no difference to him that he had never worn a uniform, never drilled a corporal's guard of soldiers, never seen a fortification except one he had visited in Barbados. With the bumptious optimism of youth he argued his case with Robert Dinwiddie, Lieutenant Governor of Virginia, and with others who might have influence, and in the end was in a degree successful. When it was decided to divide Virginia into four military districts, he was appointed one of the district adjutants—and thus, before his twenty-first birthday, became Major George Washington in 1753.

One of his principal duties as district adjutant was to travel about his Southern District, teaching county militia officers how to drill their men; but before he had time to do anything about his new chores—or even to learn much about tactics himself—a more pressing matter arose. At that time France and Great Britain were in a period of truce in their series of wars for dominance not only of Europe but of North America and other parts of the world. In 1753 France controlled Canada and the country west of the Mississippi; Britain, the thirteen Colonies. Both nations claimed the upper Ohio Valley.

In the spring of 1753 the French built a chain of forts between the shores of Lake Erie and the Allegheny River. The forts were on land now part of Pennsylvania but then claimed by Virginia, and word came from London to Governor Dinwiddie of Virginia to warn the French off. Dinwiddie had his own special reasons for being concerned: he was a member of the Ohio Company, a group of land speculators who planned to build a fort as a center for trade and settlement at the Forks of the Ohio, where the Allegheny and Monongahela rivers join to form the Ohio, the site of today's Pittsburgh. Having learned that Dinwiddie intended to send a message ordering the

French commander out of British territory, Washington rode to Williamsburg, the capital of Virginia, to volunteer to carry the letter. Dinwiddie accepted his offer at once, and Washington set out at the end of October. At Fredericksburg he picked up Jacob van Braam as his French interpreter, and at Wills Creek (now Cumberland), Maryland, he was joined by frontiersman Christopher Gist and also hired four men as "servitors."

During the rigors of his fall and winter journey, Washington kept a rough diary. On his return to Williamsburg, the Governor asked him to turn his notes into a connected account for the House of Burgesses. He had a single day for the task; his rush job in turn was given to the public printer, and the printed version is the one that survives (the printer's editing is undoubtedly responsible for removing most of Washington's frequent errors in spelling).

Wednesday, October 31st, 1753, I was commissioned and appointed by the Honourable *Robert Dinwiddie,* Esq; Governor, &c., of *Virginia,* to visit and deliver a Letter to the Commandant of the *French* Forces on the *Ohio,* and set out on the intended Journey the same Day; the next, I arrived at *Fredericksburg,* and engaged Mr. *Jacob Vanbraam,* to be my *French* Interpreter; and proceeded with him to *Alexandria,* where we provided Necessaries; from thence we went to *Winchester,* and got Baggage, Horses, &c. and from thence we pursued the new Road to *Wills*-Creek, where we arrived the 14th of *November.*

Here I engaged Mr. *Gist* to pilot us out, and also hired four others as Servitors, *Barnaby Currin,* and *John MacQuire,* Indian Traders, *Henry Steward,* and *William Jenkins,* and in Company with those Persons, left the Inhabitants the Day following.

The excessive Rains and vast Quantity of Snow that had fallen, prevented our reaching Mr. *Frazier's* an Indian Trader, at the Mouth of *Turtle*-Creek, on *Monongahela* [River], till *Thursday* the 22d. We were informed here, that Expresses were sent a few Days ago to the Traders down the River, to acquaint them with the *French* General's [Sieur de Marin, sent to build a fort at the Forks of the Ohio] death, and the Return of the major Part of the *French* Army into Winter Quarters.

The Waters were quite impassible, without swimming our Horses; which obliged us to get the Loan of a Canoe from *Frazier,* and to send *Barnaby Currin,* and *Henry Steward,* down *Monongahela,* with our Baggage, to meet us at the Forks of *Ohio,* about 10 Miles, to cross *Aligany.*

Washington's headquarters at Wills Creek, from Lossing's Mount Vernon

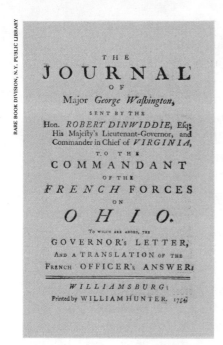

THE
JOURNAL
OF

Major *George Washington*,

SENT BY THE

Hon. *ROBERT DINWIDDIE*, Esq;
His Majesty's Lieutenant-Governor, and
Commander in Chief of *VIRGINIA*,

TO THE

COMMANDANT

OF THE

FRENCH FORCES

ON

OHIO.

To which are added, the

GOVERNOR's LETTER,

And A TRANSLATION of the

FRENCH OFFICER's ANSWER.

WILLIAMSBURG:

Printed by WILLIAM HUNTER. 1754.

Title page of the printed Journal *that Washington wrote for the House of Burgesses at Dinwiddie's request*

As I got down before the Canoe, I spent some Time in viewing the Rivers, and the Land in the Fork, which I think extremely well situated for a Fort, as it has the absolute Command of both Rivers. The Land at the Point is 20 or 25 Feet above the common Surface of the Water, and a considerable Bottom of flat, well-timbered Land all around it, very convenient for Building: The Rivers are each a Quarter of a Mile, or more, across, and run here very near at right Angles: *Aligany* bearing N.E. and *Monongahela* S.E. the former of these two is a very rapid and swift running Water, the other deep and still, without any perceptible Fall.

About two Miles from this, on the South East Side of the River, at the Place where the *Ohio* Company intended to erect a Fort, lives *Shingiss,* King of the *Delawares;* We call'd upon him, to invite him to Council at the *Loggs*-Town.

[Washington proceeded to Logstown, seventeen miles below the Forks. It was a village of Delaware, Mingo, and Shawnee Indians, but its most important chief was Tanachariston, whom the English always called the Half King, an Oneida acting as a proconsul of the Iroquois Six Nations confederacy that maintained authority over the other tribes.]

25th [November, 1753]. Came to Town four of ten *Frenchmen* that deserted from a Company at the *Cuscuscas* [an Indian village], which lies at the Mouth of this River. I got the following Account from them. They were sent from *New Orleans* with 100 Men, and 8 Canoe Loads of Provisions to this Place; where they expected to have met the same Number of Men, from the Forts this Side Lake *Erie,* to convoy them and the Stores up, who were not arrived when they ran off.

I enquired into the Situation of the *French,* on the *Missisippi,* their Number, and what Forts they had built: They inform'd me, That there were four small Forts between *New-Orleans* and the *Black-Islands* [Van Braam evidently mistook the strange word "Illinois" to be *Isles Noires,* "Black Islands"], garrison'd with about 30 or 40 Men, and a few small Pieces, in each. That at *New-Orleans,* which is near the Mouth of the *Missisippi,* there are 35 Companies, of 40 Men each, with a pretty

Our Country BY BENSON J. LOSSING, 1877

Nineteenth-century depiction of "Major Washington on his mission to the French commander"

strong Fort mounting 8 Carriage Guns; and at the *Black-Islands* there are several Companies, and a Fort with 6 Guns. The *Black-Islands* are about 130 Leagues above the Mouth of the *Ohio,* which is about 350 above *New-Orleans*: They also acquainted me, that there was a small pallisado'd Fort on the *Ohio,* at the Mouth of the *Obaish* [Wabash] about 60 Leagues from the *Missisippi*: The *Obaish* heads near the West End of Lake *Erie,* and affords the Communication between the *French* on *Missisippi* and those on the Lakes. These Deserters came up from the lower *Shanoah* [Shawanoe, now Shawnee] Town with one *Brown,* an *Indian* Trader, and were going to *Philadelphia.*

About 3 o'Clock this Evening the Half-King came to Town; I went up and invited him and *Davison,* privately, to my Tent, and desir'd him to relate some of the Particulars of his Journey to the *French* Commandant, and Reception there; and to give me an Account of the Ways and Distance. He told me, that the nearest and levellest Way was now impassable, by Reason of many large miry Savannas; that we must be obliged to go by *Venango* [an Indian village on the Allegheny], and should not get to the near Fort under 5 or 6 Night's Sleep, good Travelling. When he went to the Fort, he said he was received in a very stern Manner by the late Commander; Who ask'd him very abruptly, what he had come about, and to declare his Business, which he said he did. . . .

[Washington was elated at the chief's recounting of his speech, for the Half King told of expressing his anger at the French; on the other hand, Washington was taken aback when the Half King told of expressing his vehement opposition to having either the French or the English settle in the Ohio country. Washington said nothing of this, however, when he spoke to the Indians in council the next day. Despite his impatience to be on his way, he yielded to the Half King's request that he wait until a guard be arranged for them and took the delay with better heart when told the Indians meant to warn the French to leave.]

30th [November, 1753]. Last Night the great Men assembled to their Council-House, to consult further about this Journey, and who were to go; the Result of which was, that only three of their Chiefs, with one of their best Hunters, should be our Convoy: The Reason which they gave for not sending more, after what had been proposed at Council the 26th, was, that a greater Number might give the *French* Suspicions of some bad Design, and cause them to be treated rudely: But I rather think they could not get their Hunters in.

We set out about 9 o'Clock with the Half-King, *Jeskakake, White Thunder,* and the Hunter, and travelled on the Road to *Venango,* where we arrived the 4th of *December,* without any Thing remarkable happening but a continued Series of bad Weather.

[December 4]. This is an old *Indian* Town, situated at the Mouth of *French* Creek on *Ohio,* and lies near N. about 60 Miles from the *Loggs*-Town, but more than 70 the Way we were obliged to go.

We found the *French* Colours hoisted at a House which they drove Mr. *John Frazier,* an *English* Subject, from; I immediately repaired to it, to know where the Commander resided. There were three Officers, one of whom, Capt. *Joncaire,* inform'd me, that he had the Command of the *Ohio,* but that there was a General Officer at the near Fort, which he advised me to for an Answer. He invited us to sup with them, and treated us with the greatest Complaisance.

The Wine, as they dosed themselves pretty plentifully with it, soon banished the Restraint which at first appear'd in their Conversation, and gave a License to their Tongues to reveal their Sentiments more freely.

They told me, That it was their absolute Design to take Possession of the *Ohio,* and by G—— they would do it; for that they were sensible the *English* could raise two Men for their one; yet they knew, their Motions were too slow and dilatory to prevent any Undertaking of theirs. They pretend to have an undoubted Right to the River, from a Discovery made by one *La Sol* [La Salle] 60 Years ago; and the Rise of this Expedition is, to prevent our settling on the River or Waters of it, as they have heard of some Families moving out in Order thereto. From the best Intelligence I could get, there have been 1500 Men on this Side *Ontario* Lake, but upon the Death of the General all were recalled to

Engraving of Tanachariston, the Half King, from The Pictorial Life of George Washington *by Frost, 1853*

about 6 or 700, who were left to garrison four Forts, 150 or there abouts in each, the first of which is on *French* Creek, near a small Lake, about 60 Miles from *Venango*, near N.N.W. the next lies on Lake *Erie*, where the greatest Part of their Stores are kept, about 15 Miles from the other; from that it is 120 Miles to the carrying Place, at the Falls of Lake *Erie* [Niagara Falls] where there is a small Fort which they lodge their Goods at, in bringing them from *Montreal*, the Place that all their Stores come from: The next Fort lies about 20 Miles from this, on *Ontario* Lake; between this Fort and *Montreal* there are three others, the first of which is near opposite to the *English* Fort *Oswego*. From the Fort on Lake *Erie* to *Montreal* is about 600 Miles, which they say requires no more, if good Weather, than four Weeks Voyage, if they go in Barks or large Vessels, that they can cross the Lake; but if they come in Canoes it will require 5 or 6 Weeks, for they are oblig'd to keep under the Shore.

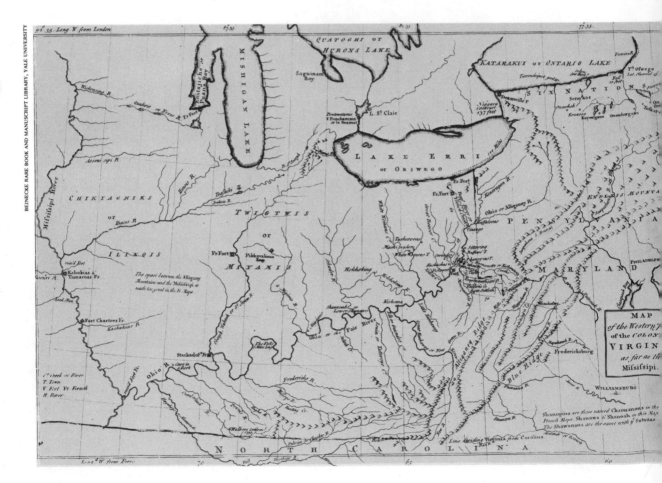

5th. Rain'd excessively all Day, which prevented our Travelling. Capt. *Joncaire* sent for the Half-King, as he had but just heard that he came with me: He affected to be much concern'd that I did not make free to bring them in before; I excused it in the best Manner I was capable, and told him I did not think their Company agreeable, as I had heard him say a good deal in Dispraise of *Indians* in general; but another Motive prevented me from bringing them into his Company; I knew he was Interpreter, and a Person of very great Influence among the *Indians,* and had lately used all possible Means to draw them over to their Interest; therefore I was desirous of giving no Opportunity that could be avoided.

When they came in, there was great Pleasure express'd at seeing them; he wonder'd how they could be so near without coming to visit him, made several trifling Presents, and applied Liquor so fast, that they were soon render'd incapable of the Business they came about, notwithstanding the Caution that was given.

6th. The Half-King came to my Tent, quite sober, and insisted very much that I should stay and hear what he had to say to the *French*; I fain would have prevented his speaking any Thing, 'til he came to the Commandant, but could not prevail: He told me, that at this Place a Council Fire was kindled, where all their Business with these People was to be transacted, and that the Management of the *Indian* Affairs was left solely to Monsieur *Joncaire.* As I was desirous of knowing the Issue of this, I agreed to stay, but sent our Horses a little Way up *French* Creek, to raft over and encamp; which I knew would make it near Night.

About 10 o'Clock they met in Council; the King spoke much the same as he had before done to the General, and offer'd the *French* Speech-Belt [a wampum belt] which had before been demanded, with the Marks of four Towns on it, which Monsieur *Joncaire* refused to receive; but desired him to carry it to the Fort to the Commander.

7th. Monsieur *La Force,* Commissary of the *French* Stores, and three other Soldiers came over to accompany us up. We found it extremely difficult getting the *Indians* off To-day, as every Stratagem had been used to prevent

The version of Washington's Journal that was printed in London included this "new map of the country as far as the Mississippi."

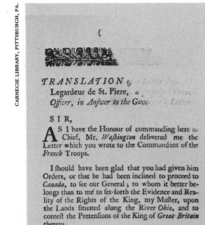

their going up with me. I had last Night left *John Davison* (the *Indian* Interpreter that I brought from the *Loggs-*Town with me) strictly charg'd not to be out of their Company, as I could not get them over to my Tent (they having some Business with *Custaloga*, to know the Reason why he did not deliver up the *French* Belt which he had in Keeping) but was obliged to send Mr. *Gist* over To-day to fetch them, which he did with great Persuasion.

At 11 o'Clock we set out for the Fort [Fort Le Boeuf], and were prevented from arriving there 'til the 11th. by excessive Rains, Snows, and bad Travelling, through many Mires and Swamps, which we were obliged to pass, to avoid crossing the Creek, which was impossible, either by fording or rafting, the Water was so high and rapid.

We passed over much good Land since we left *Venango,* and through several extensive and very rich Meadows; one of which I believe was near four Miles in Length, and considerably wide in some Places.

12th. I prepar'd early to wait upon the Commander, and was received and conducted to him by the second Officer in Command: I acquainted him with my Business, and offer'd my Commission and Letter, both of which he desired me to keep 'til the Arrival of Monsieur *Riparti,* Captain, at the next Fort, who was sent for and expected every Hour.

This Commander is a Knight of the military Order of St. *Lewis,* and named *Legardeur de St. Piere.* He is an elderly Gentleman, and has much the Air of a Soldier; he was sent over to take the Command, immediately upon the Death of the late General, and arrived here about seven Days before me.

At 2 o'Clock the Gentleman that was sent for arrived, when I offer'd the Letter, &c. again; which they receiv'd, and adjourn'd into a private Apartment for the Captain to translate, who understood a little *English;* after he had done it, the Commander desired I would walk in, and bring my Interpreter to peruse and correct it, which I did.

13th. The chief Officers retired, to hold a Council of War, which gave me an Opportunity of taking the Dimensions of the Fort, and making what Observations

Translation of the letter from "Mr. Legardeur de St. Piere," in answer to Dinwiddie's, as it appeared in Washington's printed Journal, *now in damaged condition*

I could.

It is situated on the South, or West Fork of *French* Creek, near the Water, and is almost surrounded by the Creek, and a small Branch of it which forms a Kind of an Island; four Houses compose the Sides; the Bastions are made of Piles driven into the Ground, and about 12 Feet above, and sharp at Top, with Port-Holes cut for Cannon and Loop-Holes for the small Arms to fire through; there are eight 6 lb. Pieces mounted, two in each Bastion, and one Piece of four Pound before the Gate; in the Bastions are a Guard-House, Chapel, Doctor's Lodging, and the Commander's private Store, round which are laid Plat-Forms for the Cannon and Men to stand on: There are several Barracks without the Fort, for the Soldiers Dwelling, covered, some with Bark, and some with Boards, and made chiefly of Loggs: There are also several other Houses, such as Stables, Smiths Shop, &c.

I could get no certain Account of the Number of Men here; but according to the best Judgment I could form, there are an Hundred exclusive of Officers, of which there are many. I also gave Orders to the People that were with me, to take an exact Account of the Canoes that were haled up to convey their Forces down in the Spring, which they did, and told 50 of Birch Bark, and 170 of Pine; besides many others that were block'd out, in Readiness to make.

Washington's critical meeting with St. Pierre, an illustration from Book of the Colonies *by Frost, 1846*

14*th.*   As the Snow encreased very fast, and our Horses daily became weaker, I sent them off unloaded, under the Care of *Barnaby Currin* and two others, to make all convenient Dispatch to *Venango,* and there wait our Arrival if there was a Prospect of the Rivers freezing, if not, then to continue down to *Shanapin's* Town, at the Forks of *Ohio,* and there to wait 'til we came to cross *Aligany,* intending myself to go down by Water, as I had the Offer of a Canoe or Two....

This Evening I received an Answer to his Honour the Governor's Letter from the Commandant.

[The French commandant's letter said that he had no intention of obeying Dinwiddie's demand that the French leave the country. The officer did give Washington two canoes and provisions, but for a day the French attempted unsuccessfully to cajole the Half King into remaining behind. After a cold and fatiguing seven-day trip, with four canoes of French closely following, they reached Venango on December 22.]

23d [December, 1753]. When I got Things ready to set off, I sent for the Half-King, to know whether he intended to go with us, or by Water, he told me that *White-Thunder* had hurt himself much, and was sick and unable to walk, therefore he was obliged to carry him down in a Canoe: As I found he intended to stay here a Day or two, and knew that Monsieur *Joncaire* would employ every Scheme to set him against the *English* as he had before done; I told him I hoped he would guard against his Flattery, and let no fine Speeches influence him in their Favour: He desired I might not be concerned, for he knew the *French* too well, for any Thing to engage him in their Behalf, and though he could not go down with us, he would endeavour to meet at the Forks with *Joseph Campbell,* to deliver a Speech for me to carry to his Honour the Governor. He told me he would order the young Hunter to attend us, and get Provision, *&c.* if wanted.

Our Horses were now so weak and feeble, and the Baggage heavy, as we were obliged to provide all the Necessaries that the Journey would require; that we doubted much their performing it: therefore myself and others (except the Drivers which were obliged to ride) gave up our Horses for Packs, to assist along with the Baggage; I put myself in an Indian walking Dress, and continued with them three Days, till I found there was no Probability of their getting in, in any reasonable Time; the Horses grew less able to travel every Day; the Cold increased very fast, and the Roads were becoming much worse by a deep Snow, continually freezing; and as I was uneasy to get back, to make Report of my Proceedings to his Honour the Governor, I determined to prosecute my Journey the nearest Way through the Woods, on Foot.

Accordingly I left Mr. *Vanbraam* in Charge of our Baggage, with Money and Directions, to Provide Necessaries from Place to Place for themselves and Horses, and to make the most convenient Dispatch in.

I took my necessary Papers, pulled off my Cloaths;

Washington descending the Ohio, from The Life of George Washington *by J. T. Headley published in 1856*

tied myself up in a Match Coat [a frontiersman's skin coat]; and with my Pack at my Back with my Papers and Provisions in it, and a Gun, set out with Mr. *Gist,* fitted in the same Manner, on *Wednesday* the 26th. The Day following, just after we had passed a Place called the *Murdering*-Town, where we intended to quit the Path, and steer across the Country for *Shannapins* Town, we fell in with a Party of *French* Indians, who had lain in Wait for us; one of them fired at Mr. *Gist* or me, not 15 Steps, but fortunately missed. We took this Fellow into Custody, and kept him till about 9 o'Clock at Night, and then let him go, and walked all the remaining Part of the Night without making any Stop, that we might get the Start, so far, as to be out of the Reach of their Pursuit the next Day, as we were well assured they would follow our Tract as soon as it was light: The next Day we continued travelling till quite dark, and got to the River [Allegheny] about two Miles above *Shannapins;* we expected to have found the River frozen, but it was not, only about 50 Yards from each Shore; the Ice I suppose had broken up above, for it was driving in vast Quantities.

There was no way for getting over but on a Raft, which we set about, with but one poor Hatchet, and got finished just after Sun-setting, after a whole Days Work; we got it launched, and on Board of it, and set off; but before we were Half Way over, we were jammed in the Ice in such a Manner that we expected every Moment our Raft to sink, and ourselves to perish; I put out my setting Pole to try to stop the Raft, that the Ice might pass by; when the Rapidity of the Stream threw it with so much Violence against the Pole, that it jirked me out into ten Feet Water, but I fortunately saved myself by catching hold of one of the Raft Logs; notwithstanding all our Efforts we could not get the Raft to either Shore, but were obliged, as we were near an Island, to quit our Raft and make to it.

Headley's version of Washington and Gist crossing the Allegheny River

The Cold was so extremely severe, that Mr. *Gist,* had all his Fingers, and some of his Toes frozen, and the Water was shut up so hard, that we found no Difficulty in getting off the Island, on the Ice, in the Morning, and went to Mr. *Frazier's.* We met here with 20 Warriors who were going to the *Southward* to War, but coming to a Place upon the Head of the great *Cunnaway* [Great

Kanawha River], where they found seven People killed and scalped, all but one Woman with very light Hair, they turned about and ran back, for fear the Inhabitants should rise and take them as the Authors of the Murder: They report that the People were lying about the House, and some of them much torn and eaten by Hogs: By the Marks that were left, they say they were *French* Indians of the *Ottoway* Nation, &c., that did it.

As we intended to take Horses here, and it required some Time to find them, I went up about three Miles to the Mouth of *Yaughyaughgane* [Youghiogheny River] to visit Queen *Alliquippa* [of the Delaware Nation], who had expressed great Concern that we passed her in going to the Fort. I made her a Present of a Matchcoat and a Bottle of Rum, which latter was thought much the best Present of the Two.

Tuesday the 1st. Day of *January* [1754], we left Mr. *Frazier's* House, and arrived at Mr. *Gist's* at *Monongahela* the 2d, where I bought Horse, Saddle, &c. the 6th we met 17 Horses loaded with Materials and Stores for a Fort at the Forks of *Ohio*, and the Day after some Families going out to settle: This Day we arrived at *Wills*-Creek, after as fatiguing a Journey as it is possible to conceive, rendered so by excessive bad Weather: From the first Day of *December* to the 15th, there was but one Day but it rained or snowed incessantly; and throughout the whole Journey we met with nothing but one continued Series of cold wet Weather, which occasioned very uncomfortable Lodgings, especially after we had left our Tent, which was some Screen from the Inclemency of it.

On the 11th I got to *Belvoir* where I stopped one Day to take necessary Rest, and then set out, and arrived in *Williamsburg* the 16th, and waited upon his Honour the Governor with the Letter I had brought from the *French* Commandant, and to give an Account of the Proceedings of my Journey, which I beg Leave to do by offering the foregoing, as it contains the most remarkable Occurences that happened to me.

I hope it will be sufficient to satisfy your Honour with my Proceedings; for that was my Aim in undertaking the Journey, and chief Study throughout the Prosecution of it.

Washington's accomplishment had been a noteworthy one. Although a tenderfoot, he had borne well the rigors of travel in the bitter wilderness. Sent to deliver a letter, he had found himself involved in a diplomatic battle for the allegiance of an Indian chief and had done well for an amateur against professionals. Only once had his steps lagged, the one-day stop at Belvoir "to take necessary Rest"; and it may well be that it was the captivating Sally Fairfax more than fatigue that made him break his journey there.

The news he brought was extremely upsetting to Governor Dinwiddie and others in Williamsburg, but Washington was chagrined to find that many read his report with skepticism, as largely fiction designed to gain backing for the Ohio Company. The House of Burgesses showed little interest in the Ohio country, but eventually an expedition of three hundred men was authorized. These men, it was promised, would have the help of a thousand Cherokee and Catawba warriors from the Carolinas, and the Government in London informed the Governor that three companies of regulars would also be sent from other Colonies. The expedition was to hurry to the Forks, to aid William Trent, an Indian trader, who with forty men had already begun building a fort at the juncture of the Allegheny and Monongahela rivers.

Colonel Joshua Fry was in command; George Washington, commissioned a lieutenant colonel, was second in rank. Recruiting went slowly, and it was decided that Washington should go ahead with the vanguard, leaving Colonel Fry to follow later. On April 2, 1754, Washington led 120 men out of Alexandria. He found about forty more waiting at Winchester, but had an almost impossible time obtaining transport from the farmers, who hid all but their most broken-down wagons and decrepit horses. Two weeks later, at Wills Creek, he reported extremely disheartening news to Governor Dinwiddie.

Cartouche from a map drawn in 1751 by Joshua Fry, who three years later led the expedition to the Forks, and Peter Jefferson, father of Thomas

Will's Creek [Maryland] April 25, 1754
Captain Trent's ensign, Mr. Ward, has this day arrived from the Fork of the Monongahela, and brings the disagreeable account, that the fort, on the 17th instant, was surrendered at the summons of Monsieur Contrecœur to a body of French, consisting of upwards of one thousand men, who came from Venango with eighteen pieces of cannon, sixty batteaux, and three hundred canoes. They gave him liberty to bring off all his men and working-tools, which he accordingly did the same day.

Immediately upon this information I called a council of war, to advise on proper measures to be taken in this exigency. A copy of their resolves, with the proceedings, I herewith enclose by the bearer, whom I have continued express to your Honor for more minute intelligence.

Mr. Ward has the summons with him, and a speech from the Half-King, which I also enclose, with the wampum. He is accompanied by one of the Indians mentioned therein, who were sent to see where we were, what was our strength, and to know the time to expect us out. The other young man I have prevailed upon to return to the Half-King with the following speech [pledging British friendship to the Half King and his people].

I hope my proceedings in these affairs will be satisfactory to your Honor, as I have, to the utmost of my knowledge, consulted the interest of the expedition and good of my country; whose rights, while they are asserted in so just a cause, I will defend to the last remains of life.

Hitherto the difficulties I have met with in marching have been greater, than I expect to encounter on the Ohio, when possibly I may be surrounded by the enemy, and these difficulties have been occasioned by those, who, had they acted as becomes every good subject, would have exerted their utmost abilities to forward our just designs. Out of seventy-four wagons impressed at Winchester, we got but ten after waiting a week, and some of those so badly provided with teams, that the soldiers were obliged to assist them up the hills, although it was known they had better teams at home. I doubt not that in some points I may have strained the law; but I hope, as my sole motive was to expedite the march, I shall be supported in it, should my authority be questioned, which at present I do not apprehend, unless some busybody intermeddles.

Your Honor will see by the resolves in council, that I am destined to the Monongahela with all the diligent despatch in my power. We will endeavour to make the road sufficiently good for the heaviest artillery to pass, and when we arrive at Red-stone Creek [site of an Ohio Company storehouse], fortify ourselves as strongly as the short time will allow. I doubt not that we can maintain a possession there, till we are reinforced, unless the rising of the waters shall admit the enemy's cannon to be conveyed up in canoes, and then I flatter myself we shall not be so destitute of intelligence, as not to get timely notice of it, and make a good retreat.

Governor Robert Dinwiddie

I hope you will see the absolute necessity for our having, as soon as our forces are collected, a number of cannon, some of heavy metal, with mortars and grenadoes to attack the French, and put us on an equal footing with them.

Perhaps it may also be thought advisable to invite the Cherokees, Catawbas, and Chickasaws to march to our assistance, as we are informed that six hundred Chippewas and Ottawas are marching down Scioto Creek to join the French, who are coming up the Ohio. In that case I would beg leave to recommend their being ordered to this place first, that a peace may be concluded between them and the Six Nations; for I am informed by several persons, that, as no good harmony subsists between them, their coming first to the Ohio may create great disorders, and turn out much to our disadvantage.

O n May 9 Washington was reporting his new woes to Dinwiddie: promised pack horses had not been waiting when the column arrived at Wills Creek, roadmaking was slow, Indian allies had not appeared, Captain William Trent's men returning from the Forks had been troublemakers.

Little Meadows [Pennsylvania]
9th. of May 1754

Honble. Sir

I acquainted your Honour by Mr. Ward with the determinations, which we prosecuted in 24 Days after his Departure, as soon as Waggons arrived to convey our Provisions. The want of proper Conveyances has much retarded this Expedition, and at this time, unfortunately delay'd the Detachment I have the Honour to command. Even when we came to Wills Ck. my disappointments were not less than before, for there I expected to have found a sufficient number of pack Horses provided by Captn. Trent conformable to his Promise, Majr. Carlyles Letter's and my own (that I might prosecute my first intention with light expeditious Marches) but instd. of tht., there was none in readiness, nor any in expectation, that I could perceive, which reducd me to the necessity of waitg. till Waggon's cd. be procur'd from the Branch (40 Miles distant). However in the mean time I detach'd a party of 60 Men to make and amend the Road, which party since the 25th. of Apl., and the main body since the 1st. Instt. have been laboriously employ'd, and have got no further than these Meadows abt. 20 Miles from the new Store; where we have been two Days making a Bridge across and are not done yet. The great difficulty and labour that it requires to amend and alter the Roads, prevents our Marchg. above 2, 3, or 4 Miles a Day, and I fear (tho. no diligence shall be neglected) we shall be detained some considerable time before it can be made good for the Carriages of the Artillery with Colo. Fry.

We Daily receive Intelligence from Ohio by one or other of the Trader's that are continually retreating to the Inhabitants with their Effects; they all concur, that the French are reinforced with 800 Men; and this Day by one Kalender I receiv'd an acct. which he sets forth as certain, that there is 600 Men building at the Falls of Ohio, from whence they intd. to move up to the lower Shawno Town at the Mouth of Sciodo Ck. to Erect their Fortresses. He likewise says that these forces at the Forks are Erectg. their works with their whole Force, and as he was coming met at Mr. Gists new settlemt. Monsieur La-Force with 4 Soldrs. who under the specious pretence of hunting Deserters were reconnoitreg. and discovering the Country. He also brings the agreeable news that the Half King has receiv'd, & is much pleas'd with the speech I sent them, and is now upon their March with 50 Men to meet us.

The French down the River are sending presents and invitations to all the neighbouring Indians, and practiseing every means to influence them in their Interest.

We have heard nothing from the Cawtaba's or any of the Southern Indians tho. this is the time we mostly need their assistance. I have not above 160 Effective Men with me since Captn. Trent have left us, who I discharg'd from this Detacht. & order'd them to wait your Honour's Comds. at Captn. Trents for I found them rather injurious to the other Men than Serviceable to the Expn. till they could be upon the same Establisht. with us and come under the rigr. of the Martial Law.

I am Honble. Sir with the most profound respect yr. Honour's most obt. & most Hbl. Servt.

Go: Washington

P.S. I hope yr. Hr. will excuse the papr. & wg. the want of conveniences obliges me to this.

More frustrations followed. Washington explored the Youghiogheny as a possible water route but found it obstructed by a falls. On May 27 he was writing to the Governor from a place called Great Meadows.

Gt. Meadws. [Pennsylvania]
27th. May 1754

I hereupon hurried to this place as a convenient spot. We have with Natures assistance made a good Intrenchment and by clearing the Bushes out of these Meadows prepar'd a charming field for an Encounter. I detach'd imediately upon my arrival here small light partys of horse (Wagn. Horses) to reconnoitre the Enemy and discover their strength & motion who returnd Yesterday witht. seeing any thing of them. Nevertheless we were alarmd at Night and remaind under Arms from two OClock till near Sun rise. We conceive it was our own Men as 6 of them Deserted but can't be certain whether it was them or other Enemy's. Be it as it will they were fired at by the Centrys but I believe without damage.

This Morning Mr. Gist arrivd from his place where a Detachment of 50 Men was seen Yesterday at Noon Comd. by Monsr. Laforce. He afterwards saw their tracks within 5 Miles of our Camp. I imediately detachd 75 Men in pursuit of them who I hope will overtake them before they get to red Stone where their Canoes Lie. Mr. Gist being an Eye witness of our proceedings hereupon, and waiting for this witht. knowing till just now that he intended to wait upon your Honr. obliges me to refer to him for particulars. As I expect my Messenger in to Night from the Half King I shall write more fully to morrow by the Express that came from Colo. Fry.

But before I conclude I must take the Liberty of mentioning to your Honour the gt. necessity there is for having goods out here to give for Services of the Indians. They all expect it and refuse to Scout or do any thing without saying these Services are paid well by the French. I really think was 5 or 600 Pounds worth of proper goods sent it wd. tend more to our Interest than so many Thousands given in a Lump at a treaty. I have been obligd to pay Shirts for what they have already done which I cannot continue to do.

The Numbers of the French have been greatly magnified as your Honour may see by a copy of the inclosd journal who I sent out to gain intelligence. I have receivd

Letter's from the Governor's of Pensylvania & Maryland
Copys of which I also send. I am Yr. Honrs. most Obt. &
most Hble. Servt.

GO: WASHINGTON

P.S. I hope your Honr. will excuse the Haste with which
I was obligd. to use in writing this.

Two days later Washington was writing the Governor
again from Great Meadows. After he complained at great length about the
miserable pay of Colonial officers, he eventually got around to a matter
of some importance.

[Great Meadows, Pennsylvania,
May 29, 1754]

Now, Sir, as I have answer'd your Honour's Letter, I
shall beg leave to acq't you with what has happen'd
since I wrote by Mr. Gist. I then acquainted you, that I
had detach'd a party of 75 Men to meet with 50 of the
French, who, we had Intelligence, were upon their
March towards us to Reconnoitre &ca. Ab't 9 O'clock
the same night, I receiv'd an express from the Half
King, who was Incamp'd with several of his People ab't
6 Miles of, that he had seen the Tract of two French
Men x'ing the road, and believ'd the whole body were
lying not far off, as he had an acc't of that number passing Mr. Gist.

I set out with 40 Men before 10, and was from that
time till near Sun rise before we reach'd the Indian's
Camp, hav'g March'd in [a] small path, a heavy Rain,
and a Night as Dark as it is possible to conceive. We
were frequently tumbling one over another, and often
so lost, that 15 or 20 Minutes' search would not find
the path again.

When we came to the Half King, I council'd with
him, and got his assent to go hand in hand and strike
the French. Accordingly, himself, Monacatoocha, and
a few other Indians set out with us; and when we came
to the place where the Tracts were, the Half King sent
two Indians to follow their tracts, and discover their
lodgement, which they did ab't half a mile from the Road,
in a very obscure place surrounded with Rocks. I there-
upon, in conjunction with the Half King and Monacatoocha, form'd a disposition to attack y'm on all sides,
which we accordingly did, and, after an Engagement of

ab't 15 Minutes, we killed 10, wounded one, and took 21 Prisoners. Amongst those that were killed was Monsieur Jumonville, the Commander, princip'l Officers taken is Monsieur Druillong and Mons'r La force, who your Honour has often heard me speak of as a bold Enterprising Man, and a person of great sublity and cunning. With these are two Cadets.

These Officers pretend they were coming on an Embassy; but the absurdity of this pretext is too glaring, as your Honour will see by the Instructions and Summons inclos'd. These Instructions were to reconnoitre the Country, Roads, Creeks, &ca. to Potomack, which they were ab't to do. These Enterprising Men were purposely choose out to get intelligence, which they were to send Back by some brisk dispatches, with mention of the Day that they were to serve the Summons; which could be through no other view, than to get sufficient Reinforcements to fall upon us immediately after. This, with several other Reasons, induc'd all the Officers to believe firmly, that they were sent as spys, rather than any thing else, and has occasion'd my sending them as prisoners, tho' they expected (or at least had some faint hope, of being continued as ambassadors).

Death of M. Jumonville from Headley's Life of George Washington

They, finding where we were Incamp'd, instead of coming up in a Publick manner, sought out one of the most secret Retirements, fitter for a Deserter than an Imbassador to incamp in, and s[t]ay'd there two or 3 Days, sent Spies to Reconnoitre our Camp, as we are told, tho' they deny it. Their whole Body mov'd back near 2 miles, sent off two runners to acquaint Contrecoeur with our Strength, and where we were Incamp'd. &ca. Now 36 Men w'd almost have been a Retinue for a Princely Ambassador, instead of Petit, why did they, if their designs were open, stay so long within 5 Miles of us, with't delivering his Ambassy, or acquainting me with it; His waiting c'd be with no other design, than to get Detachm't to enforce the Summons, as soon as it was given, they had no occasion to send out Spies, for the Name of Ambassador is Sacred among all Nations; but it was by the tract of these Spys, they were discover'd, and we got Intelligence of them. They w'd not have retir'd two Miles back with't delivering the Summons, and sought a sculking place (which, to do them justice, was done with g't Judgment) but for some

47

especial reason: Besides The Summons is so insolent and savours so much of Gascoigny that if two Men only had come openly to deliver it. It was too great Indulgence to have sent them back. . . .

In this Engagement we had only one Man kill'd, and two or three wounded, among which was Lieutt. Waggener slightly, a most miraculous escape, as Our Right Wing was much expos'd to their Fire and receiv'd it all. . . .

Your Honour may depend I will not be surprized let them come what hour they will; and this is as much as I can promise, but my best endeavour's shall not be wanting to deserve more, I doubt not if you hear I am beaten, but you will at the same [time,] hear that we have done our duty in fighting as long [as] there was a possibility of hope.

Washington, with his little forest skirmish, had fired the opening gun of the Seven Years' War (1754–63), whose American phase is called the French and Indian War. At the moment, however, he was concerned only with his immediate problems, which increased on May 31 when Colonel Fry died after a horseback accident and Washington assumed command of all Virginia troops. Soon after, at the age of twenty-two, he was promoted to colonel.

At Great Meadows he built Fort Necessity, a stronghold that to his untrained eye appeared sturdy enough so that he need "not fear the attack of 500 men." Indian allies drifted in, but most were women and children who consumed great amounts of scarce provisions. In mid-June Captain James MacKay arrived from South Carolina with a company of the regular British army, but he refused to take orders from Washington, since any officer holding a commission from the King outranked any Colonial officer.

Washington resumed his slow advance toward Fort Duquesne, which the French had built at the Forks of the Ohio. The Virginians had scarcely begun fortifying an advanced position when word came that the French, greatly reinforced, were moving on them. There was a hasty retreat to Fort Necessity, which was hurriedly extended and strengthened, while the Indian allies quietly vanished. Despite what Washington had written about the place being "a charming field for an encounter," the position was poor. It was low, and trenches filled with water from a steady rain that began on the morning of July 3. Before the morning was over, the French attacked.

If Washington wrote a contemporary record of the engagement, it has been lost. Long afterward, in 1786, however, he sent a memorandum to a would-be biographer, describing the fight but warning that after so many years his memory was vague on some details.

The surrender of Fort Necessity, drafted in French, was signed by Washington and dated July 3, 1754.

[October, 1786]

About 9 Oclock on the 3d. of July the Enemy advanced with Shouts, and dismal Indian yells to our Intrenchments, but was opposed by so warm, spirited, and constant a fire, that to force the works in *that way* was abandoned by them; they then, from every little rising, tree, stump, Stone, and bush kept up a constant galding fire upon us; which was returned in the best manner we could till late in the Afternn. when their fell the most tremendous rain that can be conceived, filled our trenches with Water, Wet, not only the Ammunition in the Cartouch boxes and firelocks, but that which was in a small temporary Stockade in the middle of the Intrenchment called Fort Necessity erected for the sole purpose of its security, and that of the few stores we had; and left us nothing but a few (for all were not provided with them) Bayonets for defence. In this situation and *no* prospt. of bettering it terms of capitulation were offered to us by the enemy wch. with some alterations that were insisted upon were the more readily acceded to, as we had no Salt provisions, and but indifferently supplied with fresh; which, from the heat of the weather, would not keep; and because a full third of our numbers Officers as well as privates were, by this time, killed or wounded. The next Morning we marched out with the honors of War, but were soon plundered contrary to the Articles of capitulation of great part of our Baggage by the Savages. Our Sick and wounded were left with a detachment under the care, and command of the worthy Doctr. Craik (for he was not only Surgeon to the Regiment but a lieutt. therein) with such necessaries as we could collect and the Remains of the Regimt., and the detachment of Regulars, took up their line for the interior Country. And at Winchester met 2 Companies from No. Carolina on their March to join them. These being fresh, and properly provided, were ordered to proceed to Wills's Creek and establish a post (afterwards called Fort Cumberland) for the purpose of covering the Frontiers. Where they were joined by a Company from Maryland, which, about this time, had been raized, Captn. McKay with his detachment remd. at Winchester; and the Virginia Regiment proceedd. to Alexandria in order to recruit, and get supplied with cloathing and necessarys of which they stood much in need. In this manner the Winter was employed, when advice was recd. of the force destined for this Service under the ordrs. of G. B. [General Braddock] and the arrival of Sir Jno. St. Clair the Q:Mastr. Genl with some new arrangement of Rank by which no Officer who did not *immediately* derive his Comn. from the *King* could command one *who did.* This was too degrading for G. W to submit to; accordingly, he resigned his Military employment; determining to serve the next campaign as a Volunteer.

Washington had lost thirty men killed and seventy wounded; the French admitted to two killed and seventeen wounded. Washington became something of a hero despite his defeat, although experienced military men criticized many aspects of his campaign. Moreover, the fight at Fort Necessity had wide reverberations. From the Crown in England came a promise of money and arms. Governor Horatio Sharpe of Maryland was given a King's commission and put in command of all forces that were to "be raised on this part of the continent to protect His Majesty's Dominions from the encroachments of his presumptuous enemies."

Word came that Washington's Virginia Regiment was to be broken up into independent companies, each led by a captain holding a regular commission. The plan would have reduced Washington in rank from colonel to captain; if he were unable to obtain a King's commission as captain he would have ranked below every officer, of whatever rank, who held such a commission. It was too much for his pride, and in late October of 1754 he handed his resignation to Dinwiddie.

Governor Sharpe, however, needed Washington's knowledge of the wilderness and wanted him along on the campaign he was trying to organize. He suggested that Washington might keep the title of colonel and assured him that the company he commanded would be kept on separate assignment, so that the proud Virginian would not be under the command of anyone he would have commanded as colonel. Washington refused, in a somewhat emotional letter to Sharpe's military aide.

Belvoir [Virginia], November 15th. 1754

I was favoured with your letter, from Rousby-Hall, of the 4th. Instant. It demands my best acknowledgments, for the particular marks of Esteem you have expressed therein; and for the kind assurances of his Excellency, Governour Sharp's good wishes towards me. I also thank you, and sincerely, Sir, for your friendly intention of making my situation easy, if I return to the Service; and do not doubt, could I submit to the Terms, that I should be as happy under your command, in the absence of the General, as under any gentleman's whatever: but, I think, the disparity between the present offer of a Company, and my former Rank, too great to expect any real satisfaction or enjoyment in a Corps, where I once did, or thought I had a right to, command; even if his Excellency had power to suspend the Orders received in the Secretary of Wars' Letter; which, by the bye, I am very far from thinking he either has or will attempt to do, without fuller Instructions than I believe he has: especially, too, as there has been a representation of this matter by Governour Dinwiddie, and, I believe, the Assembly of this State; we have advices, that it was received before Demmarree obtained his Letter.

All that I presume the General can do, is, to prevent the different Corps from interfering, which will occasion the Duty to be done by Corps, instead of Detachments; a very inconvenient way, as is found by experience.

You make mention in your letter of my continuing in the Service, and retaining my Colo.'s Commission. This idea has filled me with surprise: for if you think me capable of holding a Commission that has neither rank or emolument annexed to it; you must entertain a very contemptible opinion of my weakness, and believe me to be more empty than the Commission itself.

Besides, Sir, if I had time, I could enumerate many good reasons, that forbid all thoughts of my Returning; and which, to you, or any other, would, upon the strictest scrutiny, appear to be well-founded. I must be reduced to a very low Command, and subjected to that of many who have acted as my inferior Officers. In short, every Captain, bearing the Kings' Commission; every half-pay Officer, or other, appearing with such commission, would rank before me; for these reasons, I choose to submit to the loss of Health, which I have, however, already sustained (not to mention that of Effects) and the fatigue I have undergone in our first Efforts; than subject myself to the same inconveniences, and run the risque of a second disappointment. I shall have the consolation itself, of knowing, that I have opened the way when the smallness of our numbers exposed us to the attacks of a Superior Enemy; That I have hitherto stood the heat and brunt of the Day, and escaped untouched, in time of extreme danger; and that I have the Thanks of my Country, for the Services I have rendered it.

It shall not sleep in silence, my having received information, that those peremptory Orders from Home, which, you say, could not be dispensed with, for reducing the Regiments into Independant Companies, were generated, hatched, & brought from Will's-Creek. Ingenuous treatment, & plain dealing, I at least expected. It is to be hoped the project will answer; it shall meet with my acquiescence in every thing except personal Services. I herewith enclose Governour Sharp's Letter, which I beg you will return to him, with my Acknowledgments for the favour he intended me; assure him, Sir, as you truly may, of my reluctance to quit the Service, and of the pleasure I should have received in attending his Fortunes: also, inform him, that it was to obey the call of Honour, and the advice of my Friends, I declined it, and not to gratify any desire I had to leave the military line.

My inclinations are strongly bent to arms.

The length of this, & the small room I have left, tell me how necessary it is to conclude, which I will do as you always shall find Truly & sincerely, Your most hble. Servant,

GEO. WASHINGTON

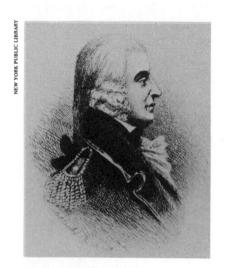

General Edward Braddock

With his military career over, at least for the time being, Washington turned to his land. Ferry Farm was to have become his on his twenty-first birthday, but he was now nearing twenty-three and his mother gave no sign of moving out. Lawrence, in his will, had left Mount Vernon to his baby daughter, with the provision that if there were no surviving children it would go to his widow until her death and then pass on to his brother George. Washington's chances of obtaining the plantation appeared thin; but Lawrence's daughter died in 1754, and his widow, who had remarried less than six months after Lawrence's death, had gone elsewhere to live with her new husband. George leased Mount Vernon from her, with eighteen resident slaves, for fifteen thousand pounds of tobacco yearly.

Thus, in December, 1754, George became the squire of Mount Vernon. But about the same time word spread through Virginia that an expedition commanded by Major General Edward Braddock was coming from Britain to drive the French from Fort Duquesne and so expel them from the upper Ohio country. Although George had resigned his commission, he still yearned for a military career, and he sent a letter when Braddock landed, congratulating him on his arrival in America—and incidentally letting him know that George Washington existed.

Washington's experience in wilderness fighting was not to be ignored, and Braddock's aide wrote to him, offering the Virginian a place on the General's staff, where he would not be subject to the humiliating distinction between regular and Colonial officers. In the latter part of March, 1755, Washington went to Alexandria, Virginia, where Braddock was organizing his expedition. He met the General, and it was agreed that Washington would join Braddock's staff at Wills Creek, Maryland. He was fascinated by his first contact with a professional army, and with the comings and goings of important Colonial leaders, and after having returned to Mount Vernon he wrote a letter to his confidant and adviser Colonel William Fairfax that reflected his pride at being part of the exciting scene.

[Mount Vernon, April 23, 1755]

I cannot think of quitting Fairfax, without embracing this last opportunity of bidding you farewell.

I this day set out for Wills Creek, where I expect to meet the Genl., and to stay—I fear too long, as our March must be regulated by the slow movements of the Train, which I am sorry to say, I think, will be tedious in advancing—very tedious indeed—as [agreeable] to the expectation I have long conceived, tho' few believ'd.

Alexandria has been honourd with 5 Governors in Consultation—a happy presage I hope, not only of the success of this Expedition, but for our little Town; for surely, such honours must have arisen from the Commodious, and pleasant situation of this place, the best constitutional qualitys for Popularity and encrease of a (now) flourishing Trade.

I have had the Honour to be introduced to the Governors; and of being well receiv'd by them all; especially Mr. Shirley, whose Character and appearance has perfectly charm'd me, as I think his every word, and every Action discovers something of the fine Gent'n., and great Politician. I heartily wish such unanimity amongst us, as appeard to Reign between him and his Assembly; when they, to expidate the Business, and forward his Journey here, sat till eleven, and twelve o'clock at Nights.

Washington first met General Edward Braddock (opposite) at this house in Alexandria, which served as his Virginia organizing headquarters.

Mount Vernon, LOSSING

Washington rode out to inspect his Bullskin plantation on the Shenandoah before joining Braddock. While there, he wrote to Sally Fairfax, asking her to correspond with him.

[Bullskin, Virginia, April 30, 1755]

Dear Madam

In order to engage your corrispondance, I think it

expedient just to deserve it; which I shall endeavour to do, by embracing the earliest, and every oppirtunity, of Writing to you.

It will be needless to expatiate on the pleasures that a communication of this kind will afford me, as it shall suffice to say—a corrispondance with my Friends is the greatest satisfaction I expect to enjoy, in the course of the Campaigne, and that none of my Friends are able to convey more real delight than you can to whom I stand indebted for so many Obligations.

If an old Proverb can claim my belief I am certainly [close to a] share of success—for surely no Man ever made a worse beginning than I have: out of 4 Horses which we brought from home, one was killd outright, and the other 3 rinderd unfit for use; so that I have been detaind here three days already, and how much longer I may continue to be so, the Womb of time must discover.

Braddock's forces moved forward at a snail's pace, methodically building a road, while the General damned the Colonists who did not deliver the wagons, horses, and supplies they had promised (only a Pennsylvanian, Benjamin Franklin, provided every one of the wagons, with teams and drivers, that he had pledged). Indians and Frenchmen wise in the ways of forest fighting struck now and then as the column moved through the woods, often at no more than two miles a day; a few men were killed, but when Washington tried to warn how unsuited the British methods were for forest warfare, he was shrugged off as the British officers expressed serene faith in their tactics and firepower. Braddock did, however, accept Washington's suggestion that a portion of the column leave some of its ponderous train of artillery and supply wagons behind and push on more rapidly before French reinforcements could reach the fort.

Washington became ill with a fever and violent head pains and had to remain behind at a supply depot on June 20 while Braddock's vanguard pushed on. Later, still painfully ill, he rejoined Braddock so as not to miss the assault on the fort, catching up with the advanced force on July 8 where it was camped only a dozen miles from Fort Duquesne. The next day the march was resumed. Early in the afternoon, the column was suddenly attacked by a much smaller force of French and Indians. The British soldiers, unable to see their enemy in the forest, hearing blood-chilling war whoops everywhere, and with their comrades falling about them, panicked completely. Only the despised Virginia Colonials, over whom Washington took command, retained some semblance of discipline. Washington wrote about it to Governor Dinwiddie.

ADVERTISEMENT

Lancaster, May 6th. 1755.

NOTICE is hereby given to all who have contracted to send Waggons and Teams, or single Horses from York County to the Army at Will's Creek, that David M'Conaughy and Michael Schwope of the said County, Gentlemen, will attend on my Behalf at York Town on Friday next, and at Philip Forney's on Saturday, to value or apprise all such Waggons, Teams and Horses, as shall appear at those Places on the said Days for that Purpose; and such as do not then appear must be valued at Will's Creek.

The Waggons that are valued at York and Forney's, are to set out immediately after the Valuation from thence for Will's Creek, under the Conduct and Direction of Persons I shall appoint for that Purpose.

The Owner or Owners of each Waggon or Set of Horses, should bring with them to the Place of Valuation, and deliver to the Apprisers, a Paper containing a Description of their several Horses in Writing, with their several Marks natural and artificial; which Paper is to be annexed to the Contract.

Each Waggon should be furnished with a Cover, that the Goods laden therein may be kept from Damage by the Rain, and the Health of the Drivers preserved, who are to lodge in the Waggons. And each Cover should be marked with the Contractor's Name in large Characters.

Each Waggon, and every Horse Driver should also be furnished with a Hook or Sickle, fit to cut that long Grass that grows in the Country beyond the Mountains.

As all the Waggons are obliged to carry a Load of Oats, or Indian Corn, Persons who have such Grain to dispose of, are desired to be cautious how they hinder the King's Service, by demanding an extravagant Price on this Occasion.

B. FRANKLIN.

Bekantmachung.

Lancaster, 6ten May, 1755.

[German-language version of the advertisement in Fraktur type]

B. Franklin.

*Franklin's successful advertisement
for horses and wagons was printed
in both English and German. The
map below of General Braddock's
defeat was drawn by a British
engineer serving in his army.*

[Fort Cumberland, Maryland, July 18, 1755]
As I am favour'd with an oppertunity, I shou'd think myself inexcusable, was I to omit givg. you some acct. of our late Engagemt. with the French on the Monongahela the 9th. Inst.

We continued our March from Fort Cumberland to Frazer's (which is within 7 Miles of Duquisne) witht. meetg. with any extraordinary event, havg. only a stragler or two picked Up by the French Indians. When we came to this place, we were attackd, (very unexpectedly I must own) by abt. 300 French and Indns.; Our numbers consisted of abt. 1300 well armd Men, chiefly regular's, who were immediately struck with such a deadly Panick, that nothing but confusion and disobedience of order's prevaild amongst them. The Officer's in Genl. behavd with incomparable bravery, for which they greatly sufferd, there being near 60 killd and woundd. A large Proportion out of the number we had! The Virginian Companies behavd like Men, and died like Soldier's; for I believe out of 3 Companys that were there that Day, scarce 30 were left alive: Captn. Peyrouny and all his Officer's down to a Corporal, were killd; Captn. Polson shard almost as hard a Fate, for only one of his Escap'd: In short the dastardly behaviour of the English Soldiers expos'd all those who were inclin'd to do their duty, to almost certain Death; and at length, in despight of every

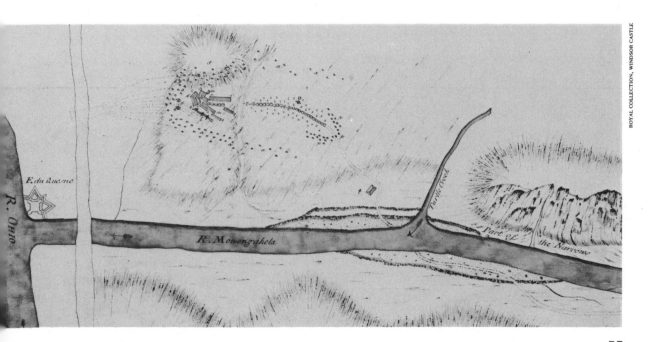

effort to the contrery broke & run as Sheep before the Hounds, leavg. the Artillery, Ammunition, Provisions and every individual thing we had with us a prize to the Enemy; and when we endeavourd to rally them in hopes of regaining our invaluable Loss, it was with as much Success as if we had attempted to have stopd the Wild Bears of the Mountains.

The Genl. was wounded behind the Shoulder, & into the Breast, of wch. he died three days after; his two Aids de Camp were both wounded, but are in a fair way of Recovering; Colo. Burton & Sir Jno. St. Clair are also wounded, and I hope will get over it; Sir Peter Halket, with many other brave Officers were killd in the Field. I luckily escap'd with't a Wound tho' I had four Bullets thro' my Coat & two Horses shot under me. It is supposed that we left 300 or more dead in the Field; abt. that number we brought off wounded; and it is imagin'd (I believe with good justice too) that two thirds of both those number's receiv'd their shots from our own cowardly Dogs of Soldiers, who gatherd themselves into a body contrary to orders 10 or 12 deep, woud then level, Fire, & shoot down the Men before them.

I Tremble at the consequences that this defeat may have upon our back setlers, who I suppose will all leave their habitation's unless their are proper measures taken for their security. Colo. Dunbar, who commands at present, intends as soon as his Men are recruited at this place to continue his March to Philda. into *Winter* Quarter's; so that there will be no Men left here unless it is the poor remains of the Virginia Troops; who now are, & will be too small to guard our Frontiers.

British military uniforms from the time of George II, worn by the soldiers fighting in America

The panic of defeat spread so far and so strongly that the rear force commander, Colonel Thomas Dunbar, assuming leadership from the dying Braddock, destroyed his artillery, transport, and supplies and retreated precipitately to Fort Cumberland at Wills Creek. There he decided that his forces were too few, too demoralized, and without sufficient artillery and other equipage to undertake any further action, and on August 2 he marched out of the frontier fort, heading for Philadelphia to go into winter quarters and leaving the border unprotected against the French and Indians except by the battered remnants of the Virginia Regiment. That same day, Washington at Mount Vernon was writing to a friend, expressing his disgust at the disaster in the wilderness.

Mount Vernon, August 2, 1755.
I must acknowledge you had great reason to be terrified with the first accts. that was given of our unhappy defeat, and I must own, I was not a little surpris'd to find that Governor Innis [James Innis, in charge of Fort Cumberland] was the means of alarming the Country with a report of that extraordinary nature, without having any better confirmation of the truth, than an affrighted waggoner's story. Its true, we have been beaten, most shamefully beaten, by a handful of Men! who only intended to molest and disturb our March; Victory was their smallest expectation, but see the wondrous works of Providence! the uncertainty of Human things! *We*, but a few moments before, believ'd our number's almost equal to the Canadian Force; *they* only expected to annoy us: Yet, contrary to all expectation, and even to the common course of things, we were totally defeated, sustain'd the loss of every thing; which they have got, are enrichen'd and strengthened by it. This, as you observe, must be an affecting story to the Colony; and will, no doubt, license the tongues of People to censure those they think most blamably; which by the by, often falls very wrongfully. I join very heartily with you in believing that when this story comes to be related in future Annals, it will meet with ridicule or indignation; for had I not been witness to the fact on that fatal Day, I sh'd scarce give credit to it now.

Dunbar's army was hardly out of sight before reports began to come in of Indians murdering isolated pioneer families on the Maryland and northwestern Virginia frontiers. In Williamsburg the General Assembly voted money to fill and equip the decimated Virginia Regiment, and Governor Dinwiddie offered George Washington an appointment not only as colonel commanding the regiment but as "commander of all the forces that now are or may be employed in the country's [Virginia's] service." Washington received his commission on August 14. At once he set to work. After having given his captains instructions for recruiting and training men, he hastened to Fort Cumberland. He reached that post on September 17, found its garrison almost demoralized, and immediately set about instilling discipline in his new command.

Fort Cumberland, September 19th. 1755
All the Men of the two Companies formed Yesterday, are to distinguish their Firelocks by some particular

mark, which the Subaltern Officers of the Companies are to enter in a Book, which they are to keep for that purpose. And if any man changes or loses his Firelock, or other Arms, he is to be confined and severely punished. The Arms of all Deserters or Dead Men, are immediately to be delivered to the Commissary, who is to pass his Receipt for them to the Commanding Officer of the Company.

Any Soldier who is guilty of any breach of the Articles of War, by Swearing, getting Drunk, or using an Obscene Language; shall be severely Punished, without the Benefit of a Court Martial.

A Court Martial to sit immediately, for Trial of all the Prisoners in the Guard.

<blockquote>
Captain Savage—President.

Members { Lieutenant Roe, Lieutenant Stewart;
Lieutenant Linn, Lieutenant Blegg.
</blockquote>

The Officers of the two Companies formed Yesterday, are to have their Rolls called over thrice every Day; which the Officers are to attend and see Done by turns, beginning with the Captain: and if any Soldier is absent without Leave, he is to be confined immediately, and

Letter of instruction from Governor Dinwiddie to Washington, August 14, 1755, after his appointment as commander of the Virginia Regiment

tried by a Court Martial, or punished at the Discretion of the Commanding Officer.

AFTER ORDERS

As Complaint has been made to me, that John Stewart, Soldier in Captain Bronaughs Company, keeps a Disorderly and riotous Assembly, constantly about him:

I do Order, that, for the future, he shall not presume to Sell any Liquor to any Soldier or any other Person whatsoever, under pain of the severest punishment.

From that time on, Washington's letters were largely of supplies that did not arrive, of orders disobeyed, of desertions, of multitudinous frustrations. In November he wrote to Lieutenant Colonel Adam Stephen, his second in command, about a serious situation.

Alexandria [Virginia] November 28, 1755

There has been such total negligence among the Recruiting Officers in general; such disregard of the Service they were employed in, and idle proceedings, that I am determined to send out none until we all meet; when each Officer shall have his own men and have only this alternative, to complete his number, or loose his Commission.

There are several officers who have been out six weeks or two months, without getting a man; spending their time in all the gaiety of pleasurable mirth, with their Relations and Friends; not attempting, or having a possible chance of Recruiting any but those who, out of their inclination to the service, will proffer themselves.

A month later he was reproving one of his company captains, John Ashby, in a letter that, except for the complaint about the man's wife, was typical of scores he had written and would write.

Winchester [Virginia] December 28, 1755

I am very much surprized to hear of the great irregularities which were allowed of in your Camp. The Rum, although sold by Joseph Coombs, I am credibly informed, is your property. There are continual complaints to me of the misbehaviour of your Wife; who I am told sows sedition among the men, and is chief of every mutiny. If she is not immediately sent from the Camp, or I hear any more complaints of such irregular Behaviour upon my arrival there; I shall take care to drive her out myself, and suspend *you.*

It is impossible to get clothing here for your men. I think none so proper for Rangers as Match-coats; therefore would advise you to procure them. Those who have not received clothing, for the future will receive their full pay without stoppages; and those already made, will be repaid them. . . .

I have sent you one of the mutiny Bills which you are (as far as it relates to the men) to have frequently read to them. Further; acquaint them, that if any Soldier deserts, altho' he return *himself*, he shall be hanged.

An intolerable situation prevailed at Fort Cumberland. Although vital to Virginia's defense, the fort was on the Maryland side of the Potomac, and arriving there early in October was one Captain John Dagworthy with a handful of Maryland troops. Dagworthy had once held a King's commission, and though his present status was cloudy, he attempted to order Washington and the Virginia troops about. Washington and his men were infuriated, and Washington wrote to Governor Dinwiddie, threatening to resign his commission unless the situation was corrected.

[Alexandria, January 14, 1756]

When I was down the Committee among other Things resolved that the Maryland and Carolina Companies shoud not be supported with our Provisions. This Resolve (I think) met with your Approbation; upon which I wrote to Colo. Stephen desiring him to acquaint Capt. Dagworthy thereof, who paid slight Regard to it, saying it was in the Kings Garrison and all the Troops had an equal Right to draw Provision with Us by his Order (as commanding Officer) and that We, after it was put there, had no Power to remove it without his Leave. I shoud therefore be glad of your Honours peremptory Orders what to do in this Case, as I dont care to act without Instructions lest it shoud appear to proceed from Pique & Resentment as having the Command disputed. This is one among the numberless Inconveniencies of having the Fort in Maryland. Capt. Dagworthy I dare venture to affirm is encouraged to say this by Governor Sharpe [of Maryland], who We know has wrote to him to keep the Command. This Capt. Dagworthy acquainted Colo. Stephen of himself.

As I have not yet heard how General Shirley has answered your Honrs. Request I fear the Success; especially as its next to an Impossibility (as Govr. Sharpe has been there to plead Capt. Dagworthy's Cause) by writing to make the General acquainted with the Nature of the Dispute. The officers have drawn up a Memorial to be presented to the General [Governor Shirley of Massachusetts], & that it may be properly strengthened they humbly beg your Sollicitation to have Us (as We have certain Advices that it is in his Power) put upon the Establishment. This woud at once put an End to Contention which is the Root of Evil & destructive to the best of Operations, and turn all our Movements into a free easy Channel. They have urged it in the warmest Manner to Me to appear personally before the General for this End, which I woud at this disagreeable Season gladly do Things being thus circumstanced if I have your Permission which I more freely ask since I have determined to resign a Commission which You were generously pleased to offer Me (and for which I shall always retain a grateful Sense of the Favour) rather than submit to the Command of a Person who I think has not such superlative Merit to balance the Inequality of Rank, however he adheres to what he calls his Right, & in which I know he is supported by Govr. Sharpe. He says that he has no Commission from the Province of Maryland but acts by Virtue of that from the King, that this was the Condition of his engaging in the Maryland Service, & when he was sent up there the first of last October was ordered by Governor Sharpe and Sr. John St. Clair not to give up his Right. To my certain Knowledge his Rank was disputed before General Braddock; who gave it in his Favour, and he accordingly took Place of every Captain upon the Expedition—except Capt. James Mercer and Capt. Rutherford whose Commissions were older than his so that I shoud not by any Means choose to act as your Honr. hinted in your last, lest I shoud be called to an Account myself.

I have during my Stay above from the 1st. Decr. to this, disposed of all the Men & Officers (that are not recruiting & can be spared from the Fort) in the best Manner I can for the Defence of the Inhabitants, and they will need no further Orders till I coud return, and the recruiting Officers are allowed till the 1st. of March to repair to their Rendezvous—which leaves at present nothing to do at the Fort but to train & discipline the Men, & prepare and salt the Provisions. For the better

Governor William Shirley

perfecting both these I have left full & clear Directions.

Besides in other Respects I think my going to the Northward might be of Service as I shoud thereby so far as they thought proper to communicate be acquainted with their Plan of Operations especially the Pennsylvanians so as to act as much as the Nature of Things woud admit in Concert.

When the Dagworthy affair got no better, Washington obtained permission from Dinwiddie to carry the Virginians' complaint to Governor William Shirley of Massachusetts, Commander in Chief of all Colonial forces. With two of his captains as aides and two servants, he set out in the first days of February, 1756. During five days in Philadelphia he spent a great deal on the new clothing that was always a weakness with him, and in New York he courted Polly Philipse, the sister-in-law of a friend and one of the wealthiest young ladies in the Colonies.

The little troop arrived in Boston on February 25. Governor Shirley gave Washington a letter stating unequivocally that the strutting Dagworthy ranked no higher than any other Colonial officer, but he did not give Washington a regular army commission, which the Virginian had deeply set his hopes on.

Washington had scarcely returned to Williamsburg on March 30 when urgent reports came in that the French and Indians, who had been immobilized during the winter, were attacking the frontier again. Washington hastened to the scene. His troubles were so many—insufficient men, provisions and pay that did not arrive, unwarranted criticism from officials safe in Williamsburg—that very soon he was writing to Governor Dinwiddie in a somewhat frantic tone.

Polly Philipse, later Mrs. Roger
Morris, in a portrait by Copley

Winchester [Virginia] April 22, 1756
This encloses several letters, and the minutes of a Council of War, which was held upon the receipt of them. Your Honor may see to what unhappy straits the distressed Inhabitants as well as I, am reduced. I am too little acquainted, Sir, with pathetic language, to attempt a description of the peoples distresses, though I have a generous soul, sensible of wrongs, and swelling for redress. But what can I do? If bleeding, dying! would glut their insatiate revenge, I would be a willing offering to savage fury, and die by inches, to save a people! I *see* their situation, know their danger, and participate their Sufferings, without having it in my power to give them further relief, than uncertain promises. In short, I see inevitable destruction in so clear a light, that, unless

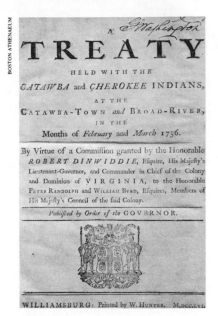

*Title page of Washington's own
copy of a treaty signed with the
Indians during the winter of 1756*

vigorous measures are taken by the Assembly, and speedy assistance sent from below, the poor Inhabitants that are now in Forts, must unavoidably fall, while the remainder of the County are flying before the barbarous Foe. In fine, the melancholy situation of the people, the little prospect of assistance; The gross and scandalous abuses cast upon the Officers in general, which is reflecting upon me in particular, for suffering misconducts of such extraordinary kinds—and the distant prospects, if any, that I can see, of gaining Honor and Reputation in the Service, are motives which cause me to lament the hour that gave me a Commission, and would induce me, at any other time than this of imminent danger, to resign without one hesitating moment, a command, which I never expect to reap either Honor or Benefit from. But, on the contrary, have almost an absolute certainty of incurring displeasure below: While the murder of poor innocent Babes and helpless families, may be laid to my account here!

The supplicating tears of the women, and moving petitions from the men, melt me into such deadly sorrow, that I solemnly declare, if I know my own mind, I could offer myself a willing Sacrifice to the butchering Enemy, provided that would contribute to the people's ease.

Lord Fairfax has ordered men from the adjacent counties: But when they will come, or in what numbers, I cannot pretend to determine. If I may judge from the success we have met with here, I have but little hopes, as three days incessant endeavours have produced but twenty men. . . .

Fortunately, the attacks soon lessened; the French and Indian parties apparently had returned in large part to Fort Duquesne. But problems continued, and one of the most pressing among many was that of widespread desertions. Washington reported on it to the Governor.

July 11, 1757.

The Deserters apprehended at Maidstone, were treated with such lenity as their subsequent behaviour convinces me was misplaced: Several of them having since deserted. This infamous practice, wherein such numbers of our own men have (by means of the villainy and ill-judged compassion of the country-people, who deem it a merit to assist Deserters) has been wonderfully successful; and is now arrived at such a height, that nothing can stop its scandalous progress, but the severest punishments, and most striking examples. Since mine of yesterday, no less than 24 more of the Draughts [drafted men] (after having received their money and clothes) deserted: notwithstanding every precaution I cou'd suggest was taken to prevent it: among others, I had all the roads way-laid in the night. Seven of those who went off last night, took that road which happened to be blocked up. Mr. Hughes (whom your Honor has been pleased to appoint adjutant) and two Soldiers, took two of them, after exchanging some Shot, and wou'd in all probability have taken them all, had he not been disabled in the right hand, & one of our Soldiers shot thro' the leg; and, it is believed, one of the Deserters was killed in the conflict.

I must again, earnestly request, your Honor will please to send me up a copy of the mutiny and desertion bill, passed the last Session of Assembly, with blank warrants to execute the Sentence of the Courts martial; without which I fear we will soon lose, not only all the draughts, but, by their going off with impunity, there is set such a bad example, as will render even the detension of the old Soldiers impracticable.

This engraving after a miniature by Charles Willson Peale was meant to show Washington at twenty-five.

Washington was a very forbearing commander but he had reached the end of his patience. Writing to Colonel John Stanwix, a regular army officer who had taken command of a new regiment on the frontier, he mentioned, among other things, a step he had taken to discourage desertions.

July 15, 1757.

No man I conceive was ever worse plagu'd than I have been with the Draughts that were sent from the several counties in this Government, to compleat its Regiment: out of 400 that were received at Fredericksburgh, and at this place, 114 have deserted, notwithstanding every precaution, except absolute confinement has been used to prevent this infamous practice. I have used the most vigorous measures to apprehend those fellows who escaped from hence (which amounted to about 30) and have succeeded so well that they are taken with the loss of one of their men, and a Soldier wounded. I have a

Gallows near 40 feet high erected (which has terrified the rest exceedingly), and I am determined, if I can be justified in the proceeding, to hang two or three on it, as an example to others.

Washington very soon put his gallows to use, as he reported in a subsequent letter to the Governor.

Fort Loudoun [Virginia], August 3, 1757. I send your Honor a copy of the proceedings of a General Court martial. Two of those condemned, namely, Ignatious Edwards, and Wm. Smith, were hanged on thursday last, just before the companies marched for their respective posts. Your Honor will, I hope excuse my hanging, instead of shooting them: It conveyed much more terror to others; and it was for example sake, we did it. They were proper objects to suffer: Edwards had deserted twice before, and Smith was accounted one of the greatest villains upon the continent. Those who were intended to be whipped, have received their punishment accordingly; and I should be glad to know what your Honor wou'd choose to have done with the rest?

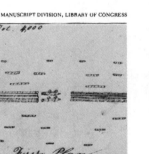

Washington submitted this plan for a line of march to General Forbes at that officer's express request.

Within three weeks, however, Washington's basically lenient nature had reasserted itself. He reported to Dinwiddie that he had freed some deserters from jail, since he found "examples of so little weight, and since those poor unhappy criminals have undergone no small pain of body and mind, in a dark room, closely ironed."

Although the chronically undermanned Virginia Regiment was never able to completely protect the frontier, it did make things more difficult for the French and Indian raiding parties. His exertions finally told on Washington; he developed a "bloody flux" (dysentery) that worsened, until by early November of 1757 he was in such distress that his physicians ordered him home at once for a long and painful convalescence. By the middle of March, 1758, he had recovered enough interest in life to call on Martha Dandridge Custis, one of the wealthiest young widows in Virginia. A week later he paid a second call, proposed marriage, and was accepted.

By the time Washington returned to duty in April, the military situation had changed. The British were making ready to put new life into their lagging war against France in America with a three-pronged offensive. One prong would be a new attempt to capture Fort Duquesne; it was to be led by Brigadier General John Forbes, and Washington would lead the Virginia Regiment (the conflict over rank had been eased by an order that any Colonial officer would be under the command of regulars only of higher rank). In late summer Washington received a letter from George William Fairfax about the progress of prenuptial remodeling at Mount Vernon. In it was enclosed a note from Sally, describing some phases of the work and also apparently teasing George about his coming marriage. Washington, as usual, burned her letter; she saved his answer, which leaves no doubt about his feelings toward her.

Camp at Fort Cumberland [Maryland]
12th. Septr. 1758

Dear Madam,

Yesterday I was honourd with your short, but very agreable favour of the first Inst. How joyfully I catch at the happy occasion of renewing a Corrispondance which I feard was dis-relished on your part, I leave to time, that never failing Expositor of all things—and to a Monitor equally as faithful in my own Breast to Testifie. In silence I now express my joy. Silence which in some cases—I wish the present—speaks more Intelligably than the sweetest Eloquence.

If you allow that any honour can be derivd from my opposition to Our present System of management you destroy the merit of it entirely in me by attributing my anxiety to the annimating prospect of possessing Mrs. Custis. When—I need not name it. Guess yourself. Shoud not my own Honour, and Country's welfare be the excitement? Tis true, I profess myself a Votary to Love. I acknowledge that a Lady is in the Case—and further I confess, that this Lady is known to you. Yes Madam, as well as she is to one, who is too sensible of her Charms to deny the Power, whose Influence he feels and must ever Submit to. I feel the force of her amiable beauties in the recollection of a thousand tender passages that I coud wish to obliterate, till I am bid to revive them. But experience alas! sadly reminds me how Impossible this is and evinces an Opinion which I have long entertaind, that there is a Destiny, which has the Sovereign controul of our Actions—not to be resisted by the strongest efforts of Human Nature.

You have drawn me my dear Madam, or rather have I drawn myself, into an honest confession of a Simple Fact. Misconstrue not my meaning—'tis obvious—doubt i[t] not, nor expose it. The World has no business to know the object of my Love, declard in this manner to you when I want to conceal it. One thing above all things in this

Romanticized nineteenth-century engraving of Martha Washington

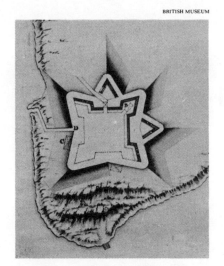

Plan showing Fort Duquesne's dominance of the Forks of the Ohio

World I wish to know, and only one person of your Acquaintance can solve me that or guess my meaning. But adieu to this, till happier times, if I ever shall see them. The hours at present are melancholy dull. Neither the rugged Toils of War, nor the gentler conflict of A — B — s [Assembly Balls?] is in my choice. I dare believe you are as happy as you say. I wish I was happy also. Mirth, good Humour, ease of Mind and — what else? cannot fail to render you so, and consummate your Wishes. . . .

I cannot easily forgive the unseasonable haste of my last Express, if he deprivd me thereby of a single word you intended to add. The time of the present messenger is, as the last might have been, entirely at your disposal. I cant expect to hear from my Friends more than this once, before the Fate of the Expedition will, some how or other be determind. I therefore beg to know when you set out for Hampton, & when you expect to Return to Belvoir again — and I shoud be glad to hear also of your speedy departure, as I shall thereby hope for your return before I get down; the disappointment of seeing [the failure to see] your Family woud give me much concern. . . .

Be assured that I am Dr. Madam, with the most unfeignd regard,

Yr. Most Obedient & Most Obligd Hble Servt.

Go: WASHINGTON

General Forbes built a new road west through Pennsylvania, while Washington protested, writing letter after letter, extolling the virtues of Braddock's road, minimizing its disadvantages, hinting that the new road was a Pennsylvania plot, and direly predicting that the expedition would never reach Fort Duquesne. Forbes was purposely moving slowly because a treaty was being arranged with the Indians; the diplomacy was successful, and the expedition reached the fort on November 25 to find that the French had burned it the night before and departed. Their Indian allies had deserted them. Washington had to leave part of his ragged Virginia Regiment in the desolate ruins to garrison the fort during the winter. He rode to Williamsburg to arrange clothing and supplies for the men who had been assigned the miserable duty. That taken care of, the young officer, not quite twenty-seven, who had once wanted a military career and had yearned to serve in the regular British army, resigned his commission as the year ended.

Chapter 3

The Squire of Mount Vernon

Martha Custis and George Washington were married on January 6, 1759, on the Custis plantation. He was almost twenty-seven years old; she was a few months older. It was destined to be a happy marriage; she brought to it a cheerful nature, personal warmth, the ability to manage a large plantation household—all the attributes of a good companion and an excellent hostess. She was considered pretty, but she was diminutive, as small as her husband was large and strong—the contrast must have been striking.

Martha's late husband had left a large estate, 17,438 acres, with other property—cash, slaves, livestock, securities—worth some twenty thousand pounds sterling, or a little over half a million dollars, as nearly as it can be translated into today's terms. One third of this went to Martha and so became Washington's on marriage, subject to restrictions preventing him from alienating or encumbering her rights in the property. The other two thirds were the property of her two children, and Washington was made the administrator of their estate. Only in relation to her two children did Martha Washington fail to show common sense. At the time of her remarriage, her son, John Parke ("Jackie") Custis, was four; her daughter, Martha Parke ("Patsy") Custis, two. Their mother indulged them shamefully and had such a morbid anxiety about leaving them that she would not accompany George on trips unless the children went along. On February 22—the day he turned twenty-seven—Washington took his seat as a member in the House of Burgesses. He had been elected a member from Frederick County the previous July, even though he was on the Forbes expedition against Fort Duquesne at the time; his fame, the efforts of his friends, and his generous provision for potables (160 gallons of rum, punch, wine, and beer) made him an easy winner.

Leaving Williamsburg, Washington set out early in April for home with his bride, stepchildren, servants, and baggage. Not until he was almost at

Mount Vernon did it occur to him that he had made no arrangements for their arrival, and he sent a messenger galloping on ahead with urgent instructions for his manager, John Alton.

Thursday Morning [April 1, 1759]

I have sent Miles on to day, to let you know that I expect to be up to Morrow, & to get the Key from Colo. Fairfax's which I desire you will take care of. You must have the House very well clean'd, & were you to make Fires in the Rooms below it wd. Air them. You must get two of the best Bedsteads put up, one in the Hall Room, and the other in the little dining Room that use to be, & have Beds made on them against we come. You must also get out the Chairs and Tables & have them very well rubd. & Cleand. The Stair case ought also to be polishd in order to make it look well.

Enquire abt. in the Neighbourhood, & get some Egg's and Chickens, and prepare in the best manner you can for our coming. You need not however take out any more of the Furniture than the Beds Tables & Chairs in Order that they may be well rubd. & cleand.

The Custis family coat of arms, as engraved on a silver salver

In preparation for the arrival of his bride, Washington had added a story to the original story-and-a-half house at Mount Vernon, but he had found little time to furnish and decorate the enlarged mansion. Making this austere domain a home and managing a large household—there were eleven house slaves—was to be Martha's task. The land was George's responsibility. He accepted the challenge gladly; his diary entries early in the following year reveal that he was a man completely absorbed in his farming.

January 1 [1760] Tuesday. Visited my Plantations and receivd an Instance of Mr. French's great Love of Money in disappointing me of some Pork because the price had risen to 22/6 [22 shillings, 6 pence] after he had engagd to let me have it at 20/.

Calld at Mr. Posseys in my way home and desird him to engage me 100 Barl. of Corn upon the best terms he coud in Maryland.

And found Mrs. Washington upon my arrival broke out with the Meazles.

Jany. 2d. Wednesy. Mrs. Barnes who came to visit Mrs. Washington yesterday returnd home in my Chariot the Weather being too bad to Travel in an open Carriage

Martha Washington 1759

THE
Bull-Finch
Being
A choice Collection
OF THE
Newest and most favourite
English Songs
Which have been
Sett to Music and Sung at
The Public Theatres & Gardens.

Printed for R. Baldwin, in Pater Noster Row,
& John Wilkie, in St. Pauls Church Yard,
LONDON.

—which together with Mrs. Washington's Indisposition confind me to the House and gave me an oppertunity of Posting my Books and putting them in good Order.

Fearing a disappointment elsewhere in Pork I was fein to take Mr. French upon his own terms & engagd them to be delivd. at my House on Monday next.

Thursday Jany. 3d.   The Weather continuing Bad & the same causes subsisting I confind myself to the House.

Morris who went to work Yesterday caught cold, and was laid up bad again—and several of the Family were taken with the Measles, but no bad Symtoms seem'd to attend any of them.

Hauled the Sein and got some fish, but was near being disappointd of my Boat by means of an Oyste[r] man who had lain at my Landing and plaged me a good deal by his disorderly behaviour.

Friday Jany. 4th.   The Weather continued Drisling and Warm, and I kept the House all day. Mrs. Washington seemg. to be very ill [I] wrote to Mr. Green [a clergy-man-physician] this afternoon desiring his Company to visit her in the Morng.

Saturday Jany. 5th. Mrs. Washington appears to be something better. Mr. Green however came to see her abt. 11 Oclock and in an hour Mrs. Fairfax arrivd. Mr. Green prescribd the needful and just as we were going to Dinnr. Captn. Walter Stuart appeard with Doctr. Laurie.

The Evening being very cold, and the wind high Mr. Fairfax went home in the Chariot & soon afterwards Mulatto Jack arrivd from Fredk. with 4 Beeves.

Sunday Jany. 6th. The Chariot not returng. time enought from Colo. Fairfax's we were prevented from Church.

Mrs. Washington was a good deal better today, but the Oyster man still continued his Disorderly behaviour at my Landing I was obligd in the most preemptory manner to order him and his Compy. away which he did not Incline to obey till next morning. . . .

Tuesday Jany. 8. Directed an Indictment to be formd by Mr. Johnston against Jno. Ballendine for a fraud in some Iron he sold me.

Got a little Butter from Mr. Dalton—and wrote to Colo. West for Pork.

In the Evening 8 of Mr. French's Hogs from his Ravensworth Quarter came down one being lost on the way as the others might as well have been for their goodness.

Nothing but the disappoin[t]ments in this Article of Pork which he himself had causd and my necessities coud possibly have obligd me to take them.

Carpenter Sam was taken with the Meazles. . . .

Saturday Jany. 12th. Sett out with Mrs. Bassett on her journey to Port Royal. The morning was clear and fine but soon clouded and promisd much Rain or other falling weather wch. is generally the case after remarkable white Frosts—as it was today. We past Occoquan [Creek] witht. any great difficulty notwithstanding the Wind was something high and Lodgd at Mr. McCraes in Dumfries—sending the Horses to the Tavern.

Here I was informd that Colo. Cocke was disgusted at my House, and left it because he saw an old Negroe there resembling his own Image.

Washington wrote Martha's name on the title page of an English song book (left) during the first year of their marriage. He acquired an English gardening book (below) for his own library the following year.

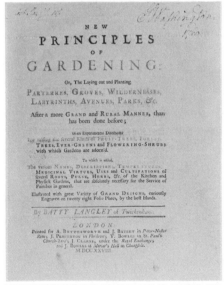

Washington was not a skilled farmer at the outset. But unlike most of his fellow Virginians, he strove to preserve the land and its fertility. He ordered from London the latest books on agriculture, and he experimented with crops and farming methods, as these additional diary entries show.

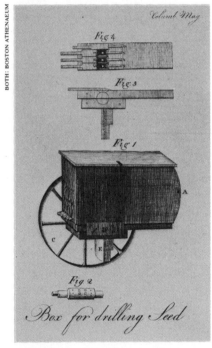

These two engravings, of a box for drilling seed and the plan for a granary (opposite), appeared in a volume of the Columbian Magazine that Washington had in his library.

Thursday April 3d [1760]. Sowd 17½ Drills of Trefoil seed in the ground adjoining the Garden, numbering from the side next the Stable (or Work shop) the residue of them viz 4 was sowd with Lucerne [alfalfa] Seed—both done with design to see how these Seeds answer in that Ground.

Sowd my Fallow Field in Oats today, and harrowd them in viz 10½ Bushels. Got done about three Oclock.

Cook Jack after laying of the Lands in this Field went to plowing in the 12 Acre Field where they were Yesterday as did the other plow abt. 5 Oclock after Pointing.

Got several Composts and laid them to dry in order to mix with the Earth brot. from the Field below to try their several Virtues.

Wind blew very fresh from South—Clouds often appeard, and sometimes threatned the near approach of Rain but a clear setting Sun seemd denoted the Contrary. . . .

Monday Apl. 14. Fine warm day, Wind Soly. and clear till the Eveng. when it clouded;

No Fish were to be catchd today neither.

Mixd my Composts in a box with ten Apartments in the following manner viz—in No. 1 is three pecks of the Earth brought from below the Hill out of the 46 Acre Field without any mixture—in No.

2. is two pecks of the said Earth and one of Marle taken out of the said Field which Marle seemd a little Inclinable to Sand.

3. Has 2 Pecks of sd. Earth and 1 of Riverside Sand.

4. Has a Peck of Horse Dung.

5. Has Mud taken out of the Creek.

6. Has Cow Dung.

7. Marle from the Gullys on the Hillside wch. seemd. to be purer than the other.

8. Sheep Dung.

9. Black Mould taken out of the Pocoson [a swamp usually dry in summer] on the Creek side.

10. Clay got just below the Garden.

All mixd with the same quantity & sort of Earth in the most effectual manner by reducing the whole to a tolerable degree of fineness & jubling them well together in a Cloth.

In each of these divisions were planted three Grains of Wheat 3 of Oats & as many of Barley all at equal distances in Rows & of equal depth (done by a Machine made for the purpose).

The Wheat Rows are next the Numberd side, the Oats in the Middle & the Barley on that side next the upper part of the Garden.

Two or three hours after sowing in this manner, and about an hour before Sun set I waterd them all equally alike with Water that had been standing in a Tub abt. two hours exposed to the Sun.

Began drawing Bricks burning Lime & Preparing for Mr. Triplet who is to be here on Wednesday to Work.

Finishd Harrowing the Clover Field, and began reharrowing of it. Got a new harrow made of smaller, and closer Tinings for Harrowing in Grain—the other being more proper for preparing the Ground for sowing.

Cook Jack's plow was stopd he being employd in setting the Lime Kiln.

Managing a plantation had its problems, but hard work usually produced results; much more frustrating was Washington's relationship with the English merchants who were his agents in selling his tobacco and in buying the endless items not available in the Colonies. Washington complained that he was underpaid for his tobacco, overcharged for the goods sent him, given inferior merchandise, and taken advantage of in various other ways. Typical of scores of laments was one to Robert Cary and Company, which handled most of Washington's overseas business.

[Mount Vernon, August 10, 1760]

By my Friend Mr. Fairfax I take the Oppertunity of acknowledging the Receipts of your several favours that have come to hand since mine of the 30th. of November last, and observe in one of them of the 14 Feby. by Crawford that you refer to another by the same Ship, but this has never yet appeard....

The Insurrance on the Tobo. pr. Falman was high I think—higher than expected; And here Gentn. I cannot forbear ushering in a Complaint of the exorbitant prices of my Goods this year all of which are come to hand (except those packages put on board Hooper): For many Years I have Imported Goods from London as well as other Ports of Britain and can truely say I never had such a penny worth before. It woud be a needless Task to innumerate every Article that I have cause to except against, let it suffice to say that Woolens, Linnens, Nails &ca. are mean in quality but not in price, for in this they excel indeed, far above any I have ever had. It has always been a Custom with me when I make out my Invoices to estimate the Charge of them, this I do, for my own satisfaction, to know whether I am too fast or not, and I seldom vary much from the real prices doing it from old Notes &ca. but the amount of your Invoice exceeds my Calculations above 25 pr. Ct. & many Articles not sent that were wrote for.

I must once again beg the favour of you never to send me any Goods but in a Potomack Ship, and for this purpose let me recommend Captn. John Johnson in an annual Ship of Mr. Russels to this River. Johnson is a person I am acquainted with, know him to be very careful and he comes past my Door in his Ship: I am certain therefore of always having my Goods Landed in Good time and Order which never yet has happend when they come into another River: This year the Charming Polly went into Rappahannock & my Goods by her, recd. at different times and in bad order. The Porter entirely Drank out [by seamen during the voyage]. There came no Invoice of Mr. Dandridges Goods to me. I suppose it was forgot to be Inclosd.

Washington imported many items from London, including "Woollens" and "Linnens" such as those advertised in the trade cards above and opposite. The trade card of his own English cabinetmaker, Philip Bell, is reproduced at right.

Six weeks later Washington was penning a letter to the same agents, plaintively claiming that rapacious London shopkeepers were making Colonists their special victims.

[Mount Vernon, September 28, 1760]

By this conveyance, & under the same cover of this Letter, you will receive Invoices of such Goods as are wanting, which please to send as there directed by Capt. Johnston in the Spring—and let me beseech you Gentn. to give the necessary directions for purchasing of them upon the best Terms. It is needless for me to particularise the sorts, quality, or taste I woud choose to have them in unless it is observd; and you may believe me when I tell you that instead of getting things good and fashionable in their several kinds we often have Articles sent Us that coud only have been usd by our Forefathers in the days of yore. 'Tis a custom, I have some Reason to believe, with many Shop keepers, and Tradesmen in London when they know Goods are bespoke for Exportation to palm sometimes old, and sometimes very slight and indifferent Goods upon Us taking care at the same time to advance 10, 15 or perhaps 20 pr. Ct. upon them. My Packages pr. the Polly Captn. Hooper are not yet come to hand, & the Lord only, knows when they will without more trouble than they are worth. As to the Busts a future day will determine my choice of them if any are wrote for. Mrs. Washington sends home a Green Sack to get cleand, or fresh dyed of the same colour; made up into a handsome Sack again woud be her choice, but if the Cloth wont afford that, then to be thrown into a genteel Night Gown. The Pyramid you sent me last year got hurt, and the broken pieces I return by this oppertunity to get New ones made by them; please to order that they be securely Packd.

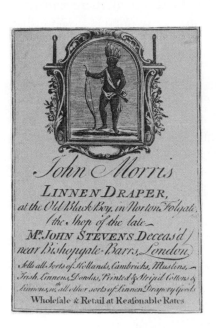

John Morris
LINNEN DRAPER,
at the Old Black Boy, in Norton Folgate,
(the Shop of the late
Mr. JOHN STEVENS Deceas'd)
near Bishopgate-Barrs, London,
Sells all Sorts of Hollands, Cambricks, Muslins,
Irish Linnens, Dowlas, Printed & Striped Cottons &
Linnens, with all other sorts of Linnen Drapery Goods
Wholesale & Retail at Reasonable Rates

Mount Vernon was badly run down when Washington inherited it; he built and repaired and bought parcels of land to round out his acres and then had to buy more slaves to work the additional land. Nor did he and Martha scrimp in satisfying their desires for fine clothes, furniture, and entertaining. As a result, Robert Cary and Company informed Washington early in 1764 that instead of having a balance in his account, he was indebted to the firm. Moreover, Jackie Custis's balance—the money from his father's estate separately deposited for him in London—had also shrunk. George Washington was quite bewildered.

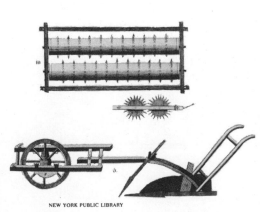

*Cultivating tools as depicted in
an eighteenth-century encyclopedia,*
Maison Rustique, *which was also
in George Washington's library*

NEW YORK PUBLIC LIBRARY

Williamsburg, May 1, 1764.
The Copy of your Letter of the 13th. of February—by
Falman—is come to hand, but for want of the Account
Inclosed in the Original I am a loss to conceive how my
balance can possibly be so much as £1811.1.1 in your
favour, or Master Custis's so little as £1407.14.7 in his;
however as the several Accts. will shew what Articles
are charged and credited—without which there can be
no judging—I shall postpone an explicit answer till
they arrive. . . .

As to my own Debt I shall have no objections to
allowing you Interest upon it untill it is discharged and
you may charge it accordingly from this time forward,
but had my Tobacco sold as I expected and the Bills
been paid according to promise I was in hopes to have
fallen very little in Arrears; however as it is otherwise
I shall endeavour to discharge the Balle. as fast as I can,
flattering myself there will be no just cause for complts.
of the Tobacco this year.

Washington was forced to admit that the merchants'
accounting was correct. He also at last faced up to a grim truth: no matter
what he did, his Mount Vernon tobacco consistently received lower prices
than that of his neighbors. Some of his 1765 diary entries reveal what he
was doing about it.

[MAY]

12
13 } Sowed Hemp at Muddy hole by Swamp.

Do [Ditto] Sowed Do above the Meadow at Doeg Run

15   Sowed Do at head of the Swamp Muddy H

16   Sowed Hemp at the head of the Meadow at Doeg
      Run & about Southwards Houses with the Barrel

JULY

22.   Began to Sow Wheat at Rivr. Plantn.

23.   Began to Sow Do. at Muddy hole

25.   Began to Sow Do. at the Mill

AUGUST

9.   Abt. 6 Oclock put some Hemp in the Rivr. to Rot. . . .

13.   Finish'd Sowing Wheat at the Rivr. Plantn. i.e.
      in the corn ground 123 Bushels it took to do it.

15.   The English Hemp i.e. the Hemp from the English
      Seed was picked at Muddy hole this day & was ripe.

15.   Began to seperate Hemp in the Neck. . . .

76

SEPTEMBER

24. Took up Flax which had been in Water since the 12th. viz 12 days.

Washington, again as can be seen from his diary, was beginning to grow hemp and flax and was greatly increasing his plantings of wheat. That year, 1765, Washington grew very little tobacco at Mount Vernon—although he continued to plant it on the Custis lands—and the next year none at all. Hemp and flax would prove unprofitable, but his production of wheat and corn greatly increased in the next three or four years; both were crops that could be sold at home, without costly shipping charges or fat commissions to London merchants. All was not work and worry at Mount Vernon, however. Washington was a social creature; he loved parties, dancing, horse races, cardplaying, the occasional drama that came to Williamsburg or Annapolis. He considered it a dull dinner when no guests were present, and once made the matter-of-fact entry in his diary, "Mrs. Possey and some young woman whose name was unknown to any body in this family dind here." In 1768 he began keeping separate entries of how his time was spent. They hardly presented a picture of a man too overworked to enjoy friends and pleasures.

JANUARY [1768]

Where, & how—my time is Spent.

1st. Fox huntg. in my own Neck with Mr. Robt. Alexander, and Mr. Colvill Catchd nothing. Captn. Posey with us.

2. Surveying some Lines of my Mt. Vernon Tract of Land.

3. At Home with Doctr. Rumney.

4. Rid to Muddy hole, D:Run, and Mill Plantn.

5. Went into the Neck.

6. Rid to Doeg Run and the Mill before Dinner. Mr. B. Fairfax and Mr. Robt. Alexander here.

7. Fox hunting with the above two Gentn. and Captn. Posey. Started but catchd nothing.

8. Hunting again in the same Comp'y. Started a Fox and run him 4 hours. Took the Hounds off at Night.

9. At Home with Mr. B: Fairfax.

10. At Home alone.

11. Running some Lines between me and Mr. Willm. Triplet.

Nineteenth-century print showing Washington and friends after a hunt

12. Attempted to go into the Neck on the Ice but it wd. not bear. In the Evening Mr. Chs. Dick, Mr. Muse & my Brother Charles came here.

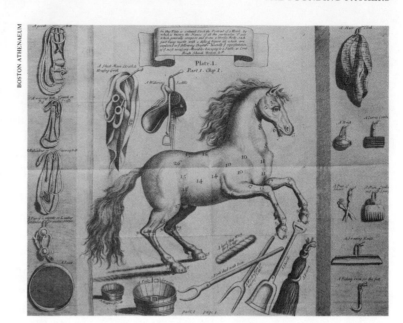

Washington, a superb horseman, owned a copy of The Compleat Horseman *containing this plate.*

13. At Home with them—Col. Fairfax, Lady, &ca.
14. Ditto—Do. Colo. Fx & famy went home in the Evening.
15. At Home with the above Gentlemen and Shooting together.
16. At home all day at Cards—it snowing.
17. At Home with Mr. Dick, &ca.
18. Went to Court and sold Colo. Colvil's L[an]d, returnd again at Night.
19. Went to Belvoir with Mr. Dick, my Bro. &ca.
20. Returnd from Do. by the Mill, Doeg Run and Muddy hole.
21. Surveyd the Water courses of my Mt. Vernon Tract of Land—taking advant. of the Ice.
22. Fox hunting with Capt. Posey, started but catchd. nothing.
23. Rid to Muddy hole & directed paths to be cut for Fox hunting.
24. Rid up to Toulston in order to Fox hunt it.
25. Confind by Rain with Mr. Fairfax and Mr. Alexander.
26. Went out with the Hounds but started no Fox. Some of the Hounds run of upon a Deer.
27. Went out again. Started a Fox ab. 10. Run him till 3 and lost him.
28. Returnd Home—found Mr. Tomi Elsey there.
29. Went to Belvoir with Mrs. W[ashingto]n, &ca. after Dinnr. Left Mr. Ellzey at home.

30. Dined at Belvoir and returnd in the Afternoon.
    Borrowed a hound from Mr. Whiting, as I did 2 from
    Mr. Alexr. the 28th.
31. At Home alone all day.

The humor in Washington's writings was infrequent and sometimes a bit heavy. One party he attended, however, did call forth some wry comments in his diary.

> Friday Feby. 15th [1760]. A Small fine Rain from No. Et. wet the Top of my Hay that had been landed last Night. It was all carted up however to the Barn & the Wet and dry seperated.
>
> Went to a Ball at Alexandria—where Musick and Dancing was the chief Entertainment. However in a convenient Room detachd for the purpose abounded great plenty of Bread and Butter, some Biscuets with Tea, & Coffee which the Drinkers of coud not Distinguish from Hot water sweetned. Be it rememberd that pocket hankerchiefs servd the purposes of Table Cloths & Napkins and that no Apologies were made for either.* (*I shall therefore distinguish this Ball by the Stile & title of the Bread & Butter Ball.)

Washington never was to father any children of his own. As a stepfather he was affectionate but overly indulgent, showing little firmness to counter Martha's doting attitude toward her children. As a result, his stepson, Jack Custis, a pleasant enough boy, grew up with little purpose in life beyond horses and clothes. Washington's concern that Jack should not lack for the best comes through clearly in a letter to the Reverend Jonathan Boucher, headmaster of a school for boys in Caroline County.

> [Mount Vernon] May 30th. 1768
> Mr. Magowan who lived several years in my Family a Tutor to Master Custis (my Son in law & Ward) having taken his departure for England leaves the young Gentleman without any Master at all at this time. I shoud be glad there fore to know if it woud be convenient for you to add him to the number of your Pupils. He is a boy of good genius, about 14 yrs. of age, untainted in his Morals, & of innocent Manners. Two yrs. and upwards he has been reading of Virgil, and was (at the time Mr. Magowan left him) entered upon the Greek Testament, tho' I presume he has grown not a little rusty in both;

having had no benefit of his Tutor since Christmas, notwithstanding he left the Country in March only.

If he come, he will have a boy [a personal slave] (well acquainted with House business, which may be made as useful as possible in your Family to keep him out of Idleness) and two Horses, to furnish him with the means of getting to Church, and elsewhere as you may permit; for he will be put entirely, and absolutely under your Tuition, and direction to manage as you think proper in all respects.

Now Sir, if you Incline to take Master Custis I shoud be glad to know what conveniencies it may be necessary for him to bring & how soon he may come, for as to his Board & Schooling (provendar for his Horses he may lay in himself) I do not think it necessary to enquire into, and will chearfully pay Ten or Twelve pounds a year extraordinary to engage your peculiar care of, and a watchful eye to him, as he is a promising boy—the last of his Family—& will possess a very large Fortune; add to this my anxiety to make him fit for more useful purposes, than a horse Racer &ca.

Jack Custis and his sister, Patsy (opposite), in twin oval portraits painted in 1772 by C. W. Peale

In May of 1773, when Jack was eighteen, Washington took him to New York, entered him in King's College (later Columbia), and rented comfortable lodgings for him and his servant. At college the youth dined with the faculty, a privilege doubtless arranged by his stepfather, for Jack boasted that no one else was similarly favored. But Jack tired of school, withdrew from college, and was married early in 1774 to Eleanor Calvert, member of a prominent Maryland family. Meanwhile Patsy Custis had been indulged as excessively as her brother, but her story was a tragic one. Washington's diary on June 14, 1768, noted that Patsy had been "seized with fitts." The fits—possibly epilepsy—continued. The family doctor did no good, nor did desperate resort to primitive remedies. An inevitable day came; Washington wrote of it to Burwell Bassett, Martha's brother-in-law.

Mount Vernon, 20th June, 1773.

It is an easier matter to conceive, than to describe the distress of this Family; especially that of the unhappy Parent of our Dear Patsy Custis, when I inform you that yesterday removed the Sweet Innocent Girl Entered into a more happy & peaceful abode than any she has met with in the afflicted Path she hitherto has trod.

She rose from Dinner about four o'clock in better health and spirits than she appeared to have been in

for some time; soon after which she was seized with one of her usual Fits, & expired in it, in less than two minutes without uttering a word, a groan, or scarce a sigh. This sudden, and unexpected blow, I scarce need add has almost reduced my poor Wife to the lowest ebb of Misery; which is encreas'd by the absence of her son, (whom I have just fixed at the College in New York from whence I returned the 8th. Inst.) and want of the balmy consolation of her Relations; which leads me more than ever to wish she could see them, and that I was Master of Arguments powerful enough to prevail upon Mrs. Dandridge [Martha's mother] to make this place her entire & absolute home. I should think as she lives a lonesome life (Betsey being married) it might suit her well, & be agreeable, both to herself & my Wife, to me most assuredly it would.

I do not purpose to add more at present, the end of my writing being only to inform you of this unhappy change.

One notable aspect of Washington's character was his insatiable desire to acquire land. By 1763 his total holdings were 9,381 acres, but he was thinking in much larger terms, and late in the summer of 1763 he entered a scheme to obtain a huge tract on the Mississippi from the Crown—a plan that eventually fell through. That same year he twice visited the Dismal Swamp, which straddles the Virginia–North Carolina border, convinced that a region of such lush vegetation must have rich soil. His summary of his trip into the Dismal Swamp was an unemotional appraisal of the area's soil and drainage possibilities.

15 *October*—1763 Memm. From Suffolk to Pocoson Swamp is reckoned about 6 Miles, and something better than 4 perhaps 5 miles from Collo. Reddick's Mill run (where the Road x's it). The land within this distance especially after passing Willis Reddicks is Level & not bad. The banks down to this (Pocoson) Swamp declines gradually, and the Swamp appears to be near 75 yds. over, but no Water in it at present. Note. Willis Reddick's Plantn. seems to be a good one, the land being level and stiff. So does Henry Riddick's above.

From Pocoson Swamp to Cyprus Swamp (which conducts more Water into the Great Dismal than any one of the many that leads into it) is about 2½ Miles. This also is dry at present, but appears to be 60 or 65

A romantic engraving of George Washington at Lake Drummond in the Dismal Swamp

yards across in the wettest part.

The next Swamp to this is calld Mossey Swamp and distant about 3 Miles. Near this place lives Jno. Reddick on good Land, but hitherto from Pocoson Swamp, the land lies flat, wet, & poor. This Swamp is 60 yards over and dry.

Between Cyprus Swamp, and the last mentioned one we went on horse back not less than ½ a mile into the great Swamp (Dismal) without any sort of difficulty the horse not sinking over the fetlocks. The first quarter however abounding in Pine and Galebury bushes, the Soil being much intermixed with Sand but afterwards it grew blacker and richer with many young Reeds & few pines and this it may be observed here is the nature of the Swamp in general.

From Mossey Swamp to a branch and a large one it is, of Oropeak (not less than 80 yards over) is reckoned 4 Miles—two Miles short of which is a large Plantation belonging to one Brindle near to which (on the south side) passes the Carolina line.

The Main Swamp of Oropeak is about ½ a Mile from this, where stands the Widow Norflets Mi[ll] and luke Sumners Plantations. This Sw[am]p cannot be less than 200 yards across but does not nevertheless discharge as much water as Cyprus Swamp.

At the Mouth of this Swamp is a very large Meadow of 2 or 3000 Acres held by Sumner, Widow Norflet, Marmaduke Norflet, Powel and others and valuable ground it is....

...we crossed from Elias Stallens (one Mile above the upper bridge on Pequemin) across to a set of People which Inhabit a small slipe of Land between the said River Pequemen & the Dismal Swamp and from thence along a new cut path through the Main Swamp a Northerly course for 5 Miles to the Inhabitants of what they call new found land which is thick settled, very rich Land, and about 6 Miles from the aforesaid River Bridge of Paspetank. The Arm of the Dismal which we passed through to get to this New land (as it is called) is 3¼ Miles Measured—Little or no timber in it, but very full of Reeds & excessive rich. Thro this we carried horses without any great difficulty.

This Land was formerly esteemed part of the Dismal but being higher tho' full of Reeds People ventured to settle upon it and as it became more open, it became more dry & is now prodigeous fine land, but subject to wets and unhealthiness.

It is to be observed here that the tide, or still Water that comes out of the Sound up Pequemen River flows up as high as Stallens, and the River does not widen much untill it passes the lower Bridge some little distance. At Ralphs ferry upon Paspetank the River is Said to be 2 Miles over, and decreases in width gradually to the bridge called River bridge where it is about 30 yards across and affords sufficient Water for New England Vessels to come up and Load.

From what observations we were capable of making it appeared, as if the Swamp had very little fall—(I mean the Waters out of the great Sw[am]p) into the heads of these Rivers which seems to be a demonstration that the Swamp is much lower on the South & East Sides because it is well known that there is a pretty considerable fall on the West side through all the drains that make into Nansemond River & the Western Branch of Elizabeth at the North End of the Dismal . . . .

This Arm of the Dismal is equaly good & Rich like the rest & runs (as we were informed) 15 or 20 Miles Easterly, and has an outlet (as some say) into Curratuck Inlet by No. West River, or Tulls Ck. but these accts, were given so indistinctly as not to be relied upon. However it is certain I believe that the Water does drain of at the East end somewhere, in which case a common causay through at the crossing place woud most certainly lay all that Arm dry.

Washington and several partners formed a company to drain and develop the Dismal Swamp and the next year, 1764, sent slaves to begin the work. Although returns from the enterprise were to be small, all his life Washington was to consider it one of his most valuable investments. There were other opportunities to be seized. When surveyors Charles Mason and Jeremiah Dixon surveyed and fixed the western limit of Pennsylvania, lands hitherto in dispute became patentable, that is, the Colony now had clear title and could make grants of land. Washington at once wrote to William Crawford, an old comrade from the Forbes expedition, who was then settled in western Pennsylvania—and was not above suggesting a bit of subterfuge if such would help obtain land.

[Mount Vernon, September 21, 1767]
From a sudden hint of your Brother Val[entin]e I wrote to you a few days ago in a hurry, since which having had more time for reflection, I am now set down in order to write more deliberately, & with greater precision to you on the Subject of my last Letter; desiring that if any thing in this shoud be found contradictory to that Letter you will wholely be governd by what I am now going to add.

I then desird the favour of you (as I understood Rights might now be had for the Lands which have fallen within the Pennsylvania Line) to look me out a Tract of about 1500, 2000, or more Acres somewhere in your Neighbourhood meaning only by this that it may be as contiguous to your own Settlemt. as such a body of good Land coud be found and about Jacobs Cabbins or somewhere on those Waters I am told this might be done. It will be easy for you to conceive that Ordinary, or even middling Land woud never answer my purpose or expectation so far from Navigation & under such a load of Expense those Lands are incumbred with. No: A Tract to please me must be rich (of which no Person can be a better judge than yourself) & if possible to be good & level; Coud such a piece of Land as this be found you woud do me a singular favour in falling upon some method to secure it immediately from the attempts of any other as nothing is more certain than that the lands cannot remain long ungranted when once it is known that Rights are to be had for them. What mode of proceeding is necessary in order to accomplish this design I am utterly at a loss to point out to you but as your own Lands are under the same Circumstances self Interest will naturally lead you to an enquiry. I am told the Land, or Surveyors Office is kept at Carlyle, if so I am of Opinion that Colo. Armstrong (an Acquaintance of mine) has something to do in the management of it & I am perswaded woud readily serve me. To him therefore at all events I will write by the first oppertunity on that Subject that the way may be prepard for your application if you shoud find it necessary to make one to him. Whatever trouble or expence you may be engagd in on my behalf you may depend upon being thankfully repaid. It is possible (but I do not know that it really is the case) that Pensylvania Customs will not admit so large a quantity of Land as I

Detail from a manuscript map of 1749 by Joshua Fry and Peter Jefferson, showing the Dismal Swamp

require, to be entered together if so this may possibly be evaded by making several Entrys to the same amount if the expence of doing which is not too heavy but this I only drop as a hint leaving the whole to your discretion & good management. If the Land can only be secur'd from others it is all I want at present. The Surveying I would choose to postpone, at least till the Spring, when if you can give me any Satisfactory Account of this matter and of what I am next going to propose I expect to pay you a visit about the last of April.

The other matter just now hinted at and which I proposed in my last is to join you in attempting to secure some of the most valuable Lands in the Kings part which I think may be accomplished after a while notwithstanding the Proclamation [the Proclamation of 1763 forbade settlement west of the Appalachians] that restrains it at present & prohibits the Settling of them at all for I can never look upon that Proclamation in any other light (but this I say between ourselves) than as a temporary expedient to quiet the Minds of the Indians & must fall of course in a few years especially when those Indians are consenting to our Occupying the Lands. Any person therefore who neglects the present oppertunity of hunting out good Lands & in some measure Marking & distinguishing them for their own (in order to keep others from settling them) will never regain it. If therefore you will be at the trouble of seeking out the Lands I will take upon me the part of securing them so soon as there is a possibility of doing it & will moreover be at all the Cost & charges of Surveying Patenting &c. after which you shall have such a reasonable proportion of the whole as we may fix upon at our first meeting as I shall find it absolutely necessary & convenient for the better furthering of the design to let some few of my friends be concern'd in the Scheme & who must also partake of the advantages....

I woud recommend it to you to keep this whole matter a profound Secret, or Trust it only with those in whom you can confide & who can assist you in bringing it to bear by their discoveries of Land and this Advice proceeds from several very good Reasons, and in the first place because I might be censur'd for the Opinion I have given in respect to the King's Proclamation & then if the Scheme I am now proposing to you was known it might

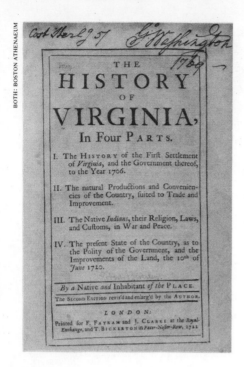

give the alarm to others & by putting them upon a Plan of the same nature (before we coud lay a proper foundation for success ourselves) set the different Interests a clashing and very probably in the end overturn the whole all which may be avoided by a Silent management & the [operation] snugly carried on by you under the pretence of hunting other Game which you may I presume effectually do at the same time you are in pursuit of Land which when fully discovered advise me of it, & if there appears but a bear possibility of succeeding any time hence I will have the Lands immediately Surveyed to keep others off & leave the rest to time & my own Assiduity to Accomplish.

If this Letter shoud reach your hands before you set out I shoud be glad to have your thoughts fully expressd on the Plan I have proposd or as soon afterwards as conveniently may be as I am desirous of knowing in time how you approve of the Scheme.

In 1754, as an incentive to recruit men for the Virginia Regiment—which eventually bled so at Fort Necessity—Governor Dinwiddie had promised 200,000 acres of frontier land as a bounty. Fifteen years later, in 1769, Washington reminded Lord Botetourt, the latest of Dinwiddie's successors, of that promise and obtained a grant of lands down the Ohio River, wherever a suitable tract might be found. The next autumn Washington set out with Dr. James Craik, who had served with him on the frontier, to select the land. By mid-October the pair was passing through an area very familiar to Washington—who was so absorbed in evaluating the land that he failed even to mention that Great Meadows had been the site of Fort Necessity and of his battle with the French sixteen years earlier. Later, however, he acquired an area including the site of his baptism in blood, just possibly from sentiment.

[October, 1770]

13. Set out about Sunrise, breakfasted at the Great Meadows 13 miles of & reachd Captn. Crawfords about 5 Oclock.

The Lands we travelld over today till we had crossed the Laurel Hill (except in small spots) was very Mountainous & indifferent—but when we came down the Hill to the Plantation of Mr. Thos. Gist the Ld. appeard charming; that which lay level being as rich & black as any thing coud possibly be. The more Hilly kind, tho of a different complexion must be good, as well from the

*Frontispiece and title page
(opposite) of Washington's copy
of a history of Virginia for which
he paid "Sterle 5/" in 1769, with
coat of arms on the frontispiece*

Crops it produces, as from the beautiful white Oaks that grows thereon. The white Oak in genl. indicates poor Land, yet this does not appear to be of that cold kind. The Land from Gists to Crawford's is very broken tho not Mountainous—in Spots exceeding Rich, & in general free from Stone. Crawfords is very fine Land; lying on Yaughyaughgani at a place commonly called Stewarts Crossing.

Sunday 14th. At Captn. Crawfords all day. Went to see a Coal Mine not far from his house on the Banks of the River. The Coal seemd to be of the very best kind, burning freely & abundance of it.

Monday 15th. Went to view some Land which Captn. Crawford had taken up for me near the Yaughyaughgani distant about 12 miles. This Tract which contains about 1600 Acres Includes some as fine Land as ever I saw—a great deal of Rich Meadow—and in general, is leveller than the Country about it. This Tract is well waterd, and has a valuable Mill Seat [Washington built a mill there five years later] (except that the Stream is rather too slight, and it is said not constant more than 7 or 8 months in the Year; but on acct. of the Fall, & other conveniences, no place can exceed it).

In going to this Land I passd through two other Tracts which Captn. Crawford had taken up for my Brothers Saml. and John. That belonging to the former, was not so rich as some I had seen; but very valuable on acct. of its levelness and little Stone, the Soil and Timber being good; that of the latter had some Bottom Land up on sml. Runs that was very good (tho narrow) the Hills very rich, but the Land in genl. broken. I intended to have visited the Land which Crawford had procurd for Lund Washington [a cousin] this day also, but time falling short, I was obligd to Postpone it making it in the Night before I got back to Crawfords where I found Colo. Stephen.

The Lands which I passed over to day were generally Hilly, and the growth chiefly white Oak, but very good notwithstanding; and what is extraordinary, & contrary to the property of all other Lands I ever saw before, the Hills are the richest Land, the Soil upon the sides and Summits of them, being as black as a Coal, & the Growth Walnut, Cherry, Spice Bushes, &ca. The flats are not so rich, and a good deal more mixd with stone.

[Two days later Washington arrived at Fort Pitt, having passed Turtle Creek on the way. Again he was too absorbed in land to note that this was memorable ground, for Braddock had suffered his ghastly defeat where Turtle Creek entered the Monongahela.]

Wednesday 17. Doctr. Craik and myself with Captn. Crawford and others arrivd at Fort Pitt, distant from the Crossing 43½ Measurd Miles. In Riding this distance we pass over a great deal of exceeding fine Land (chiefly White Oak) especially from Sweigley Creek to Turtle Creek but the whole broken; resembling (as I think all the Lands in this country does) the Loudoun Lands for Hills.

We lodgd in what is calld the Town, distant abt. 300 yards from the Fort at one Mr. Semples who keeps a very good House of Publick Entertainment; these Houses which are built of Logs, & rangd into Streets are on the Monongahela, & I suppose may be abt. 20 in Number and inhabited by Indian Traders, &ca.

The Fort [Fort Pitt] is built in the point between the Rivers Alligany & Monongahela, but not so near the pitch of it as Fort Duquesne stood. It is 5 sided & regular, two of which (next the Land) are of Brick; the others stockade. A Mote incompasses it. The Garrison consists of two Companies of Royal Irish Commanded by one Captn. Edmondson. . . .

Saturday 20. We Imbarkd in a large Canoe with sufficient stores of Provision & Necessaries, & the following Persons (besides Doctr. Craik & myself) to wit: Captn. Crawford Josh. Nicholson Robt. Bell—William Harrison—Chs. Morgan & Danl. Reardon a boy of Captn. Crawfords, & the Indians who went in a Canoe by themselves. . . .

We passd several large Island[s] which appeared to [be] very good, as the bottoms also did on each side of the River alternately; the Hills on one side being opposite to the bottoms on the other which seem generally to be abt. 3 and 4 hundred yards wide, & so vice versa. . . .

Monday 22d. As it began to Snow about Midnight, & continued pretty steadily at it, it was about 1/2 after Seven before we left our Incampment. At the distance of about 8 Miles we came to the Mouth of Yellow Creek (to the west) opposite to, or rather below which, appears to be a long bottom of very good Land, and the Assent to the Hills apparently gradual. There is another pretty large bottom of very good Land about two or 3 Miles above this. About 11 or 12 Miles from this, & just above what is called the long Island (which tho so distinguished is not very remarkable for length, breadth or goodness) comes in on the east side the River, a small Creek or Run, the name of which I coud not learn; and a Mile or two below the Island, on the West side, comes in big stony Creek (not larger in appearance than the other) on neither of which does there seem to be any large bottoms or body's of good Land. About 7 Miles from the last Mentiond Creek 28 from our last Incampment, and about 75 from Pittsburg, we came to the Mingo Town Situate on the West Side a little above the Cross Creeks.

This place contains abt. Twenty Cabbins, & 70 Inhabitants of the Six Nations.

Had we set of early, & kept pretty constantly at it, we might have reachd lower than this place Today; as the Water in many places run pretty swift, in general more so than yesterday. . . .

Upon our arrival at the Mingo Town we receivd the disagreeable news of two Traders being killd at a Town calld the Grape Vine Town, 38. miles below this; which causd us to hesitate whether we shoud proceed or not, and wait for further Intelligence.

Tuesday 23.   Several imperfect accts. coming in, agreeing that only one Person was killd, & the Indians not supposing it to be done by their People, we resolvd to pursue our passage, till we coud get some more distinct Acct. of this Transaction. Accordingly abt. 2 Oclock we set out with the two Indians which was to accompany us, in our Canoe, and in about 4 Miles came to the Mouth of a Creek calld Seulf [Sewell] Creek, on the East side; at the Mouth of which is a bottom of very good Land, as I am told there likewise is up it.

The Cross Creeks (as they are calld) are not large, that on the West side however is biggest. At the Mingo Town we found, and left, 60 odd Warriors of the Six Nations going to the Cherokee Country to proceed to war against the Cuttaba's [Catawbas]. About 10 Miles below the Town we came to two other cross Creeks

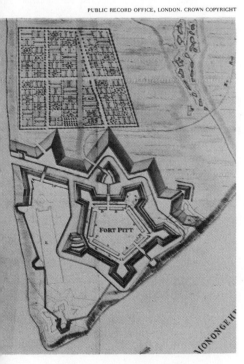

Detail of a 1761 map of Pittsburgh showing Fort Pitt on the point of land where Fort Duquesne had stood

that on the West side largest, but not big; and calld by Nicholson, French Creek. About 3 Miles or a little better below this, at the lower point of some Islands which stand contiguous to each other, we were told by the Indians with us that three men from Virginia (by Virginians they mean all the People settled upon Redstone, &ca.) had markd the Land from hence all the way to Redstone—that there was a body of exceeding fine Land lying about this place and up opposite to the Mingo Town—as also down to the Mouth of Fishing Creek. At this Place we Incampd.

[They continued downriver, with George appraising the land along the way. They learned that the trader had not been slain but had drowned trying to ford the Ohio. There was a council with friendly Indians. About 160 miles by river below Pittsburgh they came to the Great Bend, at whose foot the Great Kanawha River enters. Washington began tentatively selecting tracts of rich bottomland.]

Portion of a map made in 1755 by L. Evans showing the junction of the Ohio and Kanawha rivers

Monday 29th. ... Opposite to the Creek just below wch. we Incampd, is a pretty long bottom, & I believe tolerable wide; but abt. 8 or 9 Miles below the aforemend. Creek, & just below a pavement of Rocks on the west side, comes in a Creek with fallen Timber at the Mouth, on which the Indians say there is wide bottom's, & good Land.... Six Miles below this comes in a small Creek on the west side at the end of a small naked Island, and just above another pavement of Rocks. This Creek comes thro a Bottom of fine Land, & opposite to it (on the East side of the River) appears to be a large bottom of very fine Land also. At this place begins what they call the great Bent. 5 Miles below this again on the East side comes in (abt. 200 yds. above a little stream or Gut) another Creek; which is just below an Island, on the upper point of which are some dead standing trees, & a parcel of white bodied Sycamores. In the Mouth of this Creek lyes a Sycamore blown down by the wind; from hence an East line may be run 3 or 4 Miles; thence a North Line till it strikes the River, which I apprehend would Include about 3 or 4000 Acres of exceeding valuable Land....

Tuesday 30. We set out at 50 Minutes passed Seven; the Weather being windy and cloudy (after a Night of Rain)....

About 10 Miles below our Incampment & a little lower down than the bottom described to lye in the shape of a horse Shoe comes in a small Creek on the West side, and opposite to this on the East begins a body of flat Land which the Indians tell us runs quite across the Fork to the Falls in the Kanhawa, and must at least be 3 days walk across. If so the Flat Land containd therein must be very considerable. A Mile or two below this we Landed, and after getting a little distance from the River we came (without any rising) to a pretty lively kind of Land grown up with Hicky. & Oaks of different kinds, intermixd with Walnut, &ca. here and there. We also found many shallow Ponds, the sides of which abounding in grass, invited innumerable quantities of wild fowl among which I saw a Couple of Birds in size between a Swan and a Goose; & in colour somewhat between the two; being darker than the young Swan and of a more sutty Colour. The cry of these was as unusual as the Bird itself, as I never heard any noize resembling it before. About 5 Miles below this we Incampd in a bottom of Good Land which holds tolerably flat & rich some distance out.

Wednesday 31st. I sent the Canoe along down to the Junction of the two Rivers abt. 5 Miles, that is the Kanhawa with the Ohio—and set out upon a hunting Party to view the Land. We steerd nearly East for about 8 or 9 Miles then bore Southwardly, & westwardly, till we came to our Camp at the confluence of the Rivers. The Land from the Rivers appeard but indifferent, & very broken; whether these ridges might not be those that divide the Waters of the Ohio from the Kanhawa is not certain, but I believe they are. If so the Lands may yet be good. If not, that which lyes of the River bottoms is good for little.

November 1st. A little before eight Oclock we set of with our Canoe up the River to discover what kind of Lands lay upon the Kanhawa. The Land on both sides this River just at the Mouth is very fine; but on the East side when you get towards the Hills (which I judge to be about 6 or 700 yards from the River) it appears to be wet, & better adapted for Meadow than tillage. This bottom continues up the East side for about 2 Miles, & by going up the Ohio a good Tract might be got of bottom Land Including the old Shawna Town, which is about 3 Miles up the Ohio just above the Mouth of a Ck. where the aforementiond bottom ends on the East side the Kanhawa, which extends up it at least 50 Miles by the Indns. acct. and of great width (to be ascertaind, as we come down) in many places very rich; in others somewhat wet and pondy; fit for Meadow, but upon the whole exceeding valuable, as the Land after you get out of the Rich bottom is very good for Grain, tho not rich. We judgd we went up this River about 10 Miles today. On the East side appear to be some good bottoms but small—neither long nor wide, & the Hills back of them rather steep & poor.

Novr. 2d. We proceeded up the River with the Canoe about 4 Miles more, & then incampd & went a Hunting; killd 5 Buffaloes & wounded some others—three deer, &ca. This Country abounds in Buffalo & Wild game of

In 1773 Washington placed an ad in The Pennsylvania Gazette *offering 20,000 acres of his land on the Ohio and Great Kanawha for lease to people willing to clear and till it.*

all kinds; as also in all kinds of wild fowl, there being in the Bottoms a great many small grassy Ponds or Lakes which are full of Swans, Geese, & Ducks of different kinds.

Some of our People went up the River 4 or 5 Miles higher & found the same kind of bottom on the west side, & we were told by the Indians that it continued to the Falls which they judgd to be 50 or 60 Miles higher up. This Bottom next the Water (in most places) is very rich. As you approach to the Hills you come (in many) to a thin white Oak Land, & poor. The hills as far as we coud judge were from half a Mile to a Mile from the River; poor & steep in the parts we see, with Pine growing on them. Whether they are generally so, or not, we cannot tell but I fear they are.

Saturday 3d. We set of down the River on our return homewards, and Incampd at the Mouth; at the Beginning of the Bottom above the junction of the Rivers, and at the Mouth of a branch on the East side, I markd two Maples, an Elm, & Hoopwood Tree as A Cornr. of the Soldiers Ld. (if we can get it) intending to take all the bottom from hence to the Rapids in the Great Bent into one Survey. I also markd at the Mouth of another Gut lower down on the West side (at the lower end of the long bottom) an Ash and hoopwood for the Beginning of another of the Soldiers Survey, to extend up so as to Include all the Bottom (in a body) on the west side.

The party returned home without incident. Although Washington never saw the lands on the Great Kanawha again, his acres there would be a prized possession until the year of his death. He assumed responsibility for pressing the claims of the veterans of 1754 and had the land surveyed. Grants were made according to rank; Washington, a colonel, received fifteen thousand acres (and bought the grants of two other men for another fifty-six hundred acres). There was some grumbling later about the division. One dissatisfied veteran was George Muse, a former major, who had applied for and been given his land, though he had been a coward at Fort Necessity. When Muse complained he had received short measure, Washington fired back a letter giving a rare picture of him in anger.

[Mount Vernon, January 29, 1774]

Your impertinent Letter of the 24th. ulto., was delivered to me yesterday by Mr. Smith. As I am not accustomed to receive such from any Man, nor would have taken the same language from you personally, without letting you feel some marks of my resentiment; I would advise you to be cautious in writing me a second of the same tenour; for though I understand you were drunk when you did it, yet give me leave to tell you, that drunkness is no excuse for rudeness; and that, but for your stupidity and sottishness you might have known, by attending to the public Gazettes, (particularly Rinds of the 14th. of January last) that you had your full quantity of ten thousand acres of Land allowed you; that is, 9073 acres in the great Tract of 51,302 acres, and the remainder in the small tract of 927 acres; whilst I wanted near 500 acres of my quantity, Doctr. Craik of his, and almost every other claimant little or much of theirs. But suppose you had really fallen short 73 acres of your 10,000, do you think your superlative merit entitles you to greater indulgences than others? or that I was to make it good to you, if it did? when it was at the option of the Governor and Council to have allowed you but 500 acres in the whole, if they had been inclin'd so to do. If either of these should happen to be your opinion, I am very well convinced you will stand singular in it; & all my concern is, that I ever engag'd in behalf of so ungrateful and dirty a fellow as you are. But you may still stand in need of my assistance, as I can inform you that your affairs, in respect to these Lands, do not stand upon so solid a basis as you may imagine, & this you may take by way of hint; as your coming in for *any,* much less a *full share* may still be a disputed point, by a Gentleman who is not in this Country at this time, & who is exceedingly dissatisfyed therewith. I wrote to you [him?] a few days ago concerning the other distribution, proposing an easy method of dividing our Lands; but since I find in what temper you are, I am sorry I took the trouble of mentioning the Land, or your name in a Letter, as I do not think you merit the least assistance from

G: WASHINGTON.

Washington later described the land awarded the veterans as "the cream of the country." He had first look at the surveys and selected well: the richest land in the choice locations. He got the Governor's agreement to a plan to divide among those who had had the trouble and expense of surveying the land the acreage remaining after all claims were satisfied. There were nineteen thousand acres left over; when that pie was cut up, Washington got a 3,953-acre piece. In 1773 George was asking the Governor for still another grant, this time a bounty awarded to veterans of the French and Indian War, although his eligibility was doubtful. Only the coming of the Revolution halted this and other plans to acquire western lands.

During these years Washington showed a disinterest in political affairs beyond his immediate horizons. Even when the controversy with the mother country over taxation became a burning issue, he for a time maintained his apolitical stance. Washington was a member of the House of Burgesses when Patrick Henry made his famous speech against the Stamp Act, concluding "If *this* be treason, make the most of it." He kept no diary of his attendance and the event is not mentioned in his surviving letters. However, he was not untouched by the Stamp Act furor and wrote to Francis Dandridge, his wife's uncle, giving his measured opinion of how the act might affect trade between the Colonies and the mother country.

[Mount Vernon, September 20, 1765]

If you will permit me after six years silence—the time I have been married to your Niece—to pay my respects to you in this Epistolary way I shall think myself happy in beginning a corrispondance which cannot but be attended with pleasure on my side....

At present few things are under notice of my observation that can afford you any amusement in the recital. The Stamp Act Imposed on the Colonies by the Parliament of Great Britain engrosses the conversation of the Speculative part of the Colonists, who look upon this unconstitutional method of Taxation as a direful attack upon their Liberties, and loudly exclaim against the Violation. What may be the result of this and some other (I think I may add) ill judgd Measures, I will not undertake to determine; but this I may venture to affirm, that the advantage accrueing to the Mother Country will fall greatly short of the expectations of the Ministry; for certain it is, our whole Substance does already in a manner flow to Great Britain and that whatsoever contributes to Lesson our Importation's must be hurtful to their Manufacturers. And the Eyes of our People, already beginning to open, will perceive, that many Luxuries which we lavish our substance to Great Britain for, can well be dispensd with whilst the necessaries of Life are (mostly) to be had within ourselves. This consequently will introduce frugality, and be a necessary

German engraving of the protest in Boston against the Stamp Act

Washington did not approve of the destruction of tea at the Boston Tea Party but opposed the punishment.

stimulation to Industry. If Great Britain therefore Loads her Manufactures with heavy Taxes, will it not facilitate these Measures? They will not compel us I think to give our Money for their exports whether we will or no, & certain I am none of their Traders will part from them without a valuable consideration. Where then is the Utility of these Restrictions?

As to the Stamp Act, taken in a single view, one, & the first bad consequences attending it I take to be this. Our Courts of Judicature must inevitably be shut up; for it is impossible (or next of kin to it) under our present Circumstances that the Act of Parliam't can be complyd with were we ever so willing to enforce the execution; for not to say, which alone woud be sufficient, that we have not Money to pay the Stamps, there are many other cogent Reasons to prevent it; and if a stop be put to our judicial proceedings I fancy the Merchants of G. Britain trading to the Colonies will not be among the last to wish for a Repeal of it.

The political opinions of Washington slowly hardened. When the Crown passed new taxes on imports into the Colonies (the Townshend Acts), the Colonies resisted with nonimportation schemes. Washington sent the text of one such plan to a neighbor, George Mason; the opening portion of his letter shows a growing opposition to King and Parliament.

Mount Vernon, April 5, 1769.
Herewith you will receive a letter and Sundry papers which were forwarded to me a day or two ago by Doctor Ross of Bladensburg. I transmit them with the greater pleasure, as my own desire of knowing your sentiments upon a matter of this importance exactly coincides with the Doctors inclinations.

At a time when our lordly Masters in Great Britain will be satisfied with nothing less than the deprivation of American freedom, it seems highly necessary that some thing shou'd be done to avert the stroke and maintain the liberty which we have derived from our Ancestors; but the manner of doing it to answer the purpose effectually is the point in question.

That no man shou'd scruple, or hesitate a moment to use a-ms [arms] in defence of so valuable a blessing, on which all the good and evil of life depend; is clearly my opinion; yet A-ms I wou'd beg leave to add, should be the last resource; the denier resort. Addresses to the Throne, and remonstrances to parliament, we have already, it is said, proved the inefficacy of; how far then their attention to our rights and priviledges is to be awakened or alarmed by starving their Trade & manufactures, remains to be tryed.

Washington was present early in May, 1769, when the House of Burgesses drew up resolutions affirming, among other things, that it alone had the right to tax the people of Virginia. On receiving the resolutions, Governor Botetourt at once dissolved the House of Burgesses. Most members went to a local tavern, where they drew up an agreement to buy no taxed article from Britain. Washington was among the first to sign. Washington's point of view shifted slowly from the practical one of how parliamentary acts would affect the Colonial economy to the more philosophical one of how they infringed on the constitutional rights of citizens. Although he did not approve of the destruction of tea at the Boston Tea Party at the end of 1773, he was much opposed to the "despotick measures" laid on Boston as punishment. In the summer of 1774 Bryan Fairfax, brother of Washington's neighbor George William Fairfax, considered standing for election to the House of Burgesses. Bryan advocated a conciliatory approach to the Crown, and Washington wrote to him, commenting on Bryan's position in language showing that his own views by then were well formed.

Mount Vernon, 4 July 1774

John has just delivered to me your favor of yesterday, which I shall be obliged to answer in a more concise manner, than I could wish, as I am very much engaged in raising one of the additions to my house, which I think (perhaps it is fancy) goes on better whilst I am present, than in my absence from the workmen....

As to your political sentiments, I would heartily join you in them, so far as relates to a humble and dutiful petition to the throne, provided there was the most distant hope of success. But have we not tried this already? Have we not addressed the Lords, and remonstrated to the Commons? And to what end? Did they deign to look at our petitions? Does it not appear, as clear as the sun in its meridian brightness, that there is a regular, systematic plan formed to fix the right and practice of taxation upon us? Does not the uniform conduct of Parliament for some years past confirm this? Do not all the debates, especially those just brought to us, in the House of

COLONIAL WILLIAMSBURG

The Capitol at Williamsburg, where the House of Burgesses convened

97

Garden house at Mount Vernon

Commons on the side of government, expressly declare that America must be taxed in aid of the British funds, and that she has no longer resources within herself? Is there any thing to be expected from petitioning after this? Is not the attack upon the liberty and property of the people of Boston, before restitution of the loss to the India Company was demanded, a plain and self-evident proof of what they are aiming at? Do not the subsequent bills (not I dare say acts), for depriving the Massachusetts Bay of its charter, and for transporting offenders into colonies or to Great Britain for trial, where it is impossible from the nature of the thing that justice can be obtained, convince us that the administration is determined to stick at nothing to carry its point? Ought we not, then, to put our virtue and fortitude to the severest test?

That summer of 1774 George busied himself in adding a new wing to the Mount Vernon mansion house. He also had a sad duty to perform, auctioning off the furniture and furnishings of Belvoir, for his neighbors George William and Sally Fairfax had gone to England to live. In late August he was off to Philadelphia as one of Virginia's seven delegates to the First Continental Congress. Following his usual habit, Washington spoke little but listened and learned during the six weeks the Congress sat; he also made it a point to become acquainted socially with delegates from other Colonies. After his return to Virginia, county after county elected him to lead its militia. That the Colonies might have to fight for their rights no longer seemed impossible. And despite his quiet showing in Philadelphia the previous year, Washington was easily elected a delegate to the Second Continental Congress, which was to meet on May 10, 1775. The first news of the clashes at Lexington and Concord reached Mount Vernon on April 27. Whether Washington had any intimation of what that distant event would do to his life we cannot know. But when he drove away seven days later, bound for Philadelphia, he was not to see Mount Vernon, except in passing through, for more than eight years.

Chapter 4

Commander in Chief

Washington had not been put on a single committee in the First Continental Congress, but his experience as a military man was in demand in the Second, which convened at Philadelphia on May 10, 1775. He was made a member of groups to study the defense of New York, to draw up rules for the government of the army, to find means to supply the Colonies with ammunition. Few of the delegates expected a long conflict. Most were hopeful that the intransigent ministry of Lord North would soon be replaced by a more conciliatory one and the unpleasantness between mother country and Colonies would quickly be forgotten. But by and large, all turned with spirit to meet the challenge to their British liberties. Despite their enthusiasm, the delegates ran into a harsh and unyielding fact: they could talk and vote all they wanted, but they had little to back up their words with. The Colonies had almost no industry; they might raise an army, but they would be hard put to clothe, arm, transport, and shelter it. But Washington, pondering the first complete accounts of the fighting at Lexington and Concord, saw that the Colonials did possess one element essential for success: the spirit to stand up to British regulars. In writing to George William Fairfax in England, whose Virginia plantation he had agreed to manage, he gave his analysis of the Lexington-Concord fight.

> Philadelphia, May 31, 1775.
>
> Before this Letter can reach you, you must, undoubtedly, have received an Account of the engagement in the Massachusetts Bay between the Ministerial Troops (for we do not, nor cannot yet prevail upon ourselves to call them the King's Troops) and the Provincials of that Government; But as you may not have heard how that affair began, I inclose you the several Affidavits that were taken after the Action.
>
> General Gage acknowledges, that the detachment un-

Boston broadside listing the names of "Provincials" killed at Concord

der Lieutenant Colonel Smith was sent out to destroy private property; or, in other Words, to destroy a Magazine which self preservation obliged the Inhabitants to establish. And he also confesses, in effect at least, that his Men made a very precipitate retreat from Concord, notwithstanding the reinforcement under Lord Piercy, the last of which may serve to convince Lord Sandwich (and others of the same sentiment) that the Americans will fight for their Liberties and property, however pusilanimous, in his Lordship's Eye, they may appear in other respects.

From the best Accounts I have been able to collect of that affair; indeed from every one, I believe the fact, stripped of all colouring, to be plainly this, that if the retreat had not been as precipitate as it was (and God knows it could not well have been more so) the Ministerial Troops must have surrendered, or been totally cut off: For they had not arrived in Charlestown (under cover of their Ships) half an hour, before a powerful body of Men from Marblehead and Salem were at their heels, and must, if they had happened to have been up one hour sooner, inevitably intercepted their retreat to Charleston. Unhappy it is though to reflect, that a Brother's Sword has been sheathed in a Brother's breast, and that, the once happy and peaceful plains of America are either to be drenched with Blood, or Inhabited by Slaves. Sad alternative! But can a virtuous Man hesitate in his choice?

One of the first orders of business for Congress was to aid the New England forces besieging the British in Boston. While the delegates debated they were somewhat taken aback by news that a force of Colonials led by Benedict Arnold and Ethan Allen had captured Fort Ticonderoga on Lake George. This incident could not be blamed on aggression by British troops, as Lexington and Concord had been, but at the same time the seizure of the fort cut the British route from Canada and so eased the problem of defending the Colony of New York. Some of the nimbler minds in Congress worked out a resolution justifying the seizure as necessary to avert an invasion of the Colonies being prepared (they said) in Quebec. At the same time instructions were sent to have the artillery in the fort safely stored until Britain and the Colonies should have their differences conciliated. The cannon would prove useful before many months had passed.

Congress decided early that the New England army before Boston should become part of a united Colonial army—and that raised the question of who should have the top command. Many New Englanders favored Artemas Ward, a veteran of the French and Indian War, commander in chief of Massachusetts troops, and at the moment in command of the troops laying siege to Boston. A few championed Charles Lee, a professional soldier who had served with the British and as a soldier of fortune on the Continent, and whom many considered a top military expert. There were a few local favorites. And there was Washington. Not only was he highly regarded for his military experience and his personal qualities, but his election was urged by some, and especially John Adams, because the choice of a Virginian would help to dispel a common notion that New England was attempting to dominate the rest of the Colonies. In mid-June Washington made two brief entries in his diary.

> 14 [June, 1775]. Dined at Mr. Saml. Merediths. Spent the Evening at home.
> 15. Dined at Burn's in the Field. Spent the Eveng. on a Committee [to draft rules and regulations for the government of the army].

The diary entries do not hint that on June 14 John Adams rose to nominate Washington for Commander in Chief (as Washington modestly slipped out a side door), or that the next day Washington, still discreetly absent, was unanimously elected. On June 16 he was formally notified and made a formal acceptance.

> [Philadelphia, June 16, 1775]
> Tho' I am truly sensible of the high Honour done me in this Appointment, yet I feel great distress from a consciousness that my abilities and Military experience may not be equal to the extensive and important Trust: However, as the Congress desires I will enter upon the momentous duty, & exert every power I Possess In their Service for the Support of the glorious Cause: I beg they will accept my most cordial thanks for this distinguished testimony of their Approbation.
> But lest some unlucky event should happen unfavourable to my reputation, I beg it may be remembered by every Gentn. in the room, that I this day declare with the utmost sincerity, I do not think my self equal to the Command I am honoured with.
> As to pay, Sir, I beg leave to Assure the Congress that as no pecuniary consideration could have tempted me to have accepted this Arduous employment at the expence of my domestk. ease & happiness I do not wish to make

John Adams

any proffit from it: I will keep an exact Account of my expences; those I doubt not they will discharge & that is all I desire.

Two days later the new General wrote his wife a troubled letter, breaking the news to her. Although he spoke of returning to Mount Vernon in the fall, the air was full of uncertainty.

Philadelphia, June 18, 1775.

My Dearest:

I am now set down to write to you on a subject, which fills me with inexpressible concern, and this concern is greatly aggravated and increased, when I reflect upon the uneasiness I know it will cause you. It has been determined in Congress, that the whole army raised for the defence of the American cause shall be put under my care, and that it is necessary for me to proceed immediately to Boston to take upon me the command of it.

You may believe me, my dear Patsy, when I assure you, in the most solemn manner that, so far from seeking this appointment, I have used every endeavor in my power to avoid it, not only from my unwillingness to part with you and the family, but from a consciousness of its being a trust too great for my capacity, and that I should enjoy more real happiness in one month with you at home, than I have the most distant prospect of finding abroad, if my stay were to be seven times seven years. But as it has been a kind of destiny, that has thrown me upon this service, I shall hope that my undertaking it is designed to answer some good purpose. You might, and I suppose did perceive, from the tenor of my letters, that I was apprehensive I could not avoid this appointment,

as I did not pretend to intimate when I should return. That was the case. It was utterly out of my power to refuse this appointment, without exposing my character to such censures, as would have reflected dishonor upon myself, and have given pain to my friends. This, I am sure, could not, and ought not, to be pleasing to you, and must have lessened me considerably in my own esteem. I shall rely, therefore, confidently on that Providence, which has heretofore preserved and been bountiful to me, not doubting but that I shall return safe to you in the fall. I shall feel no pain from the toil or the danger of the campaign; my unhappiness will flow from the uneasiness I know you will feel from being left alone. I therefore beg, that you will summon your whole fortitude, and pass your time as agreeably as possible. Nothing will give me so much sincere satisfaction as to hear this, and to hear it from your own pen.

If it should be your desire to remove into Alexandria (as you once mentioned upon an occasion of this sort) I am quite pleased that you should put it into practice, and Lund Washington may be directed by you to build a kitchen and other houses there proper for your reception. If on the other hand you should rather incline to spend a good part of your time among your friends below, I wish you to do so. In short my earnest and ardent desire is that you will pursue any plan that is most likely to produce content, and a tolerable degree of tranquility; as it must add greatly to my uneasy feelings to hear that you are dissatisfied or complaining at what I really could not avoid.

As life is always uncertain, and common prudence dictates to every man the necessity of settling his temporal concerns while it is in his power, and while the mind is calm and undisturbed, I have, since I came to this place (for I had not time to do it before I left home) got Colonel Pendleton to draft a will for me, by the directions I gave him, which will I now enclose. The provision made for you in case of my death will, I hope, be agreeable: I have included the money for which I sold my land (to Doctor Mercer) in the sum given you as also all my other debts. What I owe myself is very trifling, Cary's debt excepted, and this would not have been much if the bank stock had been applied without such difficulties as he made in the transference.

Washington's appointment by Congress as Commander in Chief, dated June 19, 1775

103

I shall add nothing more at present as I have several letters to write, but to desire that you will remember me to Milly and all friends, and to assure you that I am, with the most unfeigned regard

My dear

Patcy Yr affecte

Go Washington

A letter went to Jack Custis, urging him and his wife to move to Mount Vernon while Washington was gone. To his brother John Augustine, Washington wrote of his heavy new burden of responsibility.

Philadelphia, June 20, 1775.

I am now to bid adieu to you, & to every kind of domestick ease, for a while. I am Imbarked on a wide Ocean, boundless in its prospect, & from whence, perhaps, no safe harbour is to be found. I have been called upon by the unanimous Voice of the Colonies to take Command of the Continental Army—an honour I neither sought after, nor desired, as I am thoroughly convinced, that it requires greater Abilities, and much more experience, than I am Master of, to conduct a business so extensive in its nature, and arduous in the execution; but the partiallity of the Congress, joined to a political motive, really left me without a choice; and I am now Commissioned a Generl & Commander in Chief of all the Forces now raisd, or to be raisd, for the defence of the United Colonies. That I may discharge the Trust to the Satisfaction of my Imployers, is my first wish—that I shall aim to do it, there remains as little doubt of—how far I may succeed is another point; but this I am sure of, that in the worst event, I shall have the consolation of knowing (if I act to the best of my judgment) that the blame ought to lodge upon the appointers, not the appointed, as it was by no means a thing of my own seeking, or proceeding from any hint of my friends.

I am at liberty to inform you, that the Congress, in a Committee, (which will I dare say be agreed to when reported) have consented to a Continental Currency; have ordered two million of Dollars to be struck for payment of the Troops, &ca. and have voted 15,000 Men as a Continental Army—which number will be augmented, as the strength of the British Troops will be greater than was expected at the time of passing that vote. Genl.

John Augustine Washington

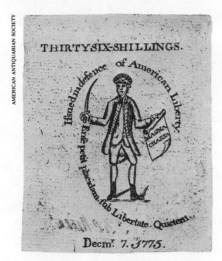

Paul Revere designed and engraved this thirty-six shilling note in 1775.

Ward, Genl. Lee, Genl. Schuyler and Genl. Putnam are appointed Major Genls. under me; the Brigadier Genls. are not yet appointed. Majr. Gates Adjutant Genl. I expect to set out tomorrow for Boston & hope to be joind there in a little time by Ten Companies of Riflemen from this Province, Maryland & Virginia. For other Articles of Intelligence, I shall refer you to the Papers, as the Printers are diligent in collecting every thing that is stirring.

I shall hope that my Friends will visit, & endeavour to keep up the spirits of my Wife as much as they can, as my departure will, I know, be a cutting stroke upon her; and on this acct. alone, I have many very disagreeable sensations. I hope you & my sister (although the distance is great) will find as much leisure this Summer, as to spend a little time at Mount Vernon.

The choice of George Washington as Commanding General, seen in the light of afterthought, was a wise one, but at the time skeptics could have been excused for doubting its wisdom. He had never commanded large bodies of men, had never led troops in battle on an open field, had never handled artillery or cavalry. Yet the various other men put forward as candidates for Commander in Chief—Charles Lee, Israel Putnam, Artemas Ward, and others—were all to fall into eclipse before the end of the war through ineptitude, improper behavior, or mischance. Congress had put the fate of America in the right hands. At the moment, the fate of the Colonies lay with the citizen-soldiers before Boston, and Washington was impatient to get there. Before setting out, he penned a short note to Martha.

Phila. June 23d. 1775.

My Dearest,

As I am within a few Minutes of leaving this City, I could not think of departing from it without dropping you a line; especially as I do not know whether it may be in my power to write again till I get to the Camp at Boston. I go fully trusting in that Providence, which has been more bountiful to me than I deserve, & in full confidence of a happy Meeting with you sometime in the Fall. I have not time to add more, as I am surrounded with Company to take leave of me. I retain an unalterable affection for you, which neither time or distance can change. My best love to Jack & Nelly, & regards for the rest of the Family concludes me with the utmost truth & sincerity, Yr. entire

Go: Washington

With Charles Lee and Philip Schuyler, newly appointed major generals, Washington started for Boston. Militia guards of honor and civic groups with speeches of welcome slowed his travel. New York, a town of about twenty-two thousand souls, gave him a tumultuous ovation, and there he intercepted an express rider carrying the first news of the Battle of Bunker Hill to Congress. He left General Schuyler in command of the Colony of New York and before proceeding found time to reply reassuringly to an address from the New York legislature, which had expressed the hope that he and the other generals would exercise their military power no longer than necessary to restore peace to the land.

Washington made his headquarters in this handsome Cambridge mansion.

Pictorial Field-Book of the Revolution
BY BENSON J. LOSSING, 1852

June 26, 1775.

At the same time that with you I deplore the unhappy necessity of such an Appointment, as that with which I am now honoured, I cannot but feel sentiments of the highest gratitude for this affecting Instance of distinction and Regard.

May your every wish be realized in the success of America, at this important and interesting Period; & be assured that the every exertion of my worthy Colleagues & myself will be equally extended to the re-establishment of Peace & Harmony between the Mother Country and the Colonies, as to the fatal, but necessary, operations of War. When we assumed the Soldier, we did not lay aside the Citizen; and we shall most sincerely rejoice with you in that happy hour when the establishment of American Liberty, upon the most firm and solid foundations, shall enable us to return to our Private Stations in the bosom of a free, peaceful and happy Country.

Washington arrived at Cambridge outside Boston on July 2 and established headquarters there. The next day he assumed command of the army from Artemas Ward, reduced to second in command as one of Congress's new major generals. Washington also delivered a major general's commission to Israel Putnam, a Connecticut Yankee of little learning but who had had a life of incredible adventure and was then fresh from heroism on Bunker Hill. Then the new commander applied himself to the onerous tasks of strengthening fortifications, instilling discipline, bolstering morale, improving camp sanitation, and taking care of the multitude of other details involved in military command. Within a day he issued his first extended orders to the army. (Note: the countersign listed daily in general orders was the password that must be given to sentries to enter the lines; the parole was a special password given only to officers of the guard and inspectors of the guard.)

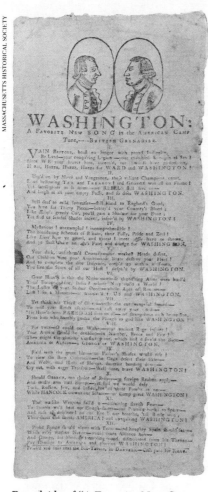

Broadside of "A Favorite New Song in the American Camp" giving a "Huzza for Ward and Washington" as Washington arrived in Cambridge

GENERAL ORDERS

Head Quarters, Cambridge, July 4th. 1775. Parole Abington. Countersign Bedford.

Exact returns to be made by the proper Officers of all the Provisions Ordnance, Ordnance Stores, Powder, Lead working Tools of all kinds, Tents, Camp Kettles, and all other Stores under their respective care, belonging to the Armies at Roxbury and Cambridge. The commanding Officer of each Regiment to make a return of the number of blankets wanted to compleat every Man with one at least.

The Hon: Artemus Ward, Charles Lee, Philip Schuyler, and Israel Putnam Esquires, are appointed Major Generals of the American Army, and due obedience is to be paid them as such. The Continental Congress not having compleated the appointments of the other officers in said army nor had sufficient time to prepare and forward their Commissions; any officer is to continue to do duty in the Rank and Station he at present holds, untill further orders.

Thomas Mifflin Esqr, is appointed by the General one of his Aid-de-Camps. Joseph Reed Esqr. is in like manner appointed Secretary to the General, and they are in future to be consider'd and regarded as such.

The Continental Congress having now taken all the Troops of the several Colonies, which have been raised, or which may be hereafter raised for the support and defence of the Liberties of America; into their Pay and Service. They are now the Troops of the UNITED PROVINCES of North America; and it is hoped that all Distinctions of Colonies will be laid aside; so that one and the same Spirit may animate the whole, and the only Contest be, who shall render, on this great and trying occasion, the most essential service to the great and common cause in which we are all engaged.

It is required and expected that exact discipline be observed, and due Subordination prevail thro' the whole Army, as a Failure in these most essential points must necessarily produce extreme Hazard, Disorder and Confusion; and end in Shameful disappointment and disgrace.

The General most earnestly requires, and expects a due observance of those articles of war, established for the Government of the army, which forbid profane cursing, swearing and drunkeness; And in like manner requires & expects, of all Officers, and Soldiers, not engaged on actual duty, a punctual attendance on divine Service, to implore the blessings of heaven upon the means used for our safety and defence.

All Officers are required and expected to pay diligent Attention, to keep their Men neat and clean—to visit them often at their quarters, and inculcate upon them the necessity of cleanliness, as essential to their health and service. They are particularly to see, that they have Straw to lay on, if to be had, and to make it known if they are destitute of this article. They are also to take care that Necessarys be provided in the Camps and frequently filled up to prevent their being offensive and unhealthy. Proper Notice will be taken of such Officers and Men, as distinguish themselves by their attention to these necessary duties.

The commanding Officer of each Regiment is to take particular care that not more than two Men of a Company be absent on furlough at the same time, unless in very extraordinary cases.

Col. Gardner is to [be] buried to morrow at 3, O'Clock, P.M. with the military Honors due to so brave and gallant an Officer, who fought, bled and died in the Cause of his country and mankind. His own Regiment, except the company at Malden, to attend on this mournful occasion. The places of those Companies in the Lines on Prospect Hill, to be supplied by Col. Glovers regiment till the funeral is over.

No Person is to be allowed to go to Fresh-water pond a fishing or on any other occasion as there may be danger of introducing the small pox into the army.

It is strictly required and commanded that there be no firing of Cannon or small Arms from any of the Lines, or elsewhere, except in case of necessary, immediate defence, or special order given for that purpose.

All Prisoners taken, Deserters coming in, Persons coming out of Boston, who can give any Intelligence; any Captures of any kind from the Enemy, are to be immediately reported and brought up to Head Quarters in Cambridge.

Capt. Griffin is appointed Aide-de-Camp to General Lee and to be regarded as such.

The Guard for the security of the Stores at Watertown, is to be increased to thirty men immediately.

A stylized woodcut of Washington taking over command of his army

A Serjeant and six men to be set as a Guard to the Hospital, and are to apply to Doctor Rand.

Complaint having been made against John White Quarter Master of Col. Nixon's Regmt. for misdemeanors in drawing out Provisions for more Men than the Regiment consisted of; a Court Martial consisting of one Captain and four Subalterns is ordered to be held on said White, who are to enquire, determine and report.

AFTER ORDERS. 10 OCLOCK

The General desires that some Carpenters be immediately set to work at Brattle's Stables, to fix up Stalls for eight Horses, and more if the Room will admit, with suitable racks, mangers, &c.

Several cases had come to General Washington's attention of officers who were setting bad examples for their troops. When a captain found guilty of cowardice was sentenced to be discharged, the General used the occasion to exhort and warn all officers.

GENERAL ORDERS

Head Quarters, Cambridge, July 7th. 1775
Parole, Dorchester. CSign Exeter.

It is with inexpressible Concern that the General upon his first Arrival in the army, should find an Officer sentenced by a General Court-Martial to be cashier'd for Cowardice. A Crime of all others, the most infamous in a Soldier, the most injurious to an Army, and the last to be forgiven; inasmuch as it may, and often does happen, that the Cowardice of a single Officer may prove the Distruction of the whole Army: The General therefore (tho' with great Concern, and more especially, as the Transaction happened before he had the Command of the Troops) thinks himself obliged, for the good of the service, to approve the Judgment of the Court-Martial with respect to Capt. John Callender, who is hereby sentenced to be cashiered. Capt. John Callender is accordingly cashiered and dismissd from all farther service in the Continental Army as an Officer.

The General having made all due inquiries, and maturely consider'd this matter is led to the above determination not only from the particular Guilt of Capt. Callender, but the fatal Consequences of such conduct to the army and to the cause of america.

He now therefore most earnestly exhorts Officers of

Life of Benjamin Franklin BY O. L. HOLLEY, 1848

Benjamin Franklin, Thomas Lynch, and Benjamin Harrison were sent to Cambridge by Congress to arrange for the maintenance of the army.

all Ranks to shew an Example of Bravery and Courage to their men; assuring them that such as do their duty in the day of Battle, as brave and good Officers, shall be honor'd with every mark of distinction and regard; their names and merits made known to the General Congress and all America: while on the other hand, he positively declares that every Officer, be his rank what it may, who shall betray his Country, dishonour the Army and his General, by basely keeping back and shrinking from his duty in any engagment; shall be held up as an infamous Coward and punish'd as such, with the utmost martial severity; and no Connections, Interest or Intercessions in his behalf will avail to prevent the strict execution of justice.

Washington discovered, when he got an accurate count of his men, that his army was woefully weak to face the British, who could strike where and when they pleased with the support of the guns of their fleet. Moreover, his fortifications were flimsy and poorly planned. Near the end of July he sent his brother John Augustine a good summary of the situation.

> Camp at Cambridge, about 5 miles from Boston,
> July 27th. 1775.
>
> On the 2d Instt. I arrived at this place after passing through a great deal of delightful Country, covered with grass.(although the Season has been dry) in a very different manner to what our Lands in Virginia are. I found a mixed multitude of People here, under very little discipline, order, or Government. I found the Enemy in Possession of a place called Bunkers Hill, on Charles Town Neck, strongly Intrenched & Fortifying themselves. I found part of our Army on two Hills (called Winter & Prospect Hills) about a Mile & quarter from the Enemy on Bunkers Hill, in a very insecure state; I found another part of the Army at this Village, and a third part at Roxbury, guarding the Entrance in and out of Boston. My whole time since I came here, has been Imployed in throwing up Lines of Defence at these three places; to secure in the first Instance, our own Troops from any attempts of the Enemy; and in the next, to cut of all Communications between their Troops and the Country; For to do this, & to prevent them from penetrating into the Country with Fire and Sword, & to harass them

Engraving of the Battle of Bunker Hill where Washington later found the enemy "strongly Intrenched"

A broadside of a Revolutionary song of 1775 describing "captain Washington" as "grown so tarnal proud"

if they do, is all that is expected of me; and if effected, must totally overthrow the designs of Administration, as the whole Force of Great Britain in the Town and Harbour of Boston, can answer no other end than to sink her under the disgrace and weight of the expence. Their Force, including Marines, Tories, &ca., are computed from the best Accts. I can get, at abt. 12,000 Men; ours, including Sick absent, &ca., at about 16,000; but then we have a cemi Circle of Eight or nine Miles to guard, to every part of wch. we are obliged to be equally attentive whilst they, situated as it were in the Centre of that Cemicircle, can bend their whole Force (having the entire command of the Water) against any one part of it with equal facility; this renders our Situation not very agreeable, though necessary; however, by incessant labour (Sundays not excepted) we are in a much better posture of defence now than when I first came. The Inclosed, though rough, will give you some small Idea of the Situation of Boston, & Bay on this side; as also of the Post they have Taken in Charles Town Neck, Bunker's Hill, and our Posts.

By very authentick Intelligence lately receivd out of Boston (from a Person who saw the returns) the number of Regulars (including I presume the Marines) the Morning of the Action on Bunkers Hill amounted to 7533 Men —their killed & wounded on that occasion amounted to

1043, whereof 92 were Officers. Our loss was 138 killed 36 Missing & 276 Wounded. The Enemy are sickly, and scarce of Fresh provisions—Beef, which is chiefly got by slaughtering their Milch Cows in Boston, sells from one shilling to 18d. Sterg. pr. lb.; & that it may not get cheaper, or more plenty, I have drove all the Stock within a considerable distance of this place back into the Country, out of the Way of the Men of War's Boats; In short, I have, & shall continue to do, every thing in my power to distress them. The Transports are all arrived & their whole Reinforcement Landed, so that I can see no reason why they should not if they ever attempt it, come boldly out and put the matter to Issue at once. If they think themselves not strong enough to do this, they surely will carry their Arms (having Ships of War & Transports ready) to some other part of the Continent, or relinquish the dispute; the last of which the Ministry, unless compelled will never agree to do. Our Works, & those of the Enemy, are so near & quite open between that we see every thing that each other is doing.

On August 1 Washington learned a shocking fact: his stock of powder, which he had been told was a barely adequate 308 barrels, was in fact a frighteningly meager ninety barrels—not enough for nine rounds per man, and with nothing for the artillery. The General enjoined the sternest kind of conservation, while carefully avoiding mention of a shortage.

GENERAL ORDERS

Head Quarters, Cambridge, August 4th. 1775
Parole, London. Countersign, Ireland.

It is with Indignation and Shame, the General observes, that notwithstanding the repeated Orders which have been given to prevent the firing of Guns, in and about Camp, that it is daily and hourly practised; that contrary to all Orders, straggling Soldiers do still pass the Guards, and fire at a Distance, where there is not the least probability of hurting the enemy, and where no other end is answer'd, but to waste Ammunition, expose themselves to the ridicule of the enemy, and keep their own Camps harrassed by frequent and continual alarms, to the hurt of every good Soldier, who is thereby disturbed of his natural rest, and will at length never be able to distinguish between a real, and a false alarm.

For these reasons, it is in the most peremptory manner forbid, any person or persons whatsoever, under any pretence, to pass the out Guards, unless authorized by the Commanding Officer of that part of the lines; signified in writing, which must be shewn to the Officer of the guard as they pass. Any person offending in this particular, will be considered in no other light, than as a common Enemy, and the Guards will have orders to fire upon them as such. The Commanding Officer of every regiment is to direct, that every man in his regiment, is made acquainted with Orders to the end, that no one may plead Ignorance and that all may be apprized of the consequence of disobedience. The Colonels of regiments and commanding Officers of Corps, to order the Rolls of every Company to be called twice a day, and every Man's Ammunition examined at evening Roll calling, and such as are found to be deficient to be confined.

The Guards are to apprehend all persons firing guns near their posts, whether Townsmen or soldiers.

At the same time, Washington appealed to Congress and to the New England Colonies for powder. His letter to Governor Nicholas Cooke of Rhode Island also solicited help in an adventure whereby powder might be obtained.

A 1775 broadside from Connecticut offers a bounty to "Any Gun-smith or Lock-maker" willing to supply arms.

Camp at Cambridge, 4th. Augst. 1775. I am now, Sir, in strict Confidence to acquaint you, that our Necessities in the Articles of Powder and Lead are so great as to require an immediate Supply. I must earnestly intreat you will fall upon some Measure to forward every Pound of each in the Colony which can possibly be spared. It is not within the Propriety or Safety of such a Correspondence to say what I might on this Subject. It is sufficient that the Case calls loudly for the most strenuous Exertions of every friend of his Country and does not admit of the least delay. No Quantity, however Small, is beneath notice and should any arrive, I beg it may be forwarded as soon as Possible. But a Supply of this kind is so precarious, not only from the Danger of the Enemy, but the opportunity of Purchasing, that I have resolved in my mind every other possible chance and listned to every proposition on the subject which could give the smallest Hope. Among others I have had one mentioned which has some Weight with me, as well as the General Officers to whom I have proposed it. One Harris is lately come from Bermuda, where there is a very considerable Magazine of Powder in a remote Part of the Island and the Inhabitants well disposed not only to our Cause in General, but to assist in this Enterprize in particular. We understand there are two Armed Vessels in your Province commanded by Men of known Activity and Spirit; one of which it is proposed to dispatch on this Errand, with such other Assistance as may be required. Harris is to go along as the Conductor of the Enterprize and to avail ourselves of his knowledge of the Island, but without any Command. I am very sensible that at first view the project may appear hazardous and its Success must depend on the Concurrence of many Circumstances; but we are in a Situation which requires us to run all Risques. No Danger is to be considered when put in Competition with the Magnitude of the Cause and the Absolute Necessity we are under of increasing our Stock. Enterprises which appear Chimerical, often prove successful from that very Circumstance, Common Sense & Prudence will Suggest Vigilance and care, when the Danger is Plain and obvious, but where little Danger is apprehended, the more the enemy is unprepared and consequently there is the fain'd Prospect of Success.

As it turned out, there was no well-stocked powder magazine on Bermuda—nor did much help to alleviate the critical powder shortage come from any source in the Colonies. Fortunately the British commander, General Gage—and after October 10 his successor, Major General Sir William Howe—made no offensive moves. Washington's patience wore thin under the constant pressure of coping with problems that seemed to have no solution. Even working with New England Yankees began to fray his Virginia temperament, and he finally exploded in a letter to Lund Washington, the cousin who was managing Mount Vernon in his absence.

Camp at Cambridge, August 20, 1775.
The People of this government have obtained a Character which they by no means deserved; their officers generally speaking are the most indifferent kind of People I ever saw. I have already broke one Colo. and five Captains for Cowardice and for drawing more Pay and Provisions than they had Men in their Companies; there is two more Colos. now under arrest, and to be tried for the

Brigadier General Horatio Gates

same offences; in short they are by no means such Troops, in any respect, as you are led to believe of them from the accts. which are published, but I need not make myself Enemies among them, by this declaration, although it is consistent with truth. I dare say the Men would fight very well (if properly Officered) although they are an exceeding dirty and nasty people; had they been properly conducted at Bunkers Hill (on the 17th of June) or those that were there properly supported, the Regulars would have met with a shameful defeat, and a much more considerable loss than they did, which is now known to be exactly 1057 killed and wounded; it was for their behaviour on that occasion that the above Officers were broke, for I never spared one that was accused of Cowardice but brot 'em to immediate Tryal.

There were endless harassing details to be taken care of. Although Brigadier General Horatio Gates, as Adjutant General, had taken charge of the administrative work of the staff and removed some of the burden from Washington, the primary responsibility was still the commander's.

GENERAL ORDERS

Head Quarters, Cambridge, July 14th. 1775
Parole, Hallifax. Countersign, Inverness.

As the Health of an Army principally depends upon Cleanliness; it is recommended in the strongest manner, to the Commanding Officer of Corps, Posts and Detachments, to be strictly diligent, in ordering the Necessarys [privies] to be filled up once a Week, and new ones dug; the Streets of the encampments and Lines to be swept daily, and all Offal and Carrion, near the camp, to be immediately buried. The Officers commanding in Barracks, or Quarters, to be answerable that they are swept every morning, and all Filth & Dirt removed from about the houses. Next to Cleanliness, nothing is more conducive to a Soldiers health, than dressing his provisions in a decent and proper manner. The Officers commanding Companies should therefore daily inspect the Camp Kitchens, and see the Men dress their Food in a wholesome way.

Head Quarters, Cambridge, August 22nd. 1775
The General does not mean to discourage the practice

of bathing, whilst the weather is warm enough to continue it; but he expressly forbids, any persons doing it, at or near the Bridge in Cambridge, where it has been observed and complained of, that many Men, lost to all sense of decency and common modesty, are running about naked upon the Bridge, whilst Passengers, and even Ladies of the first fashion in the neighbourhood, are passing over it, as if they meant to glory in their shame. The Guards and Centries at the Bridge, are to put a stop to this practice for the future.

Head Quarters, Cambridge, August 28th. 1775
As nothing is more pernicious to the health of Soldiers, nor more certainly productive of the bloody-flux; than drinking New Cyder: The General in the most possitive manner commands, the entire disuse of the same, and orders the Quarter Master General this day, to publish Advertisements, to acquaint the Inhabitants of the surrounding districts, that such of them, as are detected bringing new Cyder into the Camp, after Thursday, the last day of this month, may depend on having their casks stove.

With summer waning and the nip of early New England autumn in the air, Washington had to plan barracks for his men, provide warmer clothing, and even face the possibility that his army might melt away if the siege were not resolved before the end of the year. He expressed his forebodings to Congress in a letter to its president, John Hancock.

Camp at Cambridge, Septemr. 21st. 1775
The Connecticut & Rhode Island Troops stand engaged to the 1st. December only, & none longer than to the 1st. January. A Dissolution of the present Army therefore will take Place, unless some early Provision is made against such an Event. Most of the General Officers are of Opinion, the greater Part of them may be re-inlisted for the Winter or another Campaign, with the Indulgence of a Furlough to visit their Friends which may be regulated so as not to endanger the Service. How far it may be proper to form the new Army entirely out of the old for another Campaign, rather than from the Contingents of the several Provinces, is a Question which involves in it too many Considerations of Policy and Prudence for me to undertake to decide. It appears to be impos-

Israel Putnam (above) commanded the center division of Washington's reorganized army; Artemas Ward assumed command of the right wing.

sible to draw it from any other Source than the old Army this Winter; & as the Pay is ample, I hope a sufficient Number will engage in the Service for that Time at least: but there are various Opinions of the Temper of the Men on the Subject, & there may be great Hazard in deferring the Tryal too long.

[In the same letter, the Commander in Chief revealed that he had another campaign underway.]

I am now to inform the Honble. Congress, that encouraged by the repeated Declarations of the Canadians & Indians, & urged by their Requests; I have detached Col. Arnold with 1000 Men to penetrate into Canada by Way of Kennebeck River, & if possible, to make himself Master of Quebeck. By this manoeuvre, I propose, either to divert Carlton [Sir Guy Carleton, British commander] from St. Johns which would leave a free Passage to General Schuyler, or if this did not take Effect, Quebeck in its present defenseless State must fall into his Hands an easy Prey. I made all possible Inquiry as to the Distance, the Safety of the Rout, & the Danger of the Season, being too far advanced, but found nothing in either to deter me from proceeding, more especially, as it met with very General Approbation from all whom I consulted upon it. But that nothing might be omitted, to enable me to judge of its Propriety, & probable Consequences, I communicated it, by Express to General Schuyler, who approved of it in such Terms, that I resolved to put it into immediate Execution. They have now left this Place 7 Days, & if favoured with a good Wind, I hope soon to hear of their being safe in Kennebeck River.

Washington continued to extend and strengthen his lines, tightening his siege of Boston, which was then almost an island, connected to the mainland only by a narrow neck or peninsula. The army had been reorganized, formed into three "Grand Divisions," with the right wing, or division, under Artemas Ward, the left under Charles Lee, and the center commanded by Israel Putnam. After his powder supply had been somewhat replenished, Washington proposed to his general officers in September and again in October a concerted assault on the British lines to bring a decision. His officers disagreed, and he deferred to their opinion. To give his army more firepower, Washington assigned a special mission to Henry Knox, a twenty-five-year-old Boston bookseller, who had studied artillery and fortifications as a hobby and who would shortly become Washington's Chief of Artillery.

> [Headquarters, Cambridge, November 16, 1775]
> You are immediately to examine into the state of the artillery of this army & take an account of the Cannon Motors, Shels, Lead & Ammunition, that are wanting. When you have done that, you are to proceed in the most expeditious manner to New York; There apply to the president of the provincial Congress, and learn of him whether Col. Reed did any thing, or left any orders &c. respecting these things & get him to procure such of them as can possibly be had there. The president if he can will have them immediately sent hither: If he cannot, you must put them in a proper Channel for being Transported to this Camp with dispatch before you leave New York. After you have procured as many of these Necessaries as you can there, you must go to Major General Schuyler & get the Remainder from Ticonderoga, Crown point, or St Johns—if it should be necessary, from Quebec; if in our Hands. The want of them is so great, that no trouble or expence must be spared to obtain them. I have wrote to General Schuyler, he will give you every necessary assistance, that they may be had & forwarded to this place, with the utmost dispatch. I have given you a Warrant to the paymaster General of the Continental army for a Thousand Dollars to defray the expence attending your Journey, & procuring these articles; An Account of which you are to keep & render upon your return.
>
> Go: Washington
>
> Endeavour to procure what Flints you can.

As the first of December neared—the date on which Connecticut troops insisted their enlistments expired—Washington expressed his despair to Joseph Reed, who had returned to his law practice in Philadelphia after having served as Washington's secretary during the first months at Cambridge.

> Cambridge 28th. Novr., 1775.
> What an astonishing thing it is, that those who are employed to sign the Continental Bills should not be able, or Inclined to do it as fast as they are wanted. They

will prove the destruction of the army if they are not more attentive and diligent. Such a dearth of Publick Spirit, & want of Virtue; such stock jobbing, and fertility in all the low Arts to obtain advantages, of one kind or another, in this great change of Military arrangemt. I never saw before, and pray God I may never be witness to again. What will be the ultimate end of these Maneuvres is beyond my Scan. I tremble at the prospect. We have been till this time Enlisting about 3500 Men. To engage these I have been obliged to allow Furloughs as far as 50 Men a Regiment, & the Officers, I am persuaded, endulge as many more. The Connecticut Troops will not be prevailed upon to stay longer than their term (saving those who have enlisted for the next Campaign, & mostly on Furlough) and such a dirty, Mercenary spirit pervades the whole, that I should not be at all surprizd at any disaster that may happen. In short, after the last of this Month, our lines will be so weakened that the Minute Men and Militia must be call'd in for their defence; these, being under no kind of Government themselves, will destroy the little subordination I have been labouring to establish, and run me into one evil, whilst I am endeavouring to avoid another; but the lesser must be chosen. Could I have foreseen what I have, & am like to experience, no consideration upon Earth should have induced me to accept this Command. A regiment or any subordinate department would have been accompanied with ten times the satisfaction,—perhaps the honour.

Engraving of General Arnold's march through the Maine wilderness, from The Journal of Isaac Senter, *who accompanied the troops as surgeon*

Patriotic appeals and exhortations by Washington and other officers induced some men to re-enlist, but all but a handful of the Connecticut farmboy-soldiers insisted on going home. Washington held them until militia could arrive to fill some of the gaps, but on December 10 they left, amid general catcalls and pelting with clods. The next day, however, was one of the brightest Washington had experienced in many weeks. Martha arrived by carriage from Virginia, accompanied by her son Jack, his wife Nelly, and the wife of General Horatio Gates.

As the year drew to an end, there was good news from Canada: General Schuyler's force, led by his second in command, Brigadier General Richard Montgomery, had pushed north, captured British Forts St. John and Chambly, and then had taken Montreal. There was no news of Benedict Arnold, who had been moving with incredible hardships through the frozen wilderness of Maine toward Quebec; Washington, imminently expecting good news, would not learn for many weeks that on the last day of the year Montgomery and Arnold had joined in an unsuccessful attack on Quebec in which Montgomery had died and Arnold had been wounded.

On New Year's Day, 1776, Washington proclaimed the new army complete, with enlistments replacing all those that had expired. But far from having the twenty thousand men he considered a necessary minimum, Washington found his redoubts at some places entirely empty of defenders. Two days later King George's proclamation to Parliament, promising to crush the Colonial revolt, was first seen by the patriot army. Washington commented to Joseph Reed.

Original watercolor plan of Fort Ticonderoga made by Colonel John Trumbull at Washington's order in 1776, and then sent to Congress

Cambridge January 4th. 1776.

We are at length favoured with a sight of his Majesty's most gracious Speech, breathing sentiments of tenderness & compassion for his deluded American Subjects; the Echo is not yet come to hand; but we know what it must be; and as Lord North said, & we ought to have believed (& acted accordingly) we now know the ultimatum of British justice. The speech I send you. A volume of them was sent out by the Boston Gentry — and, farcical enough, we gave great joy to them (the red Coats I mean) without knowing or intending it, for on that day, the day which gave beginning to the new army (but before the proclamation came to hand) we had hoisted the Union Flag in compliment to the United Colonies but behold! it was received in Boston as a token of the deep Impression the Speech had made upon us, and as a signal of Submission — so we learn by a person out of Boston last night. By this time I presume they begin to think it strange that we have not made a formal surrender of our lines. Admiral Shuldham is arrivd at Boston. The 55th. and the greatest part, if not all, of the 17th. Regiment, are also got in there. The rest of the 5 Regiments from Ireland were intended for Halifax & Quebec; those for the first are arrived there, the others we know not where they are got to.

It is easier to conceive, than to describe the situation of My Mind for sometime past, & my feelings under our present Circumstances. Search the vast volumes of history through, & I much question whether a case similar to ours is to be found; to wit, to maintain a Post against the flower of the British Troops for Six Months together without [missing] and at the end of them to have one Army disbanded and another to raise within the same distance of a Reinforced Enemy. It is too much to attempt. What may be the final issue of the last manoeuvre, time only can tell. I wish this month was well over our heads. The same desire of retiring into a Chimney-Corner seized the Troops of New Hampshire, Rhode Island, & Massachusetts, (so soon as their time expired) as had work'd upon those of Connecticut, notwithstanding many of them made a tender of their Services to continue till the lines could be sufficiently strengthned. We are now left with a good deal less than half rais'd Regiments, and about 5000 Militia who only stand Ingaged to the Middle of this Month; when, according to custom, they will depart, let the necessity of their stay be never so urgent. Thus it is that for more than two Months past, I have scarcely immerged from one difficulty before I have plunged into another. How it will end God in his great goodness will direct. I am thankful for his protection to this time. We are told that we shall soon get the army compleated, but I have been told so many things which have never come to pass that I distrust every thing.

A dramatic pencil sketch of the death of General Montgomery in the Battle of Quebec, also by Trumbull

On January 9, 1776, the first detailed rolls for the new army showed Washington that he had only about eighty-two hundred men, of whom some fifty-six hundred were present and fit for duty. Later it turned out that nearly two thousand men were without muskets. To add to his already heavy burdens, word came of the defeat of Montgomery and Arnold before Quebec. One bright spot: Henry Knox returned from Fort Ticonderoga with sixty-six pieces of artillery that he had brought across frozen rivers and over rugged countryside on ox-drawn sledges. When the army's manpower was temporarily increased by the arrival of several thousand short-term militia, Washington once more considered ways of getting at the British before his strength ebbed again. He reported one such plan to Congress in a letter to its president, John Hancock.

Cambridge, 18th. Feby. 1776.

The late freezing Weather having formed some pretty strong Ice from Dorchester point to Boston Neck, and from Roxbury to the Common, thereby affording a more expanded and consequently a less dangerous Approach to the Town, I could not help thinking, notwithstanding the Militia were not all come In, and we had little or no Powder to begin our Operation by a regular Cannonade & Bombardment, that a bold & resolute Assault upon the Troops in Boston with such Men as we had (for it could not take many Men to guard our own Lines at a time when the Enemy were attacked in all Quarters) might be crown'd with success; and therefore, seeing no certain prospect of a supply of Powder on the one hand, and a certain dissolution of the Ice on the other, I called the General Officers together for their opinion (agreeably to the Resolve of Congress of the 22d. of December).

The Result will appear in the Inclosed Council of War [his officers decided such an attack would be unwise], and being almost unanimous, I must suppose to be right although, from a thorough conviction of the necessity of attempting something against the Ministerial Troops, before a Reinforcement should arrive and while we were favour'd with the Ice, I was not only ready, but willing and desirous of making the Assault; under a firm hope, if the Men would have stood by me, of a favourable Issue, notwithstanding the Enemy's advantage of Ground —Artillery,—&ca.

Perhaps the Irksomeness of my situation, may have given different Ideas to me, than those which Influenced the Gentlemen I consulted, and might have inclin'd me to put more to the hazard than was consistent with prudence. If it had, I am not sensible of it, as I endeavourd to give it all the consideration that a matter of such Importance required. True it is, & I cannot help acknowledging, that I have many disagreeable Sensations, on acct. of my Situation; for to have the Eyes of the whole Continent fixed, with anxious expectations of hearing of some great event, & to be restrain'd in every Military Operation for want of the necessary means of carrying it on, is not very pleasing; especially, as the means used to conceal my weakness from the Enemy conceals it also from our friends, and adds to their Wonder.

Major General Henry Knox by Stuart

By early spring Washington was in a position to carry out a less hazardous operation than sending his men across the ice to storm the British positions. He had accumulated enough powder to permit a modest bombardment, and on the night of March 4, 1776, began an operation that he described to his confidant Joseph Reed.

Cambridge, March 7, 1776.
The rumpus which every body expected to see between

Original drawing made by Archibald Robertson, entitled "View of Boston Showing the heights of Dorchester taken from Mount Whoredone, 1776"

the Ministerialists in Boston and our troops, has detained the bearer till this time. On Monday night I took possession of the Heights of Dorchester with two thousand men under the command of General Thomas. Previous to this, and in order to divert the enemy's attention from the real object, and to harass, we began on Saturday night a cannonade and bombardment, which with intervals was continued through the night—the same on Sunday, and on Monday, a continued roar from seven o'clock till daylight was kept up between the enemy and us. In this time we had an officer and one private killed, and four or five wounded; and through the ignorance, I suppose, of our artillery-men, burst five mortars (two thirteen inch and three ten inch), the "Congress," one of them. What damage the enemy has sustained is not known, as there has not been a creature out of Boston since. The cannonade, &c., except in the destruction of the mortars, answered our expectations fully; for although we had upwards of 300 teams in motion at the same instant, carrying on our fascines and other materials to the Neck, and the moon shining in its full lustre we were not discovered till daylight on Tuesday morning.

So soon as we were discovered, every thing seemed to be preparing for an attack, but the tide failing before they were ready, about one thousand only were able to embark in six transports in the afternoon, and these falling down towards the Castle, were drove on shore by a violent storm, which arose in the afternoon of that

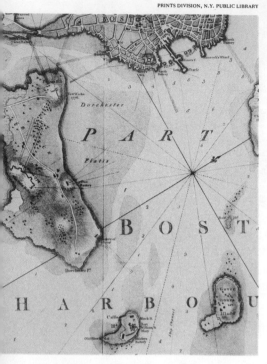

Detail from a 1776 map showing the proximity of Dorchester Neck to Boston across a narrow strip of water

day, and continued through the night; since that they have been seen returning to Boston, and whether from an apprehension that our works are now too formidable to make any impression on, or from what other causes I know not, but their hostile appearances have subsided, and they are removing their ammunition out of their magazine, whether with a view to move bag and baggage or not I cannot undertake to say, but if we had powder (and our mortars replaced, which I am about to do by new cast ones as soon as possible) I would, so soon as we were sufficiently strengthened on the heights to take possession of the point just opposite to Boston Neck, give them a dose they would not well like.

We had prepared boats, a detachment of 4000 men, &c., &c., for pushing to the west part of Boston, if they had made any formidable attack upon Dorchester. I will not lament or repine at any act of Providence because I am in a great measure a convert to Mr. Pope's opinion, that whatever is, is right, but I think everything had the appearance of a successful issue, if we had come to an engagement on that day. It was the 5th of March, which I recalled to their remembrance as a day never to be forgotton [the anniversary of the Boston Massacre]; an engagement was fully expected, and I never saw spirits higher, or more prevailing.

Washington, in short, had seized the high ground known as Dorchester Heights under cover of darkness, and by daybreak his men had fortified their positions with fascines and other devices they had brought to minimize digging in the frozen ground. The British were apparently confused at finding the heights occupied at daybreak; indecision, a wrong tide, and finally a storm kept them from counterattacking until the American positions were too strong. Shortly thereafter there were signs that the British were making ready to quit Boston. Their position would soon be untenable; from Dorchester Heights the Americans could next move to a position called Nooks Hill, where their artillery could fire down into Boston and its harbor. Within ten days or so, Washington was able to send Congress, through John Hancock, the message he had been wanting for months to dispatch.

Head Quarters Cambridge March 19th. 1776
It is with the greatest pleasure I inform you that on Sunday last the 17th. Instant, about 9th O'Clock in the forenoon the Ministerial Army evacuated the Town of

Boston, and that the Forces of the United Colonies are now in actual Possession thereof. I beg leave to congratulate you Sir, and the Honorable Congress on this happy event, and particularly as it was effected without endangering the Lives and property of the remaining unhappy Inhabitants.

I have great reason to imagine their flight was precipitated by the appearance of the Work which I had ordered to be thrown up last Saturday night, on an eminence at Dorchester, which lay nearest to Boston Neck called Newks [Nooks] Hill. The Town although it has suffered greatly, is not in so bad a state as I expected to find it, and I have a particular pleasure in being able to inform you, Sir, that your House has received no damage worth mentioning, your furniture is in tolerable Order and the family pictures are all left entire and untouched. Captn. Cazneau takes charge of the whole until he receives further Orders from you.

As soon as the Ministerial Troops had quitted the Town, I ordered a Thousand men (who had had the small pox) under command of General Putnam, to take possession of the Heights, which I shall fortify in such a manner, as to prevent their return, should they attempt it; but as they are still in the Harbour, I thought it not prudent to march off with the main body of the Army, until I should be fully satisfied they had quitted the Coast. I have therefore only detached five Regiments besides the Rifle Battalion to New York, and shall keep the remainder here 'till all suspicion of their return ceases.

The situation in which I found their Works, evidently

A 1776 broadside celebrating British evacuation of the town of Boston

*Gold medal awarded to Washington
by Congress following Boston victory*

discovered that their retreat was made with the greatest precipitation. They have left their Barracks and other works of wood at Bunkers Hill &ca. all standing, and have destroyed but a small part of their Lines. They have also left a number of fine pieces of Cannon, which they first spiked up, also a very large Iron Mortar; and (as I am informed) they have thrown another over the end of your Wharf. I have employed proper Persons to drill the Cannon, and doubt not I shall save the most of them.

I am not yet able to procure an exact List of all the Stores they have left. As soon as it can be done I shall take care to transmit it to you. From an estimate already made, by the Quarter Master General, of what he has discovered, they will amount to 25 or 30,000 £.

Part of the Powder mentioned in yours of the 6th Instant has already arrived; The remainder I have ordered to be stop'd on the Road as we shall have no occasion for it here.

The British fleet lay in the outer harbor until March 27, causing some apprehension among the Americans that Howe might return and attack them. Then it sailed away, destination unknown. New York, however, was the strategic and logical place for the royal army to strike, and Washington had started a brigade on its way there even before Howe sailed. After the British fleet disappeared, Washington started the rest of his army moving toward New York. A letter went to Artemas Ward.

Cambridge, 29th. Mar. 76

As General Green is ordered to march with the next Brigade on Monday and as General Spencer will follow with the last (leaving four or five regiments in this department for Defense, Protection of the Stores, Erection of works &c.) I should be glad, if you are not afraid of the Small Pox & Incline to continue longer in the Service that you lately talk'd of, if you would remove into Boston tomorrow or next day, & take upon you the Command and direction of Matters there.

So Washington returned command of the Boston area to the man from whom he had taken it, General Artemas Ward. He then departed Boston on April 4, hastening toward New York. Both he and his army had new confidence. They had bested the British; they believed they could do it again.

A Picture Portfolio

First in War

EVE OF INDEPENDENCE

In 1746 Benjamin Franklin wrote to England to order "two setts of Popple's Mapps of N. America" (left) to hang in the Assembly room at Philadelphia; nearly thirty years passed before relations between the mother country and her American Colonies reached the state illustrated above. And in 1774 the map was still hanging in the Pennsylvania State House when the First Continental Congress met there. Stung by Britain's hardening attitude during the tense preceding decade—years that saw the hated Stamp Act imposed and repealed, the massacre at Boston, and the tea-dumping in Boston Harbor—Congress finally took a decisive stand. "The New England governments are in a state of Rebellion," declared King George III. "Blows must decide whether they are to be subject to this country or independent." But the "Female Combatants" were more blunt: "I'll force you to Obedience you Rebellious Slut," shouts an elegant Britannia. "Liberty Liberty for ever Mother while I exist," replies an aroused America.

THE FIRST ENCOUNTERS

On April 27, 1775, George Washington, at home in Mount Vernon, received the news of the Battle of Lexington (left, above), which had erupted a week before. It was not until the middle of June, however, that Washington, nominated by John Adams, was elected by the Second Continental Congress "to command all the Continental forces raised or to be raised for the defence of American liberty." On his way north, he learned of the burning of Charlestown and the bloody contest for Bunker Hill (left, below), which the British narrowly won with staggering casualties. His own first chance to confound the enemy came nine months later, when in one remarkable night he fortified Dorchester Heights with cannon dragged all the way from Fort Ticonderoga and forced the British to evacuate their then untenable position in Boston. The imposing portrait above by Gilbert Stuart commemorates Washington's first victory.

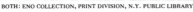

DISASTER IN NEW YORK

"I have brought the whole Army which I had in the New England Governments... to this place," Washington wrote in April, 1776. He knew that the British commander, General Howe (left), must have his eye on the Hudson River as the likeliest place to "stop the Intercourse between the northern and southern Colonies." Upon hearing of the Declaration of Independence in July, patriots toppled the statue of George III at Bowling Green (left, above). But for Washington things went from bad to worse. He suffered defeats on Long Island and at Kip's Bay before moving his army to Harlem Heights, after the British disembarked in New York—impressively Venetian as rendered at far left by a contemporary German artist. The final disaster came in November when the British took Fort Washington (above), while Washington watched in impotent fury from the New Jersey shore.

133

TEN DAYS OF VICTORY

The depths to which Washington had sunk between September, 1776, when he had written firmly from Harlem Heights, "I am resolved not to be forced from this ground while I have life," and December, when from a camp in Pennsylvania he cried, "I think the game is pretty near up," reveal the agonizing toll of his forced retreat south across New Jersey. He picked Christmas night to undertake a brilliant and dramatic stroke that was to have an electric effect on the morale of his "wretched remains of a broken army" and on the country as a whole. During the night, which he described to Congress as "very severe," he ferried his troops across the ice-clogged Delaware River, to which he points in the painting above, and totally surprised the drowsy, holiday-happy Hessian soldiers at Trenton. Their commander, Colonel Johann Rall, was killed, although the painting above, right, shows him surrendering to a Washington whose arm is extended to aid him. Washington hoped to strike again at once but encountered British reinforcements under Lord Cornwallis. While a few men kept his campfires burning in the night, Washington slipped out and struck the enemy's rear guard at Princeton. At right, Washington on horseback directs the artillery that routed the British redcoats and brought a second brilliant victory on January 3, 1777.

The Capture of the Hessians at Trenton BY JOHN TRUMBULL; YALE UNIVERSITY ART GALLERY

"A DREARY KIND OF PLACE"

The year following the Jersey victories was a dismal one. Battles at Brandywine Creek and Germantown were lost and Howe marched into Philadelphia. Washington chose Valley Forge, "a dreary kind of place" he called it, for his winter headquarters of 1777–78 (right). It was a rugged winter of suffering and despair, a point emphasized in the nineteenth-century painting below. The one good thing was the appearance of European professionals, including the Prussian drillmaster Baron von Steuben (left), who helped make Washington's army a far more viable force.

WASHINGTON AND HIS GENERALS

In this painting done after his death by an unknown hand, Washington is surrounded by his generals, among whom can tentatively be identified: Anthony Wayne (right foreground); Lafayette (in profile to his left); Greene and a round-faced Israel Putnam (to his right); Knox (far left).

CONFLICT AT MONMOUTH

Sir Henry Clinton (left, above) replaced Howe at Philadelphia in May, 1778, and decided to risk the long overland trek to New York. Determined to attack his enemy's strung-out lines, Washington put Charles Lee in charge of an advanced pursuit force that caught up with Clinton at Monmouth, New Jersey. Instead of pressing his attack, Lee for some still unknown reason ordered a retreat. A furious Washington, seen above at the moment of rallying the retreating soldiers, and "swearing like an angel from Heaven," removed Lee from command—hence *The Suspended General* (left) drawn by the famous Polish volunteer Thaddeus Kosciusko. Monmouth was the last major northern battle; after 1778, the emphasis shifted south, and French aid began to turn the tide of war.

VICTORY AT YORKTOWN

The young Marquis de Lafayette (right, above) was one of France's earliest volunteers in the American cause and a proud witness as the British troops passed in surrender between the French and American lines (above) following their defeat at Yorktown on October 19, 1781. Colonel David Humphreys, a Washington aide, had the honor of presenting the captured colors to Congress (right).

A SOLDIER'S ADIEU

More than a year passed between the British surrender at Yorktown and the signing of preliminary articles of peace at Paris in November, 1782; another year went by before the last British troops departed from New York. On December 4, 1783, Washington rode triumphantly back into the city he had been forced to retreat from in 1776 and there bade farewell to the officers who had served him so long and so faithfully. "Such a scene of sorrow and weeping I had never before witnessed," recalled one officer of the meeting in Fraunces Tavern (below). "That we should see his face no more in this world seemed to me utterly insupportable." After embracing each, Washington, too moved to speak, walked to the waterfront where a barge was waiting to take him across the Hudson River to the Jersey shore (left) and from which "out in the stream, our great and beloved General waved his hat and bid us a silent adieu."

Chapter **5**

Times That Tried
Men's Souls

Washington arrived in New York on April 13, 1776, afraid that he would find the sea-borne British already there. But Howe had taken his army to Halifax to reload and refit. The British had left Boston so hurriedly and had abandoned so much materiel that there was a great deal of sorting out to do, and shortages to be made up, before they would be ready for another campaign. General Charles Lee, now gone to South Carolina to ward off a British assault on Charleston, had started preparations for the defenses of New York, and Washington pushed on with the task. The entrance to the East River, which divides Manhattan and Long Island, was blocked with sunken vessels and other obstructions and was guarded by cannon on lower Manhattan and on the opposite high ground on Long Island known as Brooklyn Heights. On the west side of Manhattan the Hudson, or North, River was too wide and deep to be barred with sunken obstructions or effectively commanded by cannon fire; but that side of the island, unlike the East River shore, was mainly rocky and precipitous and unsuited for landings. In the city itself, which occupied only the lower tip of Manhattan, there were barricades on every street leading to the water, and trenches and earthworks laced the countryside above the town. While the American army waited and tried to make ready, Washington wrote to his brother John Augustine, once more giving him a good summary of the situation.

> [New York, April 29, 1776]
> Since my arrival at this place, I have been favour'd with two or three of your Letters, and thank you for your kind and frequent remembrance of me. If I shd. not write to you, as often as you do to me, you must attribute it to its true cause, and that is the hurry, and multiplicity of business in which I am constantly engaged from the time I rise out of my Bed till I go into it again.

146

I wrote to you a pretty full Acct. just before I left Cambridge of the movemts. of the two Armies, and now refer to it—since that, I have brought the whole Army which I had in the New England Governments (five Regiments excepted, & left behind for the defence of Boston and the Stores we have there) to this place; and Eight days ago, Detached four Regiments for Canada; and am now Imbarking Six more for the same place, as there are reasons to believe that a push will be made there this Campaign, and things in that Country not being in a very promising way, either with respect to the Canadians or Indian's. These Detachments have weaken'd us very considerably in this important post, where I am sorry to add, there are too many inimical persons; but as our Affairs in Canada can derive no support but what is sent to them, and the Militia may be called in here, it was thought best to strengthen that Quarter at the expence of this; but I am affraid we are rather too late in doing of it; from the Eastern Army (under my immediate Command) it was impossible to do it sooner.

We have already gone great lengths in fortifying this City & the Hudson River; a fortnight more will put us in a very respectable posture of Defence, the Works we have already constructed, and which they found we were about to erect, have put the King's Ships to flight; for instead of laying within Pistol shot of the Wharves, and their Centrys conversing with Ours (whilst they received every necessary that the Country afforded) they have now gone down to the Hook, near 30 Miles from this place, the last Harbour they can get to, and I have prevaild upon the Comee. of safety to forbid every kind of Intercourse between the Inhabitants of this Colony and the Enemy; this I was resolved upon effecting; but thought it best to bring it about, through that Channel, as I now can pursue my own measures in support of their resolves.

Mrs. Washington is still here, and talks of taking the Small Pox [infection with virus to produce a light—hopefully—case], but I doubt her resolution. Mr. and Mrs. Custis will set out in a few days for Maryland. I did not write to you by the 'Squire, because his departure in the first place, was sudden; in the next, I had but little to say. I am very sorry to hear that my Sister was

Washington's first headquarters in New York City were here on Pearl Street and later at 1 Broadway.

Indisposed with a sore Breast when you last wrote. I hope she is now recover'd of it, and that all your Family are well; that they may continue so, & that our once happy Country may escape the depredations & Calamities attending on War, is the fervent prayer of dr. Sir,

Go: WASHINGTON

Mrs. Washington, Mr. & Mrs. Custis join in love to my Sister the rest of the Family. With afn. G.W.

A month later New York was still waiting for the British, and Washington had occasion to send a short note to John Hancock about a subject of considerable interest.

New York, May 18. 1776

I do myself the honor to transmit to you the Inclosed letters and papers I received this morning in the state they now are, which contain sundry matters of Intelligence of the most Interesting nature.

As the Consideration of them may lead to important consequences and the adoption of several measures in the Military line, I have thought It advisable for Genl. Gates to attend Congress; he will follow to morrow and satisfie & explain to them some points they may wish to be informed of, in the course of their deliberations, not having an Opportunity at this time to submit my thoughts to them, upon these Interesting Accounts.

Among the "sundry matters of Intelligence of the most Interesting nature" that Washington enclosed were copies of treaties between England and the rulers of the petty German states of Hesse-Cassel, Brunswick, and Hanau, by which the German princes agreed to furnish soldiers to fight in America. These were the mercenaries who would be known and hated as Hessians, and their use by the Crown was to prove a last straw to many Americans who had still hoped that differences between motherland and Colonies could be conciliated. Washington expressed his own feelings about England and independence to his brother John Augustine after he learned that the Virginia Convention, the congress of that state, had voted unanimously to instruct its delegates in Philadelphia to propose that the Second Continental Congress declare the Colonies to be free and independent states.

Philadelphia, May 31, 1776.

Since my arrival at this place, where I came at the request of Congress, to settle some matters relative to

German mercenaries (opposite, above, and below), who came to fight in America, were bitterly hated.

the ensuing Campaign I have received your Letter of the 18th. from Williamsburg, & think I stand indebted to you for another, which came to hand sometime ago, in New York.

I am very glad to find that the Virginia Convention have passed so noble a vote, with so much unanimity—things have come to that pass now, as to convince us, that we have nothing more to expect from the justice of G. Britain—also, that she is capable of the most delusive Arts, for I am satisfied that no Commissioners ever were design'd, except Hessians & other Foreigners; and that the Idea was only to deceive, & throw us off our guard. The first it has too effectually accomplished, as many Members of Congress, in short, the representation of whole Provences, are still feeding themselves upon the dainty food of reconciliation; and tho' they will not allow that the expectation of it has any influence upon their judgments (with respect to their preparations for defence) it is but too obvious that it has an operation upon every part of their conduct and is a clog to their proceedings. It is not in the nature of things to be otherwise, for no Man, that entertains a hope of seeing this dispute speedily, and equitably adjusted by Commissioners, will go to the same expence, and run the same hazards to prepare for the worst event as he who believes that he must conquer, or submit to unconditional terms, & its concomitants, such as Confiscation, hanging, &c., &c.

Still the British did not appear before New York. In the meantime, the campaign in Canada had gone from bad to disastrous, and Washington was reporting that almost everything in the North was lost. His only bright news in this letter to John Hancock was from Boston, where blockading ships had been driven from the outer harbor.

New York, June 23d. 1776

I herewith transmit you an extract of a Letter from Genl. Ward which came to hand by last nights post containing the agreeable Intelligence of their having Obliged the Kings Ships to leave Nantasket Road, and of Two Transports more being taken by our Armed Vessels with Two hundred and Ten Highland Troops on board.

I sincerely wish the like success had attended our Arms in another Quarter, but It has not. In Canada

IN PROVINCIAL CONGRESS,

NEW-YORK, JUNE 13, 1776.

WHEREAS this Congress have been informed by the Continental Congress, and have great Reason to believe that an Invasion of this Colony will very shortly be made.

RESOLVED UNANIMOUSLY, That it be, and it is hereby recommended to all the Officers in the Militia in this Colony, forthwith to review the same, and give Orders that they prepare themselves, and be ready to march whenever they may be called upon.

ORDERED, That the aforegoing Resolution be published in the public News-Papers, and printed in Hand-Bills to be distributed.

Extract from the Minutes,

ROBERT BENSON, Sec'ry.

A June 13, 1776, broadside that called on the militia to prepare was followed in just over two weeks by the British fleet's entry into New York Harbor, as sketched at right.

the situation of our Affairs is truly alarming. The Inclosed Copies of Genls. Schuyler, Sullivan, & Arnold's Letters will inform you, that Genl. Thompson has met with a repulse at three Rivers, and is now a Prisoner in the hands of Genl. Burgoyne, who these accounts say is arrived with a considerable Army: nor do they seem to promise an end of our misfortunes here; It is greatly to be feared that the next advices from thence will be, that our shattered, divided & broken Army, as you will see by the return, have been obliged to abandon the Country and retreat, to avoid a greater calamity, that of being cut off or becoming prisoners. I will be done upon the Subject & leave you to draw such conclusions, as you conceive from the state of facts are most likely to result, only adding my apprehensions that one of the latter events, either that they are cutt off or become Prisoners, has already happened If they did not retreat while they had an opportunity.

Horatio Gates, formerly Adjutant General, had been made a major general and sent to Canada to try to save the situation, but he could do nothing. As the weeks passed, the defeat would become total: Benedict Arnold would be forced to give up Montreal as the rest of the American army, dispirited, sick, decimated by capture and smallpox, retreated into upper New York. Then on June 29 the first vessels of the British fleet came into New York Harbor; by the time all had dropped anchor there were 110 ships with some ten thousand men aboard. The Americans braced for action, but Howe only established camp on Staten Island. The word soon came in through the effective patriot spy system that the British general was waiting for another fleet under his older brother Admiral Richard Howe (Lord Howe) with troop transports carrying, among others, the first of the Hessians. To the dismay of Washington, the stream of reinforcements also included General Sir Henry Clinton and his forces, returned from their repulse at Charleston by Charles Lee. Rumors had spread that Congress had declared the Colonies independent of England, but not until July 9 was official word received in New York. Washington inserted a solemn announcement in the General Orders.

Head Quarters, New York, July 9th. 1776. The Hon. the Continental Congress, impelled by the dictates of duty, policy and necessity, having been pleased to dissolve the Connection which subsisted between this Country, and Great Britain, and to declare the United Colonies of North America, free and independent STATES: The several brigades are to be drawn up this evening on their respective Parades, at six OClock, when the declaration of Congress, shewing the grounds & reasons of this measure, is to be read with an audible voice.

The General hopes this important Event will serve as a fresh incentive to every officer, and soldier, to act with Fidelity and Courage, as knowing that now the peace and safety of his Country depends (under God) solely on the success of our arms: And that he is now in the service of a State, possessed of sufficient power to reward his

Johann Heinrich Ramberg, a German artist, drew his interpretation of the signing of the Declaration of Independence (above), while an American printmaker celebrated it by showing thirteen hands "Warm'd by one Heart, United in one Band."

AMERICAN INDEPENDENCE
Declared July 4th 1776

GOD SAVE AMERICA!

merit, and advance him to the highest Honors of a free Country.

The Brigade Majors are to receive, at the Adjutant Generals Office, several of the Declarations to be delivered to the Brigadiers General, and the Colonels of Regiments.

The Declaration of Independence was read to all regiments, there was cheering, and in the evening a number of zealous patriots, among them some soldiers, toppled the equestrian statue of George III in Bowling Green. It was an act that the Commander in Chief deplored in his next General Orders.

> Head Quarters, New York, July 10th. 1776.
> 'Tho the General doubts not the persons, who pulled down and mutilated the Statue, in the Broad way, last night, were actuated by Zeal in the public cause; yet it has so much the appearance of riot and want of order, in the Army, that he disapproves the manner, and directs that in future these things shall be avoided by the Soldiery, and left to be executed by proper authority.

On July 12 the British sent five ships up the Hudson River. Some American guns on the Manhattan bluffs opened fire, but in his General Orders the next day Washington remarked, more in sorrow than in anger, on the behavior of many of his cannoneers.

> Head Quarters, New York, July 13th. 1776.
> The General was sorry to observe Yesterday that many of the officers and a number of men instead of attending to their duty at the Beat of the Drum; continued along the banks of the North River, gazing at the Ships; such unsoldierly Conduct must grieve every good officer, and give the enemy a *mean* opinion of the Army, as nothing shews the brave and good Soldier more than in case of Alarms, cooly and calmly repairing to his post, and there waiting his orders; whereas a weak curiosity at such a time makes a man look mean and contemptible.

In other words, many American artillerymen had behaved like yokels, ignoring calls to man their guns and running instead to gape at the ships sailing by. The enemy craft went up the Hudson as far as the wide reach called the Tappan Zee, where they cut off American communications between Albany and New York for six weeks—until frightened away by an American attack with fire rafts. British reinforcements kept arriving in New York Harbor through the second half of July and the first part of August. Washington was greatly outnumbered; moreover, a large part of his forces were militia, enlisted for two or three months, with little training, and most of them were ready to break for home if the going got hard. Approximately ten thousand American troops (a scourge of illness had laid low many others) opposed some thirty thousand trained enemy troops, although Washington's forces were later augmented by additional militia. With his small force, Washington had to defend a front of more than fifteen miles, from western Long Island to upper Manhattan. Howe could strike with his full force anywhere he chose, and he chose Long Island, with the American positions on rocky Brooklyn Heights as his objective. On August 22, in a smooth operation, he put ashore fifteen thousand men and equipment in a matter of hours. Later Washington described the Battle of Long Island to Hancock, without quite admitting that it had been a near disaster.

> New York, Augt. 31st. 1776
> Inclination as well as duty, would have Induced me to give Congress the earliest information of my removal and that of the Troops from Long Island & Its dependencies to this City the night before last, but the extreme fatigue, which myself and Family [his military staff] have undergone as much from the Weather since the Engagement of the 27th. rendered me & them entirely

unfit to take a pen in hand. Since Monday scarce any of us have been out of the Lines till our passage across the East River was effected yesterday morning & for Forty Eight Hours preceeding that I had hardly been of my Horse and never closed my Eyes so that I was quite unfit to write or dictate till this Morning.

Our Retreat was made without any Loss of Men or Ammunition and in better order than I expected from Troops in the situation ours were. We brought off all our Cannon & Stores, except a few heavy pieces, which in the condition the earth was by a long continued rain we found upon Trial impracticable. The Wheels of the Carriages Sinking up to the Hobs rendered It impossible for our whole force to drag them. We left but little Provisions on the Island except some Cattle which had been driven within our lines and which after many attempts to force across the water we found impossible to effect circumstanced as we were. I have Inclosed a copy of the council of War held previous to the Retreat, to which I beg leave to refer Congress for the reasons or many of them, that led to the adoption of that measure. Yesterday Evening and last Night a party of our Men were employed in bringing our Stores, Cannon, Tents &ca. from Governors Island, which they nearly compleated. Some of the Heavy Cannon remain there still, but I expect will be got away to day.

In the Engagement on the 27th. Generals Sullivan

Nineteenth-century engraving (above) of the American retreat from Long Island and a sketch (below) made by an English officer aboard one of Howe's ships in New York Harbor just after that disastrous defeat

General John Sullivan

& Stirling were made prisoners. The former has been permitted on his parole to return for a little time. From Lord Stirling I had a Letter by Genl. Sullivan, a Copy of which I have the Honor to transmit. That contains his Information of the Engagement with his Brigade. It is not so full and certain as I could wish, he was hurried most probably as his Letter was unfinished. Nor have I been yet able to obtain an exact amount of our Loss, we suppose it from 700 to a Thousand killed & taken. Genl. Sullivan says Lord Howe is extremely desirous of seeing some of the Members of Congress for which purpose he was allowed to come out & to communicate to them what has passed between him & his Lordship. I have consented to his going to Philadelphia, as I do not mean or conceive It right to withhold or prevent him from giving such Information as he possesses in this Instance.

I am much hurried & engaged in arranging and making new Dispositions of our Forces, The movements of the Enemy requiring them to be immediately had, and therefore have only time to add that I am with my best regards to Congress, and to you.

The British, using an unguarded road, had fallen on the rear of the regiments of General John Sullivan and the man the Americans knew as Lord Stirling for his claim to an extinct Scottish earldom. The enemy was suddenly on the slopes of Brooklyn Heights itself and might easily have carried the redoubts against the panicky, green defenders if Howe, probably with grim memories of Bunker Hill, had not held them back. Washington's water-borne rescue of his army—transported across the East River to Manhattan on a foggy night—was a marvel of secrecy, but no retreat is a cause for rejoicing. Through John Hancock, Washington gave Congress his views of a basic weakness of the Army.

New York, Septr. the 2d. 1776
As my Intelligence of late has been rather unfavorable and would be received with anxiety & concern, peculiarly happy should I esteem myself, were it in my power at this time to transmit such information to Congress, as would be more pleasing and agreeable to their wishes But unfortunately for me—unfortunately for them, It is not.

Our situation is truly distressing. The Check our Detachment sustained on the 27th. Ulto. has dispirited

John Glover's Marblehead regiment evacuated Washington's troops from Long Island, where General Israel Putnam had been in overall charge; Glover (above) in a facsimile of a Trumbull drawing and Putnam (below) from a Trumbull sketch.

too great a proportion of our Troops and filled their minds with apprehension and dispair. The Militia instead of calling forth their utmost efforts to a brave and manly opposition in order to repair our Losses, are dismayed, Intractable, and Impatient to return. Great numbers of them have gone off; in some instances almost by whole Regiments, by half ones & by Companies at a time. This circumstance of Itself, Independent of others, when fronted by a well appointed Enemy, superior in number to our whole collected force, would be sufficiently disagreeable, but when their example has Infected another part of the Army,—when their want of discipline & refusal of almost every kind of restraint & government, have produced a like conduct but too common to the whole, and an entire disregard of that order and subordination necessary to the well doing of an Army and which had been inculcated before, as well as the nature of our Military establishment would admit of, our condition is still more alarming, and with the deepest concern I am obliged to confess my want of confidence in the generality of the Troops. All these circumstances fully confirm the opinion I ever entertained and which I more than once in my letters took the liberty of mentioning to Congress, that no dependence could be put in a Militia or other Troops than those enlisted and embodied for a longer period than our regulations heretofore have prescribed. I am persuaded and as fully convinced, as I am of any one fact that has happened, that our liberties must of necessity be greatly hazarded, If not entirely lost If their defence is left to any but a permanent standing Army,—I mean one to exist during the War. Nor would the expence Incident to the support of such a body of Troops as would be competent almost to every exigency, far exceed that which is daily incurred by calling in succour and New Inlistments and which when effected are not attended with any good consequences. Men who have been free and subject to no controul, cannot be reduced to order in an Instant, and the priviledges & exemptions they claim and will have Influence the conduct of others, and the aid derived from them is nearly counterbalanced by the disorder, Irregularity and confusion they occasion. I can not find that the Bounty of Ten Dollars is likely to produce the desired effect. When men can get double that

157

sum to engage for a month or two in the Militia & that Militia frequently called out, It is hardly to be expected. The addition of Land might have a considerable Influence on a permanent Inlistment. Our number of men at present fit for duty are under 20,000. They were so by the last returns and best accounts I could get after the Engagement on Long Island, — since which numbers have deserted.

Washington had a demonstration of the dismal weakness of poorly trained short-term militia when British and Hessians landed above New York on Kip's Bay (between 32nd and 38th Streets on the East River side of today's Manhattan) on September 15. Again he was reporting to John Hancock as president of Congress.

Head Qrs. at Col. Roger Morris's House,
September 16, 1776.

...about Eleven oClock [the enemy ships] in the East River began a most severe and heavy Cannonade to scour the Grounds and cover the landing of their Troops between Turtle Bay and the City, where Breast Works had been thrown up to oppose them. As soon as I heard the Firing, I road with all possible dispatch towards the place of landing when to my great surprize and mortification I found the Troops that had been posted in the Lines retreating with the utmost precipitation, and those ordered to support them, Parsons's & Fellows's Brigades, flying in every direction and in the greatest confusion, notwithstanding the exertions of their Generals to form them. I used every means in my power to rally and get them into some order but my attempts were fruitless and ineffectual and on the appearance of a

After the British had landed at Kip's Bay, as drawn on the spot (left), British officers used the Kip family mansion as headquarters (above), while Washington took refuge in the house of his friend Colonel Morris.

BOTH: *Pictorial Field-Book of the Revolution,* LOSSING

small party of the Enemy, not more than Sixty or Seventy, their disorder increased and they ran away in the greatest confusion without firing a single Shot. Finding that no confidence was to be placed in these Brigades and apprehending that another part of the Enemy might pass over to Harlem plains and cut of the retreat to this place, I sent orders to secure the Heights in the best manner with the Troops that were stationed on and near them, which being done; the retreat was effected with but little or no loss of Men, tho' of a considerable part of our Baggage occasioned by this disgraceful and dastardly conduct. Most of our Heavy Cannon and a part of our Stores and Provisions, which we were about removing was unavoidably left in the City, tho' every means after It had been determined in Council to evacuate the post had been used to prevent It. We are now encamped with the Main body of the Army on the Heights of Harlem, where I should hope the Enemy would meet with a defeat in case of an Attack, If the generality of our Troops would behave with tolerable bravery, but, experience to my extreme affliction has convinced me that this is rather to be wished for than expected. However I trust, that there are many who will act like men, and shew themselves worthy of the blessings of Freedom. I have sent out some reconoitring parties to gain Intelligence If possible of the disposition of the Enemy and shall inform Congress of every material event by the earliest Opportunity.

Although his forces were temporarily safe on rocky Harlem Heights in northern Manhattan, the Commander in Chief was thoroughly discouraged. Then, only the day after the disgraceful conduct of the militia at Kip's Bay, American units attacked and drove into retreat British forces that had ventured near Harlem Heights. The Battle of Harlem was a relatively minor clash, but it greatly raised patriot morale; the redcoats were not invincible. But one victory did not solve Washington's main problem; his forces were melting away as weary or homesick farm boys simply left and trudged the dirt roads leading home. Washington told his cousin Lund of his problems and his anguish.

Col. Morris's, on the Heights of Harlem.
September 30, 1776.
Your letter of the 18th., which is the only one received and unanswered, now lies before me. The amazement

159

which you seem to be in at the unaccountable measures which have been adopted by [Congress] would be a good deal increased if I had time to unfold the whole system of their management since this time twelve months. I do not know how to account for the unfortunate steps which have been taken but from that fatal idea of conciliation which prevailed so long—fatal, I call it, because from my soul I wish it may [not] prove so, though my fears lead me to think there is too much danger of it. This time last year I pointed out the evil consequences of short enlistments, the expenses of militia, and the little dependence that was to be placed in them. I assured [Congress] that the longer they delayed raising a standing army the more difficult and chargeable would they find it to get one, and that, at the same time that the militia would answer no valuable purpose, the frequent calling them in would be attended with an expense that they could have no conception of. Whether, as I have said before, the unfortunate hope of reconciliation was the cause, or the fear of a standing army prevailed, I will not undertake to say; but the policy was to engage men for twelve months only. The consequence of which, you have had great bodies of militia in pay that never were in camp: you have had immense quantities of provisions drawn by men that never rendered you one hour's service (at least usefully), and this in the most profuse

A contemporary, but highly fanciful, German engraving of the British troops marching into New York City

and wasteful way. Your stores have been expended, every kind of military [discipline?] destroyed by them; your numbers fluctuating, uncertain, and forever far short of report—at no one time, I believe, equal to twenty thousand men fit for duty. At present our numbers fit for duty (by this day's report) amount to 14,759, besides 3,427 on command, and the enemy within stone's throw of us. It is true a body of militia are again ordered out, but they come without any conveniences and soon return. I discharged a regiment the other day that had in it fourteen rank and file fit for duty only, and several that had less than fifty. In short, such is my situation that if I were to wish the bitterest curse to an enemy on this side of the grave, I should put him in my stead with my feelings; and yet I do not know what plan of conduct to pursue. I see the impossibility of serving with reputation, or doing any essential service to the cause by continuing in command, and yet I am told that if I quit the command inevitable ruin will follow, from the distraction that will ensue. In confidence I tell you that I never was in such an unhappy, divided state since I was born. To lose all comfort and happiness on the one hand, whilst I am fully persuaded that under such a system of management as has been adopted, I cannot have the least chance for reputation, nor those allowances made which the nature of the case requires; and to be

Another fanciful view by the same artist of the disastrous fire that swept New York after Howe's entry

BOTH: ENO COLLECTION, PRINTS DIVISION, N.Y. PUBLIC LIBRARY

161

told, on the other, that if I leave the service all will be lost, is, at the same time that I am bereft of every peaceful moment, distressing to a degree. But I will be done with the subject, with the precaution to you that it is not a fit one to be publicly known or discussed. If I fall, it may not be amiss that these circumstances be known, and declaration made in credit to the justice of my character. And if the men will stand by me (which by the by I despair of), I am resolved not to be forced from this ground while I have life; and a few days will determine the point, if the enemy should not change their plan of operations; for they certainly will not—I am sure they ought not—to waste the season that is now fast advancing, and must be precious to them. I thought to have given you a more explicit account of my situation, expectation, and feelings, but I have not time. I am wearied to death all day with a variety of perplexing circumstances—disturbed at the conduct of the militia, whose behavior and want of discipline has done great injury to the other troops, who never had officers, except in a few instances, worth the bread they eat. My time, in short, is so much engrossed that I have not leisure for corresponding, unless it is on mere matters of public business.

In this engraving of the Battle of Harlem Heights, one of Washington's only successes in New York, the 42nd Highlanders are seen scurrying over a fence in disorganized retreat.

On October 12, 1776, Howe landed troops at Throgs Neck in what is now the Bronx, with the obvious intent of cutting the American line of communication with the country to the north. Washington skillfully evaded the trap by withdrawing. He later gave John Augustine Washington an account of subsequent events.

White Plains [New York], November 6, 1776. Whilst we lay at the upper end of York [Manhattan] Island (or the heights of Harlem) How suddenly Landed from the best accts. we cd. get, about 16,000 Men above us, on a place called Frogs point on the East River, or Sound, this obliged Us, as his design was evidently to surround us, & cut of our Communication with the Country, thereby stopping all Supplies of Provisions (of which we were very scant) to remove our Camp and out Flank him, which we have done, & by degrees got strongly posted on advantageous Grounds at this place....

Novr. 19, at Hackensac [New Jersey]. I began this Letter at the White plains as you will see by the first part of it; but by the time I had got thus far the Enemy advanced a Second time (for they had done it once before, & after engaging some Troops which I had posted on a Hill, and driving them from it with the loss of abt. 300 killed & wounded to them, & little more than half the number to us) as if they meant a genel. Attack but finding us ready to receive them, & upon such ground as they could not approach without loss, they filed of & retreated towards New York.

As it was conceived that this Manoeuvre was done with a design to attack Fort Washington (near Harlem heights) or to throw a body of Troops into the Jersey's, or what might be still worse, aim a stroke at Philadelphia, I hastend over on this side [New Jersey] with abt. 5000 Men by a round about March (wch. we were obliged to take on Acct. of the shipping opposing the passage at all the lower Ferries) of near 65 Miles, but did not get hear time enough to take Measures to save Fort Washington tho I got here myself a day or two before it surrendered, which happened on the 16th. Instt. after making a defence of about 4 or 5 hours only. . . .

This is a most unfortunate affair, and has given me great Mortification as we have lost not only two thousand Men that were there, but a good deal of Artillery, & some of the best Arms we had. And what adds to my Mortification is that this Post, after the last Ships went past it, was held contrary to my Wishes & opinion; as I conceived it to be a dangerous one: but being determind on by a full Council of General Officers, and recieving a resolution of Congress strongly expressive of their desires, that the Channel of the River (which we had been labouring to stop for a long while at this place) might be obstructed, if possible, & knowing that this could not be done unless there were Batteries to protect the Obstruction I did not care to give an absolute Order for withdrawing the Garrison till I could get round & see the Situation of things & then it became too late as the Fort was Invested.

General Nathanael Greene

The grievous loss of men and supplies at Fort Washington must be laid at the Commander in Chief's door. Washington had believed this last American stronghold on Manhattan should be abandoned; General Nathanael Greene, who was in command of the fort, wanted to defend it. Washington, as he so often did, yielded. His reluctance to impose his decisions was a flaw in leadership; it would disappear only as he came to recognize that since his was the ultimate responsibility, his must also be the final decision. Troubles multiplied. Reporting to the president of Congress on the situation in New Jersey, Washington had not finished his letter before he was forced to tell of a fresh disaster.

This map of New York Island, drawn by a man who served under General Howe, shows Fort Washington almost dead center with Fort Lee across the Hudson River in New Jersey.

[Hackensack] November 21. The unhappy affair of the 16th. has been succeeded by further Misfortunes.

Yesterday Morning a large body of the Enemy landed between Dobb's Ferry and Fort Lee. Their object was evidently to inclose the whole of our Troops and stores that lay between the North and Hackensack Rivers, which form a narrow neck of Land. For this purpose they formed and Marched, as soon as they had ascended the Heights towards the Fort. Upon the first information of their movements, our men were ordered to meet them, but finding their numbers greatly superior and that they were extending themselves It was thought proper to withdraw our Men, which was effected and their retreat secured over Hackensack Bridge. We lost the whole of the Cannon that was at the Fort except two twelve pounders, and a great deal of Baggage, between two & three hundred Tents, about a thousand Barrels of Flour and other stores in the Quarter Master's Department. This loss was inevitable. As many of the stores had been removed, as circumstances & time would admit of. The Ammunition had been happily got away. Our present situation between Hackensack & Passaick Rivers, being exactly similar to our late one, and our force here by no means adequate to an Opposition, that will promise the smallest probability of Success, we are taking measures to retire over the Waters of the latter, when the best dispositions will be formed, that Circumstances will admit of.

The Commander in Chief's spare words did not tell the entire dramatic story. He himself had galloped to warn the garrison of Fort Lee (across the Hudson from Fort Washington) that the British were coming and had hurried the men out so fast that those preparing a meal could not wait for kettles to cool enough to pack. Even so, they barely won a race with the enemy to a bridge over the Hackensack River and escape. Washington now wrote to General Charles Lee, who had been left in com-

164

mand of a force north of Manhattan, directing him to rejoin the main army in New Jersey. Unknown to the commander, another letter had been inserted with his by Joseph Reed, his former secretary and confidant and now Adjutant General. "I do not mean to flatter or praise you at the expense of any other," Reed wrote in part to Lee, "but I confess I do think it is entirely owing to you that this army, and the liberties of America, so far as they are dependent on it, are not totally cut off." Reed heaped more praise on Lee, whose self-esteem as a professional soldier was already monumental, blamed Washington for the loss of Fort Washington, and declared, "Oh! General, an indecisive mind is one of the greatest misfortunes that can befall an army; how often have I lamented it in this campaign." Washington sent several urgent messages to Lee, all in the same vein.

New Ark [New Jersey], Novemr. 27th. 1776.

I last night received the favour of your Letter of the 25th. My former Letters were so full and explicit, as to the Necessity of your Marching, as early as possible, that it is unnecessary to add more on that Head. I confess I expected you would have been sooner in motion. The force here, when joined by yours, will not be adequate to any great opposition; at present it is weak, and it has been more owing to the badness of the weather, that the Enemy's progress has been checked, than any resistance we could make. They are now pushing this way, part of 'em have passed the Passaic. Their plan is not entirely unfolded, but I shall not be surprized, if Philadelphia should turn out the object of their Movement. The distress of the Troops, for want of Cloaths, I feel much, but what can I do? Having formed an enterprize against Roger's &c. I wish you may have succeeded.

Engraving after an original water color of the landing of the British forces in New Jersey on November 20

But Lee was not obeying the order to bring his forces to New Jersey. Lee's motives are still obscure. He may have hoped for a victory of his own over British forces in his area, which would enhance his military reputation at Washington's expense. Undoubtedly he also feared the effect of the march on his own disintegrating army. And he strongly disagreed with his commander's current military plans. In the meantime he wrote to Joseph Reed, thanking the Adjutant General for his kind letter and saying, among other things, "Lament with you that fatal indecision of mind which in war is a much greater disqualification than stupidity, or even want of personal courage." Reed was away when the letter arrived, and Washington, thinking it some Army matter, opened it. He recognized it, as he later put it, as "an echo" of one Reed must have written to Lee, but sent it on to Reed with an apology.

Brunswick [New Jersey], Novr. 30th. 1776.
The inclosed was put into my hands by an Express from
the White Plains. Having no Idea of its being a Private
Letter, much less suspecting the tendency of the correspondence, I opened it, as I had done all other Letters
to you, from the same place and Peekskill, upon the
business of your Office, as I conceived and found them
to be.

This, as it is the truth, must be my excuse for seeing the
contents of a Letter, which neither inclination or intention would have prompted me to.

I thank you for the trouble and fatigue you have undergone in your Journey to Burlington, and sincerely wish
that your labours may be crowned with the desired
success.

Reed sent his resignation to Congress; Washington
urged him to stay on for the good of the country. Reed did remain, but it
was a long time before the tension between the two was eased. As the ragged
American Army retreated across New Jersey, its Jersey militiamen melted
away, and citizens hastened to buy immunity from British reprisals by
swearing allegiance to King George. In early December the Army reached
temporary safety when it crossed the Delaware into Pennsylvania, taking
every boat it could find to hamper pursuit. And all the while Washington
was calling on Charles Lee to hurry to his assistance, while that self-seeking
man now argued that he could do more good hanging on the flanks of
Howe's army. In one of his periodic letters to his cousin Lund, Washington
described his dangerous situation and imparted the news of Lee's capture.

Falls of the Delaware, Southside,
December 10, 1776.

Dear Lund:

I wish to Heaven it was in my power to give you a
more favorable account of our situation than it is. Our
numbers, quite inadequate to the task of opposing that
part of the army under the command of General Howe,
being reduced by sickness, desertion, and political
deaths (on or before the 1st. instant, and having no assistance from the militia,) were obliged to retire before
the enemy, who were perfectly well informed of our
situation till we came to this place, where I have no idea
of being able to make a stand, as my numbers, till joined
by the Philadelphia militia, did not exceed three thousand
men fit for duty. Now we may be about five thousand to

oppose Howe's whole army, that part of it excepted which sailed under the command of Gen. Clinton. I tremble for Philadelphia. Nothing, in my opinion, but Gen. Lee's speedy arrival, who has been long expected, though still at a distance (with about three thousand men,) can save it. We have brought over and destroyed all the boats we could lay our hands on upon the Jersey shore for many miles above and below this place; but it is next to impossible to guard a shore for sixty miles, with less than half the enemy's numbers; when by force or strategem they may suddenly attempt a passage in many different places. At present they are encamped or quartered along the other shore above and below us (rather this place, for we are obliged to keep a face towards them) for fifteen miles.

December 17, ten miles above the Falls. I have since moved up to this place, to be more convenient to our great and extensive defences of this river. Hitherto, by our destruction of the boats, and vigilance in watching the fords of the river above the falls (which are now rather high,) we have prevented them from crossing; but how long we shall be able to do it God only knows, as they are still hovering about the river. And if every thing else fails, will wait till the 1st. of January, when there will be no other men to oppose them but militia, none of which but those from Philadelphia, mentioned in the first part of the letter, are yet come (though I am told some are expected from the back counties). When I say none but militia, I am to except the Virginia regiments and the shattered remains of Smallwood's, which, by fatigue, want of clothes, &c., are reduced to nothing—Weedon, which was the strongest, not having more than between one hundred and thirty to one hundred and forty men fit for duty, the rest being in the hospitals. The unhappy policy of short enlistments and a dependence upon militia will, I fear, prove the downfall of our cause, though early pointed out with an almost prophetic spirit! Our cause has also received a severe blow in the captivity of Gen. Lee. Unhappy man! Taken by his own imprudence, going three or four miles from his own camp, and within twenty of the enemy, notice of which by a rascally Tory was given, a party of light horse seized him in the morning after travelling all night, and carried him off in high triumph and with

General Joseph Reed

every mark of indignity, not even suffering him to get his hat or surtout coat. The troops that were under his command are not yet come up with us, though they, I think, may be expected to-morrow. A large part of the Jerseys have given every proof of disaffection that they can do, and this part of Pennsylvania are equally inimical. In short, your imagination can scarce extend to a situation more distressing than mine. Our only dependence now is upon the speedy enlistment of a new army. If this fails, I think the game will be pretty well up, as, from disaffection and want of spirit and fortitude, the inhabitants, instead of resistance, are offering submission and taking protection from Gen. Howe in Jersey.

The capture of General Charles Lee by a British scouting party was mourned by many prominent patriots and celebrated by the British as a loss to the American cause of its best trained and most competent general. In fact, Washington was well rid of a man whom even he had described as "fickle," though he was as bemused as everyone else by Lee's self-proclaimed military talents. As 1776 drew to a close, Washington gave way to despair; to his brother John Augustine he suggested that the American cause might well be lost.

Camp, near the Falls of Trenton,
December 18, 1776.

Since I came on this side, I have been join'd by about 2000 of the City Militia, and understand that some of the Country Militia (from the back Counties,) are on their way; *but we are in a very disaffected part of the Provence, and between you and me, I think our Affairs are in a very bad situation; not so much from the apprehension of Genl. Howe's Army, as from the defection of New York, Jerseys, and Pensylvania. In short, the Conduct of the Jerseys has been most Infamous. Instead of turning out to defend their Country and affording aid to our Army, they are making their submissions as fast as they can. If they the Jerseys had given us any* support, we might have made a stand at Hackensack and after that at Brunswick, but the few Militia that were in Arms, disbanded themselves and left the poor remains of our Army to make the best we could of it.

I have no doubt but that General Howe will still make an attempt upon Philadelphia this Winter. I see nothing to oppose him a fortnight hence, as the time

Capture of Charles Lee

General Sir William Howe

of all the Troops, except those of Virginia (reduced almost to nothing,) and Smallwood's Regiment of Maryland, (equally as bad) will expire in less than that time. In a word my dear Sir, *if every nerve is not strain'd* to recruit the New Army with all possible expedition, *I think the game is pretty near up, owing, in a great measure, to the insidious Arts of the Enemy, and disaffection of the Colonies before mentioned, but* principally to the accursed policy of short Inlistments, and placing too great a dependence on the Militia the Evil consequences of which were foretold 15 Months ago with a spirit almost Prophetick.

The soldiers of the weary little Army were ragged, hungry, cold, often sick, and much of Washington's effort was devoted to obtaining for them the common necessities of life. To Robert Morris, who had remained in Philadelphia to procure supplies for the Army after the other members of Congress had fled to Baltimore, he made a plea for clothing for his troops.

> Camp above the Falls at Trenton,
> Decr. 22d. 1776.
>
> Your favour of yesterday [a letter saying 856 blankets were being sent to the Army] came duely to hand, and I thank you for the several agreeable articles of Intelligence therein contain'd. For godsake hurry Mr. Mease [James Mease, Clothier-General of the Army] with the Cloathing as nothing will contribute more to facilitate the recruiting Service than warm & comfortable Cloathing to those who engage.

On the day he wrote to Morris, Washington sent the Pennsylvania Council of Safety a message even more eloquent in what it said of the state of the patriot Army.

> Head Quarters, Buck County,
> December 22, 1776.
>
> Your Collection of old cloathes for the use of the army, deserves my warmest thanks; they are of the greatest use and shall be distributed where they are most wanted. I think if the Committee or some proper persons were appointed to go thro' the County of Bucks and make a Collection of Blankets &c., in the manner you have done in Philadelphia, it would be better than doing it in a

Military Way by me; for many people, who would be willing to contribute or sell, if asked so to do by their Neighbours or Acquaintances, feel themselves hurt when the demand is made, backed by an Armed force. But I would at the same time remark, that if any, who can spare without inconvenience, refuse to do it, I would immediately give proper assistance to take from them.

I have not a Musket to furnish the Militia who are without arms, this demand upon me makes it necessary to remind you, that it will be needless for those to come down who have no Arms, except they will consent to work upon the Fortifications instead of taking their Tour of Military Duty; if they will do that, they may be most usefully employed.

By the end of 1776 the American cause was indeed at low ebb. On December 23 there appeared a pamphlet, the first of Thomas Paine's *Crisis* papers, which began, "These are the times that try men's souls." But three days later, the morning after Christmas, Washington struck at the celebration-befuddled Hessian camp at Trenton. He made a happy report to Congress.

Head Quarters, Newton, December 27, 1776. I have the pleasure of Congratulating you upon the success of an enterprize which I had formed against a Detachment of the Enemy lying in Trenton, and which was executed yesterday Morning. The Evening of the 25th. I ordered the troops intended for this service to parade back of McKonkey's Ferry, that they might begin to pass as soon as it grew dark, imagining we should be able to throw them all over, with the necessary Artillery, by 12 O'Clock, and that we might easily arrive at Trenton by five in the Morning, the distance being about nine miles. But the Quantity of Ice, made that Night, impeded the passage of the Boats so much, that it was three o'clock before the Artillery could all be got over, & near four, before the troops took up their line of march.

This made me despair of surprizing the Town, as I well knew we could not reach it before the day was fairly broke, but as I was certain there was no making a retreat without being discovered, and harassed on repassing the river, I determined to push on at all Events. I formed my detachments into two divisions

The War of Independence BY BENSON J. LOSSING, 1850

Engraving of Washington crossing the Delaware from Lossing's The War of Independence, *1850 (above); a German engraving (below) shows the prisoners taken at Trenton being marched through Philadelphia.*

one to March by the lower or river road, the other by the upper or Pennington Road. As the divisions had nearly the same distance to march, I ordered each of them, immediately upon forcing the out guards, to push directly into the Town, that they might charge the enemy before they had time to form. The upper division arrived at the enemy's advanced post, exactly at eight oclock, and in three minutes after I found from the fire on the lower road that, that division had also got up. The Out guards made but small opposition tho' for their numbers, they behaved very well, keeping up a constant retreating fire from behind houses. We presently saw their main body formed, but from their motions, they seemed undetermined how to act.

Being hard pressed by our troops, who had already got possession of part of their Artillery, they attempted to file off by a road on their right leading to Princeton, but perceiving their intention, I threw a body of troops in their way which immediately checked them. Finding from our disposition that they were surrounded, and that they must inevitably be cut to pieces if they made any further resistance, they agreed to lay down their arms. The number, that submitted in this manner, was 23 Officers and 886 Men. Col. Rall the commanding officer with seven others were found wounded in the town. I dont exactly know how many they had killed, but I fancy not above twenty or thirty, as they never made any regular stand. Our loss is very trifling indeed, only two officers and one or two privates wounded.

I find, that the detachment of the enemy consisted of the three Hessian Regiments of Lanspatch, Kniphausen and Rohl amounting to about 1500 Men, and a troop of British light horse, but immediately upon the begining of the attack, all those who were not killed or taken, pushed directly down the Road towards Burdentown. These would likewise have fallen into our hands, could my plan have been compleatly carried into execution. Genl. Ewing was to have crossed before day at Trenton ferry, and taken possession of the bridge leading out of town but the quantity of Ice was so great, that tho he did every thing in his Power to effect it, he could not get over.

This difficulty also hindered General Cadwallader from crossing with the Pennsylvania militia, from Bristol, he got part of his foot over, but finding it impossible to embark his artillery, he was obliged to desist. I am fully confident, that could the troops under Generals Ewing and Cadwallader have passed the river, I should have been able, with their assistance, to have driven the enemy from all their posts below Trenton. But the number I had with me, being inferior to theirs below me, and a strong battalion of light infantry at Princeton above me I thought it most prudent to return the same evening with my prisoners and the artillery we had taken. We found no stores of any consequence in the Town. In justice to the officers and men, I must add, that their behaviour upon this occasion, reflects the highest honor upon them. The difficulty of passing the river in a very severe night, and their march thro' a violent storm of snow and hail, did not in the least abate their ardour. But when they came to the charge, each seemed to vie with the other in pressing forward, and were I to give a preference to any particular corps, I should do great injustice to the others.

Colonel Baylor, my first Aid de Camp, will have the honor of delivering this to you, and from him you may be made acquainted with many other particulars; his spirited behaviour upon every occasion, requires me to recommend him to your particular notice. I have the honor to be with great respect Sir your most Obedt. Servt.

G. WASHINGTON

P.S. Inclosed you have a particular list of the prisoners, artillery and other stores.

General Hugh Mercer, who was killed in the Battle of Princeton, 1777

The effect on both civilian and Army morale was electric. Men whose terms of enlistment were to have expired at the end of the year agreed to stay on for another six weeks to see the campaign through. The next battle of that campaign came on January 2, when Lord Cornwallis, one of Howe's generals, confronted Washington on Assunpink Creek near Trenton as night fell. The American position was precarious, but Washington had a few men keep the American campfires blazing during the night, while the patriot Army circled the enemy camp, attacked and defeated a British force at Princeton, and then retired before Cornwallis could bring his main army to the rescue. The American Army then went into winter quarters at Morristown, in a region protected by natural defenses of rocky hills. It was a location that threatened the enemy supply line if the British attempted any move toward Philadelphia, and so forced

Howe to retire into eastern New Jersey. Washington busied himself with the details of command, from recruiting his depleted ranks to prodding Congress for pay and clothing for his men. No problem was more onerous than that of dealing with an influx of French officers, many claiming commissions conferred by Congress or by Silas Deane, the American representative in Paris, most speaking no English, all expecting high rank. He complained to Congress.

Preliminary drawing by Trumbull for his painting Battle of Princeton

Head Quarters, Morristown,
February 11, 1777.

I was yesterday waited upon by two French Gentlemen, Monsr. Romand de Lisle, and Robillard. The first produced a Commission signed by you in Novemr. last appointing him a Major of Artillery, but, by the inclosed Letter from him to me, he claims much higher Rank under the promise of Congress, that of Commandant of the Continental Artillery. Whether any such promise was made, I leave you to determine.

Robillard claims a Captaincy of Artillery, but, upon what he grounds his pretentions, I do not know. I never saw him but once before, and that was upon his way from Boston to Philada.

Washington's headquarters at
Morristown, New Jersey

You cannot conceive what a weight these kind of people are upon the Service, and upon me in particular, few of them have any knowledge of the Branches which they profess to understand, and those that have, are entirely useless as officers, from their ignorance of the English Language. I wish it were possible to make them understand, when Commissions are granted to them, that they are to make themselves Masters of the english Language in some degree, before they can be attached to any particular Corps.

Not all the French volunteers were useless baggage. Some, experts in military engineering, Washington could not have done without. The Marquis de Lafayette, an arrival during the summer of 1777, whom Congress saw fit to make a major general although he was not yet twenty and had had no military experience, soon became a confidant of Washington's. Martha came to Morristown in mid-March, 1777, for a two-month stay that relieved the tedium of winter quarters. There were occasional clashes between American and enemy units but nothing decisive. Then on June 30, 1777, Howe left Amboy, his last base in New Jersey. A week or so later came dispiriting news: General John Burgoyne, moving down from Canada, had captured Fort Ticonderoga without firing a shot, opening the way south to the Hudson. Washington was sure Howe would move up the Hudson to meet Burgoyne and thus split New England from the rest of the nation, but the British commander only engaged in a game of hide-and-seek that kept the puzzled American leader shuttling his army here and there. He told John Augustine Washington about it.

Germantown, near Philada., Augt. 5th., 1777. Your favors of the 21st. of June from Westmoreland, and 10th. ulto. from Fredericksburg, are both to hand. Since Genl. Howes remove from the Jerseys, the Troops under my Command have been more harrassed by Marching, & Counter Marching, than by any thing that has happend to them in the course of the Campaign.

After Genl. Howe had Imbarkd his Troops, the presumption that he woud operate upon the North [Hudson] River, to form a junction with General Burgoyne, was so strong, that I removed from Middle Brook to Morristown, & from Morristown to the Clove (a narrow pass leading through the Highlands) about 18 Miles from the River. Indeed, upon some pretty strong presumptive evidence, I threw two divisions over the North River. In this Situation we lay till about the 24th. ulto., when,

Washington's camp-chest

Receiving certain Information that the Fleet had actually Saild from Sandy hook (the outer point of New York harbour) and the concurring Sentiment of every one, (tho I acknowledge my doubts of it were strong) that Philadelphia was the object We counter Marchd, and got to Coryells Ferry on the Delaware (abt. 33 Miles above the City) on the 27th. where I lay till I receiv'd Information from Congress that the Enemy were actually at the Capes of Delaware. This brought us in great haste to this place for defence of the City, but in less than 24 hours after our arrival we got Accts. of the disappearance of the Fleet on the 31st.; since which nothing having been heard of them, we remain here in a very irksome state of suspense. Some imagine that they are gone to the Southward, whilst a Majority (in whose opinion upon this occasion I concur) are satisfied they are gone to the Eastward. The fatigue however, & Injury, which Men must Sustain by long Marches in such extreme heat as we have felt for the last five days, must keep us quiet till we hear something of the destination of the Enemy.

The Marquis de Lafayette by Peale

Howe's transports at last showed up on Chesapeake Bay south of Philadelphia, where the British disembarked and began moving toward the capital. Washington chose to make his stand on a creek called the Brandywine, twenty miles or so from the city. His first brief report of the clash to John Hancock was made the night of the battle.

At Midnight, Chester, September 11, 1777.
I am sorry to inform you, that in this day's engagement we have been obliged to leave the enemy masters of the field. Unfortunately the intelligence received of the enemy's advancing up the Brandywine, and crossing at a ford about six miles above us, was uncertain and contradictory, notwithstanding all my pains to get the best. This prevented my making a disposition adequate to the force with which the enemy attacked us on the right; in consequence of which the troops first engaged, were obliged to retire before they could be reinforced. In the midst of the attack on our right, that body of the enemy which remained on the other side of Chad's Ford, crossed it, and attacked the division there under the command of General Wayne, and the light Troops under Genl. Maxwell who, after a severe conflict, re-

The Battle of Germantown, 1777

tired. The Militia under the command of Major Genl. Armstrong, being posted at a ford, about two Miles below Chad's, had no opportunity of engaging. But altho' we fought under many disadvantages and were from the causes above mentioned obliged to retire, yet our loss of Men is not, I am persuaded, very considerable, I beleive much less than the enemys. We have also lost about seven or eight pieces of cannon, according to the best information I can at present obtain. The baggage having been previously moved off is all secure, saving the men's Blankets; which being at their backs, many of them doubtless are lost.

I have directed all the Troops to Assemble behind Chester, where they are now arranging for the night. Notwithstanding the misfortune of the day, I am happy to find the troops in good spirits; and I hope another time we shall compensate for the losses now sustained.

The Marquis La Fayette was wounded in the leg, and Genl. Woodford in the hand. Divers other Officers were wounded, and some slain; but the number of either cannot now be ascertained. I have the honor To be Sir Your obedient hub. Servant

GO: WASHINGTON

P.S. It has not been in my power to send you earlier intelligence; the present being the first leisure moment I have had since the action.

While it was true that the Americans were outnumbered and that many of Washington's troops were local militia of questionable dependability, nevertheless the battle was poorly fought by Washington. He had done little reconnaissance and so was unable to evaluate reports of the enemy movements. One of his biographers says he fought like a man in a daze. Later, as the two armies maneuvered, Howe feinted the Americans out of position and sent Cornwallis's division to take unopposed possession of Philadelphia. As for Washington, he awaited his opportunity and struck on October 4 against Howe's main forces at Germantown. It was an audacious move; the American troops attacked at dawn and were rolling back the enemy in confused fighting in heavy fog when, for some unknown reason, panic spread through the patriot forces and sent them tumbling to the rear. The headlong flight was checked, but the advantage of surprise was lost and Washington was forced to retreat. In the midst of war, Washington and General Howe maintained a formal correspondence on such matters as prisoner exchange—and one nonmilitary subject.

October 6, 1777.

General Washington's compliments to General Howe. He does himself the pleasure to return him a Dog, which accidentally fell into his hands, and by the inscription on the Collar, appears to belong to General Howe.

On October 15, 1777, Washington announced to his troops the defeat of General Burgoyne by Horatio Gates at the Battle of Saratoga in upper New York. Washington had heard of the victory only indirectly; no word had come from Gates, who should have reported to his superior officer. Writing to congratulate Gates, Washington mildly reproved his subordinate officer.

Head Qrs. near White Marsh 15 Miles from Philada.
Octobr. 30 1777

By this Opportunity, I do myself the pleasure to congratulate you on the signal success of the Army under your command, in compelling Genl. Burgoyne and his whole force, to surrender themselves prisoners of War. An event that does the highest honor to the American Arms, and which, I hope, will be attended with the most extensive and happy consequences. At the same time, I cannot but regret, that a matter of such magnitude and so interesting to our general operations, should have reached me by report only, or thro' the Channel of Letters, not bearing that authenticity, which the importance of it required, and which it would have received by a line under your signature, stating the simple fact.

View of General Burgoyne's army encamped on the west bank of the Hudson River before his defeat

Gates's failure to inform Washington had been no oversight. His victory and his soaring popularity had opened new vistas. He saw himself as the commander of a northern department coequal with Washington's southern command—and very likely he would soon be called upon to take supreme command to save the nation. When Gates finally did write to Washington, he loftily notified the Commander in Chief that henceforth he would report directly to Congress, which—Gates suggested—would keep Washington sufficiently informed. When Horatio Gates had sent his first report of the victory at Saratoga to Congress, his courier had been his aide, Colonel James Wilkinson, a young man of sociable habits. Wilkinson tarried on his errand for an evening of conviviality at an inn where several of Washington's officers were staying. His tongue was loosened, and he boasted that General Gates had received a letter from one of Washington's brigadier generals, Thomas Conway, an Irish-born Frenchman, in which Conway had made remarks derogatory to the Commander in Chief. One of Washington's loyal officers reported the incident to the commander. Although Washington was well aware that he had detractors, the letter from Conway to Gates, men who he did not know were even acquainted with each other, was his first indication of a widespread intrigue to discredit him and have him ousted. It would become known as the Conway Cabal, more for reasons of euphony than because its leading figure was Brigadier General Thomas Conway.

For the moment, Washington had more pressing problems. Hard winter was coming on, and the Army had to find cold-weather quarters. Washington chose a region protected by streams and bluffs not only because it was easily defensible, but because, less than twenty miles from Philadelphia, the nearness of his Army would keep the British on the qui vive. On December 20, for the first time, he used the date line "Valley Forge" from the new winter headquarters.

Medal struck in honor of General Gates for his victory at Saratoga

Pictorial Field-Book of the Revolution, LOSSING

178

Chapter 6

The Long Road
to Yorktown

Ceneral Howe took the British army into snug winter quarters in Philadelphia on December 9, 1777. Washington's men found no comforts
when they trudged through the snow to their own winter quarters at Valley
Forge shortly after the middle of December. Valley Forge lay about twenty
miles northwest of Philadelphia, an area of rolling land in the angle where
Valley Creek joins the Schuylkill River, protected by bluffs on all sides. Its
natural defenses were strong, but it offered no amenities except for a few
farms and plenty of timber for firewood and cabins. Getting his men into
"huts" was one of the Commander in Chief's first considerations. Two days
before he arrived at Valley Forge, he had laid down specifications for housing.

> Head Quarters, at the Gulph, Decr. 18, 1777.
> The Colonels, or commanding officers of regiments, with
> their Captains, are immediately to cause their men to
> be divided into squads of twelve, and see that each squad
> have their proportion of tools, and set about a hut for
> themselves: And as an encouragement to industry and art,
> the General promises to reward the party in each regi-
> ment, which finishes their hut in the quickest, and most
> workmanlike manner, with *twelve* dollars. And as there
> is reason to believe, that boards, for covering, may be
> found scarce and difficult to be got—He offers *One
> hundred* dollars to any officer or soldier, who in the
> opinion of three Gentlemen, he shall appoint as judges,
> shall substitute some other covering, that may be cheaper
> and quicker made, and will in every respect answer
> the end.
> The Soldier's huts are to be of the following dimensions
> —viz—fourteen by sixteen each—sides, ends and roofs
> made with logs, and the roof made tight with split slabs,

179

or in some other way—the sides made tight with clay—fireplace made of wood and secured with clay on the inside eighteen inches thick, this fire place to be in the rear of the hut—the door to be in the end next the street—the doors to be made of split oak-slabs, unless boards can be procured—Side-walls to be six and a half feet high—the officers huts to form a line in the rear of the troops, one hut to be allowed to each General Officer, one to the staff of each brigade—one to the field officers of each regiment—one to the staff of each regiment—one to the commissioned officers of two companies, and one to every twelve non-commissioned officers and soldiers.

It is doubtful if the British army could have housed itself without lumber and nails, but the Americans were largely farm boys, skilled with an axe. Even so, building log cabins for eleven thousand men takes time, and meanwhile the icy chill of canvas tents could have been borne with a better will if the men had not lacked everything else. In a letter to Congress, Washington gave way to frustration and anger over the sad state of affairs.

Valley Forge December 23d. 1777.
Full as I was in my representation of matters in the Commissary's department yesterday, fresh and more powerful reasons oblige me to add, that I am now convinced, beyond a doubt, that unless some great and Capital change suddenly takes place in that line, this Army must inevitably be reduced to one or other of these three things; starve, dissolve or disperse in order to obtain subsistence in the best manner they can; rest assured Sir, this is not an exaggerated picture, and that I have abundant reason to support what I say.

Yesterday afternoon, receiving information that the Enemy, in force, had left the City and were advancing towards Derby, with apparent design to forage, and draw subsistance from that part of the Country, I ordered the Troops to be in readiness, that I might give every opposition in my power; when behold, to my great mortification, I was not only informed, but convinced, that the Men were unable to stir on Acct. of Provision, and that a dangerous mutiny, begun the night before, and which with difficulty was suppressed by the spirited exertion of some Officers, was still much to be apprehended for want of this article.

"Washington forma il Campo a Valle-fucina"—an Italian version of log-cabin building at Valley Forge

This brought forth the only Commissary in the purchasing line, in this Camp; and with him, this melancholy and alarming truth, that he had not a single hoof of any kind to slaughter, and not more than 25. Barrels of Flour! From hence form an opinion of our situation, when I add, that he could not tell when to expect any.

The huts were not completed until about mid-January, and only when all the men were housed did Washington move from his own hut into the farmhouse that he made his headquarters. Many of the huts were still without straw to cover the cold earthen floors, the men were ill-supplied with blankets, most were in rags. In the midst of his other troubles, Washington had to contend with the Conway Cabal, that collection of oddly assorted characters whose common denominator was a wish to see a new Commander in Chief: Horatio Gates, or possibly the still-captive Charles Lee, or even the loudmouthed braggart Conway. The faction had enough influence in Congress to have Conway promoted to Major General in December, 1777, although Washington was emphatically opposed to such an advance in rank. Conway was made Inspector General of the Army, charged with putting into effect a new system of drill and maneuver. The intriguers hoped that an outraged Washington would resign, but when Conway presented himself at headquarters, Washington merely sent him a blunt letter concerning his appointment.

Head Qurs., Decemr. 30th. 1777.

I am favoured with your Letter of Yesterday, in which you propose (in order to loose no time) to begin with the instructions of the Troops.

You will observe by the Resolution of Congress relative to your appointment, that the Board of War is to furnish a set of Instructions, according to which the Troops are to be Manoeuvred. As you have made no mention of having received them, I suppose they are not come to you. When they do, I shall issue any Orders which may be judged necessary to have them carried into immediate Execution.

Your appointment of Inspector General to the Army, I believe has not given the least uneasiness to any Officer in it. By consulting your own feelings upon the appointment of the Baron De Kalb [whom Conway claimed he had outranked in France] you may judge what must be the Sensations of those Brigadiers, who by your promotion are superceded. I am told they are determined to remonstrate against it; for my own part

Horatio Gates, drawn from life by Du Simitière, engraved by Prevost

I have nothing to do in the appointment of Genl. Officers, and shall always afford every Countenance and due respect to those appointed by Congress, taking it for granted, that prior to any Resolve of that nature, they take a dispassionate view, of the merits of the Officer to be promoted, and consider every consequence that can result from such a procedure; nor have I any other wish on that Head, but that good attentive Officers may be chosen, and no Extraordinary promotion take place, but where the merit of the Officer is so generally acknowledged as to obviate every reasonable cause of dissatisfaction thereat.

Conway vented his frustration with a couple of insulting letters to Washington, who did not deign to answer. Close on the heels of this episode, General Gates wrote to Washington. He had just learned that the commander knew about the letter from Conway that his aide Colonel Wilkinson had talked about so freely one evening in a tavern. The letter had been "stealingly copied," he said. Not so, replied Washington.

Valley Forge January 4th. 1778. Your Letter of the 8th. Ulto. came to my hands a few days ago, and to my great surprise informed me, that a copy of it had been sent to Congress, for what reason, I find myself unable to account; but, as some end doubtless was intended to be answered by it, I am laid under the disagreeable necessity of returning my answer through the same channel, lest any member of that Honble. Body, should harbour an unfavourable suspicion of my having practiced some indirect means to come at the contents of the confidential Letters between you and General Conway.

I am to inform you then, that Colo. Wilkinson in his way to Congress in the month of October last, fell in with Lord Stirling at Reading; and, not in confidence that I ever understood, informed his Aid de Camp Major McWilliams that General Conway had written thus to you,

"Heaven has been determined to save your Country; or a weak General and bad Counsellors would have ruined it."

Lord Stirling from motives of friendship, transmitted the account with this remark. "The inclosed was communicated by Colo. Wilkinson to Major McWilliams; such wicked duplicity of conduct I shall always think

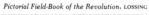

Pictorial Field-Book of the Revolution, LOSSING

House of Isaac Potts, Washington's headquarters at Valley Forge

Colonel James Wilkinson
by Charles Willson Peale

it my duty to detect."

In consequence of this information, and without having any thing more in view than merely to shew that Gentleman, that I was not unapprized of his intriguing disposition, I wrote him a Letter in these words. "Sir. A Letter which I received last night contained the following paragraph.

"In a Letter from Genl. Conway to Genl. Gates he says, Heaven has been determined to save your Country; or a weak General and bad Counsellors (one of whom, by the bye, he was) would have ruined it. "I am Sir &ca."

Neither this Letter, nor the information which occasioned it was ever, directly, or indirectly communicated by me to a single officer in this Army (out of my own family) excepting the Marquis De la Fayette, who, having been spoken to on the Subject by General Conway, applied for, and saw, under injunctions of secresy, the Letter which contained Wilkenson's information; so desirous was I of concealing every matter that could, in its consequences, give the smallest Interruption to the tranquility of this Army, or afford a gleam of hope to the Enemy by dissentions therein.

Thus Sir, with an openess and candour which I hope will ever characterize and mark my conduct, have I complied with your request. The only concern I feel upon the occasion, finding how matters stand, is, that in doing this, I have necessarily been obliged to name a Gentleman whom I am persuaded (although I never exchanged a Word with him upon the Subject) thought he was rather doing an act of Justice, than committing an act of infidility; and sure I am, that, till Lord Stirling's Letter came to my hands, I never knew that General Conway (whom I viewed in the light of a stranger to you) was a correspondent of yours, much less did I suspect that I was the subject of your confidential Letters. Pardon me then for adding, that so far from conceiving that the safety of the States can be affected, or in the smallest degree injured, by a discovery of this kind, or, that I should be called upon in such solemn terms to point out the author, that I considered the information as coming from yourself, and given with a friendly view to forewarn, and consequently forearm me, against a secret enemy, or in other words, a dangerous incendiary; in which character, sooner or later, this

Country will know General Conway. But, in this, as in other matters of late, I have found myself mistaken.

The matter led to a quibbling debate by letter that was unlike Washington, but in the end Gates disengaged himself by disclaiming any personal connection with Conway and denying ties with any faction. Washington, probably with tongue in cheek, accepted the proffered olive branch.

> Valley Forge Feby. 24th., 1778.
>
> I yesterday received your favor of the 19th. Instt. I am as averse to controversy, as any man, and had I not been forced into it, you never would have had occasion to impute to me, even the Shadow of a disposition towards it. Your repeatedly and Solemnly disclaiming any offensive views, in those matters, which have been the subject of our past correspondence, makes me willing to close with the desire, you express, of burying them hereafter in silence, and as far as future events will permit, oblivion. My temper leads me to peace and harmony with all men; and it is peculiarly my wish, to avoid any personal feuds or dissentions with those, who are embarked in the same great national interest with myself; as every difference of this kind must in its consequences be very injurious.

There were influential men in the Conway Cabal, but most of the Army and probably most of the nation remained staunchly loyal to Washington. A number of brigadier generals protested to Congress the promotion of Conway over the heads of abler men. "We have commanded [with?] him in the field and are totally unacquainted with any superior Act of Merit which could entitle him to rise above us," they wrote. Collectively, the brigadiers had enough political influence in their states to make many members of Congress back away from Conway. In January the intriguers, through the Board of War, which they dominated, conceived a winter attack on Canada to be led by the Marquis de Lafayette with General Thomas Conway second in command. But Lafayette absolutely refused to have Conway and threatened Congress with his resignation and those of a number of other French officers if the Board insisted. Later, when he reached Albany, he found supplies for a winter campaign so miserably inadequate that he castigated the Board of War for even thinking about an invasion, to the extreme discomfiture of that body. By early spring the Conway Cabal was in confusion and retreat. Wilkinson and Gates had almost fought a duel. Thomas Mifflin, Washington's former aide, onetime Quartermaster General, and a leading intriguer, publicly proclaimed that the Commander in Chief was the best friend he ever had. And Conway, who often threatened resignation to frighten Congress into giving him what he wanted, did it once too often and found his bluff called by delegates disenchanted with him. While he fenced with the Conway Cabal, Washington had to cope with the privation that marked Valley Forge. Two months after having moved to the encampment he was still crying crisis in a joint letter to three supply officers.

Head Qurs. Valley Feby. 15th. 1778.
I am constrained to inform you, that the situation of the Army is most critical and alarming for want of provision of the Meat kind. Many of the Troops for four days and some longer, have not drawn the smallest supplies of this Article. This being the case, it is needless to add [more] to convince you of their distress. They have been on the point of dispersing and without the earliest releif, no address or authority will be sufficient to keep them long together. Their patience and endurance are great, but the demands of nature must be satisfied. I must therefore, Gentlemen, in the most urgent terms, request and entreat your immediate and more active exertions to procure and forward to Camp, as expeditiously as possible, all the provision of the Meat kind which it may be in your power to obtain. I would not have you wait till you collect a large quantity, but wish you to send on supplies, as fast as you can get them. The troops must have instant relief or we shall have reason to apprehend the worst consequences. I need not mention to you the necessity of secrecy in an affair of such delicacy. Your own prudence and discretion will point it out. . . .
P.S. The State of Forage is the same with that of provision, and a supply is materially wanted. Without it and very speedily, we shall have not a Horse left.

George Washington and the Town of Reading in Pennsylvania by BENNETT J. NOLAN, 1931

Major General Thomas Conway

The darkness lightened. On March 12, 1778, Washington wrote Governor George Clinton of New York that "by the exertions of our Friends in different quarters, the Army has been pretty well supplied" since mid-February. Martha had been at Valley Forge since early February, creating, as always, some bit of social gaiety among the small circle of officers' wives. Washington, though beset by problems, was not too busy to spare a moment for a young woman.

185

Camp-Valley-Forge 18th. Mar. 1778
General Washington having been informed, lately, of the honor done him by Miss Kitty Livingston in wishing for a lock of his Hair, takes the liberty of inclosing one, accompanied by his most respectful compliments.

The day before he sent Miss Livingston the lock of hair, the Commander in Chief issued a brief General Order that was going to have far-reaching effects on the Continental Army.

Pictorial Field-Book of the Revolution, LOSSING

Banner of Washington's Life Guard

Head-Quarters V. Forge
March 17th. 1778. Tuesday.
Parole Robinson. Countersigns Radnor, Ringwood.

One hundred chosen men are to be annexed to the Guard of the Commander in Chief for the purpose of forming a Corps to be instructed in the Manoeuvres necessary to be introduced in the Army and serve as a Model for the execution of them. As the General's guard is composed intirely of Virginians the one hundred draughts are to be taken from the troops of the other States.

What it meant was that the Baron von Steuben, former officer under Frederick the Great of Prussia, was now drillmaster of the American Army. His system of training and reorganizing the Army, starting with the squad of one hundred as a model, created for the first time a disciplined American armed force. Also, France had for some time been sending arms and supplies to the new nation, and official recognition was expected. When Washington received formal notification of the alliance from Congress, he issued orders to the Army for celebration.

GENERAL ORDERS

Head-Quarters V. Forge Tuesday May 5th. 1778.
It having pleased the Almighty ruler of the Universe propitiously to defend the Cause of the United American States and finally by raising us up a powerful Friend among the Princes of the Earth to establish our liberty and Independence upon lasting foundations, it becomes us to set apart a day for gratefully acknowledging the divine Goodness & celebrating the important Event which we owe to his benign Interposition.

The several Brigades are to be assembled for this Purpose at nine o'Clock tomorrow morning when their Chaplains will communicate the Intelligence contain'd

G. Washington

In CONGRESS, 29th March, 1779.

CONGRESS *judging it of the greatest importance to prescribe some invariable rules for the order and discipline of the troops, especially for the purpose of introducing an uniformity in their formation and manœuvres, and in the service of the camp:*

ORDERED, *That the following regulations be observed by all the troops of the United States, and that all general and other officers cause the same to be executed with all possible exactness.*

By Order,

JOHN JAY, PRESIDENT.

Attest.

CHARLES THOMPSON,
Secretary.

Two pages, above and below, of the special presentation copy given to Washington by Baron von Steuben of his manual, Regulations for the Order and Discipline of the Troops of the United States

in the Postscript to the Pennsylvania Gazette of the 2nd. instant and offer up a thanksgiving and deliver a discourse suitable to the Occasion. At half after ten o'Clock a Cannon will be fired, which is to be a signal for the men to be under Arms. The Brigade Inspectors will then inspect their Dress and Arms, form the Battalions according to instructions given them and announce to the Commanding Officers of Brigades that the Battalions are formed. The Brigadiers or Commandants will then appoint the Field Officers to command the Battalions, after which each Battalion will be ordered to load & ground their Arms.

At half after eleven a second Cannon be fired as a signal for the march upon which the several Brigades will begin their march by wheeling to the right by Platoons & proceed by the nearest way to the left of their ground in the new Position; this will be pointed out by the Brigade Inspectors. A third signal will be given upon which there will be discharge of thirteen Cannon; When the thirteen has fired a runing fire of the Infantry will begin on the right of Woodford's and continue throughout the whole front line, it will then be taken on the left of the second line and continue to the right. Upon a signal given, the whole Army will *Huzza!* "Long Live the King of France." The Artillery then begins again and fires thirteen rounds, this will be succeeded by a second general discharge of the Musquetry in a runing fire—*Huzza!*—"And long live the friendly European Powers." Then the last discharge of thirteen Pieces of Artillery will be given, followed by a General runing fire and *Huzza!* "To the American States".

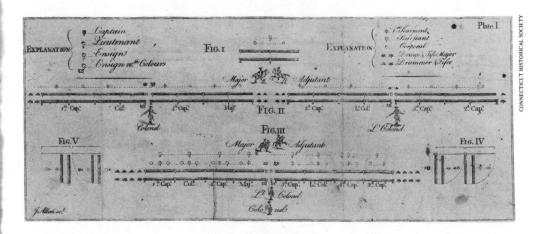

The English print above condemns the Americans for their alliance with France, while the French print at right shows Washington holding the Declaration of Independence and the formal treaty signed in 1778.

The review was the first showing of the Steuben-trained Army and went off smoothly. A disciplined soldiery was one of the good things to come out of Valley Forge; it would soon have a chance to prove its mettle. With the coming of spring, Major General Charles Lee returned after a year and a half as a prisoner, freed in exchange for a British officer. Washington had feared that Lee, a onetime British officer, might be hanged as a traitor; in fact, Lee and Lord Howe had been on such friendly terms that Lee had worked out for the British a plan for defeating the American Army. On June 18 the British army—now commanded by Sir Henry Clinton, who had succeeded Howe in May—left Philadelphia and started overland toward New York. The next day Washington led his forces out of Valley Forge in cautious pursuit. When he proposed to his generals that an attack be made on the rear of the strung-out enemy column, General Lee was so vehemently opposed that he at first declined to lead the attack force, although he was the ranking officer. Americans, he said, could not possibly stand up to European soldiers in open battle. He changed his mind and accepted the command only when it was offered to Lafayette. The clash took place near Monmouth Court House (now Freehold), New Jersey. Washington's first report to Congress was simply a statement that an encounter was shaping up in almost intolerably hot weather.

Before the Army left Valley Forge, Congress directed Washington to administer an oath of allegiance to each of his officers. This one is signed by Major General Stirling.

English Town, 6 Miles from Monmouth Court House
June 28th. 1778. 1/2 after 11.A.M.

I am now here with the main body of the Army and presing hard to come up with the Enemy. They encamped yesterday at Monmouth Court House, having almost the whole of his front, particularly his left wing, secured by a marsh and thick wood and his rear by a difficult defile, from whence he moved very early this morning. Our advance, from the rainy weather and the intense heat when it was fair (tho' these may have been equally disadvantageous to the Enemy) has been greatly delayed. Several of our men have fallen Sick from these causes, and a few unfortunately have fainted and died in a little time after. We have a select and strong detachment more forward under the general Command of Major Genl. Lee, with orders to attack their rear, if possible. Whether it will be able to come up with them, is a matter of some doubt; especially before they get into strong grounds. Besides this, Morgan with his Corps and some bodies of Militia are on their flanks. I cannot determine yet at what place they intend to embark. Some think they will push for Sandy Hook, whilst other suppose they mean to go to shoal harbour. The latter opinion seems to be founded in the greatest probability, as from intelligence several Vessels and Craft are lying there. We have made a few prisoners, and they have lost a good many men by desertion. I cannot ascertain their number, as they came in to our advanced parties & pushed immediately into the [Country]. I think five or Six hundred at least, have come in the whole. The deserters are chiefly foreigners.

The following day, the Commander in Chief sent Congress a brief and strangely uninformative account of the battle.

Fields near Monmouth Court House
29th. June 1778.

I have the honor to inform you that about seven OClock yesterday Morning both Armies advanced on each other. About 12 they met on the Grounds near Monmouth Court House, when an action commenced. We forced the Enemy from the Field and encamped on the Ground. They took a strong post in our front, secured on both flanks by Morasses and thick Woods, where they re-

189

mained till about 12 at Night, and then retreated. I cannot at this time go into a detail of Matters. When opportunity will permit I shall take the liberty of transmitting Congress a more particular account of the proceedings of the day.

Plan of the Battle of Monmouth

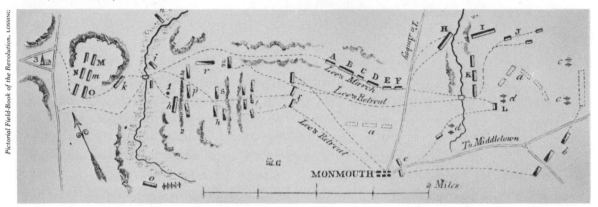

Washington made a complete report two days later, but in his detailed recounting of the movements of regiments and brigades, the curious actions of General Lee were obscured. To his brother Jack he was more outspoken.

Brunswick in New Jersey July 4th. 1778. Your Letter of the 20th Ulto. came to my hands last Night. Before this will have reached you, the Acct. of the Battle of Monmouth probably will get to Virginia; which, from an unfortunate, and bad beginning, turned out a glorious and happy day.

The Enemy evacuated Philadelphia on the 18th. Instt.—at ten oclock that day I got intelligence of it, and by two oclock, or soon after, had Six Brigades on their March for the Jerseys, & followed with the whole Army next Morning. On the 21st. we compleated our passage over the Delaware at Coryells ferry (abt. 33 Miles above Philadelphia) distance from Valley forge near 40 Miles. From this Ferry we moved down towards the Enemy, and on the 27th. got within Six Miles of them.

General Lee having the command of the Van of the Army, consisting of full 5000 chosen Men, was ordered to begin the Attack next Morning so soon as the enemy began their March, to be supported by me. But, strange to tell! when he came up with the enemy, a retreat

Sir Henry Clinton

commenced; whether by his order, or from other causes, is now the subject of enquiry, & consequently improper to be discanted on, as he is in arrest, and a Court Martial sitting for tryal of him. A Retreat however was the fact, be the causes as they may; and the disorder arising from it would have proved fatal to the Army had not that bountiful Providence which has never failed us in the hour of distress, enabled me to form a Regiment or two (of those that were retreating) in the face of the Enemy, and under their fire, by which means a stand was made long enough (the place through which the enemy were pursuing being narrow) to form the Troops that were advancing, upon an advantageous piece of Ground in the rear. Hence our affairs took a favourable turn, & from being pursued, we drove the Enemy back, over the ground they had followed us, recovered the field of Battle, and possessed ourselves of their dead—but, as they retreated behind a Morass very difficult to pass, & had both Flanks secured with thick Woods, it was found impracticable with Men fainting with fatigue, heat, and want of water, to do any thing more that Night. In the Morning we expected to renew the Action, when behold the enemy had stole off as Silent as the Grave in the Night after having sent away their wounded. Getting a Nights March of us, and having but ten Miles to a strong post, it was judged inexpedient to follow them any further, but move towards the North River least they should have any design upon our posts there.

Major General Charles Lee

Lee had almost turned the Battle of Monmouth into a disaster. After one brief clash in which an American regiment turned back an enemy cavalry charge, Lee had ordered a retreat but told only the regiment next to him, leaving other units to discover that they had been left unsupported. Washington had come up just in time to stem the withdrawal. Lee had babbled about saving the Army from disaster by his retreat, but Washington, unconvinced, had Lee court-martialed. Lee was found guilty of disobeying orders, of misbehavior before the enemy, and of disrespect for the Commander in Chief, but was given the strangely light sentence of suspension from command for one year. However, he wrote a letter so insulting to Congress that those gentlemen took his commission away entirely.

France and Britain went to war in June; a joint Franco-American action in July against a British garrison in Rhode Island ended abortively when a storm scattered the French fleet. Otherwise the summer and fall of 1778 passed rather uneventfully, and in December Washington went into winter quarters at Middlebrook (Bound Brook), New Jersey. The Army passed the cold months "better clad and more healthy than they had ever been since the formation of the army," according to Washington, although food was hardly in bountiful supply yet. In the spring of 1779 Washington sent one of his periodic summaries to his brother Jack.

Middlebrook May 12th. 1779.
[It is] my opinion, that the enemy will strain every nerve to push the War with vigor this Campaign. By Accts. from England as late as March it appears evident that Seven Regiments besides two of the new raised scotch Corps, recruits for the Guards, & for other Regiments now in America were on the Point of embarking. The whole it is said would amt. to 12 or 1300 Men; but whether they will go to the West Indies, Georgia, or New York or in part to all, remains to be determined. My own opinion of the matter is, that they will Garrison New York & Rhode Isld. strongly, & push their successes to the Southward vigorously.... By a Bill which has passed both Houses of Parliament every parish in the Kingdom is called upon to furnish two Men. These it is said will be immediately had, & will amount in the whole to 27000 recruits for their Army. In aid of these, all the Indians from the extremest North to the South, are bribed to cut our throats, & have already begun the work of devastation in most places on our frontiers. We, on the other hand, have been dreaming of Peace and Independence, and striving to enrich ourselves on the spoils & ruin of our Country, by preying upon the very vitals of it. In a word, our

This engraving of the siege of Rhode Island in 1778 appeared in Gentleman's Magazine *the next year.*

conduct has been the very reverse of the enemy's, for while they were doing every thing to prepare vigorously for the Campaign now opening, we were doing nothing— nay, worse than nothing—but considering how cautious I intended to be, I have said more than enough; & shall add no more on this head, but lament, which I do most pathetically that decay of public virtue with which people were inspired at the beginning of this contest. Speculation—peculation—with all their concomitants, have taken such deep root in almost every Soil, that little else but money making is attended to—the great business may get forward as it can. . . .

I am very apprehensive for the fate of Charlestown. A detachment of between 3 & 4000 Men left New York the 5th. Instt. intended, as is conjectured, to reinforce the enemy in Georgia. This will leave them abt. 8 or 9000 strong at New York and abt. 5000 at Rhode Isld. which they can unite in a few hours at any time. I have ordered all the Virginia levies to Georgia under the command of Genl. Scott. They are to be formed into Regiments, & Officers go from the Troops of that State, in this Camp, to command them. It is much to be feared that this aid will prove very inadequate without vigorous measures are adopted by Virginia & No. Carolina to assist their Sister State. Let them bear in mind how much better it is to oppose the enemy at a distance than at their own homes.

We have, and still do flatter ourselves, with an acknowledgment of our Independance by Spain; and that she will take an active part against G. Britain. Should an event of this kind take place, it would, I should hope, give a decisive turn to our affairs—but as my imagination is not sufficiently fertile to suggest a good reason for the delay, I am inclined to think that the Ministry hath hit upon some device to keep Spain amused while she tries the issue of another Campaign; if not with a view of conquest—to obtain better terms. This campaign is certainly big of events; & requires all our exertions— wisdom—fortitude—& virtue.

Except for a minor but morale-building action in July against a fort at Stony Point on the Hudson, there was little military action in which Washington had any direct part during 1779, and little had been accomplished by the time cold weather came once more. Washington again made his headquarters at Morristown, New Jersey, where he had spent the winter of 1776–77. It was to be Valley Forge all over again, only worse. The soldiers huddled in tents while huts were being built. An officer wrote that "many a good lad [had] nothing to cover him from his hips to his toes, save his blanket." To cap everything, the winter was one of the most bitterly cold in memory. Washington early warned Congress that the situation was desperate, and he sent letters in like vein to the governors of New York, New Jersey, Pennsylvania, Delaware, and Maryland.

Head Qurs. Morris Town 16th. Decr. 1779. The situation of the Army with respect to supplies is beyond description alarming. It has been five or Six weeks past on half allowance: and we have not more than three days bread at a third allowance on hand, nor any where within reach. When this is exhausted, we must depend on the precarious gleanings of the neighbouring country. Our Magazines are absolutely empty every where and our commisaries entirely destitute of Money or Credit to replenish them. We have never experienced a like extremity at any period of the War. We have often felt temporary want, from accidental delay in forwarding supplies; but we always had something in our Magazines and means of procuring more. Neither one nor the other is at present the case. This representation is the result of a minute examination of our resources. Unless some extraordinary and immediate exertions be made by the States, from which we draw our supplies, there is every appearance that the Army will infallibly disband in a fortnight. I think it my duty to lay this candid view of our situation before your Excellency and to entreat the vigorous interposition of the State to rescue us from the danger of an event, which if it did not prove the total ruin of our affairs, would at least give them a shock, from which they would not easily recover and plunge us into a train of new and still more perplexing embarrassments, than any we have hitherto felt.

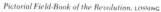

View of Stony Point

On the day before Christmas, Washington had to order that corn meant for horses be ground into meal for the men. On the second day of 1780, a violent and deadly two-day blizzard began, piling drifts as high as six feet. Hungry soldiers took to raiding at night, pillaging farmers of food until Washington organized a system of requisitioning grain and

Washington was elected a member of the American Philosophical Society of Philadelphia in March of 1780.

cattle and paying for them in the Continental currency the farmers would not accept voluntarily. The measure helped for a while, but destitution lasted far into the spring—with serious consequences. Washington wrote to Governor Jonathan Trumbull of Connecticut about an incident involving troops from his state.

Head Qurs. Morris Town May 26th. 1780. It is with infinite pain I inform you, that we are reduced to a situation of extremity for want of meat. On several days of late the troops have been entirely destitute of any, and for a considerable time past they have been at best, at a half, a quarter, an Eighth allowance of this Essential Article of Provision. The Men have borne their distress with a firmness and patience never exceeded, and every possible praise is due the Officers for encouraging them to it, by precept, by exhortation, by example. But there are certain bounds beyond which it is impossible for human Nature to go. We are arrived at these. The want of provision last night produced a Mutiny in the Army of a very alarming kind. Two Regiments of the Connecticut line got under Arms and but for the timely notice and exertions of their Officers, it is most likely it would have been the case with the whole, with a determination to return home. After a long expostulation by their Officers and some of the Pennsylvania line who had come to their assistance they were prevailed on to go into their Huts. But this without relief can only be momentary. I will not dwell longer upon this melancholy subject, being fully convinced that Your Excellency will hasten to us every possible relief in your power.

The Connecticut soldiers who mutinied had had no meat in ten days; neither they nor any other troops had been paid for five months. The Army was melting away, with state governments doing little about replacement recruiting. One bright spot for Washington was the return in May, 1780, of Lafayette from a year-and-a-half furlough in France. The young marquis, whose relationship with Washington had become almost that of father and son, brought the inspiriting news that six French men-of-war and six thousand troops were on their way to America. Then, to counter these good tidings came the grim word from South Carolina that on May 12 Charleston had fallen to General Clinton, with fifty-five hundred prisoners taken, the worst American defeat of the war. The day after having learned of the loss of Charleston, Washington wrote to Joseph Jones, delegate to Congress from Virginia, to express himself—as he would many times in coming years—on the need for the states to surrender some of their prerogatives to create a stronger Congress.

Morristown May 31st. 1780.

I have been honoured with your favour in answer to my Letter respecting the appointment of a Committee; and with two other of later date—the last containing General Woodford's account of the situation of things at Charlestown, at the time of his writing. I thank you for them all. Unhappily that place (Charles town) the Garrison in it, &c. (as appears by the New York account, which I have transmitted to Congress) have been in the hands of the Enemy since the 12th. Instant.

Certain I am, that unless Congress speaks in a more decisive tone; unless they are vested with powers by the several States, competent to the great purposes of War, or assume them as matter of right; and they, and the States respectively, act with more energy than they hitherto have done, that our cause is lost. We can no longer drudge on in the old way. By ill-timing the adoption of measures; by delays in the execution of them or by unwarrantable jealousies, we incur enormous expences, and derive no benefit from them. One State will comply with a requisition of Congress, another neglects to do it. A third executes it by halves, and all differ, either in the manner; the matter; or so much in point of time, that we are always working up Hill and ever shall (while such a System as the present one, or rather want of one prevails) be unable to apply our strength or resources to any advantage.

This, My Dear Sir, is plain language to a Member of Congress; but it is the language of Truth and friendship.

Detail of a map of the siege of Charleston from Stedman's history of the American Revolution, 1794

It is the result of long thinking, close application, and strict observation. I see one head gradually changing into thirteen. I see one Army branching into thirteen; and instead of its looking up to Congress, as the supreme controuling power of the United States, are considering themselves as dependent on their respective States. In a word, I see the powers of Congress declining too fast for the consequence and respect which is due to them as the Great representative Body of America, and am fearful of the consequences.

British General Clinton returned to New York from Charleston, leaving General Cornwallis to carry on the campaign in the South. Washington braced for action, but Clinton, after a bit of skirmishing in New Jersey, again settled down in New York City. Transports with a French army under the Comte de Rochambeau arrived at Newport, Rhode Island, but almost immediately were bottled up by a blockading British fleet. As for the American Army, by mid-August it had received only six thousand of the 16,500 recruits the states had been asked to supply. The states were equally remiss in providing supplies, so much so that the Army was forced to requisition its own food from the countryside; in a land heavy with a bountiful harvest the men were still hungry and half naked. Washington sent letters of implied warning to the governors of the New England and Middle Atlantic States.

Head Quarters near the liberty Pole Bergen County
27th. August 1780

A contemporary engraving caricatured Rochambeau reviewing French troops.

The Honorable the Committee of cooperation having returned to Congress, I am under the disagreeable necessity of informing Your Excellency, that the army is again reduced to an extremity of distress for want of Provision. The greater part of it had been without meat from the 21st. to the 26th. To endeavour to obtain some relief, I moved down to this place, with a view of stripping the lower parts of the Country of its Cattle, which, after a most rigorous exaction, is found to afford between two and three days supply only, and those consisting of milch cows and calves of one or two years old. When this scanty pittance is consumed, I know not what will be our next resource, as the Commissary can give me no certain information of more than 120 head of Cattle expected from Pennsylvania, and about 150 from Massachusetts. I mean in time to supply our immediate wants.

Pictorial Field-Book of the Revolution, LOSSING

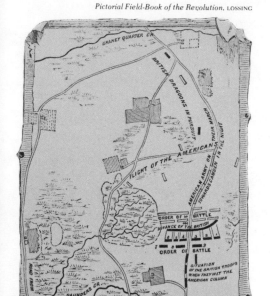

Plan of the battle fought near the town of Camden, S.C., August, 1780

Military coercion is no longer of any avail, as nothing further can possibly be collected from the Country in which we are obliged to take a position, without depriving the Inhabitants of the last morsel. This mode of subsisting, supposing the desired end could be answered by it, besides being in the highest degree distressing to individuals, is attended with ruin to the morals and discipline of the Army. During the few days which we have been obliged to send out small parties to procure Provisions for themselves, the most enormous excesses have been committed.

It has been no inconsiderable support of our cause, to have had it in our power to contrast the conduct of our army with that of the Enemy, and to convince the Inhabitants that while their rights were wantonly violated by the British Troops, by ours they were respected. This distinction must unhappily now cease, and we must assume the odious character of the plunderers, instead of the protectors of the People, the direct consequence of which must be to alienate their minds from the army, and insensibly from the cause.

We have not yet been absolutely without flour, but we have *this* day but *one* days supply in Camp, and I am not certain that there is a single barrel between this and Trenton. I shall be obliged therefore to draw down one or two hundred barrels, from a small Magazine which I had endeavoured to establish at West Point, for the security of the Garrison in case of a sudden investiture.

From the above state of facts, it may be foreseen that this army cannot possibly remain much longer together, unless very vigorous and immediate measures are taken by the States to comply with the requisitions made upon them. The Commissary General has neither the means nor the power of procuring supplies. He is only to receive them from the several Agents. Without a speedy change of circumstances, this dilemma must be involved; either the Army must disband, or what is, if possible, worse, subsist upon the plunder of the People.

I would fain flatter myself that a knowledge of our situation will produce the desired relief—not a relief of a few days, as has generally heretofore been the case, but a supply equal to the establishment of magazines for the Winter. If these are not formed, before the Roads are broken up by the Weather, we shall certainly experience the same difficulties and distresses the ensuing Winter, which we did the last. Altho' the Troops have upon every occasion hitherto, borne their wants with unparalled patience, it will be dangerous to trust too often to a repetition of the causes of discontent.

There was more bad news from the South, where General Horatio Gates, sent to recoup American fortunes, had been so badly defeated at Camden, South Carolina, that he did not stop retreating for 180 miles. In September, Washington went to Hartford, Connecticut, to meet General Rochambeau and discuss future joint strategy. On his return he stopped at West Point to inspect the vital Hudson River fortress and to pay a call on his friend General Benedict Arnold. He arrived at the Beverly Robinson house across the river from West Point, where Arnold made his headquarters, to find a puzzling situation that grew ominous as the day progressed. He summarized it for Congress the next day.

Robinsons House in the Highlands
Septr. 26th. 1780.

I have the honour to inform Congress, that I arrived here yesterday about 12 O'Clock on my return from Hartford. Some hours previous to my arrival, Major General Arnold went from his quarters which were at this place and as it was supposed, over the River to the Garrison at West point, whither I proceeded myself in order to visit the Post. I found General Arnold had not been there during the day, and on my return to His Quarters he was still absent. In the mean time a packet had arrived from Lieut. Colo. Jamison announcing the capture of a John Anderson who was endeavouring to go to New York, with the several interesting and important papers, mentioned below, all in the hand writing of General Arnold. This was also accompanied with a letter from the Prisoner, avowing himself to be Major John Andre Adjutant General of the British Army relating the manner of his capture and endeavouring to shew that he did not come under the description of a Spy. From these several circumstances and information that the General seemed to be thrown into some degree of agitation, on receiving a letter a little time before he went from his Quarters, I was led to conclude immediately that he had heard of Major Andre's captivity and that he would, if possible, escape to the Enemy and

The War of Independence, LOSSING

The Beverly Robinson house, in which General Arnold had his headquarters

An engraving of West Point, as it appeared at the close of war, from the old New York Magazine

accordingly took such measures as appeared the most probable to apprehend him. But he had embarked in a barge and proceeded down the River under a flag to the Vulture Ship of War which lay some miles below Stony and Verplank's Points. He wrote me after he got on board, a letter of which the inclosed is a Copy. Major Andre is not arrived yet, but I hope he is secure and that he will be here to day. I have been and am taking proper precautions, which I trust will prove effectual, to prevent the important consequences which this conduct on the part of Genl. Arnold was intended to produce. I do not know the party that took Major Andre, but it is said it consisted only of a few Militia, who acted in such a manner upon the Occasion, as does them the highest honour and proves them to be Men of great Virtue. They were offered, I am informed, a large sum of Money for his release and as many Goods as they would demand, but without any effect.

Washington's inspection had revealed the West Point defenses to be woefully neglected and the garrison so disposed that it could have put up little effective resistance to an enemy attack. The reasons why one of Washington's most brilliant and dependable combat generals should have turned traitor are complex and even today are not entirely understood, but one contributory cause was that on three or four occasions in the past, promotions Arnold had abundantly earned had gone to lesser men because of the workings of state politics, leaving him deeply embittered. Arnold had escaped. Major André was not so fortunate. The decision of the court-martial in his case was inevitable.

The capture of Major André

GENERAL ORDERS

Head Quarters Orangetown
Sunday October 1st. 1780.

The Board of General officers appointed to examine into the Case of Major Andre have reported.

1st. "That he came on shore from the Vulture sloop of War in the night of the 21st. of September last on an interview with General Arnold in a private and secret manner."

2dly. "That he changed his dress within our Lines and under a feigned name and in a disguised habit passed our works at Stoney and Vere-Planks Points the Evening of the 22d. of September last at Tarrytown in a disguised habit being then on his way to New York;

and when taken he had in his possession several Papers which contain'd intelligence for the Enemy."

The Board having maturely considered these Facts do also report to his Excellency General Washington

"That Major Andre Adjutant General to the British Army ought to be considered as a spy from the Enemy and that agreeable to the Law and usage of nations it is their opinion he ought to suffer Death."

The Commander in Chief directs the execution of the above Sentence in the usual way this afternoon at five o'clock precisely.

André, young, handsome, chivalrous, was greatly disturbed that he was to be hanged like a criminal rather than shot like an officer and a gentleman. He pleaded with Washington to die before a firing squad, but he had been captured in civilian clothes, and the military code is rigid. His execution was delayed one day when General Clinton made a

A broadside printed in Providence, Rhode Island, after death of André

special appeal for his young adjutant; Washington offered to trade André for Arnold, but the deal was unacceptable, and André died on the gallows.

The Army went into winter quarters in December as usual, with Washington's headquarters at New Windsor near West Point, although units were spread from West Point to Morristown to ease the supply problem. Food and clothing scarcities were so severe that for the first time Washington made no attempt to hold troops through the winter but directed his officers to let men drift away as their enlistments expired in order to diminish the number of hungry mouths. Then early in January, 1781, occurred an event the Commander in Chief had been dreading. Among those to whom he later sent a report were the New England governors, in a circular letter.

Head Qurs. New Windsor 5th. Janry. 1781. It is with extreme anxiety and pain of mind, I find myself constrained to inform *your Excellency,* that the event I have long apprehended would be the consequence of the complicated distresses of the Army, has at length taken place. On the night of the 1st. instant, a mutiny was excited by the non Commissioned Officers and Privates of the Pennsylvania Line, which soon became so universal as to defy all opposition; in attempting to quell this tumult, in the first instance, some Officers were killed, others wounded, and the lives of several common Soldiers lost. Deaf to the arguments, entreaties & utmost efforts of *all their Officers* to stop them, they moved off from Morris Town the place of their cantonment, with their Arms, and Six pieces of Artillery. And from accounts just received by General Wayne's Aid de Camp, they were still in a body, on their March to Philadelphia to demand a redress of their grievances. At what point this defection will stop, or how extensive it may prove, God only knows; at present the troops at the important Posts in this vicinity remain quiet, not being acquainted with this unhappy and alarming affair, but how long they will remain so cannot be ascertained, as they labor under some of the pressing hardships with the troops who have revolted.

The aggravated Calamities and distresses that have resulted from the Total want of Pay for nearly twelve months, the want of Clothing at a severe Season, and not unfrequently the want of Provisions, are beyond description. The circumstances will now point out much more forcibly what ought to be done, than any thing that can possibly be said by me on the subject.

*Letter from Washington to Congress,
describing the mutiny of his troops*

The mutiny had been caused by resentment over food, pay, terms of enlistment, and bounties. These grievances led to action. Pennsylvania authorities negotiated with the mutineers, ending the rebellion, but at a cost of discharging more than half the twenty-four hundred men of the Pennsylvania division, men who swore that they had served more than three years (written records were sketchy). Inspired by the success of the Pennsylvanians as well as by their own misery, New Jersey troops mutinied on January 20, 1781. But Washington's attitude differed from that of the Pennsylvania authorities; his orders to Major General Robert Howe at West Point were unequivocal.

[West Point, January 22, 1781]

You are to take the command of the detachment, which

Cornwallis Retreating !

PHILADELPHIA, April 7, 1781.

Extract of a Letter from Major-General *Greene*, dated
CAMP, at *Buffelo Creek, March* 23, 1781.

"ON the 16th Inftant I wrote your Excellency, giving an Account of an Action which happened at Guilford Court-Houfe the Day before. I was then perfuaded that notwithftanding we were obliged to give up the Ground, we had reaped the Advantage of the Action. Circumftances fince confirm me in Opinion that the Enemy were too much gauled to improve their Succefs. We lay at the Iron-Works three Days, preparing ourfelves for another Action, and expecting the Enemy to advance: But of a fudden they took their Departure, leaving behind them evident Marks of Diftrefs. All our wounded at Guilford, which had fallen into their Hands, and 70 of their own, too bad to move, were left at New-Garden. Moft of their Officers fuffered—Lord Cornwallis had his Horfe fhot under him—Col. Steward, of the Guards was killed, General O Hara and Cols, Tarlton and Webfter, wounded. Only three Field-Officers efcaped, if Reports, which feem to be authentic, can be relied on.

Our Army are in good Spirits, notwithftanding our Sufferings, and are advancing towards the Enemy; they are retreating to Crofs-Creek.

In South-Carolina, Generals Sumpter and Marian have gained feveral little Advantages. In one the Enemy loft 60 Men, who had under their Care a large Quantity of Stores, which were taken, but by an unfortunate Miftake were afterwards re-taken.

Publifhed by Order,
CHARLES THOMSON, Secretary.

§†§ Printed at N. WILLIS's Office.

Broadside containing an extract of a letter from General Nathanael Greene, telling of enemy's retreat

has been ordered to march from this Post against the Mutineers of the Jersey line. You will rendezvous the whole of your command at Ringwood or Pomptons as you find best from circumstances. The object of your detachment is to compel the Mutineers to unconditional submission, and I am to desire you will grant no terms while they are with Arms in their hands in a state of resistance. The manner of executing this I leave to your discretion according to circumstances. If you succeed in compelling the revolted Troops to a surrender you will instantly execute a few of the most active and incendiary leaders.

You will endeavour to collect such of the Jersey Troops to your standards as have not followed the pernicious example of their associates, and you will also try to avail yourself of the services of the Militia, representing to them how dangerous to Civil Liberty the precedent is of Armed Soldiers dictating terms to their Country.

The mutinous troops were taken by surprise, two ringleaders summarily executed, their officers restored to command. Then Washington appointed a commission to look into their grievances.

More and more the South became the main arena of war. General Nathanael Greene, who had replaced the defeated Horatio Gates the previous December, reorganized his army and fought so skillfully, though outnumbered and unable to win a decisive battle, that he forced the British out of all Georgia and the Carolinas, except the seaport towns of Savannah and Charleston. Meanwhile, Washington wanted to strike at New York; the French General Rochambeau, at Cornwallis's army in Virginia. The decision was taken out of Washington's hands when word came that the French Admiral the Comte de Grasse would bring his West Indies fleet into Chesapeake Bay in August and be available to help in a Virginia campaign but would not venture north to New York. The overland movement of the allied armies was carefully designed to leave Clinton in the dark as to its objective until the last moment; not till they were on their way did Washington even inform Congress.

Head Quarters Chatham 27th. Augst. 1781
I have the Honor to inform Congress, that my Expectation of the Arrival of the Fleet of Monsr. De Grasse, in the Chesapeak Bay—with some other Circumstances, of which Congress were informed in my Letter of the 2d. of Augt. & in which very little Alterations have since taken place—have induced me to make an Alteration

in the concerted Operations of this Campaign. I am now on my March with a very considerable Detachment of the American Army and the whole of the French Troops, for Virginia.

As I expect a few Days will bring me to Philadelphia, I shall then have the Honor to open my Motives & Intentions to Congress, more fully than it may be prudent to do by Letter at this Distance.

Washington wrote ahead to Lafayette, who commanded a small force harassing Cornwallis at Yorktown, Virginia, telling him to hold fast. More notable than what he said was the location from which he wrote.

French view of de Grasse's fleet

Mount Vernon Septr. 10th. 1781.
We are thus far, My Dear Marquis, on our way to you. The Count De Rochambeau has just arrived: General Chattelus will be here and we propose (after resting tomorrow) to be at Fredericksburg on the Night of the 12th.: The 13th. we shall reach New Castle, and the next Day we expect the pleasure of seeing you at your Encampment.

Should there be any danger as we approach you, I shall be obliged if you will send a party of Horse towards New Kent Court House to meet us. With great personal regd etc.

P.S. I hope you will keep Lord Cornwallis safe, without Provisions or Forage untill we arrive. Adieu.

Washington spent three days at Mount Vernon, the first since he had become Commander in Chief six years earlier. He met his three stepgranddaughters and an infant stepgrandson for the first time. And his stepson, Jack Custis, announced that he had decided to serve his country by joining Washington's staff. Cornwallis had taken his army to Yorktown on Chesapeake Bay, expecting support by a British fleet. Instead, de Grasse's fleet arrived at the end of August, established a blockade, and landed troops to join Lafayette's small force. On September 28 Washington and Rochambeau marched in with the allied armies and began the siege of Yorktown. Two days later, as Washington wrote to George Weedon, a Brigadier General, Cornwallis's lines were already being forced in.

Camp before York 30th. Septr. 1781.
I have just received your favor of Yesterday. Last Night the Enemy evacuated their exterior Works, and have left

205

A French engraving of "Le General Washington" has an inset view of the "Journée mémorable" of surrender. Opposite: a battle plan drawn in 1781 by a New York artilleryman

us in full possession of Pigeon Quarter, and some other work which they had occupied, contracting their defence near the Town. The circumstance has created a jealousy in some Minds similar to yours, that Lord Cornwallis may throw himself with his Troops upon the Gloucester side [the town of Gloucester was across the James River from Yorktown], and endeavour, by a rapid movement, to attempt an Escape: I can hardly persuade myself that he will make such a push: He ought to be watched however on every point. You will therefore pay the utmost attention to all their movements approaching as near as you can with safety and prudence so as not to hazard too much. In case any intention of an escape should be discovered, you will give me the most instantaneous information, and at the same time give immediate Notice to the Inhabitants to remove from their probable Route all the Cattle and Horses that can be of use to them; and at the same time give every impediment to their march that you possibly can, that I may have time to throw my Army in their Front.

I am this Day informed that some Troops are crossing to Glosesster; whether these are to replace a Corps of Germans which are said to have come from that side Yesterday, or for some other purpose I cannot say. Three Boats with Men I saw cross myself.

From then on, Washington's reports to Congress were always of constricting lines drawing closer to Yorktown, of siege guns battering Cornwallis's defenses. At last he received from the British commander a message he had awaited for years; it asked for a twenty-four-hour cessation of hostilities. His reply was terse.

Camp before York 17. Octr. 1781.
I have had the honour of receiving your Lordships letter of this date.

An ardent desire to spare the further effusion of Blood, will readily incline me to listen to such terms for the surrender of your Posts of York & Gloucester, as are admissible.

I wish previously to the meeting of Commissioners that your Lordships proposals in writing, may be sent to the American Lines, for which purpose a suspension of hostilities during two hours, from the Delivery of this letter will be granted.

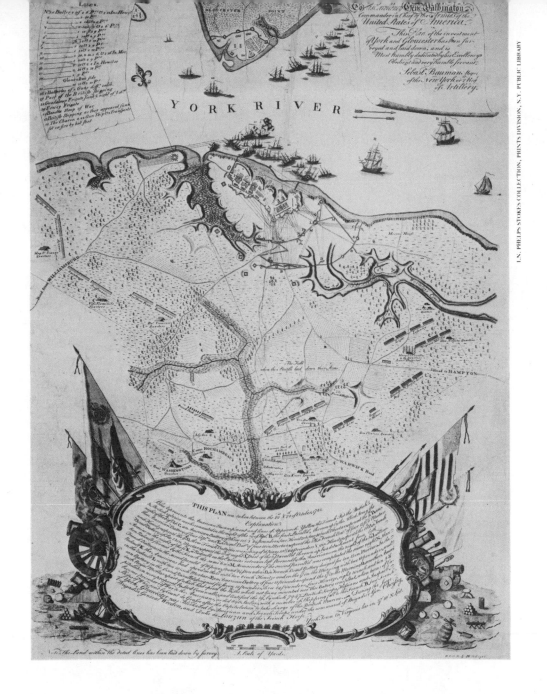

The surrender terms were worked out, the capitulation was signed on October 19, 1781, and the next day the British army, almost eight thousand strong, marched out between the ranked allied armies to give up their arms, with the immaculately uniformed French on one side and the ragged Continentals on the other. Cornwallis, bitter with humiliation, did not appear at the ceremony but sent his second in command. As for Washington, now that a magnificent victory was his, he found himself with surprisingly little to say in his report to Congress.

Head Quarters near York 19th. Octr. 1781.

I have the Honor to inform Congress, that a Reduction

of the British Army under the Command of Lord Cornwallis, is most happily effected. The unremitting Ardor which actuated every Officer & Soldier in the combined Army on this Occasion, has principally led to this Important Event, at an earlier period than my most sanguine Hopes had induced me to expect.

The singular Spirit of Emulation, which animated the whole Army from the first Commencement of our Operations, has filled my Mind with the highest pleasure & Satisfaction—and had given me the happiest presages of Success.

On the 17th. instant, a Letter was received from Lord Cornwallis, proposing a Meeting of Commissioners, to consult on Terms for the Surrender of the Posts of York & Gloucester. This Letter (the first which had passed between us) opened a Correspondence, a Copy of which I do myself the Honor to inclose; that Correspondence was followed by the Definitive Capitulation, which was agreed to, & Signed on the 19th. Copy of which is also herewith transmitted—and which I hope, will meet the Approbation of Congress.

On October 24 General Clinton arrived off Chesapeake Bay with a relieving army of seven thousand but put back to New York when he found he was too late to help Cornwallis. De Grasse and the French fleet prepared to return to the West Indies, while the French army planned to go into winter quarters in Virginia. But Washington made ready to return north; the war was not over as long as Clinton and the main British army remained in New York.

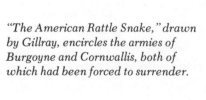

"The American Rattle Snake," drawn by Gillray, encircles the armies of Burgoyne and Cornwallis, both of which had been forced to surrender.

Chapter 7

"I Resign with Satisfaction"

When the British marched out of Yorktown to give up their arms, their band played in dirge time a popular song of the day, "The World Turned Upside-down." If the song expressed something of the astonishment and humiliation of the King's troops at surrendering to the ragged rebel forces, it also said something for the emotions in the hearts of the American troops, who were probably hard-put to realize that the scene was actually taking place, after all the years of defeat and privation and false hopes. That only the help of a French army and fleet had made the victory possible diminished their satisfaction very little. Washington had scant time to pause and savor his victory. The Army had to be established near the main British force in New York again. And he had a myriad of duties to attend to before he could leave Yorktown. Troops had to be sent south to reinforce Nathanael Greene in South Carolina. Care had to be provided for enemy sick and wounded. Arrangements had to be made either to use or store matériel captured from the enemy. The list went on and on — and only so much could be left to subordinates. Affairs were enough in hand to let Washington depart on November 5, 1781. But the next day he was sending a message to his secretary, Jonathan Trumbull, Jr., explaining that he had been tragically delayed and asking Trumbull to send the rest of Washington's staff on to Mount Vernon.

> Eltham [Virginia], November 6, 1781
> I came here in time to see Mr. Custis breathe his last. About Eight o'clock yesterday Evening he expired. The deep and solemn distress of the Mother, and affliction of the Wife of this amiable young Man, requires every comfort in my power to afford them; the last rights of the deceased I must also see performed; these will take me three or four days; when I shall proceed with Mrs. Washington and Mrs. Custis to Mount Vernon.

As the dirty tavern you are now at cannot be very comfortable; and in spite of Mr. Sterne's [novelist Laurence Sterne] observation the House of Mourning not very agreeable; it is my wish, that all of the Gentn. of my family, except yourself, who I beg may come here and remain with me; may proceed on at their leizure to Mount Vernon, and wait for me there. Colo. Cobb will join you on the road at the Tavern we breakfasted at (this side Ruffens).

John Parke Custis had joined his stepfather in Yorktown and had served briefly as a civilian aide. His belated gesture cost him his life; he had contracted "camp fever"—probably typhus—and had gone to Eltham, the home of his uncle Burwell Bassett, some thirty miles from Yorktown. His wife, mother, and oldest daughter, only five, had been summoned; Washington had arrived only hours before he died. After the funeral and other melancholy duties had been taken care of, Washington went on to Mount Vernon. He had looked forward to a few days of quiet at home, but Jack's death had cast a pall over the household, and with two grieving women about, he was probably happy to have his staff with him to keep him busy. One letter, with some observations on the future of the war, went to the Marquis de Lafayette, who was about to leave America and return to his home in France.

> Mount Vernon Virga. Novr. 15th. 1781.
> Not 'till the 5th. My dear Marquis, was I able to leave York; providing for the detachment that was to go Southerly; Embarking the Troops that were to go Northerly; making a distribution of the Ordnance and Stores for various purposes; and disposing of the Officers and other Prisoners to their respective places of destination would not admit of my leaving that part of the Country sooner. . . .
>
> As you expressed a desire to know, My sentiments respecting the operations of next Campaign before your departure for France, I will without a tedious display of reasoning, declare in one Word, that the advantages of it to America and the honour and Glory of it to the allied Arms in these States, must depend *absolutely* upon the Naval force which is employed in these Seas, and the time of its appearance, next year. No Land force can act decisively, unless it is accompanied by a Maritime superiority; nor can more than negative advantages be expected without it; For proof of this, we have only to

Life of George Washington, HEADLEY

A highly romantic rendering of the death in 1781 of John Parke Custis

recur to the instances of the ease and facility with which the British shifted their Ground, as advantages were to be obtained at either extremity of the Continent, and to their late heavy loss the moment they failed in their naval superiority. To point out the further advantages which might have been obtained in the course of this Year if Count de Grasse could have waited and would have covered a further operation to the Southward, is unnecessary; because a doubt did not, nor does at this moment remain upon any Mans mind of the total extirpation of the British force in the Carolina's and Georgia, if he could have extended his co-operation two Months longer.

It follows then as certain as that Night succeeds the day, that without a decisive Naval force we can do nothing definitive; and with it every thing honourable and glorious. A constant naval superiority would terminate the War speedily; without it, I do not know that it will ever be terminated honourably. If this force should appear early, we shall have the whole Campaign before us. The Months of June to September inclusive, are well adapted for operating in any of the States to the Northward of this; and the remaining Months are equally well suited to those South of it; In which time with such means, I think much, I will add, every thing, might be expected.

How far the policy of Congress may carry them, towards filling their Continental Battalions does not lay with me to determine. This measure (before and since the capitulation) has been strongly recommended [to] me. Should it be adopted by that Body, and executed with energy in the several States, I think our force (comprehending the Auxiliary Troops now here) will be fully competent to all the purposes of the American War, provided the British force on this Continent remains nearly as it now is; but as this is a contingency which depends very much upon political manoeuvres in Europe, and as it is uncertain how far *we* may be in a State of preparation at the opening of the next Campaign, the propriety of augmenting the present Army under the command of Count de Rochambeau is a question worthy of consideration, but as it lies with Congress to determine, I shall be silent on the subject.

If I should be deprived of the pleasure of a personal

interview with you, before your departure, permit me, my dear Marquis, to adopt this method of making you a tender of my ardent Vows for a propitious Voyage, a gracious reception from your Prince, an honourable reward for your services, a happy meeting with your Lady and friends and a safe return in the Spring to My Dear Marquis. . . .

His victory had made Washington a hero; even many who had once called him incompetent joined in the paeans. While he was at Mount Vernon he was already finding himself busy replying to eulogistic letters from Congress and other well-wishers. To his neighbors at Alexandria, Virginia, went a letter of thanks that differed from most only in being a bit more personal.

[Mount Vernon] November 20th. 1781.
I accept with peculiar satisfaction the very kind and affectionate address of the citizens of Alexandria, the long acquaintance which in former times I have had of their Sincerity and cordiality, stamps it with particular Value, and permit me to say, that to make a peaceful return to this agreeable Society of my Fellow Citizens, is among the most ardent of my Wishes, and would prove my greatest comfort for all the toils and Vicissitudes which I have experienced during my absence.

The great director of events has carried us through a variety of Scenes, during this long and bloody Contest, in which we have been for Seven Campaigns most nobly struling. The present prospect is pleasing. The late success at York Town is very promising, but on our own improvement depend its future good consequences. A vigorous prosecution of this success, will, in all probability procure us what we have so long wished to secure, an establishment of peace, Liberty and Independence. A Relaxation of our exertions at this moment may cost us many more toilsome Campaigns, and be attended with the most unhappy consequences.

Your condolence for the loss of that amiable youth Mr. Custis, affects me most tenderly; [his] loss, I trust, will be compensated to you, in some other Worthy representative.

Amidst all the Vicissitudes of time or fortune, be assured Gentlemen, that I shall ever regard with particular affection the Citizens and Inhabitants of Alexandria.

Companion likenesses of Martha and George Washington drawn in 1782 are among earliest engraved portraits.

On November 20 George and Martha Washington left Mount Vernon. The next day they were in Annapolis, where for two days Washington was wined and dined and addressed by the mayor, the governor and legislature of Maryland, and groups of citizens. Then they proceeded to Philadelphia and more acclaim. Even at the theater Washington sat through laudatory prologues in painful embarrassment. While the Army went into winter quarters again, at Newburgh on the Hudson, Washington remained in Philadelphia, for Congress had many things to discuss with him about the future of the war. Most of the problems involved recruiting men or raising money. In March of 1781 the thirteen states had at last united formally under the Articles of Confederation. The union was a weak one; Congress, its only executive body, could make war but could obtain the necessary men and money only by asking the states for them—with no power to compel any state to comply. The Commander in Chief sent a circular letter to the chief executives of all thirteen states.

Philadelphia 22 Janry. 1782.

Although it may be somewhat out of my province, to address your Excellency on a subject not immediately of a Military nature, yet I consider it so nearly connected with and so essential to the operations under my direction, that I flatter myself my interference will not be deemed impertinent.

Upon applying to the Supcrintendant of Finance to know how far I might depend upon him for the Pay, feeding and Clothing of the Army for the current year, and for the Sums necessary to put it and keep it in motion, he very candidly laid open to me the State of our Monied affairs, and convinced me, that although the assistances we had derived from abroad were considerable, yet they would be by no means adequate to our expences. He informed me further: that to make up the deficiency, the States had been called upon by Congress, for eight Million of Dollars for the service of the Year 1782, and shewed me the copy of a Circular letter from himself to the several Legislatures, in which he had so fully and clearly pointed out the necessity of a compliance with the requisition, that it is needless for me to say more on that head, than that I Intirely concur with him in opinion, so far as he has gone into the matter. But there are other reasons which could not be so well known to him as they are to me, as having come under my immediate observation and which therefore I shall take the liberty to mention.

Your Excellency cannot but remember the ferment

Engraved after drawings by Benjamin Blyth, these hand-colored portraits were published by J. Coles in Boston.

into which the whole Army was thrown twelve Months ago, for the want of pay and a regular supply of Clothing and Provisions: and with how much difficulty they were brought into temper, by a partial supply of the two first, and a promise of more regular supplies of all in future. Those promises the Soldiery now begin to claim and although we shall be able to satisfy them tolerably in respect to Clothing, and perfectly in regard to Provision (if the Financier is enabled to comply with his Contracts) yet there is no prospect of obtaining pay, until part of the money required of the States can be brought into the public Treasury. You cannot conceive the uneasiness which arises from the total want of so essential an Article as Money, and the real difficulties in which the officers in particular are involved on that account. The favourable aspect of our affairs, and the hopes that matters are in a train to afford them relief contributes to keep them quiet but I cannot answer for the effects of a disappointment. . . .

To bring this War to a speedy and happy conclusion, must be the fervent wish of every lover of his Country; & sure I am, that no means are so likely to effect these as vigorous preparations for another Campaign. Whether then we consult our true interest, Substantial oeconomy, or sound policy, we shall find that relaxation and langour are of all things to be avoided. Conduct of that kind on our part will produce fresh hopes and new exertions on that of the Enemy; whereby the War, which has already held beyond the general expectation, may be protracted to such a length, that the people groaning under the burthen of it and despairing of success, may think any change, a change for the better.

I will close with a request, that your Excelly. will be good enough to take the first opportunity of laying these my sentiments before the Legislature of your State. From the attention they have [ever] been pleased to pay to any former requisitions or representations of mine, I am encouraged to hope that the present, which is equally important with any I have ever made, will meet with a favourable reception.

A detail from a cartoon of 1782, "The Horrors of War," shows America with a dagger in her breast begging an indifferent England to "forego this bloody warfare."

As spring neared, Washington expected a resurgence of enemy military activity and was increasingly concerned about the failure of the states to prepare for that time. One of those to whom he expressed his concern was James McHenry, aide to Lafayette until three months earlier, when he had resigned to serve in the Maryland legislature.

Philadelphia March 12th. 1782.

Never, since the commencement of the present revolution, has there been, in my judgment, a period when vigorous measures were more consonant with sound policy than the present. The Speech of the British King and the Addresses of the Lords and Commons are evincive proofs to my Mind of two things, namely their wishes to prosecute the American War, and their fears of the consequences. My Opinion, therefore, of the matter is, that the Minister will obtain supplies for the current Year, prepare vigorously for another Campaign, and then prosecute the War or treat of Peace as circumstances and fortuitous events may justify; and that nothing will contribute more to the first, than a relaxation, or apparent supineness on the part of these States. The debates upon the addresses evidently prove what I have here advanced to be true. For these addresses, as explained, are meant to answer any purpose the Ministers may have in view. What madness then can be greater, or policy and oeconomy worse, than to let the Enemy again rise upon our folly and want of exertion? Shall we not be justly chargeable for all the Blood and Treasure which shall be wasted in a lingering War, procrastinated by the false expectation of Peace, or timid measures for the prosecution of it? Surely we shall, and much is to be lamented that our endeavours do not at all times accord with our wishes; each State is anxious to see the end of our Warfare accomplished, but shrinks when it is called upon for the means: and either withholds them altogether, or grants them in such [a] way as to defeat the End. Such, it is to be feared, will be the case in many instances respecting the requisitions of Men and Money.

I have the pleasure, however, to inform you, that the Assembly of this State [Pennsylvania], now setting, have passed their supply Bill without a dissenting voice, and that a laudable spirit seems to pervade all the members of that Body; but I fear notwithstanding, they will be deficient of their Quota of Men. It is idle, at this late period of the War, when enthusiasm is cooled, if not done away; when the Minds of that class of Men who are

Another 1782 cartoon shows the reconciliation between America and her "Dear Mama," Britannia.

proper subjects for Soldiers, are poisoned by the high Bounties which have been given; and the knowledge of the distresses of the Army so generally diffused through every State; to suppose that our Battalions can be compleated by voluntary enlistment; the attempt is vain and we are only deceiving ourselves and injuring the cause by making the experiment. There is no other *effectual* method to get Men suddenly, but that of classing the People, and compelling each Class to furnish a Recruit. Here every Man is interested; every Man becomes a recruiting Officer. If our necessities for Men did not press, I should prefer the mode of voluntary Inlistment to all others to obtain them; as it does, I am sure it will not answer, and that the Season for enterprise will be upon us long ere we are ready for the Field.

The anxious state of suspense in which we have been for some time, and still remain, respecting the Naval engagement in the West Indies and attempt upon Brimstone Hill in the Island of St. Kitts, is disagreeable beyond description. The issue of these must be very interesting and may give a very unfavourable turn to affairs in that Quarter, and to America in its consequences.

Only six days after Washington had given McHenry such a categorical statement of the aggressive plans of the British Crown, he had obtained fresher news that made him modify his views of enemy intentions and caused him to write in a different vein to Nathanael Greene, the talented commander of American forces in the South.

Philadelphia 18th. March 1782.
It gives me the more pain to hear of your distresses for want of Clothing or other necessaries, as you are at so great a distance that you cannot be suddenly relieved, even if we had the means. I am not however without hopes, that should the War be continued to the Southward (of which I have my doubts, for reasons which I shall presently give) matters will be put into much better train than they have hitherto been. The arrangements made already by the Superintendant of Finance have been attended with infinite public advantages, and he is extending those arrangements as fast as circumstances will possibly admit....

By late advices from Europe and from the declara-

Lord North as caricatured by Sayers

tions of the British Ministers themselves, it appears, that they have done with all thoughts of an excursive War, and that they mean to send small if any further reinforcements to America. It may be also tolerably plainly seen, that they do not mean to hold all their present Posts, and that New York will be occupied in preference to any other. Hence, and from other indications, I am induced to believe that an evacuation of the Southern States will take place. Should this happen, we must concentre our force as the Enemy do theirs: You will therefore, upon the appearance of such an event, immediately make preparations for the march of the army under your command to the northward. What Troops shall in that case be left in the Southern States will be a matter of future discussion.

The information that Washington sent to Greene was accurate. The British had had their fill of the fight to subdue the Colonies. On February 27, 1782, the House of Commons voted against carrying on the war in America and a few days later authorized the Government to negotiate a peace settlement. On March 20 came the resignation of Lord North, Prime Minister since 1770, whose coercive acts had driven the Colonies into revolt. He was replaced by Lord Rockingham, who had long advocated American independence. There was a shake-up in the military, too; Sir Guy Carleton, long-time commander in Canada, replaced Sir Henry Clinton as British Commander in Chief in America and arrived in New York on May 5. In spite of these changes, Washington remained very skeptical of British intentions, as he told Governor George Clinton.

[Newburgh] May 7th. 1782.

It seems we are coming to a period, when we are exceedingly in danger of being imposed upon by the Insiduous measures of our Enemy. You have doubtless seen the Intelligence from New York and the Debates in Parliament upon the American War, which the Country it seems are catching at as a prelude to a speedy peace, upon principles of Independence. I will only mention to your Excellency that I have perused the several motions which have been made and the Debates thereon with great attention, and upon serious consideration am obliged to say, that the whole appears to me merely delusory, calculated to quiet the Minds of their own people, & to lull the exertions of ours, and that finding themselves hard pushed in other quarters, they want to amuse us in America, whilst they attend to other parts of their Empire; which being secured, they will have time and means to revert to this continent again, with hopes of success.

An idea of American Independence, on its true principles, dont appear thro' the whole debates; but an idea of reconnecting us to the British Nation, by dissolving our connexion with France, is too prevalent.

Washington's mistrust in no way lessened when on May 9 he received from General Carleton a letter saying that Carleton and Admiral Robert Digby, the British naval commander, were joined "in the commission of peace." Washington continued to denounce accounts from England as an "opiate to increase that stupor into which we have fallen." While most Americans relaxed at the prospect of peace, he worked out a comprehensive and grandiose strategy for winning the war with attacks on Canada, New York, Charleston, Savannah, and perhaps even Bermuda. But the Army did not march, and Washington had other problems.

GENERAL ORDERS

Head Quarters Newburgh Thursday 16 May 82
Parole. Signs.

The General is extremely concerned to learn that an Article so salutary as that of distilled Liquors was expected to be when properly used, and which was designed for the comfort and refreshment of the troops has been in many instances productive of very ill consequences. He calls the attention of officers of every grade to remedy these abuses and to watch over the health of their men, for which purpose he suggests the expedient of keeping liquor Rolls in every Corps, from which the Name of every soldier shall be struck off who addicts himself to drunkenness or injures his Constitution by intemperence. Such soldiers as are Struck off are not to draw liquor on any occasion, but are to receive other articles in lieu thereof. The Quarter Masters upon receiving such commuted Articles are to receipt for the ful amount of the rations included in the returns: that there may be no irregularity in the Accounts.

On May 22 Washington received from Colonel Lewis Nicola, a respected officer, a long letter in which Nicola discussed the sad situation of the unpaid Army, blamed the situation on the inefficiency of

Congress and of republican government in general, and proposed the solution: make Washington a king. Possibly some other designation might be wise, Nicola conceded, because "some people have so connected the ideas of tyranny and monarchy as to find it very difficult to seperate them." Washington replied at once.

Newburgh May 22d. 1782.

With a mixture of great surprise and astonishment, I have read with attention the sentiments you have submitted to my perusal. Be assured, Sir, no occurrence in the course of the War, has given me more painful sensations than your information of there being such Ideas existing in the Army as you have expressed, and I must view with abhorrence and reprehend with severity. For the present the communication of them will rest in my own bosom, unless some further agitation of the matter, shall make a disclosure necessary.

I am much at a loss to conceive, what part of my conduct, could have given encouragement to an address, which to me seems big with the greatest mischiefs that can befall my Country. If I am not deceived in the knowledge of myself, you could not have found a person to whom your schemes are more disagreeable: At the same time, in justice to my own feelings, I must add, that no Man possesses a more sincere wish to see ample justice done to the Army than I do, and as far as my powers and influence, in a constitutional way, extend, they shall be employed to the utmost of my abilities to effect it, should there be any occasion. Let me conjure you then, if you have any regard for your Country; concern for yourself, or posterity, or respect for me, to banish these thoughts from your Mind, and never communicate, as from yourself, or any one else, a sentiment of the like Nature.

The War of Independence, LOSSING

Washington's headquarters, Newburgh, New York

Washington might reprove Nicola, but this would not stop the talk. More and more officers and men would become convinced during the days ahead that only by retaining their weapons when peace came, and brandishing them if necessary, would they obtain the months of back pay owing to them. Washington would meet the problem again. As for the prospects for peace, Washington continued skeptical. His attitude toward British peace proposals is well typified by the way he let them pass with only a perfunctory mention in a letter to the Comte de Rochambeau, still with the French army in Virginia.

Head Quarters 28th. May 1782.
Since the information I conveyed to your Excellency by the Baron Closen, the amusement of Peace, held out by our Enemies, has been much augmented by the arrival of Sir Guy Carleton in New York, who announces himself as Commander in Chief in America, with powers of conciliation to these States. These Ideas, pleasing as their first prospect might have been, are now, I believe, beginning to be generally viewed in their proper Colours; as merely delusory and vain, and I hope will not be attended with such consequences as the Enemy seem to flatter themselves with.

The Alliance Frigate you will hear is safe arrived in New London. A Cutter also from France in 25 Days passage, is in at Salem. Her dispatches are gone to Congress You will probably know their contents as early as I shall.

Our accounts of the action in the West Indies between the two Fleets remain very uncertain and vague. From repeated publications in New York, compared with those I collected from other parts, I confess, I form too many reasons to fear, that the matter has not passed so favorably to our friend the Count de Grasse as you seem to imagine A little time will disclose the whole to us; and I sincerely hope it may dispel my apprehensions.

The action between French and British fleets to which Washington had referred had gone badly for the French. It was a new reason for foreboding; Washington was certain that a victorious Britain would lose interest in peace. Meanwhile, the Army had little to do, and Washington filled the void, as commanders always have, with drill and spit and polish.

GENERAL ORDERS

Head Quarters Newburgh Saturday June 8. 82
The General was highly pleased with the appearance of the first Massachusetts Brigade yesterday under Arms, and was very well satisfied with their Manoeuvering: the firing might have been better, and he fears the Locks or flints of the Musketts were in bad order, as many of them missed fire. The Officers commanding the Light Infantry should impress upon the men the necessity of taking deliberate Aim whenever they fire and see that they do it when it is in their power. It is the effect of the shot not the report of the Gun that can discomfit the Enemy and

if a bad habit is acquired at exercise it will prevail in real Action and so vice versa.

Although Washington continued to argue that the enemy's talk of peace was designed only to throw Americans off guard, the evidences of an approaching end to hostilities seemed very real. Benjamin Franklin had begun talks with the British in Paris in April. On July 11 the British evacuated Savannah. But when Lord Rockingham died after only a few months as British Prime Minister, Washington predicted to James McHenry that a new ministry would discard Rockingham's peace policy.

Verplanks point Septr. 12th. 1782. Our prospects of Peace is vanishing. The Death of the Marquis of Rockingham, has given a shock to the New Administration, and disordered its whole System. Fox, Burke, Lord John Cavendish, Lord Keppel (and I believe others) have left it; Earl Shelburne takes the lead, as first Lord of the Treasury; to which Office he was appointed by the King, the moment the vacancy happened, by the death of Lord Rockingham. This Nobleman declares, that the Sun of Great Britain will set the moment American Independency is acknowledged, and that no Man has ever heard him give an assent to the measure. The Duke of Richmond, on the other hand, asserts, that the Ministry, of which Lord Shelburne is one, came into Office upon the express condition and pledged to each other, that America should be declared Independent, that he will watch him and the moment he finds him departing therefrom, he will quit Administration, and give it every opposition in his power. That the King will push the War, as long as the Nation will find Men or Money, admits not of a doubt in my Mind. The whole tenor of his conduct, as well as his last proroguing Speech on the 11th. of July, plainly indicate it; and shews, in a clear point of view, the impolicy of relaxation on our parts. If we are wise, let us prepare for the worst; there is nothing which will so soon produce a speedy and honourable Peace as a state of preparation for War, and we must either do this, or lay our account to patch up an inglorious Peace after all the Toil, Blood, and Treasure we have spent. This has been my uniform Opinion. A Doctrine I have endeavoured, amidst the torrent of expectation of an approaching Peace, to inculcate; and what I am sure the event will justify me in.

The Marquis of Rockingham

Despite Washington's pessimism, there was no discernible change in British policy. Washington had moved his army to Verplanck's Point on the Hudson, so that French and American armies might camp near each other, ready to cooperate if the British should act. The French, moving up from Virginia, arrived in mid-September. It was an occasion for many reunions of old Yorktown comrades, but American officers were at a great disadvantage in the mutual entertaining that went on—as Washington complained to the Secretary at War in detailing the discontents and grievances eating into the hearts of officers and men.

Head Quarters, [Verplanck's Point]
Octr. 2nd. 1782.

My dear Sir:

Painful as the task is, to describe the dark side of our Affairs, it some times becomes a matter of indispensable necessity. Without disguise or palliation, I will inform you candidly of the discontents which, at this moment, prevail universally throughout the Army.

The complaint of Evils which they suppose almost remediless, are, the total want of Money, or the means of existing from one day to another, the heavy debts they have already incurred, the loss of Credit, the distress of their Families (i.e. such as are married) at home, and the prospect of Poverty and Misery before them. It is vain Sir, to suppose that Military Men will acquiesce *contently* with bare Rations, when those in the Civil Walk of life (unacquainted with half the hardships they endure) are regularly paid the emoluments of Office; while the human Mind is influenced by the same passions, and have the same inclinations to endulge, it cannot be. A Military Man has the same turn to sociability, as a person in Civil Life: He conceives himself equally called upon to live up to his rank; and his Pride is hurt, when circumstances restrain him: Only conceive then, the mortification they (even the General Officers) must suffer when they cannot invite a French Officer, a visiting Friend, or traveling acquaintance to a better repast than stinking Whiskey (and not always that) and a bit of Beef without Vegitables, will afford them.

The Officers also complain of other hardships which they think might and ought to be remedied without delay, vizt. the stopping Promotions where there have been vacancies open for a long time, the withholding Commissions from those who are justly entitled to them and have Warrants, or Certificates of their appointments from the

Detail from a British cartoon, "The Blessings of Peace," showing Peace as a witch on a broom flying toward Great Britain's setting sun

Executives of their States, and particularly the leaving the compensation for their services in a loose equivocal state, without ascertaining their claims upon the public, or making Provision for the future payment of them.

While I premise, that tho' no one that I have seen or heard of, appears opposed to the principle of reducing the Army as circumstances may require; Yet I cannot help fearing the Result of the measure in contemplation, under present circumstances, when I see such a number of Men, goaded by a thousand Stings of reflexion on the past, and of anticipation on the future, about to be turned into the World, soured by penury and what they call the ingratitude of the Public, involved in debts, without one Farthing of Money to carry them home, after having spent the flower of their days and many of them their patrimonies in establishing the freedom and Independence of their Country, and suffered every thing human Nature is capable of enduring on this side of Death. I repeat it, these irritable circumstances, without one thing to sooth their feelings, or *frighten* the gloomy prospects, I cannot avoid apprehending that a train of evils will follow, of a very serious and distressing Nature. On the other hand, could the Officers be placed in as good a situation, as when they came into Service, the contention, I am persuaded, would be, not who should continue in the Field, but who should retire to private Life.

I wish not to heighten the shades of the Picture, so far as the real Life would justify me in doing, or I would give Anecdotes of Patriotism and distress which have scarcely ever been paralleled; never surpassed in the history of Mankind. But you may rely upon it, the patience and long sufferance of this Army are almost exhausted, and that there never was so great a spirit of discontent as at this instant. While in the Field, I think it may be kept from breaking out into acts of outrage; but when we retire into Winter Quarters (unless the Storm is previously dissipated) I cannot be at ease, respecting the consequences. It is high time for a Peace.

To you, My Dear Sir, I need not be more particular in describing my anxiety and the Grounds of it. You are too well acquainted from your own service, with the real sufferings of the Army to require a longer detail: I will therefore only add, that exclusive of the common hardships of a Military life, our Troops have been, and still

Detail from same cartoon of 1783 with Franklin (1) crowning the young republic between her allies, the kings of France and Spain

Trumbull sketch for an unfinished painting of the peace treaty signing at Paris in 1783; Benjamin Franklin is at center.

are obliged to perform more services, foreign to their proper duty, without gratuity or reward, than the Soldiers of any other Army: For example, the immense labours expended in doing the duties of Artificers, in erecting Fortifications and Military Works; the fatigue of Building themselves Barracks, or Huts annually; and of cutting and transporting Wood for the use of all our Posts and Garrisons, without any expence whatever to the public.

Of this Letter, (which from the tenor of it must be considered in some degree of a Private nature) you may make such use as you shall think proper, since the principal objects of it were, by displaying the merits, the hardships, the disposition and critical state of the Army, to give information that might eventually be useful....

Secretary at War Benjamin Lincoln had been a major general in the Continental Army and well understood what Washington was saying. He replied in a private letter, the gist of which was that one cannot get blood from a turnip: Congress could pay the Army only if the states provided the money, and the states were showing no interest in honoring their debts to the men who had given so much for so long. Washington had returned to his Newburgh headquarters in October, and in December the French army left American shores for the West Indies. That same month the British evacuated Charleston, though it would be weeks before Washington learned of the event. And in Paris on November 30, 1782, a provisional treaty of peace had been signed recognizing American independence. Months would pass before that news would reach America, and in the meantime Washington continued to preach caution in accepting British earnests of peaceful intentions. But though he talked preparedness and even planned a little for a campaign in 1784, he too was affected by the general atmosphere of relaxation. He was finding time to write again to Lund Washington about Mount Vernon affairs and even got off a letter to his nephew Bushrod, son of his brother John Augustine. Washington was much given to quoting maxims, usually of his own coining, when he advised the young, and his letter to Bushrod (who would one day be an associate justice of the United States Supreme Court) is a fine example of his use of this prose form.

Newburgh Jany. 15th. 1783.

Dear Bushrod:

You will be surprized perhaps at receiving a Letter from me; but if the end is answered for which it is written, I shall not think my time misspent.

Your Father, who seems to entertain a very favourable Opinion of your prudence, and I hope you merit it; in one or two of his Letters to me, speaks of the difficulty he is under to make you remittances. Whether this arises from the scantiness of his Funds or the extensiveness of your demands, is matter of conjecture with me. I hope it is not the latter, because common prudence, and every other consideration which ought to have weight in a reflecting Mind, is opposed to your requiring more than his conveniency and a regard to his other Children will enable him to pay; and because he holds up no Idea in his Letter, which would support me in the conclusion. Yet when I take a view of the inexperience of Youth; the temptations in, and vices of Cities; and the distresses to which our Virginia Gentlemen are driven by an accumulation of Taxes, and the want of a market; I am almost inclined to ascribe it in part to both. Therefore, as a Friend, I give you the following advice.

Let the object which carried you to Philadelphia, be always before your Eyes. Remember, that it is not the mere study of the Law, but to become eminent in the profession of it, which is to yield honour and profit; the first was your choice, let the second be your ambition: And that dissipation is incompatible with both.

That the Company in which you will improve most, will be least expensive to you; and yet I am not such a Stoick as to suppose you will, or to think it right that you ought, always to be in Company with Senators and Philosophers; but of the Young and Juvenile kind, let me advise you to be choice. It is easy to make acquaintances, but very difficult to shake them off; however irksome and unprofitable they are found, after we have once committed ourselves to them; the indiscretions and scrapes, which very often they involuntarily lead one into, proves equally distressing and disgraceful.

Be courteous to all, but intimate with few, and let those few be well tried before you give them your confidence. True friendship is a Plant of slow Growth, and must undergo and withstand the shocks of adversity before it is entitled to the appellation.

Let your *Heart* feel for the afflictions and distresses of every one, and let your *hand* give in proportion to your Purse; remembering always the estimation of the Widows Mite. But that it is not every one who asketh, that deserveth Charity: All however are worthy of the inquiry or the deserving may suffer.

Mount Vernon, LOSSING

Bushrod Washington

Do not conceive that fine Clothes make fine Men, any more than fine Feathers make fine Birds. A plain genteel Dress is more admired and obtains more credit than Lace and embroidery in the Eyes of the Judicious and Sensible.

The last thing I shall mention, is first of importance; and that is, to avoid Gaming. This is a vice which is productive of every possible evil: Equally injurious to the morals and Health of its votaries. It is the Child of avarice, The Brother of inequity, and Father of mischief. It has been the ruin of many worthy Familys; the loss of many a Man's honour and the cause of Suicide. To all those who enter the lists, it is equally fascinating; The Successful Gamester pushes his good fortune 'till it is over taken by a reverse: The loosing Gamester, in hopes of retrieving past misfortunes, goes on from bad to worse, 'till grown desperate, he pushes at every thing; and looses his all. In a word, few gain by this abominable practice (the profit, if any, being diffused) while thousands are injured.

Perhaps you will say my conduct has anticipated the advice, and that "not one of these cases apply to me." I shall be heartily glad of it. It will add not a little to my happiness, to find those, to whom I am so nearly connected, pursuing the right Walk of life: It will be the sure Road to my Favour, and to those honours, and places of profit, which their Country can bestow, as merit rarely goes unrewarded.

The day after he wrote to Bushrod, Washington sent a letter to his brother Jack—Bushrod's father—and discussed some painful family matters.

Newburgh 16th. Jany. 1783.
Since the letter which Bushrod delivered me in Philadelphia, I have received your favors of the 24th. of July from Westmoreland—and 12th. of Novr. from Berkley.

The latter gave me extreme pain. In Gods name how did my Brothr. Saml. contrive to get himself so enormously in debt? Was it by purchases? By misfortunes? or shear indolence & inattention to business? From whatever cause it proceeded, the matter is now the same, & curiosity only prompts the enquiry—as it does to know what will be saved, & how it is disposed of. In the list of his debts did it appear that I had a claim upon him for the

Samuel Washington

purchase money of the Land I sold Pendleton on Bullskin? I have never received a farthing for it yet, and think I have been informed by him that he was to pay it.

I have heard a favourable acct. of Bushrod, and doubt not but his prudence will direct him to a proper line of Conduct. I have given him my sentiments on this head; & perswade myself that, with the advice of Mr. Wilson, to whose friendship as well as instruction in his profession I recommended him and the admontion of others, he will stand as good a chance as most youth of his age to avoid the Vices of large Cities, which have their advantages & disadvantages in fitting a Man for the great theatre of public Life.

I have lately received a letter from my Mother in which she complains much *of the Knavery of the Overseer at the little Falls Quarter*—that She says she can get nothing from him. It is pretty evident I believe, that I get nothing from thence, while I have the annual rent of between Eighty & an hundred pounds to pay. *The whole profit of the Plantation according to her Acct. is applied to his own use*—which is rather hard upon me as I had no earthly inducement to meddle with it but to comply with her wish, and to free her from care. This like every other matter of private concern, with me, has been totally neglected; but it is too much while I am suffering in every other way (and hardly able to keep my own Estate from Sale) to be saddled with all the expence of hers & not be able to derive the smallest return from it. . . .

While I am talking of my Mother and her concerns, I am impelled to mention somethings which has given, and still continues to give me pain. About two years ago a Gentleman of my acquaintance informed me that it was in contemplation to move for a pension for her in the Virginia Assembly—That he did not suppose I knew of the Measure—or that it would be agreeable to me to have it done—but wished to know my sentiments on it. I instantly wrote him that it was new & astonishing to me & begged that he would prevent the motion if possible, or oppose it if made; for I was sure she had not a Child that would not share the last farthing with her & that would not be hurt at the idea of her becoming a Pensioner—or in other Words receiving charity. Since *then* I have heard nothing of *that* matter; but I learn from very good authority that she is upon all occasions, & in all Companies

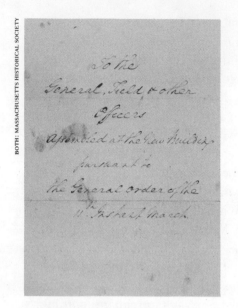

Above and opposite, the first two pages of Washington's speech to his officers, Newburgh, March 15, 1783

complaining of the hardness of the times—of her wants & distresses; & if not in direct terms, at least by strong innuendos inviting favors which not only makes *her* appear in an unfavourable point of view but *those* also who are connected with her. That she can have no *real* wants that may not be supplied I am sure of—*imaginary* wants are indefinite, & oftentimes insatiable, because they are boundless & always changing. The reason of my mentioning these matters to you is, that you may enquire into her real wants and see what is necessary to make her comfortable. If the Rent is insufficient to do this, while I have any thing I will part with it to make her so; & wish you to take measures in my behalf accordingly—at the same time I wish you to represent to her in delicate terms the impropriety of her complaints & acceptance of favors even where they are voluntarily offered from any but relations. It will not do to touch upon this subject in a letter to her—& therefore I have avoided it.

Physically, the Army was passing the winter well. In February Washington could write to one of his generals that the troops were "better covered, better Clothed and better fed, than they have ever been in any former Winter Quarters." But morale was low. On March 10 Washington was given a copy of a call to all officers for a mass meeting the next day to consider ways to obtain a just settlement of their grievances. The Newburgh Address, as this appeal to the Army came to be known, was from an anonymous hand (later identified as an aide to General Horatio Gates) and was skillfully and emotionally written. The writer spoke at length of the ingratitude of the country, wondered what the soldiers could expect during peace if they were treated so shabbily while they still bore arms, and finally came to his point: the Army should not disband until it had obtained justice. Dismayed and alarmed at this call for insurgency by the military, Washington denounced it in General Orders the next morning.

Head Quarters Newburgh
Tuesday March 11th. 1783.

The Commander in Chief having heard that a General meeting of the officers of the Army was proposed to be held this day at the Newbuilding in an ananommous paper which was circulated yesterday by some unknown person conceives (altho he is fully persuaded that the good sense of the officers would induce them to pay very little attention to such an irregular invitation) his duty as well as the reputation and true interest of the Army requires his disapprobation of such disorderly proceedings, at the same time he requests the General & Field officers with one officer from each company and a proper representation of the Staff of the Army will assemble at 12 o'clock on Saturday next at the Newbuilding to hear the report of the Committee of the Army to Congress.

After mature deliberation they will devise what further measures ought to be adopted as most rational and best calculated to attain the just and important object in view. The senior officer in Rank present will be pleased to preside and report the result of the Deliberations to the Commander in Chief.

Washington's action headed off the mass meeting of officers, but another Newburgh Address appeared. Its principal argument was that Washington, by the tone of his General Orders, had indicated that he was actually on the side of the insurgents. It became plain to Washington that he would have to appear in person at a new meeting scheduled for March 15. The meeting hall, which Washington referred to as the Newbuilding, was a large structure built by the troops some weeks earlier for use as an assembly and dance hall. It was filled to overflowing with officers, some plainly resentful. After he apologized for finding it necessary to address them and explained that he had put his thoughts in writing because the occasion was too important for misunderstandings, Washington began to read.

[Newburgh, March 15, 1783]

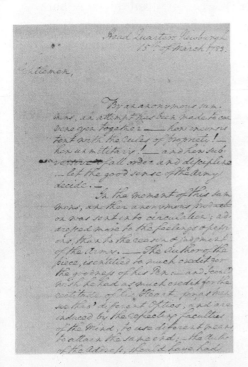

By an anonymous Summons, an attempt has been made to convene you together; how inconsistent with the rules of propriety, how unmilitary, and how subversive of all good order & discipline, let the good sense of the Army decide.

In the moment of this summons, another anonymous production was sent into circulation, addressed more to the feelings and passions, than to the reason and judgment of the Army. The author of the Piece, is entitled to much credit for the goodness of his pen, and I could wish he had as much credit for the rectitude of his heart; for as Men see through different optics, and are induced by the reflecting faculties of the mind, to use different means to obtain the same end, the author of the Address, should have had more Charity, than to mark for suspicion the Man who should recommend moderation & longer forbearance, or in other words, who should not think as he thinks, and act as he advises.

229

But he had another plan in view, in which candour and liberality of sentiment, regard to justice, and love of Country, have no part; and he was right to insinuate the darkest suspicions, to effect the blackest designs.

That the address is drawn with great art, and is designed to answer the most insidious purposes, that it is calculated to impress the mind, with an idea of premeditated injustice in the Sovereign power of the United States, and rouse all those Resentments which must unavoidably flow from such a belief, that the secret mover of this scheme (whoever he may be) intended to take advantage of the passions, while they were warmed, by the recollection of past distresses without giving time for cool, deliberate thinking, and that composure of mind which is so necessary to give dignity and Stability to measures is rendered too obvious, by the mode of conducting the business to need other proof, than a reference to the proceeding.

Thus much, Gentlemen, I have thought it incumbent on me to observe to you, to shew upon what principles I opposed the irregular & hasty meeting, which was proposed to have been held on Tuesday last and not because I wanted a disposition to give you every opportunity consistent with your own honour, and the dignity of the Army, to make known your grievances. If my conduct heretofore has not evinced to you that I have been a faithful friend to the Army, my declaration of it at this time would be equally unavailing and improper: but as I was among the first who embarked in the cause of our Common Country; as I have never left your side one moment, but when called from you on public duty; as I have been the constant companion & witness of your distresses, and not among the last to feel and acknowledge your Merits; as I have ever considered my own Military reputation as inseparably connected with that of the Army; as my heart has ever expanded with joy, when I have heard its praises, and my indignation has arisen when the mouth of detraction has been opened against it, it can scarcely be supposed, at this late state of War, that I am indifferent to its interests. But how are they to be promoted? The way is plain says the anonymous addresser, if War continues, remove into the unsettled Country; there establish yourselves, and leave an ungrateful Country to defend

At the end of the war Washington submitted his expense account to Congress, including this last item of Mrs. Washington's travel expenses.

Discharge of a sergeant from the American Army signed by Washington

itself. But who are they to defend. Our Wives, our Children, our farms and other property which we leave behind us? Or, in the State of hostile seperation, are we to take the two first (the latter cannot be removed) to perish in a Wilderness with hunger, cold and nakedness? If Peace takes place, never sheath your swords (says he) untill you have obtained full and ample justice. This dreadful alternative, of either deserting our Country, in the extremest hour of distress, or turning our Arms against it (which is the apparent object, unless Congress can be compelled into instant compliance) has something so shocking in it, that humanity revolts at the idea. My God! what can this writer have in view by recommending such measures? Can he be a friend to the Army? Can he be a friend to this Country? Rather is he not an insidious foe? some emissary, perhaps from New York, plotting the ruin of both, by sowing the seeds of discord and separation between the Civil and Military Powers of the Continent, and what a compliment does he pay to our understandings, when he recommends measures, in either alternative, impracticable in their nature....

I cannot...in justice to my own belief, & what I have great reason to conceive is the intention of Congress, conclude this address, without giving it, as my decided opinion, that that Honourable body entertain exalted sentiments of the services of the Army, and from a full conviction of its merits and sufferings, will do it complete justice. That their endeavours to discover and establish funds for this purpose, have been unwearied, and will not cease, till they have succeeded, I have no doubt; but like all other large bodies, where there is a variety of different interests to reconcile, their deliberations are slow. Why then should we distrust them? and in consequence of that distrust, adopt measures, which may cast a shade over that glory, which has been so justly acquired and tarnish the reputation of an Army, which is celebrated through all Europe, for its fortitude and Patriotism, and for what is this done; to bring the object we seek nearer? No! most certainly, in my opinion it will cast it at a greater distance....

While I give you these assurances, and pledge myself in the most unequivocal manner, to exert whatever ability I am possessed of, in your favour, let me entreat you Gentlemen, on your part not to take any measures, which, viewed in the calm light of reason, will lessen the dignity, and sully the Glory you have hitherto maintained. Let me request you to rely on the plighted faith of your Country, and place a full confidence in the purity of the intentions of Congress, that previous to your dissolution as an Army, they will cause all your [accounts] to be fairly liquidated, as directed in their Resolutions which were published to you two days ago, and that they will adopt the most effectual measures in their power, to render ample justice to you for your faithful and meritorious services. And let me conjure you, in the name of our Common Country, as you value your own sacred honour, as you respect the rights of humanity, and as you regard the Military and National character of America, to express your utmost horror and detestation of the Man, who wishes, under any specious pretences, to overturn the liberties of our Country, and who wickedly attempts to open the flood-gates of Civil discord, and deluge our rising Empire in blood. By thus determining, and thus acting, you will pursue the plain and direct road to the attainment of your wishes; you will defeat the insidious designs of our Enemies, who are compelled to resort from open force to secret artifice; you will give one more distinguished proof of unexampled patriotism and patient virtue, rising superior to the pressure of the most complicated sufferings; and you will, by the dignity of your conduct, afford occasion for posterity to say, when speaking of the glorious example you have exhibited to Mankind, had this day been wanting, the World had never seen the last stage of perfection, to which human nature is capable of attaining.

It was an effective exhortation, but the resentment of many officers ran deep, and the intriguers might well have swayed the meeting if Washington had left the hall at the end of his address. Instead, he took a paper from his pocket, saying he would read a letter from a member of Congress to show what the delegates were trying to do for the Army. He began reading, faltered over the cramped text, and then drew out a pair of spectacles as his audience watched in surprise. Only recently had he been fitted for glasses; few of his officers had seen him wearing them. "Gentlemen," he said as he hooked them behind his ears, "you must pardon me. I have grown gray in your service and now find myself growing blind." The simple act and words did more than all eloquence could have achieved and brought tears to the eyes of many in his audience. The officers voted overwhelmingly their confidence in Congress, restated their patriotism, and dissociated themselves from the Newburgh Addresses.

On March 12 a ship at last brought the provisional peace treaty of November 30. But it was an anticlimax; the treaty did not become effective until France and Britain also agreed on peace terms. Word of that happy event came two weeks later, and so Britain and her former Colonies were at peace after eight years—although the formal end to hostilities had to await ratification of the final treaty by Congress. Washington announced that action in General Orders.

Friday April 18th. 1783.
The Commander in Chief orders the Cessation of Hostilities between the United States of America and the King of Great Britain to be publickly proclaimed tomorrow at 12 o'clock at the Newbuilding, and that the Proclamation which will be communicated herewith, be read tomorrow evening at the head of every regiment & corps of the army—After which the Chaplains with the several Brigades will render thanks to almighty God for all his mercies, particularly for his over ruling the wrath of man to his own glory, and causing the rage of war to cease amongst the nations.

Altho the proclamation before alluded to, extends only to the prohibition of hostilities and not to the annunciation of a general peace, yet it must afford the most rational and sincere satisfaction to every benevolent mind—as it puts a period to a long and doubtful contest, stops the effusion of human blood, opens the prospect to a more splendid scene, and like another morning star, promises the approach of a brighter day then hath hitherto illuminated the Western Hemisphere. On such a happy day, a day which is the harbinger of Peace, a day which compleats the eighth year of the war, it would be ingratitude not to rejoice!—it would be insensibility not to participate in the general felicity.

The Commander in Chief far from endeavoring to stifle the feelings of Joy in his own bosom, offers his most cordial Congratulations on the occasion to all the Officers of every denomination—to all the Troops of the United States in General, and in particular to those gallant and persevering men who had resolved to defend the rights of their invaded country so long as the war should continue—For these are the men who ought to

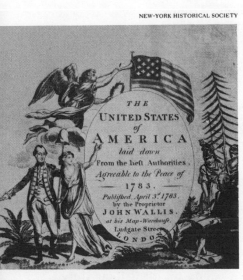

Cartouche from a map of the United States "laid down from the best Authorities Agreeable to the Peace of 1783"; Washington stands at left.

be considered as the [pride] and boast of the American Army; And, who crowned with well earned laurels, may soon withdraw from the field of Glory, to the more tranquil walks of civil life.

Congress, eager to get soldiers off the public payroll, ordered Washington to furlough men even though the drafting and ratification of a definitive peace treaty would not be completed for many months. The Commander in Chief had insisted that men leaving the Army should do so with at least three months' pay in their pockets, but there was no money to make good on the promise, and appeals to the states brought in nothing. The best that Robert Morris, financial wizard of the Revolution, could propose, was that each man be given a note calling on his home state to give him three months' pay. Morris had difficulty even finding money to buy paper on which to print the notes, and many veterans straggled home bearing only their muskets, which Congress had handsomely voted to give them as a parting gift. Disaffection was in the air, and trouble came. Washington wrote to the president of Congress on first hearing of it.

Head Qurs. Newburgh
Evening June 24th. 1783.

It was not until 3 O'Clock this Afternoon that I had the first intimation of the infamous and outrageous Mutiny of a part of the Pennsylvania Troops, it was then I received your Excellency's Letter of the 21st. by your Express, and agreeable to your request contained in it, I instantly ordered three complete Regiments of Infantry and a Detachment of Artillery to be put in motion as soon as possible; this Corps (which you will observe by the Return is a large proportion of our whole force) will consist of upwards of 1500 Effectives. As all the Troops who composed this gallant little Army, as well those who were furloughed, as those who remain in service, are Men of tried fidelity I could not have occasion to make any choice of Corps, and I have only to regret, that there exists a necessity, they should be employed on so disagreeable a service. I dare say, however, they will on this and all other occasions perform their duty as brave and faithful Soldiers.

Silhouette of Robert Morris

Washington was deeply chagrined by mutiny in an army whose loyalty he had defended, but he pointed out that the trouble-makers were "Recruits and Soldiers of a day," most of them having been in the service for only a brief time and having borne little of the burden of the war in comparison with the main Army, which had not revolted. He sent some fifteen hundred troops, almost the entire remaining Army, to take care of what he euphemistically called "the unhappy Irregularities of the troops in Philadelphia"; then, left in Newburgh with little to do, he informed Congress, "I have resolved to wear away a little time in performing a tour to the northward." Starting on July 18, he visited Saratoga, Lake George, Lake Champlain, Ticonderoga, and other places made famous by the war in the North. With the war receding, he was less interested in the strategic value of the country than in its land values, and he bid on at least three tracts of upper New York State land. He was back in Newburgh on August 6, to discover Martha ill with a fever and to find a letter from Congress summoning him to Princeton, New Jersey, where Congress had moved because of the mutiny scare. In the latter part of August, Washington moved his headquarters to a farmhouse at Rocky Hill near Princeton. He was entertained, spent much time tying up loose ends left by the disbanding of the Army, and conferred with Congress on the size and organization of a peacetime Army. Martha returned to Virginia, while he finished his business with Congress. By the middle of November Washington was at West Point, replying briefly to a letter from Sir Guy Carleton.

> West Point, Novr. 14th. 1783.
>
> I had the honor yesterday, to receive, by Major Beckwith, your Excellency's favor of the 12th. To day I will see the Governor of this State, & concert with him the necessary arrangements for taking possession of the City of New York & other Posts mentioned in your Letter, at the times therein specified For the information of which, you will please to accept my thanks.

General Carleton had announced that he would evacuate Manhattan, Long Island, and Staten Island over a period of two or three days beginning November 21. There were postponements of a few days, but at last it was accomplished, and Washington led the small remnant of his army into New York while the British boarded ship. His report to the president of Congress was of the utmost brevity.

> New York 3d. Decem. 1783.
>
> In my last Letter to your Excellency, I had the honor to acquaint Congress with the arrangement Sir Guy Carleton had made for the evacuation of New York on the 23d. ulto. I have now to inform you, that the embarkation was postponed two days on account of the badness of the weather.
>
> On the 25th. Novr. the British Troops left this City,

*First and last pages of General
Washington's farewell address to the
Army, his last official document
as commander, November 2, 1783*

& a Detachment of our army marched into it. The civil power was immediately put in possession, & I have the happiness to assure you that the most perfect regularity & good order have prevailed ever since; on which pleasing events I congratulate your Excellency & Congress.

At noon on December 4, Washington met for the last time with some of his officers in New York's Fraunces Tavern. Only a few were there: three major generals, a single brigadier general, a colonel or two, a number of lower grades. Washington tried to eat something from the table of food but could not manage, then filled a glass with wine and signaled the others to do the same. "With a heart full of love and gratitude, I now take leave of you," he said in a choked voice. "I most devoutly wish that your later days may be as prosperous and happy as your former ones have been glorious and honorable." They drank in silence, then Washington asked each to come to him. Starting with Henry Knox they came, and he embraced each without speaking. Then still too moved to speak, he walked out of the tavern and to the waterfront, where he boarded a waiting boat to be rowed to the New Jersey shore. He was in a hurry, but as he rode south he had to pause to receive the formal expressions of esteem of citizens and politicians: the people of New Brunswick, the legislature of New Jersey, the merchants of Philadelphia, the Executive Council of Pennsylvania, many others. And to each he had to make an appropriate response, as in his remarks at Baltimore.

Washington leaving New York

Baltimore December 18th. 1783.

The acceptable manner in which you have wellcomed my arrival in the Town of Baltimore, and the happy terms in which you have communicated the congratulations of its Inhabitants, lay me under the greatest obligations.

Be pleased, Gentlemen, to receive this last public acknowledgement for the repeated instances of your politeness, and to believe, it is my earnest wish that the Commerce, the Improvements, and universal prosperity of this flourishing Town, may, if possible, encrease with even more rapidity than they have hitherto done.

He finally reached Annapolis, Maryland, to which Congress had taken its deliberations early in November. There were some odds and ends of Army business: several officers had asked to be recommended for service in any peacetime Army that might be formed; an officer wounded and partially disabled in 1776 had asked Washington to present his petition for a pension. There were three days and nights of dinners and balls, and then Congress formally received the Commander in Chief. He was escorted into the chamber, bowed, and read a statement of his purpose in being there.

Annapolis 23d. Decr. 1783.

The great events on which my resignation depended having at length taken place, I have now the honor of offering my sincere congratulations to Congress, & of presenting myself before them to surrender into their hands the trust committed to me, and to claim the indulgence of retiring from the service of my Country.

Happy in the confirmation of our Independence & Sovereignty, & pleased with the opportunity afforded the United States of becoming a respectable Nation, I resign with satisfaction the appointment I accepted with diffidence; a diffidence in my abilities to accomplish so arduous a task, which however was superseded by a confidence in the rectitude of our cause, the support of the Supreme power of the Union, and the patronage of Heaven.

The Successful termination of the War has verified the most sanguine expectations, & my gratitude for the interposition of Providence, & the assistance I have received from my Countrymen, encreases with every review of the momentous Contest.

While I repeat my obligations to the army in general, I should do injustice to my own feelings not to acknowledge in this place the peculiar services & distinguished merits of the Gentlemen who have been attached to my person during the war. It was impossible the choice of confidential officers to compose my family, should have been more fortunate; permit me, Sir, to recommend in particular, those who have continued in Service to the present moment, as worthy of the favorable notice & patronage of Congress.

I consider it an indispensable duty to close this last solemn act of my official life, by commending the interests of our dearest Country to the protection of Almighty God, & those who have the superintendence of them, to his holy keeping.

Having now finished the work assigned me, I retire from the great Theatre of Action; & bidding an affectionate farewell to this August Body under whose orders I have so long acted, I here offer my Commission & take my leave of all the employments of public life.

At the close of his address Washington drew from his pocket the commission he had received in 1775 and handed it to the president of Congress. He was no longer Commander in Chief but simply George Washington, Virginia planter. His horse was waiting when he left Congress shortly after noon. He rode hard the rest of that day and most of the next, and turned into the driveway of Mount Vernon well before the early winter twilight of Christmas Eve had fallen.

Broadside of a circular letter from Washington to the governors of the states on resigning his command

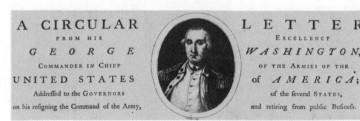

A Picture Portfolio

A Lifetime Haven

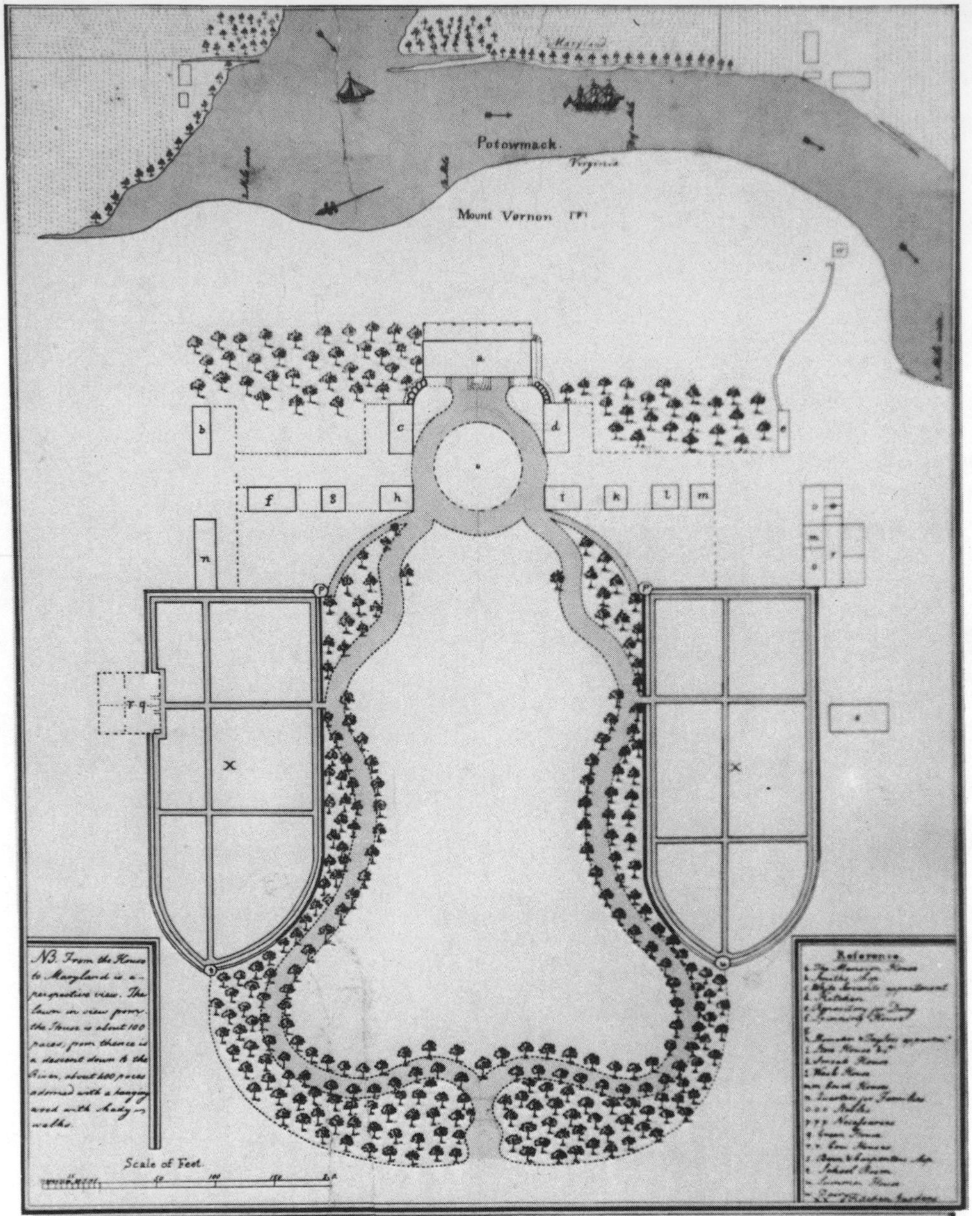
Maryland
Potowmack
Virginia
Mount Vernon
N.B. From the House to Maryland is a perspective view. The lawn in view from the House is about 100 paces; from thence is a descent down to the River, about 400 paces adorned with a hanging wood with shady walks.
Reference
Scale of Feet

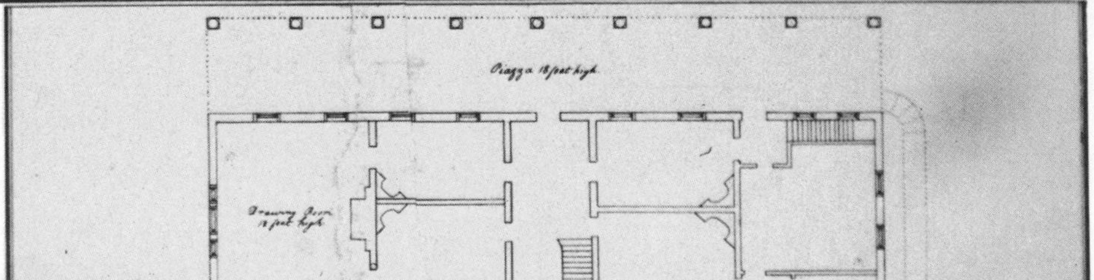
Piazza 18 feet high
Drawing Room 18 feet high

"THE SIMPLICITY OF RURAL LIFE"

George Washington first saw the quiet acres of what was to become Mount Vernon, sloping down to the broad Potomac (below), when his father moved the family there from a farm farther south. He was three years old. The plantation was not to be his until some years after the untimely death, in 1751, of his older half-brother and "best friend" Lawrence (right), who had himself inherited it. Mount Vernon blossomed under Washington's meticulous and loving supervision. The plan at left shows the handsome layout of the house and grounds in 1787. Despite its comfort, Washington, in extending an invitation to a European visitor, offered only "the simplicity of rural life."

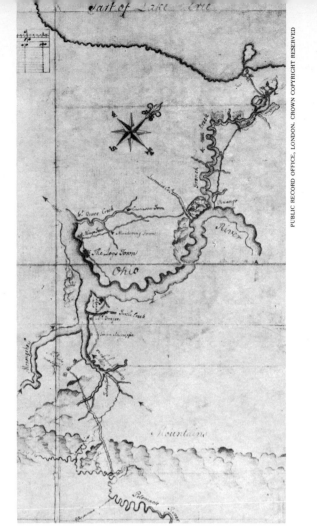

A RUGGED MANHOOD

Before Lawrence died, George, not yet twenty-one and with no qualifications except that of a surveyor (above), applied for his brother's job as Adjutant General of Virginia. And when Virginia was divided into four districts, he was appointed one of the four adjutants with the rank of major. Thus commenced the military career that was to bring him fame. Charles Willson Peale's portrait (left) shows him in the uniform he had designed for his regiment; he was described by a friend of those early manhood days as "straight as an Indian, measuring six feet two inches in his stockings and weighing 175 pounds.... His movements and gestures are graceful, his walk majestic, and he is a splendid horseman." Almost immediately he was sent by Virginia's governor to determine the strength of the French forces at the Forks of the Ohio. His own map of this mission (right, above) indicates his rigorous route. That he kept up both his surveying and mapmaking is attested by the survey map he made of Mount Vernon in 1766 (right).

The George Washington Atlas, WASHINGTON, D.C., 1932. N.Y. PUBLIC LIBRARY

AN ENDURING RELATIONSHIP

Washington's marriage to the widow Martha Dandridge Custis, when both were twenty-seven, was—like the house to which he brought her—a lifetime haven. Seen in a portrait the year before her marriage (left, above), Martha was a plump and tiny woman, barely five feet tall. She ran the large establishment at Mount Vernon, viewed from the west front in this 1792 painting, with skill and good humor, and she made it into a home to which Washington always longed to return. If there was any dark side to their married life, it was in the fact that they had no children together. Martha had brought to the marriage two small children (left). Overindulged by both mother and stepfather, "Jackie" was described later as "exeedingly indolent." "Patsy," an epileptic, died at seventeen.

SOUTHERN HOSPITALITY

The Washingtons enjoyed company, and throughout the pleasant years at Mount Vernon there was always a great deal of it. In the 1780's Washington conceived of the long porch with its graceful two-story pillars as a splendid spot from which to watch for guests arriving by boat and to entertain them. Lafayette, a frequent and favorite house guest, is seen below in an idealized painting, chatting with his adopted father, while Martha, her grandchildren, servants, and dogs complete the tranquil scene. The architect Benjamin Latrobe visited Mount Vernon in 1796 and drew the family at tea one afternoon on the spacious piazza—a view complete with Washington peering through a telescope between the lofty pillars (right). He then sketched the aging Virginia planter's profile (right, below) "while he was looking to discover a distant vessel in the Potomac, in which he expected some of his friends from Alexandria."

Sketch of General Washington, Stolen at Mount Vernon while he was looking to discover a distant Vessel on the Potowmac, in which he expected some of his friends from Alexandria.

247

METROPOLITAN MUSEUM OF ART, GIFT OF EDGAR WILLIAM AND BERNICE CHRYSLER GARBISCH, 1962

A CROWNING DOVE

Washington suffered two long and painful periods of separation from his beloved Mount Vernon. First were the years of the Revolution, when he took no leave of any kind and saw his home and four unknown grandchildren for the first time in seven years on his way south to Yorktown. The second, and perhaps harder, wrench came after an all-too-satisfying respite when his country called upon him to become its first President in 1789, as commemorated in the painting by Frederick Kemmelmeyer at left. Once again, as Washington confided to his diary, "I bade adieu to Mount Vernon, to private life, and to domestic felicity, and with a mind oppressed with more anxious and painful sensation than I have words to express, set out...." Before this last personal sacrifice, Washington had crowned his lovely house with a Dove of Peace weathervane (above) that was to welcome him home for good in 1797, after two strenuous terms of office devoted to setting the nation on the road to its destiny.

Chapter **8**

The Nation Adrift

After eight and a half years as Commander in Chief, when it had often seemed that few besides himself much cared whether the war was won or lost, Washington was at last free to do the things he had so long dreamed of. He hunted fox, he visited old neighbors, he took stock of the condition of his fields and buildings, he made plans for the future. Lund Washington had managed Mount Vernon probably to the best of his ability, but Lund was no hand at bookkeeping, and Mount Vernon had become a large operation. Its lands extended ten miles along the Potomac and inland as much as four miles. Besides the main, or mansion house, establishment, which amounted to a community in itself, there were five smaller dependent farms. Plantation operations included a flour mill, a ferry, looms, carpentry and blacksmith shops, a fishery, later a distillery. There were herds of horses and cattle, flocks of sheep, and an unknown number of swine, which ran wild in the woods. To work this huge establishment, Washington had two hundred or more slaves, both black and white overseers, artisans, and technicians of one kind or another. Lund also had an aversion to travel, and thus had not collected rents from tenants on Washington's lands in the West. Furthermore, Washington's papers were in disorder; they had become jumbled during several hurried removals on alarms that British raiders were coming, and so Washington had no way of determining just where his accounts stood. But he did know that he had lost a great deal of money. Those things would have to be taken care of in good time. First, almost immediately on arriving home, he turned his attention to the house. In 1774 he had added a south wing; in 1776 he had had Lund add a balancing north wing, whose interior was still unfinished. He wrote to Samuel Vaughan of London, then visiting in Philadelphia, for advice on one point.

Mot. Vernon 14th. Jany. 1784.

The torpid state into which the severity of the season has thrown things—the interruption of the post, occasioned by bad roads, and frozen rivers — & a want of other conveyance consequent thereof, must plead my excuse for not thanking you sooner for the polite attention you were pleased to shew me, while I was in Philada.; & for the friendly offers you obligingly made me, before I left that city. But though my acknowledgements of them come late, I pray you to be persuaded that they are not less sincere, nor are they less gratefully offered on that account.

Colo. Humphreys (one of my late Aid de Camp's) who accompanied me to Virginia, & is now on his return home, will do me the favor of presenting this letter to you, & of handing Mr. Higgins's observations on Cements, which you were pleased to lend me, & from which I have extracted such parts as I mean to carry into practice.

I found my new room, towards the completion of which you kindly offered your house-joiner, so far advanced in the wooden part of it, the Doors, Windows & floors being done, as to render it unnecessary to remove your workman with his Tools (the distance being great) to finish the other parts; especially as I incline to do it in [stucco], (which, if I understood you right, is the present taste in England), & more especially as you may find occasion for him in the execution of your own purposes as the Spring advances. And now my good sir, as I have touched upon the business of stuccoing, permit me to ask you if the rooms with which it is encrusted are painted, generally; or are they left of the natural colour which is given by the cement made according to Mr. Higgins's mode of preparing it? And also, whether the rooms thus finished are stuccoed below the surbase (chair high) or from thence upwards only?

These are trifling questions to trouble you with, but I am sure you will have goodness enough to excuse, & answer them. Please to make a tender of my best respects to Mrs. Vaughan & the rest of the family, & accept the compliments of the season from Mrs. W——n & myself who join in expression of the pleasure we shou'd feel in seeing you under our roof.

Washington's bookplate was engraved for him in 1772 by S. Valliscure of London. The Metropolitan Museum has the original copper plate.

Although Washington might cry poverty, he did not let his debts interfere with his style of living, and not until 1787 was the north wing completed to his satisfaction; it was given over almost entirely

251

to a two-story banqueting hall. Even while enjoying to the utmost his return to the role of Virginia country gentleman, Washington could not put aside his concern for the nation he had done so much to create. Less than a month after returning home he was writing to Benjamin Harrison, Governor of Virginia, to express himself on what could be a fatal weakness in the Government.

Mount Vernon 18th. Jany. 1784.

I have just had The pleasure to receive your letter of the 8th. For the friendly & affectionate terms in which you have welcomed my return to this Country & to private life; & for the favourable light in which you are pleased to consider, & express your sense of my past services, you have my warmest & most grateful acknowledgments.

That the prospect before us is, as you justly observe, fair, none can deny; but what use we shall make of it, is exceedingly problematical; not but that I believe, all things will come right at last; but like a young heir, come a little prematurely to a large inheritance, we shall wanton and run riot until we have brought our reputation to the brink of ruin, & then like him shall have to labor with the current of opinion when *compelled* perhaps, to do what prudence & common policy pointed out as plain as any problem in Euclid, in the first instance.

The disinclination of the individual States to yield competent powers to Congress for the Fœderal Government, their unreasonable jealousy of that body & of one another & the disposition which seems to pervade each, of being all-wise and all-powerful within itself, will, if there is not a change in the system be our downfal as a Nation. This is as clear to me as the A, B, C; & I think we have opposed Great Britain, & have arrived at the present state of peace & independency, to very little purpose, if we cannot conquer our own prejudices. The powers of Europe begin to see this, & our newly acquired friends the British, are already & professedly acting upon this ground; & wisely too, if we are determined to persevere in our folly. They know that individual opposition to their measures is futile, & *boast* that we are not sufficiently united as a Nation to give a general one! Is not the indignity alone, of this declaration, while we are in the very act of peace-making & conciliation, sufficient to stimulate us to vest more extensive & adequate powers in the sovereign of these United States? For my

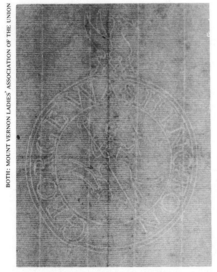

A watermark on Washington's stationery shows Britannia holding a sprig of foliage and sitting on a plough.

Decorative motifs from a china set, derived from the Society of the Cincinnati, the select group of Revolutionary officers, headed by George Washington

own part, altho' I am returned to, & am now mingled with the class of private citizens, & like them must suffer all the evils of a Tyranny, or of too great an extension of fœderal powers; I have no fears arising from this source; in my mind, but I have many, & powerful ones indeed which predict the worst consequences from a half-starved, limping Government, that appears to be always moving upon crutches, & tottering at every step. Men, chosen as the Delegates in Congress are, cannot officially be dangerous—they depend upon the breath—nay, they are so much the creatures of the people, under the present Constitution, that they can have no views (which could possibly be carried into execution) nor any interests, distinct from those of their constituents. My political creed therefore is, to be wise in the choice of Delegates—support them like Gentlemen while they are our representatives—give them competent powers for all federal purposes—support them in the due exercise thereof—& lastly, to compel them to close attendance in Congress during their delegation. These things under the present mode for, & termination of elections, aided by annual instead of constant Sessions, would, or I am exceedingly mistaken, make us one of the most wealthy, happy, respectable & powerful Nations, that ever inhabited the terrestrial Globe—without them, we shall in my opinion soon be every thing which is the direct reverse of them.

I shall look for you, in the first part of next month, with such other friends as may incline to accompany you, with great pleasure, being with best respects to Mrs. Harrison, in which Mrs. Washington joins me....

Despite his continuing deep interest in the course of the nation, there is little doubt that Washington was quite convinced that his days in public life were over. A number of his letters echo this conviction. One such went to the Marquis de Chastellux, French philosopher and writer, who had been a major general in Rochambeau's army during the war and had become a close friend to Washington.

Mount Vernon 1st. Feby. 1784.

I have had the honor to receive your favor of the 23d. of August from L'Orient. I hope this Letter will find you in the circle of your friends at Paris, well recovered from the fatigues of your long & wearisome inspection on

In 1784 Washington was admitted to membership in Charleston's library.

The Order of the Cincinnati, worn by Society members

the frontiers of the Kingdom.

I am at length become a private citizen of America, on the banks of the Patowmac; where under my own Vine & my own Fig tree—free from the bustle of a camp & the intrigues of a Court, I shall view the busy world, "in the calm light of mild philosophy"—& with that serenity of mind, which the Soldier in his pursuit of glory, & the Statesman of fame, have not time to enjoy. I am not only retired from all public employments; but I am retiring within myself & shall tread the private walks of life with heartfelt satisfaction.

After seeing New York evacuated by the British Forces on the 25th. of Novembr., & civil Government established in the city, I repaired to Congress, & surrendered into their hands, all my powers, with my Commission on the 23d. of Decemr. and arrived at this Cottage on Christmas eve, where I have been close locked up ever since in Frost & Snow.

Actually, when Washington wrote to Chastellux, he still had not found the serenity about which he wrote. For years his life had been the life of the army camp, and he had lived by its rhythms, from the first drumbeat of reveille in the morning to the sound of tattoo at night. Each morning during those years he had waked to face seemingly insoluble problems: could he feed his men, where could he obtain clothing for them, dare he face the British with his inferior numbers, would he even have an army in two or three months? In a letter to Major General Henry Knox, soon to be appointed Secretary at War, he revealed how long it had taken him to stop thinking as Commander in Chief.

Mount Vernon 20th. Feby. 1784.

The bad weather, & the great care which the Post riders take of themselves, prevented your Letters of the 3d. & 9th. of last month from getting to my hands 'till the 10th. of this. Setting off next morning for Fredericksburg to pay my duty to an aged mother, & not returning 'till yesterday, will be admitted I hope, as a sufficient apology for my silence until now.

I am much obliged by the trouble you have taken to report the state of the Garrison & Stores, together with the disposition of the Troops at West-Point, to me; and think the allowance of rations, or subsistence money, to such Officers as could not retire at that inclement season, was not only perfectly humane, but perfectly just also—and that it must appear so to Congress....

I am just beginning to experience that ease, & freedom from public cares which, however desireable, takes some time to realize; for strange as it may seem, it is never the less true, that it was not 'till lately, I could get the better of my usual custom of ruminating as soon as I waked in the morning, on the business of the ensuing day —& of my surprize at finding, after having revolved many things in my mind, that I was no longer a public Man, or had any thing to do with public transactions.

I feel now however, as I conceive a wearied traveller must do, who after treading many a painful step with a heavy burthen on his shoulders, is eased of the latter, having reached the haven to which all the former were directed; & from his house-top is looking back & tracing with an eager Eye, the meanders by which he escaped the Quicksands & mires which lay in his way; & into which, none but the all-powerful guide, & great dispencer of human events could have prevented his falling.

The Marquis de Chastellux

The problems of having to hold together and lead an army were, of course, replaced by other knotty questions. Washington found it difficult to put the affairs of Mount Vernon in order because of the confused state of his papers. He wrote here and there seeking information that would help him get some grip on things, especially the status of his land holdings in the West. A letter to John Stephenson, a business acquaintance, was a masterpiece in combining condolences, a request for information, and a dun for payment of a debt.

Fredericksg. 13th. Feby. 1784.

After condoling with you on the unhappy fate of your Brother William, which I do very sincerely; & upon the Death of your brother Vale., I should be glad to get a copy from both their Books, or Memos. of the accounts as they stand between us; which are of long standing, & I fear not a little intricate. I write to you Sir, because I do not know (if you are not one yourself) who are the Executors or Administrators of those deceased Gentlemen. There were also some Land transactions, in partnership & otherwise between your Brother William & me, which I wish to have an account of. If it is in your power therefore, or you should have come across any warrants, Entries, Memoms. or papers relative to this business, which can give me insight into the matter, I shall be much obliged to you for the information.

There is also a Bond in my possession from your deceased brother Hugh (for whose Death I am also very much concerned) with your name, or that of your brother James's to it (I am not certain which as I am from home, & have accidentally met with this good and direct opportunity) for a Sum of money due to me from your Fathers Estate; which I wish to know when it can be settled & paid, as the situation of my private Affairs makes it absolutely necessary to close my Accounts & to receive payment as soon as possible.

Fielding Lewis, Washington's nephew

When Washington's nephew Fielding Lewis, son of his sister Betty, wrote asking for a loan, Washington's answer was definite and a bit sharp.

Mount Vernon 27th. Feby. 1784.

Dear Fieldg.:

You very much mistake my circumstances when you suppose me in a condition to advance money. I made no money from my Estate during the nine years I was absent from it, & brought none home with me. Those who owed me, for the most part, took advantage of the depreciation & paid me off with six pence in the pound. Those to whom I was indebted, I have yet to pay, without other means, if they will not wait, than selling part of my Estate; or distressing those who were too honest to take advantage of the tender Laws to quit scores with me.

This relation of my circumstances, which is a true one, is alone sufficient (without adding that my living under the best oeconomy I can use, must unavoidably be expensive,) to convince you of my inability to advance money.

I have heard with pleasure that you are industrious. Convince people by your mode of living that you are sober & frugal also; and I persuade myself your creditors will grant you every indulgence they can. It would be no small inducement to me, if it should ever be in my power, to assist you. Your Father's advice to you in his Letter of the 8th. of October 1778 is worthy the goodness of his own heart, & very excellent to follow; if I could say anything to enforce it, it should not be wanting.

I shall always be glad to see you here. Your Aunt joins me in best wishes & I am, &ca.

P.S. There was a great space between the 23d. of September 1778, when you were called upon by your Father for a specific list of your Debts, & his death: how happen'd it that in all that time you did not comply with his request? And what do they amount to now? His Letters to you are returned, & I hope will get safe to hand.

Tobias Lear, a portrait by Sharples

In time Washington's records were put in order. During 1786 he hired as his secretary Tobias Lear, a New Hampshire Yankee, who was to serve him through his first term as President and again during the last year of his life. Lear performed the small miracle of reorganizing Washington's papers. The result was not encouraging; his records showed that Washington had lost some ten thousand pounds sterling, partly because many of his debtors had taken advantage of wartime inflation to pay him off in near-worthless money, partly because most of the debts still owing him had become uncollectible. Mount Vernon was constantly bulging with visitors, some of them friends Washington welcomed, most of them strangers. Many were only travelers caught by the night, for the public road to Alexandria ran nearby, and there was no inn. A few were people who had simply come to see the famous man, to gawk like spectators at a zoo. There were painters and sculptors to immortalize him on canvas or in marble, and would-be historians and biographers wanting to look at his papers. His diary lists only a fraction of the visitors: those who were friends or who came with recommendations from friends or were notable for some reason. He was occasionally exasperated by strangers demanding favors.

Monday, 10th [October, 1785]. A Mr. Jno. Lowe, on his way to Bishop Seabury [Samuel Seabury, first

Protestant Episcopal Bishop of Connecticut] for Ordination, called & dined here. Could not give him more than a general certificate founded on information, respecting his character; having no acquaintance with him, nor any desire to open a Corrispondence with the *new* ordained Bishop.

The boldness and presumption of some of these self-invited guests is past understanding. Because Washington was a public figure, he was considered fair game for all manner of outrageous demands from those who happened by Mount Vernon.

> *Saturday, 5th* [November, 1785]. ...Mr. Robert Washington of Chotanck, Mr. Lund Washington & Mr. Lawrence Washington dined here, as did Colo. Gilpin and Mr. Noah Webster. The 4 first went away afterwards. The last stayed all Night. In the afternoon a Mr. Lee came here to sollicit Charity for his Mother who represented herself, as having nine children—a bad husband—and no support. He also stayed the Evening.

His account book for the date shows that Washington gave this dubious beggar the generous sum of two pounds, eight shillings. There is no way of knowing how often Washington was taken advantage of by charlatans. Probably most of the uninvited were just who they claimed to be—but not always.

> *Sunday, 19th* [March, 1786]. ...A Gentleman calling himself the Count de Cheize D'arteignan Officer of the French Guards came here to dinner; but bringing no letters of introduction, nor any authentic testimonials of his being either; I was at a loss how to receive, or treat him. He stayed dinner and the evening.

The count, of whom Washington continued to be suspicious, remained for two days, then went on. He was obviously a fraud, for the French army lists of that day contain no such name. Most of these visitors had horses that had to be stabled and fed at Washington's expense; many had servants who also drew on the food resources of the plantation. Washington once said that Mount Vernon could be compared to "a well-resorted tavern." He fed his guests generously, and they always joined the Washington family for the midday meal. The table was almost always filled, often with a dozen or more: family, friends, and strangers. As a Virginia gentleman, Washington would accept no pay, not even from chance travelers caught at his door by storm or nightfall. Besides the visitors who came to his door, he received endless letters asking for favors, endorsement of books, a kind word about limping odes dedicated to him, and the like. He wrote to David Humphreys, his wartime aide-de-camp, complaining about the endless demands on his time and patience.

> Mount Vernon, February 7, 1785.
>
> My dear Humphreys:
>
> In my last, by the Marquis de la Fayette, I gave you reason to believe that when I was more at lcizure, you should receive a long letter from me; however agreeable this might be to my wishes, the period it is to be feared, will never arrive. I can with truth assure you, that at no period of the war have I been obliged to write half as much as I now do, from necessity. I have been enquiring for sometime past, for a person in the character of Secretary or clerk to live with me [the position eventually filled by Tobias Lear]; but hitherto unsuccessfully. What with letters (often of an unmeaning nature) from foreigners. Enquiries after Dick, Tom, and Harry who *may have been* in some part, or at *sometime,* in the Continental service. Letters, or certificates of service for those who want to go out of their own State. Introductions; applications for copies of Papers; references of a thousand old matters with which I *ought* not to be troubled, more than the Great Mogul, but which must receive an answer of some kind, deprive me of my usual exercise; and without relief, may be injurious to me as I already begin to feel the weight, and oppression of it in my head, and am assured by the *faculty,* if I do not change my course, I shall certainly sink under it.

A printed invitation to dine, sent in 1788 to Mr. and Mrs. Thomas Porter, newlyweds from Alexandria

On September 1, 1784, Washington set out upon a journey to the West. He had three main purposes: to revisit his lands on the Kanawha River, which he had last seen in 1770 when he had gone down the Ohio to select bounty lands for himself and other veterans of the Fort Necessity campaign; to take care of a couple of irritating situations of long standing on his lands in Pennsylvania; and to find a point where a navigable headwater of the Potomac closely approached a navigable headwater of the Ohio. With Washington were his nephew Bushrod, Dr. James Craik, who had been his companion in 1770, and Craik's son William. By the morning of the third day they were sixty miles from Mount Vernon. Following is an extract from Washington's diary.

3d [September, 1784]. Having business to transact
with my Tenants in Berkeley; & others, who were
directed to meet me at my Brother's (Colo. Charles
Washington's), I left Doctr. Craik and the Baggage to
follow slowly, and set out myself about Sunrise for that
place—where after Breakfasting at Keys' ferry I arrived
about 11 Oclock—Distant abt. 17 Miles.

Colo. Warner Washington [George's uncle], Mr.
Wormeley, Genl. Morgan, Mr. Snickers and many other
Gentlemen came here to see me—& one object of my
journey being to obtain information of the nearest and
best communication between the Eastern & Western
Waters; & to facilitate as much as in me lay the Inland
Navigation of the Potomack; I conversed a good deal with
Genl. Morgan on this subject, who said, a plan was in
contemplation to extend a road from Winchester to the
Western Waters to avoid if possible an interference with
any other State—but I could not discover that Either
himself, or others, were able to point it out with precision. He seemed to have no doubt but that the Counties
of Frederk., Berkeley & Hampshire would contribute
freely towards the extension of the Navigation of Poto-

mack; as well as towards opening a road from East to West.

4th. Having finished my business with my Tenants (so far at least as partial payments could put a close to it)— and provided a waggon for the transportation of my Baggage to the Warm springs (or Town of Bath) to give relief to my Horses, which from the extrem[e] heat of the weather began to rub & gaul, I set out after dinner, and reached Captn. Stroads a Substantial farmers betwn. Opeckon Creek & Martinsburgh—distant by estimation 14 Miles from my Brothers.

Finding the Captn. an intelligent Man, and one who had been several times in the Western Country—tho' not much on the communication between the North Branch of Potomack, & the Waters of Monongahela—I held much conversation with him—the result of which, so far as it respected the object I had in view, was,—that there are two Glades which go under the denomination of the Great glades—one, on the Waters of the Yohiogany, the other on those of Cheat River; and distinguished by the name of the Sandy Creek Glades—that the Road to the first goes by the head of Patterson Creek—that from the Accts. he has had of it, it is rough;—the distance he knows not—that there is a way to the Sandy Creek Glades from the great crossing of Yohiogany (on Braddocks Road) & a very good one; but how far the Waters of Potomack above Fort Cumberland, & the Cheat river from its Mouth are navigable, he professes not to know— and equally ignorant is he of the distance between them.

He says that old Captn. Thos. Swearengen has informed him, that the navigable water of the little Kanhawa comes within a small distance of the Navigable Waters of the Monongahela, & that a good road, along a ridge, may be had between the two—& a young Man who we found at his House just (the Evening before) from Kentucke, told us, that he left the Ohio River at Weeling (Colo. David Shepperds), & in about 40 Miles came to red stone old Fort on the Monongahela, 50 Miles from its Mouth.

Two pages from the diary kept by Washington on his journey west

There was more in the same vein. Washington was pursuing the problem of finding a practical route from the Potomac to the

Ohio. The headwaters of the two rivers almost interlace in the Allegheny Mountains, but the region was still largely wilderness, and he had to depend on often conflicting accounts by local inhabitants. Washington was not moved by some sudden enthusiasm; he knew that if settlers west of the mountains were not kept tied to the East by communications and commerce, then inevitably their trade would go down the west-flowing rivers to the Mississippi, and the United States would in time become two nations. The next day he arrived at Berkeley Springs, or Bath, as it had been renamed in 1776, where he had once taken his doomed brother Lawrence and later his stepdaughter Patsy in their vain searches for health.

5th [September, 1784]. Dispatched my Waggon (with the Baggage) at daylight; and at 7 Oclock followed it. Bated [Baited, stopped for food] at one Snodgrasses, on Back Creek—and dined there; About 5 Oclock P.M. we arrived at the Springs, or Town of Bath after travelling the whole day through a drizling rain, 30 Miles.

6th. Remained at Bath all day and was shewed the Model of a Boat constructed by the ingenious Mr. Rumsey, for ascending rapid currents by mechanism; the principles of this were not only shewn, & fully explained to me, but to my very great satisfaction, exhibited in practice in private, under the injunction of Secresy, untill he saw the effect of an application he was about to make to the assembly of this State, for a reward.

The model, & its operation upon the water, which had been made to run pretty swift, not only convinced me of what I before thought next to, if not quite impracticable, but that it might be turned to the greatest possible utility in inland Navigation; and in rapid currents; that are shallow—and what adds vastly to the value of the discovery, is the simplicity of its works; as they may be made by a common boat builder or carpenter, and kept in order as easy as a plow, or any common impliment of husbandry on a farm.

Having obtained a Plan of this Town (Bath) and ascertained the situation of my lots therein, which I examined; it appears that the disposition of a dwelling House; Kitchen & Stable cannot be more advantageously placed than they are marked in the copy I have taken from the plan of the Town; to which I refer for recollection, of my design; & Mr. Rumsey being willing to undertake those Buildings, I have agreed with him to have them finished by the 10th. of next July. The

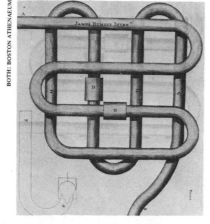

Engraving from Columbian Magazine, *in Washington's library, of a boiler invented by James Rumsey*

dwelling House is to be 36 feet by 24. . . .

Meeting with the Revd. Mr. Balmain at this place, he says the distance from Staunton to the Sweet Springs is 95 Miles; that is, 50 to what are commonly called the Augusta Springs & 45 afterwards. This differs widely from Captn. Strodes Acct., and both say they have travelled the Road.

From Colo. Bruce whom I also found at this place, I was informed that he had travelled from the North Branch of Potomack to the Waters of Yaughiogany, and Monongahela—that the Potomk. where it may be made Navigable—for instance where McCulloughs path crosses it, 40 Miles above the old fort (Cumberland), is but about 6 Miles to a pretty large branch of the Yohiogany, but how far it is practicable to make the latter navigable he knows not, never having explored it any length downwards.

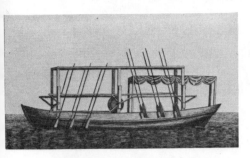

The copy of Columbian Magazine *also contained "Plan for Mr. Fitch's Steam Boat," an early competitor to the "ingenious" Rumsey's boat.*

Again Washington noted much more about the navigability of this or that tributary of the Potomac and the Ohio, and of the feasibility of roads to connect them. James Rumsey, whom Washington met at Bath, had showed him a model of an odd craft, an arrangement of two hulls with a paddle wheel between them. The current of the stream turned the paddle wheel, which in turn activated poles that pushed against the bottom of the stream and forced the craft against the current. Washington, enthusiastic, was certain it was the solution to upriver travel. On September 10 he headed north into Pennsylvania to take care of some matters there before continuing on to his lands on the Kanawha River. His business with Gilbert Simpson was of an annoying nature. Simpson, in a partnership arrangement, was supposed to be operating a gristmill on land owned by Washington. Although Washington claimed to have put twelve hundred pounds into the venture over the years without getting a penny back, his artful partner had always been able to charm him out of his anger.

10th [September, 1784].   Set off a little after 5 Oclock altho' the morning was very unpromising. Finding from the rains that had fallen, and description of the Roads, part of which between the old Town & this place (old Fort Cumberland) we had passed, that the progress of my Baggage would be tedeous, I resolved (it being Necessary) to leave it to follow; and proceed on myself to Gilbert Simpson's, to prepare for the Sale which I had advertised of my moiety of the property in co-partnership with him— and to make arrangements for my trip to the Kanhawa, if the temper & disposition of the Indians should render it advisable to proceed. Accordingly, leaving Doctr. Craik, his Son, and my Nephew with it, I set out with one Servant only. Dined at a Mr. Gwins at the Fork of the Roads leading to Winchester and the old Town, distant from the latter abt. 20 Miles & lodged at Tumbersons at the little Meadows....

The Road from the Old Town to Fort Cumberland we found tolerably good, as it also was from the latter to Gwins, except the Mountain which was pretty long (tho' not steep) in the assent and discent; but from Gwins to Tumberson's it is intolerably bad—there being many steep pinches of the Mountain—deep & Miry places—and very stony ground to pass over. After leaving the Waters of Wills Creek which extends up the Mountain (Alligeny) two or three Miles as the road goes, we fell next on those of George's Creek, which are small—after them upon Savage River which are more considerable; tho' from the present appearance of them, does not seem capable of Navigation....

12th. Left Daughtertys about 6 Oclock,—stopped a while at the Great Meadows [site of Fort Necessity and Washington's defeat; then owned by Washington], and viewed a tenament I have there, which appears to have been but little improved, tho capable of being turned to great advantage, as the whole of the ground called the Meadows may be reclaimed at an easy comparitive expence & is a very good stand for a Tavern. Much Hay may be cut here when the ground is laid down in Grass & the upland, East of the Meadow, is good for grain....

In passing over the Mountains, I met numbers of Persons & Pack horses going in with Ginsang; & for salt & other articles at the Markets below; from most of whom I made enquiries of the Nature of the Country between the little Kanhawa and ten miles Creek (which had been represented as a short and easy portage) and to my surprize found the Accts. wch. had been given were so far from the truth that numbers with whom I conversed assured me that the distance between was very considerable—that ten miles Ck. was not navigable even for Canoes more than a Mile from its mouth and few of them, altho I saw many who lived on different parts of this Creek would pretend to guess at the

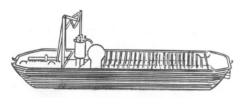

Plan of Rumsey's steamboat (above) and his proposals for forming a company to enable him to build it

distance.

I also endeavoured to get the best acct. I could of the Navigation of Cheat River, & find that the line which divides the States of Virginia & Pensylvania crosses the Monongahela above the Mouth of it; wch. gives the Command thereof to Pensylvania—that where the River (Cheat) goes through the Laurel hill, the Navigation is difficult; not from shallow, or rapid water, but from an immense quantity of large Stones, which stand so thick as to render the passage even of a short Canoe impracticable—but I could meet with no person who seemed to have any accurate knowledge of the Country between the navigable or such part as could be made so, of this River & the North Branch of Potomack. All seem to agree however that it is rought & a good way not to be found.

The Accts. given by those Whom I met of the late Murders, & general dissatisfaction of the Indians, occasioned by the attempts of our people to settle on the No. West side of the Ohio, which they claim as their territory; and our delay to hold a treaty with them, which they say is indicative of a hostile temper on our part, makes it rather improper for me to proceed to the Kanhawa agreeably to my original intention, especially as I learnt from some of them (one in particular) who lately left the Settlement of Kentucke that the Indians were generally in arms & gone, or going, to attack some of our Settlements below—and that a Party who had drove Cattle to Detroit had one of their Company & several of their Cattle killed by the Indians—but as these Accts. will either be contradicted or confirmed by some whom I may meet at my Sale the 15th. Instt. my final determination shall be postponed 'till then.

13th. I visited my Mill, and the several tenements on this Tract (on which Simpson lives). I do not find the land in *general* equal to my expectation of it. Some part indeed is as rich as can be, some othe[r] part is but indifferent—the levellest is the coldest, and of the meanest quality—that which is most broken is the richest; tho' some of the hills are not of the first quality.

The tenements with respect to buildings, are but indifferently improved—each have Meadow and arable, but in no great quantity. The Mill was quite destitute

Mount Vernon. LOSSING

Silhouette of Dr. James Craik

of Water. The works & House appear to be in very bad condition—and no reservoir of Water—the stream as it runs, is all the resource it has. Formerly there was a dam to stop the Water; but that giving way it is brought in a narrow confined & trifling race to the forebay, wch. and the trunk, which conveys the water to the Wheel are in bad order. In a word, little rent, or good is to be expected from the present aspect of her.

14th. Remained at Mr. Gilbert Simpsons all day. Before Noon Colo. Willm. Butler and the Officer Commanding the Garrison at Fort Pitt, a Capt. Lucket came here. As they confirmed the reports of the discontented temper of the Indians and the Mischiefs done by some parties of them—and the former advised me not to prosecute my intended trip to the Great Kanhawa, I resolved to decline it.

This day also the people who lives on my land on Millers run came here to set forth their pretensions to it; & to enquire into my right. After much conversation, & attempts in them to discover all the flaws they could in my Deed, &ca.—& to establish a fair and up right intention in themselves;—and after much councelling which proceeded from a division of opinion among themselves—they resolved (as all who live on the Land were not here) to give me their definite determination when I should come to the Land, which I told them would probably happen on Friday or Saturday next.

15th. This being the day appointed for the Sale of my moiety of the Co-partnership stock—Many People were gathered (more out of curiosity I believe than from other motives) but no great Sale made. My Mill I could obtain no bid for, altho I offered an exemption from the payment of Rent 15 Months. The Plantation on which Mr. Simpson lives rented well—Viz. for 500 Bushels of Wheat payable at any place with in the County that I, or my Agent should direct. The little chance of getting a good offer in money for Rent, induced me to set it up to be bid for in Wheat....

16th. Continued at Simpsons all day in order to finish the business which was begun yesterday—Gave leases to some of my Tents. on the Land whereon I now am.

17th. Detained here by a settled Rain the whole day—

which gave me time to close my accts. with Gilbert Simpson, & put a final end to my Partnership with him. Agreed this day with a Major Thomas Freeman to superintend my business over the Mountains, upon terms to be inserted in his Instructions.

In settling up with Simpson, Washington apparently got the worst of the deal once again, for in his ledger under Simpson's account is a notation, "Settled [by Simpson] by a payment in depreciated paper Money." This accomplished, Washington was off to another tract of land, the one from which "the people who lives on my land on Millers run," as he noted in his diary, had come to Simpson's to talk to him on September 14. These people, religious dissenters from Europe, had moved onto Washington's land in 1773, virtually evicting the man who was living there to protect Washington's rights.

18th [September, 1784]. Set out with Doctr. Craik for my Land on Miller's run (a branch of Shurtees [Chartier's] Creek). Crossed the Monongahela at Deboirs Ferry—16 miles from Simpsons—bated at one Hamiltons about 4 Miles from it, in Washington County, and lodged at a Colo. Cannons on the Waters of Shurtees Creek—a kind hospitable Man; & sensible.

Most of the Land over which we passed was hilly— some of it very rich—others thin. Between a Colo. Cooks and the Ferry the Land was rich but broken. About Shurtee, & from thence to Colo. Cannons, the soil is very luxurient and very uneven.

19th. Being Sunday, and the People living on my Land, *apparently* very religious, it was thought best to postpone going among them till tomorrow—but rode to a Doctr. Johnsons who had the Keeping of Colo. Crawfords (surveying) records—but not finding him at home was disappointed in the business which carried me there.

20th. Went early this Morning to view my Land, & to receive the final determination of those who live upon it. Having obtained a Pilot near the Land I went ...first to the plantation of Samuel McBride, who has about

5 Acres of Meadow—&
30 of arable Land

under good fencing—a Logged dwelling house with a punchion roof, & stable, or small barn, of the same kind—the Land rather hilly, but good, chiefly white oak....[Here follow similar descriptions of the farms of a dozen other settlers.]

The foregoing are all the Improvements upon this Tract which contains 2813 acres.

The Land is leveller than is common to be met with in this Part of the Country, and good; the principal part of it is white oak, intermixed in many places with black oak; and is estemed a valuable tract.

Dined at David Reeds, after which Mr. James Scot & Squire Reed began to enquire whether I would part with the Land, & upon what terms; adding, that tho' they did not conceive they could be disposed, yet to avoid contention, they would buy, if my terms were moderate. I told them I had no inclination to sell; however, after hearing a great deal of their hardships, their Religious principles (which had brought them together as a society of Ceceders) and unwillingness to seperate or remove; I told them I would make them a last offer and this was—the whole tract at 25/. pr. Acre, the money to be paid at 3 annual payments with Interest;—or to become Tenants upon leases of 999 years, at the annual Rent of Ten pounds pr. [   ] pr. Ann.—The former they had a long consultation upon, & asked if I wd. take that price at a longer credit, without Interest, and being answered in the negative they then determined to stand suit for the Land; but it having been suggested that there were among them some who were disposed to relinquish their claim, I told them I would receive their answers individually; and accordingly calling upon them as they stood...they severally answered, that they meant to stand suit, & abide the Issue of the Law.

This business being thus finished, I returned to Colo. Cannons in company with himself, Colo. Nevil, Captn. Swearingen (high Sherif) & a Captn. Richie, who had accompanied me to the Land.

21st. Accompanied by Colo. Cannon & Captn. Swearingen who attended me to Debores ferry on the Monongahela which seperates the Counties of Fayette & Washington, I returned to Gilbert Simpson's in the Afternoon; after dining at one Wickermans Mill near the Monongahela.

Colo. Cannon, Captn. Sweringin & Captn. Richie

all promised to hunt up the Evidences which could prove my possession & improvement of the Land before any of the present Occupiers saw it.

$\quad$ Washington was angry and determined to prosecute the case vigorously, for he considered the settlers as squatters who had spurned his fair offer to let them buy or rent. It was not until 1786, however, that the case was finally decided; Washington's 1771 survey was somehow missing from land office records, and other records had flaws. Eventually, though, he won his case. But that lay in the future. Now, with his business concluded and the trip to the Kanawha canceled by Indian hostility, he started for home, still gathering voluminous information on Potomac-Ohio routes and even going so far as to work out combinations of streams and portages by which the fur trade of the Northwest could be funneled through Detroit and down into Virginia. He arrived home on October 4, 1784, and soon was lobbying to urge the legislatures of Maryland and Virginia to authorize improvement of navigation on the Potomac, which the two states shared as a common boundary. He later described the results to his friend former Major General Benjamin Lincoln.

Major General Benjamin Lincoln

$\quad$ Mount Vernon 5th. Feby. 1785.
We have nothing stirring in this quarter worthy of observation, except the passing of two Acts by the Assemblies of Virginia & Maryland (exactly similar) for improving & extending the navigation of the river Potomac from tide water, as high up as it shall be found practicable, & communicating it by good roads with the nearest navigable waters to the Westward: which acts in their consequences, may be of great political, as well as commercial advantages: the first to the confederation, as it may tie the Settlers of the Western Territory to the Atlantic States by interest, which is the only knot that will hold. Whilst those of Virginia & Maryland will be more immediately benefited by the large field it opens for the latter. Books for receiving subscriptions are to be opened at Alexandria & other places the 8th. instant, & continue so until the 10th. of May; as the navigable part of the business is to be undertaken by a company to be incorporated for the purpose.

$\quad$ The Potomac Company was formed, and Washington was named its president. That same summer, 1785, he and the other directors made the first of several inspections, beginning just above the Great

Falls of the Potomac, not far upstream from where the city of Washington would rise. His diary detailed the difficulties they found.

Wednesday, 3d [August, 1785]. ... Having provided Canoes and being joined by Mr. Rumsay the principal Manager, & Mr. Stewart an Assistant to him, in carrying on the Works, we proceeded to examine the falls [Seneca Falls]; and beginning at the head of them went through the whole by water, and continued from the foot of them to the Great fall—After which, returning back to a Spring on the Maryland Side between the Seneca & Great Falls, we partook (about 5 O'clock) of another cold Collation which a Colo. Orme a Mr. Turner & others of the Neighbourhood, had provided and returned back by the way of Mr. Bealls Mill to our old Quarters at Mr. Goldsboroughs—The distance as estimated 8 Miles.

The Water through these Falls is of sufficient depth for good Navigation; and as formidable as I had conceived them to be; but by no means impracticable. The principal difficulties lye in rocks which occasion a crooked passage. These once removed, renders the passage safe without the aid of Locks & may be effected for the sum mentioned in Mr. Jno. Ballendine's estimate (the largest extant) but in a different manner than that proposed by him. It appearing to me, and was so, unanimously determined by the Board of Directors, that a channel through the bed of the river in a strait direction, and as Much in the course of the current as may be, without a grt. increase of labour & expence, would be preferable to that through the Gut which was the choice of Mr. Ballendine for a Canal with Locks— the last of which we thought unnecessary, & the first more expensive in the first instance, besides being liable to many inconveniences which the other is not as it would, probably be frequently choaked with drift wood—Ice—and other rubbish which would be thrown therein through the several inlets already made by the rapidity of the currts. in freshes and others which probably would be made thereby; whereas a navigation through the bed of the river when once made will, in all probability, remain forever, as the currt. here will rather clear than contribute to choak the passage. It is true, no track path [towpath] can be had in a navigation thus ordered, nor does there appear a necessity for it. Tracking, constitutes a large part of Mr. Ballendine's

The Great Falls of the Potomac, a formidable but not "impracticable" obstacle to Washington's canal

estimate—The want of which, in the rapid parts of the river, (if Mr. Rumsey's plan for working Boats against stream by the force of mechanical powers should fail) may be supplied by chains buoyed up to haul by which would be equally easy, more certain, and less dangerous than setting up with Poles....

Thursday, 4th. In order to be more certain of the advantages and disadvantages of the Navigation proposed by Mr. Ballendine, through the Gut, we took a more particular view of it—walking down one side & returning on the other and were more fully convinced of the impropriety of its adoption first, because it would be more expensive in the first instance—and secondly because it would be subject to the ravages of freshes &ca. as already mentioned without any superiority over the one proposed through the bed of the River unless a track path should be preferable to hauling up by a Chain with buoys.

Engaged nine labourers with whom to *commence* the Work.

Friday, 5th. ...After Breakfast, and after directing Mr. Rumsey when he had marked the way and set the labourers to Work to meet us at Harpers ferry on the Evening of the morrow at Harpers Ferry (at the conflux of the Shannondoah with the Potomack) myself and the Directors set out for the same place by way of Frederick Town (Maryland). Dined at a Dutch man's 2 Miles above the Mo[uth] of Monocasy & reached the former about 5 Oclock. Drank Tea—supped—and lodged at Govr. Johnsons.

In the Evening the Bells rang, & Guns were fired; & a Committee waited upon me by order of the Gentlemen of the Town to request that I wd. stay next day and partake of a public dinner which the Town were desirous of giving me—But as arrangements had been made, and the time for examining the Shannondoah Falls, previous to the day fixed for receiving labourers into pay, was short I found it most expedient to decline the honor.

The group went up the Potomac as far as Harpers Ferry. Although the Potomac canal long remained a project close to Wash-

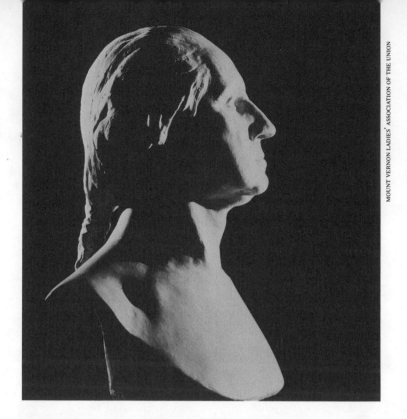

Bust of Washington made by the
famous sculptor Houdon in 1785;
persons familiar with Washington
thought it the best likeness.

ington's heart, it was never to amount to anything during his lifetime. James Rumsey's self-poling boat proved impracticable, and canal building was difficult and expensive beyond the resources of the company. Earlier that same year Washington had made a poignant little pilgrimage; he had ridden over to the ruins of Belvoir, onetime home of George William Fairfax and his wife Sally, who had once bewitched the young George Washington. The Fairfaxes now lived in England; Belvoir, empty, had burned during the war years. Within its halls, as an awkward teen-ager, Washington had first come in contact with the exciting world of Virginia society. Now he wrote to Fairfax, expressing the wistful hope that he and his wife might return to Belvoir.

> Mount Vernon 27th. Feby. 1785.
> I cannot at this moment recur to the contents of those letters of mine to you which I suspect have miscarried; further than that they were all expressive of an earnest wish to see you & Mrs. Fairfax once more fixed in this country; & to beg that you would consider Mt. Vernon as your home until you could build with convenience — in which request Mrs. Washington joins very sincerely. I never look towards Belvoir, without having this upper most in my mind. But alas! Belvoir is no more! I took a ride there the other day to visit the ruins, & ruins indeed they are. The dwelling house & the two brick buildings in front, underwent the ravages of the fire; the walls of which are very much injured: the other

Houses are sinking under the depredation of time &
inattention, & I believe are now scarcely worth repairing. In a word, the whole are, or very soon will be a
heap of ruin. When I viewed them—when I considered
that the happiest moments of my life had been spent
there—when I could not trace a room in the house (now
all rubbish) that did not bring to my mind the recollection of pleasing scenes; I was obliged to fly from them;
& came home with painful sensations, & sorrowing for
the contrast. Mrs. Morton still lives at your Barn quarter.
The management of your business is entrusted to one
Muse (son to a Colonel of that name, whom you cannot
have forgotten)—he is, I am told, a very active & industrious man; but in what sort of order he has your Estate,
I am unable to inform you, never having seen him since
my return to Virginia.

Despite his enthusiasm for canals and the time he gave
to a wide-ranging correspondence, Washington was, above all, a farmer.
He continued endlessly to try new plants and new methods, and to go
about it as scientifically as he knew how. His diaries recorded agricultural
experiments, as they had before the war.

> *Monday, 25th* [April, 1785]. ...Got the ground, on the
> North side of the gate—between the outer ditch & the
> Sweet brier hedge in a proper state of preparation to
> receive grass seed; and for making a compleat experimt.
> of the Plaister of Paris as a manure. Accordingly, I divided
> it into equal sections; by a line from the Center of the
> old gate, between the New Gardon Houses, stretched
> to the outer ditch at which they were 18 1/2 feet apart
> and 16 apart at the outer edge of the Holly berries by
> the Sweet brier hedge. Each of these Sections contained
> 655 square feet. On the 1st. that is, the one next the road
> I sprinkled 5 pints of the Plaister in powder—on the 2d.
> 4 pints—on the 3d. 3 pints—on the 4th. 2 pts. on the
> 5th. one pint—and on the 6th. none. On the 7th. 8th.
> 9th. 10th. & 11th. 5, 4, 3, 2 & 1 pints again; and on
> the 12th. nothing—and on the 13th. 14th. 15. 16 &
> 17th.—5, 4, 3, 2 & 1 in the same manner as before. On
> these three grand divisions (as they may be called) I
> sowed Orchard Grass Seed. But before I did this, I
> harrowed the first grand division with a heavy Iron
> toothed harrow. The 2d. grand division was gone over

with a Bush harrow (without the Iron harrow)—and the third grand division was only rolled without either of the above harrowings. The whole of this ground was, in quality, as nearly alike as ground cou'd well be—and this experiment, if the grass seed comes up well, will show first, what quantity is most proper for an acre (the above [amt.] being, as nearly as may be, in the proportion of 1, 2, 3, 4, & 5 Bushels to the acre)—and secondly, whether burying the Powder of Paris deep (as a heavy harrow will do it)—shallow—or spreading it on the surface only, is best.

But alas! for all Washington's efforts, Mount Vernon never quite lived up to his hopes. Before the war, he had given up growing tobacco, partly because his harvest always brought prices lower than the prevailing rate and partly because it exhausted the land and renewing it with organic manures was more expensive than buying new land. He had done better with crops such as wheat and corn, but his best expectations were always disappointed. In 1785 it was drought and an infestation of chinch bugs that gave him a severe setback.

Friday, 22d. [July]. ...Rid to the Ferry—Dogue run and Muddy hole Plantations.

Mr. Lund Washington & his wife dined here. And Mr. Thompson went away after Breakfast.

The leaves of the locust Trees this year, as the last, began to fade, & many of them dye. The Black Gum Trees which I had transplanted to my avenues or Serpentine Walks, & which put out leaf and looked well at first, are all dead, so are the Poplars, and most of the Mulberrys. The Crab apple trees also, which were transplanted into the Shrubberies & the Papaws are also dead, as also the Sassafras in a great degree—The Pines wholly—& several of the Cedars—as also the Hemlock almost entirely. The live Oak which I thought was dead is putting out shoots from the bottom and have appearances of doing well....

Thursday, 11th [August]. ...The Drought, the effects of which were visible when I left home, had, by this (no rain having fallen in my absence) greatly affected vegetation. The grass was quite burnt & crisp under foot—Gardens parched—and the young Trees in my Shrubberies, notwithstanding they had been watered

THE
BOTANICAL MAGAZINE;
OR,
Flower-Garden Displayed:

IN WHICH
The moſt Ornamental FOREIGN PLANTS, cultivated in the Open Ground, the Green-Houſe, and the Stove, will be accurately repreſented in their natural Colours.

TO WHICH WILL BE ADDED,

Their Names, Claſs, Order, Generic and Specific Characters according to the celebrated LINNÆUS; their Places of Growth, and Times of Flowering:

TOGETHER WITH

THE MOST APPROVED METHODS OF CULTURE.

A WORK
Intended for the Use of

Such LADIES, GENTLEMEN, and GARDENERS, as wiſh to become ſcientifically acquainted with the Plants they cultivate.

LONDON:

Printed for W. CURTIS, at his BOTANIC-GARDEN, Lambeth-Marſh; and Sold by all Bookſellers, Stationers, and News Carriers, in Town and Country.

M DCC LXXXVII.

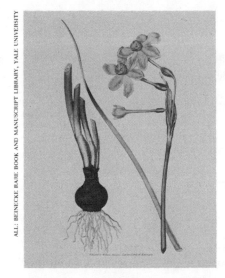

Washington subscribed to England's Botanical Magazine *(left), in which these plates of the Jonquil (top) and the Sessile Trillium appeared.*

(as it is said) according to my direction were much on the decline. In a word nature had put on a melancholy look—everything seeming to droop....

Saturday, 13th. ...Rid to my Muddy hole and Neck Plantations; and beheld Corn in a melancholy situation, fired in most places to the Ear with little appearance of yielding if rain should soon come & a certainty of making nothing if it did not. Attempts had been made at both these Plantations to sow Wheat, but stirring the ground in the parched condition it was in, had so affected the Corn as to cause well grounded apprehensions that it would die if not restored by seasonable & sufficient Rains. This put a stop to further seeding which is almost as bad as the injury done by it to the Corn as latter sowing in old Corn ground seldom produces. At the first mentioned place about 30 Bushels had been sowed—at the latter less.

The two kinds of Chinese Seeds which had appeared before I left home were destroyed either by the drought or insects. That between the 8th. & 9th. stakes in the 2d. row was entirely eradicated—indeed some kind of fly, or bug, had begun to prey up on the leaves before I left home. The other was broke of near the ground & cannot I fear recover....

Monday, 15th. ...Rid to my Plantations at the Ferry, Dogue run and Muddy hole. Found the two first were suffering as I had described the other two on Saturday—and that both had discontinued sowing of Wheat after putting about 30 Bushels at each place in the ground.

My Overseer at the Ferry (Fairfax) ascribes the wretched condition of his Corn to the bug which has proved so destructive to both Wheat and Corn on James River and elsewhere equally with the drought & shewed me hundreds of them & their young under the blades at the lower joints of the stock. The Corn is effected by their sucking the juices which occasions a gradual decline of the whole plant. He also shewed me a piece of course grass that was quite killed by them, by the same kind of operation.

When other Potomac plantations were still green and fruitful, Washington's trees died and his crops wilted in dry weather, for the

hard truth was that Mount Vernon was set on mediocre land. Its topsoil
overlay heavy clay into which water was slow to soak. Heavy rains ran off
instead of sinking in, eroding precious topsoil, while in spring the fields
were so slow to absorb standing water that they were always late in being
worked and planted. In such a situation Washington's efforts to restore
fertility accomplished little. Mount Vernon had also become overburdened
with excess workers. Washington's diary for February, 1786, listed 216
slaves of all ages at Mount Vernon and its five dependent farms. He had
adopted the humane policy of rarely selling a slave unless the slave was
willing, and since Washington was a good, if strict, master, few left. The
birth rate was high, and as a result there were more hands to feed than the
plantation could profitably employ. Moreover, Washington was troubled by
slavery. As a Southerner he had once accepted it as part of the normal order
of things, but time had brought doubts. His mixed feelings on the subject
appeared in a letter to Robert Morris of Philadelphia.

*Details from two nineteenth-century
paintings include slaves at Mount
Vernon as domestics in the house
(above) and field hands (opposite).*

Mt. Vernon, 12th. April 1786.
I give you the trouble of this letter at the instance of
Mr. Dalby of Alexandria; who is called to Philadelphia
to attend what he conceives to be a vexatious law-suit
respecting a slave of his, which a Society of Quakers in
the city (formed for such purposes) have attempted to
liberate. The merits of this case will no doubt appear
upon trial; but from Mr. Dalby's state of the matter, it
should seem that this Society is not only acting repug-
nant to justice so far as its conduct concerns strangers,
but, in my opinion extremely impolitickly with respect
to the State—the City in particular; & without being
able, (but by acts of tyranny & oppression) to accomplish
their own ends. He says the conduct of this society is
not sanctioned by Law: had the case been otherwise,
whatever my opinion of the Law might have been, my
respect for the policy of the State would on this occasion
have appeared in my silence; because against the penal-
ties of promulgated Laws one may guard; but there is
no avoiding the snares of individuals, or of private
societies—and if the practice of this Society of which Mr.
Dalby speaks, is not discountenanced, none of those
whose *misfortune* it is to have slaves as attendants, will
visit the City if they can possibly avoid it; because by
so doing they hazard their property—or they must be at
the expence (& this will not always succeed) of providing
servants of another description for the trip.
I hope it will not be conceived from these observations,
that it is my wish to hold the unhappy people, who are

the subject of this letter, in slavery. I can only say that there is not a man living who wishes more sincerely than I do, to see a plan adopted for the abolition of it — but there is only one proper and effectual mode by which it can be accomplished, & that is by Legislative authority; and this, as far as my suffrage will go, shall never be wanting. But when slaves who are happy & content to remain with their present masters, are tampered with & seduced to leave them; when masters are taken unawares by these practices; when a conduct of this sort begets discontent on one side and resentment on the other, & when it happens to fall on a man whose purse will not measure with that of the Society, & he loses his property for want of means to defend it — it is oppression in the latter case, & not humanity in any; because it introduces more evils than it can cure.

I will make no apology for writing to you on this subject; for if Mr. Dalby has not misconceived the matter, an evil exists which requires a remedy; if he has, my intentions have been good though I may have been too precipitate in this address.

As 1786 wore on, Washington became increasingly concerned about the state of the nation. Under the Articles of Confederation the United States was little more than a collection of thirteen quasi nations. States levied import duties on each other's commerce and issued their own money. Congress was impotent; it could not tax, and its only means of income was to beg from the states, which seldom responded. By 1786, Congress was no longer able to pay even the interest on the national debt. Washington's somber outlook was typified by the following extract from a letter to the Marquis de Lafayette.

Mount Vernon, May 10, 1786.
It is one of the evils of democratical governments, that the people, not always seeing & frequently misled, must often feel before they can act right — but then evils of this nature seldom fail to work their own cure. It is to be lamented nevertheless that the remedies are so slow, & that those who may wish to apply them seasonably are not attended to before they suffer in person, in interest & in reputation. I am not without hopes that matters will soon take a more favourable turn in the fœderal Constitution. The discerning part of the community have long since seen the necessity of giving adequate powers to

The State House at Annapolis

Congress for national purposes; & the ignorant & designing must yield to it 'ere long. Several late acts of the different Legislatures have a tendency thereto; among these, the Impost which is now acceded to by every State in the Union, (tho' clogged a little by that of New York) will enable Congress to support the national credit in pecuniary matters better than it has been; whilst a measure, in which this state [Virginia] has taken the lead at its last session, will it is to be hoped give efficient powers to that Body for all commercial purposes. This is a nomination of some of its first characters to meet other Commissioners from the several States in order to consider of & decide upon such powers as shall be necessary for the sovereign power of them to act under; which are to be reported to the respective Legislatures at their autumnal sessions for, it is to be hoped, final adoption: thereby avoiding those tedious & futile deliberations, which result from recommendations & partial concurrences; at the same time that it places it at once in the power of Congress to meet European Nations upon decisive & equal ground. All the Legislatures which I have heard from, have come into the proposition, & have made very judicious appointments. Much good is expected from this measure, and it is regretted by many that more objects were not embraced by the meeting. A General Convention is talked of by many for the purpose of revising & correcting the defects of the fœderal government; but whilst this is the wish of some, it is the dread of others from an opinion that matters are not yet sufficiently ripe for such an event.

The meeting of commissioners from the several states to which Washington referred was to be held at Annapolis. Virginia and Maryland, after having reached agreement on navigation of the Potomac, had joined in inviting all the states to send delegates to try in the same spirit to solve their mutual trade problems. Only five states were represented when the meeting convened in September, 1786, and nothing could be accomplished. Undaunted, the delegates issued a call for all the states to send delegates to Philadelphia the following May for a much broader purpose: to discuss all matters necessary "to render the constitution of the Federal Government adequate to the exigencies of the Union."

Not long after getting a report of the disappointing outcome of the Annapolis Convention, Washington received distressing news from Massachusetts. In the postwar depression, many New England farmers and small property owners were having their property seized to satisfy claims for unpaid debts and taxes. In Massachusetts, when petitions for relief were ignored by the legislature, the protesters in late August began mass demonstrations to intimidate courts and prevent legal action against debtors. Then, afraid they might be indicted for treason, the insurgents marched on Springfield to frighten the state's Supreme Court. Violence was avoided when both insurgents and militia agreed to go home. Washington, receiving his news in bits and pieces, got an overly sensational picture of the situation. He poured out his feelings to Henry ("Light-Horse Harry") Lee, one of his wartime officers and soon to be Governor of Virginia, who had suggested that Washington go to Massachusetts and use his influence to end the rebellion.

Mount Vernon 31st. Octr. 1786.

I am indebted to you for your several favors of the 1st., 11th. & 17th. of this inst. & shall reply to them in the order of their dates; but first let me thank you for the interesting communications imparted by them.

The picture which you have exhibited, & the accounts which are published of the commotions, & temper of numerous bodies in the Eastern States, are equally to be lamented & deprecated. They exhibit a melancholy proof of what our trans-Atlantic foe has predicted; & of another thing perhaps, which is still more to be regretted, & is yet more unaccountable, that mankind when left to themselves are unfit for their own Government. I am mortified beyond expression when I view the clouds which have spread over the brightest morn that ever dawned upon any Country. In a word, I am lost in amazement when I behold what intrigue, the interested views of desperate characters, ignorance & jealousy of the minor part, are capable of effecting, as a scourge on the major part of our fellow Citizens of the Union; for it is hardly to be supposed that the great body of the people, tho' they will not act, can be so short sighted, or enveloped in darkness as not to see rays of a distant sun thro' all this mist of intoxication & folly.

You talk, my good Sir, of employing influence to appease the present tumults in Massachusetts. I know not where that influence is to be found; and if attainable, that it would be a proper remedy for the disorders. Influence is no Government. Let us have one by which our lives, liberties & properties will be secured; or let us know the worst at once. Under these impressions,

"Light-Horse Harry" Lee

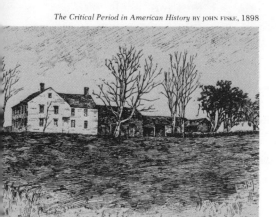

The Critical Period in American History BY JOHN FISKE, 1898

House in which Shays was captured

my humble opinion is, that there is a call for decision. Know precisely what the insurgents aim at. If they have *real* grievances, redress them if possible; or acknowledge the justice of them, & your inability to do it in the present moment. If they have not, employ the force of government against them at once. If this is inadequate, *all* will be convinced that the superstructure is bad, or wants support. To be more exposed in the eyes of the world, and more contemptible than we already are, is hardly possible. To delay one or the other of these, is to exasperate on the one hand, or give confidence on the other, & will add to their numbers; for, like snowballs, such bodies encrease by every movement, unless there is something in the way to obstruct & crumble them before the weight is too great & irresistible.

These are my sentiments. Precedents are dangerous things—let the reins of government then be braced & held with a steady hand, & every violation of the Constitution be reprehended: if defective, let it be amended, but not suffered to be trampled upon whilst it has an existence.

The protest, which had become known as Shays' Rebellion from its leader, Daniel Shays, a captain during the Revolution, flared up again in late December when the insurgents returned to Springfield planning to seize arms from the national arsenal there. Early in the new year they were dispersed by troops under Benjamin Lincoln. Shays fled to Vermont; he and a number of other leaders were condemned to death, and large numbers of others were disfranchised, a punishment that Washington considered too severe. Writing to Lincoln, Washington commented on the outcome.

Mount Vernon March 23d. 1787.
Ever since the disorders in your State began to grow serious I have been peculiarly anxious to hear from that quarter; General Knox has, from time to time, transmitted to me the state of affairs as they came to his hands; but nothing has given such full and satisfactory information as the particular detail of events which you have been so good as to favor me with, and for which you will please to accept my warmest and most grateful acknowledgements. Permit me also, my dear Sir, to offer you my sincerest congratulations upon your success. The suppression of those tumults

Governor James Bowdoin

and insurrections with so little bloodshed, is an event as happy as it was unexpected; it must have been peculiarly agreeable to you, being placed in so delicate and critical a situation. I am extremely happy to find that your sentiments upon the disfranchising act [are] such as they are; upon my first seeing it, I formed an opinion perfectly coincident with yours, viz., that measures more generally lenient might have produced equally as good an effect without entirely alieniating the affections of the people from the government; as it now stands, it affects a large body of men, some of them, perhaps, it deprives of the means of gaining a livelihood; the friends and connections of those people will feel themselves wounded in a degree, and I think it will rob the State of a number of its inhabitants if it produces nothing worse.

It gives me great pleasure to hear that your Eastern settlements succeeds so well. The sincere regard which I have for you will always make your prosperity a part of my happiness.

In Massachusetts, Governor James Bowdoin was defeated in the next election, Shays and other condemned leaders were soon pardoned, and the harassed debtors obtained through the ballot the changes they had failed to win by marching. Although conservatives took Shays' Rebellion as proof that a republican government was unworkable, most thinking Americans saw it as an indication of the need for a stronger government, one that could handle, or better yet, prevent, such crises. The rebellion thus unintentionally created strong sentiment in favor of the approaching convention to review the confederation. Washington wanted no personal part in the convention, and many of his close friends urged him not to go; if it should be a failure, his reputation, more than that of any other man, would suffer. But once again he answered the call of duty. In early May, 1787, as the time for his departure for Philadelphia neared, he wrote to Robert Morris to politely decline a thoughtful invitation.

Mount Vernon May 5th. 1787.
When your favor of the 23d. Ult. was sent here from the Post Office, I was at Fredericksburg (to which place I had been called, suddenly, by Express) to bid, as I was prepared to expect, the last adieu to an honoured parent, and an affectionate Sister whose watchful attention to my Mother during her illness had brought to deaths door. The latter I hope is now out of danger, but the former

cannot long Survive the disorder which had reduced her to a Skeleton, tho' she is somewhat amended.

I do not know how, sufficiently, to express my thankfulness to Mrs. Morris and you for your kind invitation to lodge at your house, and though I could not be more happy any where, yet as there is great reason to apprehend that the business of the Convention (from the tardiness of some States, and the discordant opinions of others) will not be brought to a speedy conclusion, I cannot prevail on my self to give so much trouble to a private family as such a length of time must do. I hope therefore that Mrs. Morris and you will not take it a miss that I decline the polite and obliging offer you have made me.

Mrs. Washington is become too Domestick, and too attentive to two little Grand Children to leave home, and I can assure you, Sir, that it was not until after a long struggle I could obtain my own consent to appear again in a public theatre. My first remaining wish being, to glide gently down the stream of life in tranquil retirement till I shall arrive at the world of Spirits.

The Morris house in Philadelphia, in which Washington made his home

Washington left Mount Vernon on May 9, 1787. Almost immediately on arriving in Philadelphia he accepted Robert Morris's renewed invitation and moved into the financier's mansion. When he arrived at the State House (today called Independence Hall) on May 14 for the opening session, only the Pennsylvania and Virginia delegations were present—hardly a quorum. While foreboding grew in Washington's heart, delegates from other states leisurely drifted in during the following days. Meanwhile, the Virginia delegation, ignoring the fact that the convention had been called only to revise the Articles of Confederation, drafted a plan for a completely new form of government to be presented to the convention. At last Washington was able to record in his diary that the meeting to revise the Articles of Confederation had been convened.

> *Friday, 25th* [May, 1787].   Another Delegate coming in from the State of New Jersey gave it a representation and encreased the number to Seven which forming a quoram of the 13 the Members present resolved to organize the body; when, by a unanimous vote I was called up to the Chair as President of the body. Majr. William Jackson was appointed Secretary—and a Comee. was chosen consisting of (Mr. Wythe, Mr. Hamilton and Mr. Chs. Pinkney chosen) 3 Members to

prepare rules & regulations for conducting the business—and after appointing door keepers the Convention adjourned till Monday, (10 oclock) to give time to the Comee. to report the matters referred to them.

Returned many visits (in the forenoon) today. Dined at Mr. Thos. Willings—and sp[en]t the evening at my lodgings.

Unfortunately for posterity, the delegates voted to keep their deliberations secret, and Washington's diary henceforth reveals little more than where he dined and had tea. Meanwhile, in what has since become known as the Constitutional Convention, the delegates decided to scrap completely the Articles of Confederation and then debated through the hot summer over the form of the new government. In 1787 they had no precedents. The Virginia Plan, calling for judicial, legislative, and executive branches of the national government, was accepted as the basis for discussion. But should the executive be one man or three, a Southerner, a Westerner, and a Northerner? A one-house legislature or two? Should the upper house be elected by the people or chosen by the lower house? Should?—there were a hundred vexing problems. How often Washington despaired during the deliberations we cannot know. As presiding officer, he carefully kept a neutral stance; moreover, the Revolution had taught him a great deal about seemingly hopeless causes. At least once he expressed pessimism in a letter to Alexander Hamilton, who had left the convention for a time.

First page of Washington's copy of the first printed draft of the Constitution, August 6, 1787

Philadelphia 10th. July [17]87.

I thank you for your communication of the 3d. When I refer you to the State of the Councils which prevailed at the period you left this City—and add, that they are now, if possible, in a worse train than ever; you will find but little ground on which the hope of a good establishment can be formed. In a word, I *almost* despair of seeing a favourable issue to the proceedings of the Convention, and do therefore repent having had any agency in the business.

The Men who oppose a strong & energetic government are, in my opinion, narrow minded politicians, or are under the influence of local views. The apprehension expressed by them that the *people* will not accede to the form proposed is the *ostensible*, not the *real* cause of the opposition—but admitting that the present sentiment is as they prognosticate, the question ought nevertheless to be, is it or is it not, the best form? If the former, recommend it, and it will assuredly obtain mauger opposition. I am sorry you went away. I wish you were back. The crisis is equally important and alarming, and no opposition under such circumstances should discourage exertions till the signature is fixed. I will not, at this time trouble you with more than my best wishes and sincere regards.

Voting record of convention on the question of a single executive (right), one of the many problems considered before adoption of the Constitution; Washington was the first to sign the document (opposite, above); following this, "Members adjourned to the City Tavern" (far right).

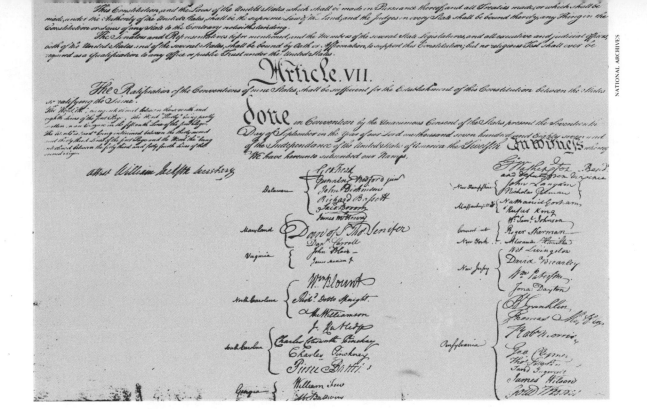

Despite their differences, the men at Philadelphia, from states large and small and representing divergent economic interests, did compromise their many disagreements to create a constitution that—if completely satisfactory to none—all but three delegates present were willing to accept. (Rhode Island, which had stubbornly refused to send delegates to the convention, was not represented at the final signing, and part of the New York delegation had left earlier.) Washington, on the final day, ended his prohibition against mentioning convention proceedings in his diary.

Monday, 17th [September, 1787]. Met in Convention when the Constitution received the Unanimous assent of 11 States and Colo. Hamilton's from New York (the only delegate from thence in Convention) and was subscribed to by every Member present except Govr. [Edmund] Randolph and Colo. [George] Mason from Virginia—& Mr. [Elbridge] Gerry from Massachusetts.

The business being thus closed, the Members adjourned to the City Tavern, dined together and took a cordial leave of each other—after which I returned to my lodgings—did some business with, and received the papers from the secretary of the Convention, and retired to meditate on the momentous w[or]k which had been executed, after not less than five, for a large part of the time Six, and sometimes 7 hours sitting every day, [except] sundays & the ten days adjournment to give a Comee. opportunity & time to arrange the business for more than four Months.

The next day Washington left for Mount Vernon. Although as president of the convention he had taken little part in the debate, his commanding presence had been a powerful factor in the creation of the new Constitution. James Monroe, an opponent of the document, had written to Jefferson, "Be assured, his influence carried the government." After his return to Virginia, Washington wrote to his friends advocating ratification of the Constitution. He alternated between optimism and deep gloom as one state convention after another slowly and often heatedly deliberated before voting on ratification. By the end of May, 1788, eight states had ratified; only one more was needed to make the Constitution operative, and the convention in Virginia met on June 2. Washington's spirits were now up, now down, as he followed the daily exchanges in Richmond. The final vote came on June 25; one of those to whom Washington wrote in high spirits was Benjamin Lincoln.

In this engraving from the cover of a 1788 almanac, Washington and Franklin, pulled by thirteen men, escort the Constitution to ratification.

Mount Vernon June 29th. 1788.
I beg you will accept my thanks for the communications handed to me in your letter of the 3d. instant—and my congratulations on the encreasing good dispositions of the Citizens of your State of which the late elections are strongly indicative. No one *can* rejoice more than I do at every step the people of this great Country take to preserve the Union, establish good order and government—and to render the Nation happy at home and respectable abroad. No Country upon Earth ever had it more in its power to attain these blessings than United America. Wonderously strange then, and Much to be regretted indeed would it be, were we to neglect the means and to depart from the road which providence has pointed us to, so plainly—I cannot believe it will ever come to pass. The great Governor of the Universe has led us too long and too far on the road to happiness and glory to forsake us in the midst of it. By folly and improper conduct, proceeding from a variety of causes, we may now and then get bewildered; but I hope and trust that there is good sense and virtue enough left to recover the right path before we shall be entirely lost. You will, before this letter can have reached you, have heard of the Ratification of the new Government by this State. The final question without previous amendments was taken the 25th. Ayes 89—Noes 79;

New Hampshire ratified Constitution on June 21; Virginia, a rising pillar in this drawing, four days later.

Independent Chronicle and Universal Advertiser, 1788

but something recommendatory, or declaratory of the rights [accompanied] the ultimate decision. This account and the News of the adoption by New Hampshire arrived in Alexandria nearly about the same time on Friday evening; and, as you will suppose, was cause for great rejoicing among the Inhabitants who have not I believe an Antifederalist among them. Our Accounts from Richmond are, that the debates, through all the different Stages of the business, though [brisk] and animated, have been conducted with great dignity and temper; that the final decision exhibited [an] auful and solomn scene, and that there is every reason to expect a perfect acquiescence therein by the minority — not only from the declaration of Mr. Henry, the great Leader of it, who has signified that though he can never be reconciled to the Constitution in its present form, and shall give it every *constitutional* opposition in his power yet that he will submit to it peaceably, as he thinks every good Citizen ought to do when it is in exercise and that he will both by precept and example inculcate this doctrine to all around him.

There is little doubt entertained here *now* of the ratification of the proposed Constitution by North Carolina; and however great the opposition to it may be in New York the leaders thereof will, I should conceive, consider well the consequences before they reject it. With respect to Rhode Island, the power that governs there has so far baffled all calculation on this question that no man would chuse to hasard an opinion lest he might be suspected of participating in its phrensy.

New York ratified in July, 1788, making eleven states. But North Carolina put off action until November of 1789, waiting for the new government to submit a proposed Bill of Rights to the states. Rhode Island, still intransigent, refused even to call a convention until 1790; then it voted to join the year-old Union. Congress — the old Congress — set March 4, 1789, as the day for the new government to go into effect. It had been pretty generally assumed that the first President could be only one man, George Washington. Although Washington was very reticent about discussing the matter, when his friend and former aide Alexander Hamilton wrote to say very candidly that the survival of the new government might well depend on his becoming President, Washington admitted that he had heard the possibility mentioned.

Mount Vernon October 3d. 1788.
In acknowledging the receipt of your candid and kind letter by the last Post; little more is incumbent upon me, than to thank you sincerely for the frankness with which you communicated your sentiments, and to assure you that the same manly tone of intercourse will always be more than barely wellcome, Indeed it will be highly acceptable to me. I am particularly glad, in the present instance; you have dealt thus freely and like a friend. Although I could not help observing from several publications and letters that my name had been sometimes spoken of, and that it was possible the *Contingency* which is the subject of your letter might happen; yet I thought it best to maintain a guarded silence and to [seek] the *counsel* of my best friends (which I certainly hold in the highest estimation) rather than to hazard an imputation unfriendly to the delicacy of my feelings. For, situated as I am, I could hardly bring the question into the slightest discussion, or ask an opinion even in the most confidential manner; without betraying, in my Judgment, some impropriety of conduct, or without feeling an apprehension that a premature display of anxiety, might be construed into a vain-glorious desire of pushing myself into notice as a Candidate. Now, if I am not grossly deceived in myself, I should unfeignedly rejoice, in case the Electors, by giving their votes in favor of some other person, would save me from the dreaded Dilemma of being forced to accept or refuse. If that may not be—I am, in the next place, earnestly desirous of searching out the truth, and of knowing whether there does not exist a probability that the government would be just as happily and effectually carried into execution, without my aid, as with it. I am *truly* solicitous to obtain all the previous information which the circumstances will afford, and to determine (when the determination can with propriety be no longer postponed) according to the principles of right reason, and the dictates of a clear conscience; without too great a referrence to the unforeseen consequences, which may affect my person or reputation. Untill that period, I may fairly hold myself open to conviction—though I allow your sentiments to have weight in them; and I shall not pass by your arguments without giving them as dispassionate a consideration, as I can possibly bestow

upon them.

In taking a survey of the subject in whatever point of light I have been able to place it; I will not suppress the acknowledgment, my Dr. Sir that I have always felt a kind of gloom upon my mind, as often as I have been taught to expect, I might, and perhaps must ere long be called to make a decision. You will, I am well assured, believe the assertion (though I have little expectation it would gain credit from those who are less acquainted with me) that if I should receive the appointment and if I should be prevailed upon to accept it; the acceptance would be attended with more diffidence and reluctance than ever I experienced before in my life. It would be, however, with a fixed and sole determination of lending whatever assistance might be in my power to promote the public, weal, in hopes that at a convenient and an early period, my services might be dispensed with, and that I might be permitted once more to retire—to pass an unclouded evening, after the stormy day of life, in the bosom of domestic tranquility.

But why these anticipations? If the friends to the Constitution conceive that my administering the government will be a means of its acceleration and strength, is it not probable that the adversaries of it may entertain the same ideas and of course make it an object of opposition? That many of this description will become Electors, I can have no doubt of: any more than that their opposition will extend to any character who (from whatever cause) would be likely to thwart their measures. It might be impolite in them to make this declaration *previous* to the Election, but I shall be out in my conjectures if they do not act conformably thereto—and from that the seeming moderation by which they appear to be actuated at present is neither more nor less than a finesse to lull and deceive. Their plan of opposition is systemised, and a regular intercourse, I have much reason to believe between the Leaders of it in the several States is formed to render it more effectual.

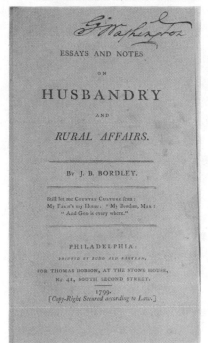

One of the last books Washington purchased on his favorite subject

Washington had given up his sword in 1783 and had returned to Mount Vernon with every hope and intention of spending the rest of his days there. It was becoming clear to him that once again he was going to have to say good-by to the place he loved so much.

Chapter 9

President of All the People

During the late summer and fall of 1788 George Washington was a worried man. He had already agonized—now optimistic, now gloomy—during the state-by-state ratification proceedings of the Constitution, wondering if the document would ever be approved. Now the Constitution had been ratified by eleven of the thirteen states, more than enough to make it operative; and Washington was anxiously following the elections to see if the senators, representatives, and presidential electors were Federalist or Antifederalist, supporters of the new nation envisioned in the Constitution or its enemies. Although the Antifederalists had failed to block the Constitution, it was possible that they might achieve enough power in the new government to wreck it from within. But Washington's apprehensions proved groundless. The senators-elect and representatives-elect proved to be overwhelmingly Federalist in sentiment, although the legislature of Washington's own Virginia, which was dominated by violently Antifederalist Patrick Henry, named two Antifederalist senators (senators were then chosen by state legislatures). The large majority of presidential electors were also Federalists. By the beginning of 1789 Washington was again able to view the future optimistically as he wrote to Lafayette. On the subject of himself as President-to-be, which everyone else took almost for granted, his references were modestly oblique.

Mount Vernon Jany. 29th. 1789.

My dear Marqs.:

By the last Post, I was favored with the receipt of your letter, dated the 5th. of September last. Notwithstanding the distance of its date, it was peculiarly welcome to me: for I had not, in the mean time received any satisfactory advices respecting yourself or your country. By that letter, my mind was placed much more at its ease, on both those subjects, than it had been for many months.

The last letter, which I had the pleasure of writing to you, was forwarded by Mr. Gouverneur Morris. Since his departure from America, nothing very material has occurred. The minds of men, however, have not been in a stagnant State. But patriotism, instead of faction, has generally agitated them. It is not a matter of wonder, that, in proportion as we approached to the time fixed for the organization and operation of the new government, their anxiety should have been encreased, rather than diminished. The choice of Senators, Representatives and Electors, whh. (excepting in that of the last description) took place at different times, in the different States, has afforded abundant topics for domestic News, since the beginning of Autumn. I need not enumerate the several particulars, as I imagine you see most of them detailed, in the American Gazettes. I will content myself with only saying, that the elections have been hitherto vastly more favorable than we could have expected, that federal sentiments seem to be growing with uncommon rapidity, and that this encreasing unanimity is not less indicative of the good disposition than the good sense of the Americans. Did it not savour so much of partiality for my Countrymen I might add, that I cannot help flattering myself the new Congress on account of the self-created respectability and various talents of its Members, will not be inferior to any Assembly in the world. From these and some other circumstances, I really entertain greater hopes, that America will not finally disappoint the expectations of her Friends, than I have at almost any former period. Still however, in such a fickle state of existence I would not be too sanguine in indulging myself with the contemplation of scenes of uninterrupted prosperity; lest some unforeseen mischance or perverseness should occasion the greater mortification, by blasting the enjoyment in the very bud.

I can say little or nothing new, in consequence of the repetition of your opinion, on the expediency there will be, for my accepting the office to which you refer. Your sentiments, indeed, coincide much more nearly with those of my other friends, than with my own feelings. In truth my difficulties encrease and magnify as I [draw] towards the period, when, according to the common belief, it will be necessary for me to give a definitive answer, in one way or another. Should the circumstances render

Broadside announcing ratification of the Constitution by Virginia

291

it, in a manner inevitably necessary, to be in the affirmative: Be assured, my dear Sir, I shall assume the task with the most unfeigned reluctance, and with a real diffidence for which I shall probably receive no credit from the world. If I know my own heart, nothing short of a conviction of duty will induce me again to take an active part in public affairs—and, in that case, if I can form a plan for my own conduct, my endeavours shall be unremittingly exerted (even at the hazard of former fame or present popularity) to extricate my country from the embarrassments in which it is entangled, [through] want of credit; and to establish, a general system of policy, which, if pursued will ensure permanent felicity to the Commonwealth. I think, I see a *path*, as clear and direct as a ray of light, which leads to the attainment of that object. Nothing but harmony, honesty, industry and frugality are necessary to make us a great and happy people. Happily the present posture of affairs and the prevailing disposition of my countrymen promise to co-operate in establishing those four great and essential pillars of public felicity....

While you are quarrelling among yourselves in Europe —while one King is running mad—and others acting as if they were already so, by cutting the throats of the subjects of their neighbours: I think you need not doubt, My Dear Marquis we shall continue in tranquility here— And that population will be progressive so long as there shall continue to be so many easy means for obtaining a subsistence, and so ample a field for the exertion of talents and industry.

History of the United States BY JOHN FROST, 1836

As depicted in this old woodcut, Charles Thomson, secretary of the Congress and Washington's friend, comes to inform him of nomination.

Although Washington wrote of still being undecided about the Presidency, the truth was that he had already virtually decided that he would serve, thinking it possible that after the new government was running smoothly he might resign. On February 4, 1789, the electors met in their respective states and cast their ballots. The result was not to be announced officially for another month, but it was not a secret to keep: the final tally showed that the sixty-nine electors had voted unanimously for Washington for President. Among the vice-presidential choices, John Adams received the most votes, thirty-four. Under the timetable set by the old Congress, the new government was to come into being on March 4 when Congress officially convened at New York and the president pro tempore of the Senate formally opened the electors' ballots. As the date approached,

Washington's spirits once more fell at the news that Congress was showing no haste to assemble. There was no quorum on March 4, nor was there one a full month later. When Henry Knox informed him that Congress's dilatoriness had already cost the country £300,000 in spring import duties missed, Washington replied that that was not the worst part of it.

Mount Vernon April 10th. 1789.

The cloth & Buttons which accompanied your favor of the 30th. Ult., came safe by Colo. Hanson; and really do credit to the Manufactures of this Country. As it requires Six more of the large (engraved) button to trim the Coat in the manner I wish it to be [a coat of American-made cloth Washington was to wear at his inauguration], I would thank you, my good Sir, for procuring that number and retaining them in your hands until my arrival at New York.

Not to contemplate (though it is a serious object) the loss which you say the General Government will sustain in the article of Impost, the stupor, or listlessness with which our public measures seem to be pervaded, is, to me, matter of deep regret. Indeed it has so strange an appearance that I cannot but wonder how men who sollicit public confidence or who are even prevailed upon to accept of it can reconcile such conduct with their own feelings of propriety. The delay is inauspicious to say the best of it — and the World must contemn it. With sentiments of sincerest friendship, I am etc.

PS. The advices by the Mail of this Evening will, surely, inform us of a Quorum in both Houses of Congress.

Charles Thomson

At last enough senators and representatives did reach New York over the muddy spring roads to make a quorum, and the electoral votes were solemnly counted. On April 14 Charles Thomson, secretary of Congress and an old friend of Washington's, rode up to Mount Vernon. After the two men had greeted each other, Thomson made a short speech informing Washington that he had been elected and then read a letter from the president pro tempore of the Senate. Washington responded by reading his acceptance speech.

[Mount Vernon, April 14, 1789]

I have been accustomed to pay so much respect to the opinion of my fellow-citizens, that the knowledge of their having given their unanimous suffrages in my favour, scarcely leaves me the alternative for an option. I can not, I believe, give a greater evidence of my

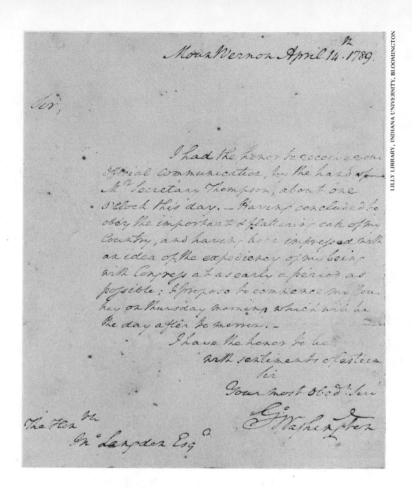

In addition to his acceptance speech, Washington wrote this letter to John Langdon, president pro tempore of the Senate, accepting the "important flattering call of my Country."

sensibility of the honor which they have done me than by accepting the appointment.

I am so much affected by this fresh proof of my Country's Esteem and Confidence that silence can best explain my gratitude. While I realize the arduous nature of the Task which is imposed upon me, and feel my own inability to perform it, I wish however that there may not be reason for regretting the Choice — for indeed all I can promise is only to accomplish that which can be done by an honest zeal.

Upon considering how long time some of the Gentlemen of both Houses of Congress have been at New-York — how anxiously desirous they must be to proceed to business — and how deeply the public mind appears to be impressed with the necessity of doing it speedily, I can not find myself at liberty to delay my journey. I shall therefore be in readiness to set out the day after tomorrow and shall be happy in the pleasure of your company; for you will permit me to say that it is a peculiar gratification to have received the communication from You.

Two days later, in midmorning of April 16, Washington's coach rolled out of the Mount Vernon drive. Washington was accompanied by Thomson and by David Humphreys, a wartime aide who had been going through Washington's papers with some intention of writing a biography. The President-elect recorded his emotions on leaving in his diary, a journal whose entries were usually quite matter-of-fact.

> April 16 [1789]. —About ten o'clock I bade adieu to Mount Vernon, to private life, and to domestic felicity; and, with a mind oppressed with more anxious and painful sensations than I have words to express, set out for New York in company with Mr. Thompson and Colonel Humphreys, with the best disposition to render service to my country in obedience to its call, but with less hope of answering its expectations.

The first leg of his journey took Washington not much more than half a dozen miles before he stopped at Alexandria for a farewell dinner with his old friends and neighbors. Only a couple of hours earlier he had felt a deep stab at leaving Mount Vernon; once again he was overcome by the poignancy of parting and the uncertainties of the future as he said his formal good-by to people he had known for many years.

[Alexandria, April 16, 1789]

> Gentlemen:
>
> Although I ought not to conceal, yet I cannot describe, the painful emotions which I felt in being called upon to determine whether I would accept or refuse the Presidency of the United States.
>
> The unanimity in the choice, the opinion of my friends, communicated from different parts of Europe, as well as of America, the apparent wish of those, who were not altogether satisfied with the Constitution in its present form, and an ardent desire on my own part, to be instrumental in conciliating the good will of my countrymen towards each other have induced an acceptance.
>
> Those who have known me best (and you, my fellow citizens, are from your situation, in that number) know better than any others my love of retirement is so great, that no earthly consideration, short of a conviction of duty, could have prevailed upon me to depart from my resolution, *"never more to take any share in transactions. of a public nature"*—For, at my age, and in my circumstances, what possible advantages could I propose to

Washington's triumphal journey to New York was drawn by Peale (above and right, below) for a contemporary magazine. George Cruikshank drew the young ladies at Trenton (right).

myself, from embarking again on the tempestuous and uncertain ocean of public-life?

I do not feel myself under the necessity of making public declarations, in order to convince you, Gentlemen, of my attachment to yourselves, and regard for your interests. The whole tenor of my life has been open to your inspection; and my pas[t] actions, rather than my present declarations, must be the pledge of my future conduct.

In the meantime I thank you most sincerely for the expressions of kindness contained in your valedictory address. It is true, just after having bade adieu to my domestic connections, this tender proof of your friendship is but too well calculated still farther to awaken my sensibility, and encrease my regret at parting from the enjoyments of private life.

All that now remains for me is to commit myself and you to the protection of that beneficent Being, who on a former occasion hath happily brought us together, after a long and distressing separation. Perhaps the same gracious Providence will again indulge us with the same heartfelt felicity. But words, my fellow-citizens, fail me: *Unutterable sensations must then be left to more expressive silence: while, from an aching heart, I bid you all, my affectionate friends, and kind neighbours, farewell*[!]

The journey to New York took on the aspects of a triumphal march. Everywhere, except where the country was sparsely settled, troops of horsemen escorted him in almost unbroken relays, so that Washington often rode for hours in a cloud of dust. At Gray's Ferry near Philadelphia a floating bridge across the Schuylkill River was walled with branches of laurel and cedar and a leafy arch had been erected at each end. As Washington, astride a horse provided for the occasion, started through this floating bower, a child hidden in the greenery of the arch lowered a laurel wreath until it was suspended just above his head. First plans had been to drop the wreath on Washington's head, but it was decided that this might be a bit unnerving even to a hero. Philadelphia outdid itself in acclaiming the President-elect with roaring cannon, pealing churchbells, cheering crowds, and five addresses, to each of which Washington replied briefly. Washington was probably less than overjoyed when informed that the Philadelphia City Troop of Horse meant to escort him all the way to Princeton, for such ceremony and honor slowed his progress. Thus, when the morning turned out to be threatening, he took advantage of the situation in a way that got rid of the escort without hurting any feelings.

City-Tavern [Philadelphia]
Tuesday morning April 21 1789.
General Washington presents his compliments to the President of the State, and requests his Excellency to communicate the General's best thanks to the Officers and Gentlemen of the several Corps who did him the honor to form his escort to Philadelphia. General Washington having made his arrangements to be at the place of embarkation for New York, at a particular hour, will find himself under the necessity of leaving this City about ten o'clock—But, as the weather is likely to prove unfavorable, he must absolutely insist that the military Gentlemen of Philadelphia will not attend him in the manner they had proposed. He is so perfectly satisfied with their good intentions, that it will be impossible for them, by taking any unnecessary trouble, to make any addition to the proofs of their attachment, or the motives of his gratitude.

The bridge his army had defended against the British at Assunpink Creek near Trenton was now turned into a tunnel of green. On its face was a banner bearing the motto "The Defenders of the Mothers will also Defend the Daughters," and lining the entrance to the bridge were rows of matrons and girls of all ages. As Washington came between their ranks, a chorus of young ladies burst into a song of welcome. At the concluding lines—"Strew, ye fair, his way with flowers;/Strew your Hero's way with flowers"—small girls with baskets stepped out and spread flowers before Washington's horse. Washington, visibly moved, thanked the ladies, and that evening found time to write a note addressed to "the Ladies of Trenton who assembled at the Triumphal Arch."

David Humphreys

Trenton April 21st. 1789.
General Washington cannot leave this place without expressing his acknowledgments, to the Matrons and Young Ladies who received him in so Novel & grateful a manner at the Triumphal Arch in Trenton, for the exquisite sensation he experienced in that affecting moment. The astonishing contrast between his former and actual situation at the same spot—the elegant taste with which it was adorned for the present occasion—and the innocent appearance of the *white-robed Choir* who met him with the gratulatory song, have made such impressions on his remembrance, as, he assures them, will never be effaced.

On April 23 Washington reached Elizabeth Town Point, New Jersey, to be rowed in a barge about fifteen miles across the bay to New York, where his reception was tumultuous. He was not even given an opportunity to change his clothes before he was hauled away to a banquet and an evening of viewing the illuminated transparencies in the city's windows. For a week, while Congress fussed about arrangements for the inauguration, Washington received visits from committees, was called on by members of Congress, and was bothered from morning till night by a stream of visitors whose principal motive in wishing to see him, apparently, was curiosity. Shortly after noon on April 30 Washington was escorted to the halls of Congress at Wall and Broad streets. So that the enormous crowds might see the historic event, the oath was taken on a small balcony. Washington promised to execute faithfully the office of President and to preserve, protect, and defend the Constitution to the best of his ability, in exactly the same words that have been repeated by every President since. Then, while the cheers still rolled through the crowds, the new Chief Executive returned inside and made his inaugural speech. It was brief. Washington's recommendations to Congress went no further than to warn against such things as pettiness, "local prejudices," "party animosities," and the like. He cautiously endorsed a Bill of Rights while warning against hasty tinkering with the main substance of the Constitution, and he called frequently on the Almighty for guidance.

[New York, April 30, 1789]
Fellow Citizens of the Senate and of the House of Representatives.

Among the vicissitudes incident to Life, no event could have filled me with greater anxieties than that, of which the notification was transmitted by your order and received on the fourteenth day of the present month.

Washington's reception in New York

Inauguration of Washington

On the one hand, I was summon'd by my Country, whose Voice I can never hear but with veneration and love, from a retreat which I had chosen with the fondest predilection, and in my flattering hopes, with an immutable decision, as the assylum of my declining years, a retreat which was rendered every day more necessary as well as more dear to me, by the addition of habit to inclination and of frequent interruptions in my health to the gradual waste committed on it by time. On the other hand, the magnitude and difficulty of the Trust to which the voice of my country called me, being sufficient to awaken in the wisest and most experienced of her Citizens, a distrustful scrutiny into his qualifications, could not but overwhelm with despondence, one, who (inheriting inferior endowments from Nature and unpractised in the duties of civil administration) ought to be peculiarly conscious of his own deficencies. In this conflict of emotions, all I dare aver, is, that it has been my faithful study to collect my duty from a just appreciation of every circumstance by which it might be affected. All I dare hope, is, that if in executing this Task, I have been too much swayed by a grateful remembrance of former instances or by an affectionate sensibility to this transcendent proof of the confidence of my fellow Citizens; and have thence too little consulted my incapacity as well as disinclination for the weighty and untried cares before me; my error will be palliated by the motives which misled me, and its consequences be judged by my Country with some share of the partiality in which they originated.

Such being the impressions under which I have in obedience to the public summons repaired to the present station; it would be peculiarly improper to omit in this first official act my fervent supplications to that Almighty Being who rules over the Universe, who presides in the Councils of Nations and whose providential aids can supply every human defect, that his benediction may consecrate, to the Liberties and happiness of the people of the United States, a Government instituted by themselves for these essential purposes: and may enable every instrument employed in its administration, to execute with success the functions allotted to his charge.... By the article establishing the executive department, it is made the duty of the President

After his inauguration, Washington walked to St. Paul's Church (right of Brick Presbyterian Church), where prayers were offered for success.

"to recommend to your consideration such measures as he shall judge necessary and expedient." The circumstances under which I now meet you, will acquit me from entering into that subject, farther than to refer to the great consitutional Charter under which you are assembled; and which in defining your powers, designates the objects to which your attention is to be given. It will be more consistent with those circumstances and far more congenial with the feelings which actuate me to substitute in place of a recommendation of particular measures, the tribute that is due to the talents, the rectitude and the patriotism which adorn the Characters selected to devise and adopt them. In these honorable qualifications, I behold the surest pledges that as on one side, no local prejudices or attachments; no seperate views, nor party animosities, will misdirect the comprehensive and equal Eye which ought to watch over this great assemblage of communities and interests; so, on another that the foundations of our national policy will be laid in the pure and immutable principles of private morality; and the preeminence of free Government be exemplified by all the attributes, which can win the affections of its citizens and command the respect of the world....

Besides the ordinary objects submitted to your care, it will remain with your judgment to decide, how far an exercise of the occasional power delegated by the fifth article of the Constitution is rendered expedient at the present juncture, by the nature of objections which have been urged against the System, or by the degree of inquietude which has given birth to them. Instead of undertaking particular recommendations on this subject, in which I could be guided by no lights derived from official opportunities, I shall again give way to my entire confidence in your discernment and pursuit of the public good—For I assure myself that whilst you carefully avoid every alteration which might endanger the benefits of an United and effective government or which ought to await the future lessons of experience; a reverence for the characteristic rights of freemen, and a regard for the public harmony, will sufficiently influence your deliberations on the question, how far the former can be impregnably fortified or the latter be safely and advantageously promoted.

Washington also proposed that he receive no salary but only be reimbursed for his expenses, as he had been during the Revolution. Congress, however, fixed a salary of twenty-five thousand dollars a year, and although Washington drew only his expenses, over four years they amounted almost exactly to what the salary would have been. The new President was in a world without precedents, and it was important that he act carefully and wisely. He moved early to put the presidential social life in order; it was imperative that he limit the parade of visitors who called at all hours and also that he cut down on his attendance at social functions if he were to conserve his energy and get any work done. He asked Vice President Adams, Alexander Hamilton, and John Jay for their advice.

[New York, May 10, 1789]

The President of the United States wishes to avail himself of your sentiments on the following points.

1st.   Whether a line of conduct, equally distant from an association with all kinds of company on the one hand and from a total seclusion from Society on the other, ought to be adopted by him? and, in that case, how is it to be done?

2d.   What will be the least exceptionable method of bringing any system, which may be adopted on this subject, before the public and into use?

3d.   Whether, after a little time, one day in every week will not be sufficient for receiving visits of Compliment?

4th.   Whether it would tend to prompt impertinent applications & involve disagreeable consequences to have it known, that the President will, every Morning at 8 Oclock, be at leisure to give Audiences to persons who may have business with him?

5th.   Whether, when it shall have been understood that the President is not to give *general entertainment* in the Manner the Presidents of Congress have formerly done, it will be practicable to draw such a line of discrimination in regard to persons, as that Six, eight or ten official characters (including in the rotation the members of both Houses of Congress) may be invited informally or otherwise to dine with him on the days fixed for receiving Company, without exciting clamours in the rest of the Community?

6th.   Whether it would be satisfactory to the Public for the President to make about four great entertainmts. in a year on such great occasions as ... the Annaversary of the Declaration of Independence ... the Alliance with

This small mansion on the corner of Pearl and Cherry streets in New York was the first presidential abode.

France...the Peace with Great Britain...the Organization of the general Government: and whether arrangements of these two last kinds could be in danger of diverting too much of the Presidents time from business, or of producing the evils which it was intended to avoid by his living more recluse than the Presidts. of Congress have heretofore lived.

7th.   Whether there would be any impropriety in the Presidents making informal visits—that is to say, in his calling upon his Acquaintances or public Characters for the purposes of sociability or civility—and what (as to the form of doing it) might evince these visits to have been made in his private character, so as that they might not be construed into visits from the President of the United States? and in what light would his appearance *rarely at Tea* parties be considered?

8th.   Whether, during the recess of Congress, it would not be advantageous to the interests of the Union for the President to make the tour of the United States, in order to become better acquainted with their principal Characters & internal Circumstances, as well as to be more accessible to numbers of well-informed persons, who might give him useful information and advices on political subjects?

9th.   If there is a probability that either of the arrangements may take place, which will eventually cause additional expences, whether it would not be proper that these ideas should come into contemplation, at the time when Congress shall make a permanent provision for the support of the Executive?

Remarks

On the one side no augmentation can be effected in the pecuniary establishment which shall be made in the first instance, for the support of the Executive. On the other, all monies destined to that purpose beyond the actual expenditures, will be left in the Treasury of the United States or sacredly applied to the promotion of some National objects.

Many things which appear of little importance in themselves and at the beginning, may have great and durable consequences from their having been established at the commencement of a new general government. It will be much easier to commence the administration, upon a well adjusted system built on tenable grounds,

Washington used this writing table in Federal Hall when the capital was still located in New York City.

than to correct errors or alter inconveniencies after they shall have been confirmed by habit. The President in all matters of business & etiquette, can have no object but to demean himself in his public character, in such a manner as to maintain the dignity of Office, without subjecting himself to the imputation of superciliousness or unnecessary reserve. Under these impresions, he asks for your candid and undisguised Opinions.

Both Hamilton and Adams advised Washington to remain aloof. The President compromised somewhat; he set two weekly occasions: a "levee" for men and a tea for both sexes over which Martha would preside, during which, for one hour, any citizen could call and meet the President. There was also to be a weekly dinner at which the President would be host to groups of government officials. There were precedents to be set in government, too. When, for instance, a letter arrived from the King of France addressed both to the President and to Congress, Washington in informing Congress said that he would take care of the answer and left the unmistakable implication that such matters were strictly in his province.

United States September 29th. 1789.

Gentlemen of the Senate and House of Representatives:

His most Christian Majesty, by a letter dated the 7th. of June last, addressed to the President and Members of the General Congress of the United States of North America, announced the much lamented death of his son the Dauphin. The generous conduct of the French Monarch and Nation towards this Country renders every event that may affect his or their prosperity interesting to us, and I shall take care to assure him of the sensibility with which the United States participate in the affliction which a loss so much to be regretted must have occasioned both to him and them.

Louis XVI

There were hundreds of appointments for Washington to make, most of them for customs collectors and the like, but also for the high offices of the justices of the Supreme Court and the judges of the eleven district courts, as well as the members of the President's own Cabinet— although it appears that Washington himself did not use the term Cabinet. Alexander Hamilton was appointed Secretary of the Treasury; Henry Knox became Secretary of War; Thomas Jefferson, Secretary of State; and Edmund Randolph, Attorney General. John Jay, the leading diplomat of the old government, was appointed first Chief Justice of the United States. Congress adjourned on September 29, and on October 15 the President set out on a tour of New England. He kept a careful record of people and places in his diary, as he had on former travels, but now there was a difference. Previously he had been mainly interested in land and soil; now he was curious about community growth, commerce, manufacturing, and other evidences of national expansion. Following are some typical excerpts from that diary.

Thursday, 15th [October, 1789]. Commenced my Journey about 9 oclock for Boston and a tour through the Eastern States. The Chief Justice, Mr. Jay—and the Secretaries of the Treasury and War Departments accompanied me some distance out of the city. About 10 Oclock it began to Rain, and continued to do so till 11, when we arrived at the house of one Hoyatt, who keeps a Tavern at Kings-bridge, where we, that is, Major Jackson, Mr. Lear and myself, with Six Servants, which composed my Retinue, dined. After dinner through frequent light showers we proceedd. to the Tavern of a Mrs. Haviland at Rye [New York]; who keeps a very neat and decent Inn....

The distance of this days travel was 31 Miles in which we passed through (after leaving the Bridge) East Chester, New Rochel & Mameroneck; but as these places (though they have houses of worship in them) are not regularly laid out, they are scarcely to be distinquished from the intermediate farms which are very close together—and separated, as one Inclosure from another also is, by fences of Stone which are indeed easily made, as the Country is immensely stony. Upon enquiry we find their Crops of Wheat & Rye have been abundant—though of the first they had sown rather sparingly on Acct. of the destruction which had of late years been made of that grain by what is called the Hessian fly.

Friday, 16th. About 7 Oclock we left the Widow Havilands, and after passing Horse Neck, six miles distant from Rye, the Road through which is hilly and immensely stoney and trying to Wheels & Carriages, we breakfasted at Stamford [Connecticut] which is 6 miles further (at one Webbs) a tolerable good house, but not equal in appearance or reality, to Mrs. Havilds. In this Town are an Episcopal Church and a Meeting house. At Norwalk which is ten miles further we made a halt to feed our Horses. To the lower end of this town

Washington's first Cabinet included Jefferson and Hamilton (standing to his right), and Knox reading paper.

John Jay

Sea Vessels come and at the other end are Mills, Stores, and an Episcopal and Presbiterian Church. From hence to Fairfield where we dined and lodged, is 12 Miles; and part of it very rough Road, but not equal to that thro' horse Neck.... The Destructive evidences of British cruelty are yet visible both in Norwalk & Fairfield; as there are the Chimneys of many burnt houses standing in them yet. The principal export from Norwalk & Fairfield is Horses and Cattle—Salted Beef & Porke, Lumber & Indian Corn, to the West Indies—and in a small degree Wheat & Flour.

Saturday, 17th. ...[We] arrived at New haven before two Oclock; We had time to Walk through several parts of the City before Dinner. By taking the lower Road, we missed a Committee of the assembly, who had been appointed to wait upon, and escort me into town—to prepare an Address—and to conduct me when I should leave the City as far as they should judge proper. The address was presented at 7 Oclock—and at nine I received another address from the Congregational Clergy of the place. Between the rect. of the two addresses I received the Compliment of a Visit from the Govr. Mr. Huntington—the Lieut. Govr. Mr. Wolcot—and the Mayor Mr. Roger Shurman. The City of New-haven occupies a good deal of ground; but is thinly, though regularly laid out, and built. The number of Souls in it are said to be about 4000. There is an Episcopal Church and 3 Congregational Meeting Houses and a College [Yale] in which there are at this time 120 Students under the auspices of Doctr. Styles. The Harbour of this place is not good for large Vessels—abt. 16 belongs to it. The Linnen Manufacture of this place does not appear to be of so much importance as I had been led to believe—In a word I could hear but little of it. The Exports from this City are much the same as from Fairfield &ca. and flax seed (chiefly to New York). The Road from Kings bridge to this place runs as near the Sound as the Bays and Inlets will allow, but from hence to Hartford it leaves the Sound and runs more to the Northward....

Monday, 19th. Left New haven at 6 oclock, and arrived at Wallingford (13 miles) by half after 8 oclock, where we breakfasted and took a walk through the Town.... At this place (Wallingford) we see the white Mulberry growing, raised from the Seed to feed the Silkworm. We also saw samples of lustring (exceeding good) which had been manufactured from the Cocoon raised in this Town, and silk thread very fine. This, except the weaving, is the work of private families without interference with other business, and is likely to turn out a beneficial amusement.

Washington and his party—two secretaries and six servants—continued up the Connecticut River to Springfield, Massachusetts, then turned east toward Boston, the scene of his first victory over the British. He received a tremendous welcome but was forced to establish the supremacy of the President over the governor of a state. Washington had accepted an advance invitation to dine with Governor John Hancock, fully expecting that Hancock would call on him first. But when he arrived in Boston, Hancock was not among the welcomers and sent word that gout made it impossible for him to move from his house. Washington realized that Hancock, a strong advocate of states' rights, was trying to establish that when a President visited a state he did so only as a guest of the governor. He immediately canceled the dinner engagement. The message was not lost on Hancock, who sent emissaries and then came to call. Washington described the incident in his diary briefly and without comment.

Banner carried by Boston shoemakers during procession in honor of visit

Saturday, 24th [October, 1789]. ...Having engaged yesterday to take an informal dinner with the Govr. today, (but under a full persuasion that he would have waited upon me so soon as I should have arrived) I excused myself upon his not doing it, and informing me thro his Secretary that he was too much indisposed to do it, being resolved to receive the visit. Dined at my Lodgings, where the Vice-President favoured me with his Company.

Sunday, 25th. Attended Divine Service at the Episcopal Church whereof Doctor Parker is the Incumbent in the forenoon, and the Congregational Church of Mr. Thatcher in the Afternoon. Dined at my Lodgings with the Vice President. Mr. Bowdoin accompanied me to both Churches. Between the two I received a visit from the Govr., who assured me that Indisposition alone had prevented his doing it yesterday, and that he was still indisposed; but as it had been suggested that he expected to *receive* the visit from the President, which he knew was improper, he was resolved at all hazds. to pay his Compliments today. The Lt. Govr. & two of the Council to wit Heath & Russel were sent here last Night to express the Govrs. Concern that he had not been in a condition to call upon me so soon as I came to Town. I informed them in explicit terms that I should not see the Govr., unless it was at my own lodgings.

Hancock had been carried, heavily swathed in bandages, into Washington's lodgings when he called on the President; but if Washington suspected that the Governor's gout was feigned, he did not confide it to his diary. The constitutional issue was settled, and the precedence of President over governor established. On his fifth day in Boston, Washington escaped from the ceremonial and social activities and began to become better acquainted with the city.

John Hancock

Wednesday, 28th [October, 1789]. Went after an early breakfast to visit the duck Manufacture which appeared to be carrying on with spirit, and is in a prosperous way. They have manufactured 32 pieces of Duck of 30 or 40 yds. each in a week; and expect in a short time to encrease it to [   ]. They have 28 looms at work & 14 Girls spinning with Both hands (the flax being fastened to their waste). Children (girls) turn the wheels for them, and with this assistance each spinner can turn out 14 lbs. of thread pr. day when they stick to it, but as they are pd. by the piece, or work they do, there is no other restraint upon them but to come at 8 Oclock in the Morning and return at 6 in the evening. They are the daughters of decayed families, and are girls of Character—none others are admitted. The number of hands now employed in the different parts of the work is [   ] but the Managers expect to encrease them to [   ]. This is a work of public utility & private advantage. From hence I went to the Card Manufactury where I was informed about 900 hands of one kind and for one purpose or another. All kinds of Cards are made; & there are Machines for executing every part of the work in a new and expeditious manr., especially in cutting & bending the teeth wch. is done at one stroke. They have made 63,000 pr. of Cards in a year and can under sell the Imported Cards—nay Cards of this Manufactury have been smuggled into England. . . .

Thursday, 29th. Left Boston about 8 o'clock. Passed over the Bridge at Charles Town and went to see that at Malden, but proceeded to the college at Cambridge [Harvard], attended by the Vice President, Mr. Bowdoin, and a great number of Gentlemen: At this place I was shewn by Mr. Willard the President, the Philosophical Aparatus, and amongst others Popes Orary (a curious piece of Mechanism for shewing the revolutions of the Sun, Earth, and many other of the Planets,)—the library, (containing 13,000 volumes,)—and a Museum. The Bridges of Charles town and Malden are useful & noble —doing great credit to the enterprising spirit of the People of this State. From Boston, besides the number of Citizens which accompanied me to Cambridge, & many of them from hence to Lynn—the Boston Corps of Horse escorted me to the line between Middlesex and Essex County where a party of Horse with Genl. Titcomb met me, and conducted me through Marblehead (which is 4 miles out of the way, but I wanted to see it,) to Salem. The Chief employmt. of the People of Marblehead (Male) is fishing—about 110 Vessels and 800 Men and boys are engaged in this business. Their chief export is fish. About 5000 Souls are said to be in this place which has the appearance of antiquity; the Houses are old—the streets dirty—and the common people not very clean.

New York Magazine, SEPTEMBER, 1795; NEW-YORK HISTORICAL SOCIETY

A view of the bridge over Charles River, which President Washington described as "useful and noble"

Washington continued his journey, through Salem, which he thought "a neat town," on to Newburyport, and into New Hampshire, where there was another rousing welcome by militia, horsemen, and dignitaries, including the president (governor) of the state, John Sullivan, his good friend and onetime general. Two days later he crossed the river from Portsmouth, New Hampshire, to Kittery in Maine, then a province of Massachusetts. He and his party went fishing for cod, "but it not being a proper time of tide, we only caught two." From this northernmost point he began his return, asking that all ceremony be avoided. There was little pomp and circumstance in his passage through farmland and hamlets; like any other mortal, he talked with farmers about crops, asked directions and sometimes got bad advice, and occasionally had trouble finding lodgings.

Friday, 6th [November, 1789]. A little after Seven oclock, under great appearances of Rain or Snow, we left Watertown [Massachusetts], and Passing through Needham (five Miles therefrom) breakfasted at Sherburn which is 14 Miles from the former. Then passing through Holliston 5 Miles, Milford 6 More, Menden 4 More, and Uxbridge 6 More, we lodged at one Tafts 1 Miles further; the whole distance of this days travel being 36 Miles. From Watertown till you get near Needham, the Road is very level—about Needham it is hilly—then level again, and the whole pleasant and well cultivated 'till you pass Sherburn; between this and Holliston is some hilly & Rocky ground as there is in places, onwards to Uxbridge; some of wch. are very bad; Upon the whole it may be called an indifferent Rd.—diversified by good & bad land—cultivated and in woods—some high and Barren—and others low, wet and Piney. Grass and Indian Corn is the chief produce of the Farms. Rye composes a part of the culture of them, but wheat is not grown on Acct. of the blight. The Roads in every part of this State are amazingly crooked, to suit the convenience of every Mans fields; & the directions you receive from the People equally blind & ignorant; for instead of going to Watertown from Lexington, if we had proceeded to Waltham, we should in 13 Miles have saved at least Six; the distance from Lexington to Waltham being only 5 Miles and the Road from Watertown to Sherburn going with in less than two miles of the latter, (i.e. Waltham). The Clouds of the Morning vanished before the Meridian Sun, and the Afternoon was bright and pleasant. The house in Uxbridge had a good external appearance (for a Tavern) but the owner of it being from home, and the wife sick, we could not gain admittance which was the reason of my coming on to Tafts; where, though the People were obliging, the entertainment was not very inviting....

Sunday, 8th. It being contrary to Law & disagreeable to the People of this State (Connecticut) to travel on the Sabbath day—and my horses, after passing through such intolerable Roads, wanting rest, I stayed at Perkins's Tavern (which by the bye is not a good one,) all day—and a meeting House being with in few rod of the Door, I attended Morning & evening Service, and heard very lame discourses from a Mr. Pond.

On his tour Washington had avoided Rhode Island, which had not yet ratified the Constitution, and Vermont, not yet a state. He arrived back in New York on Friday afternoon, November 13, just in time for Martha's weekly tea party.

The triumphal arch and colonnade erected in Boston in front of the State House to honor the President

Congress reconvened in early January, and Washington presented his first annual message. A week later Alexander Hamilton gave Congress a plan for strengthening national credit and reducing the public debt. It was the issue that would eventually split Washington's Administration into opposing political parties. Congress had gone deeply into debt during the Revolution. The foreign debt was almost twelve million dollars. No one knew exactly what the domestic debt was—Army quartermaster foraging parties, for instance, had given thousands of hastily written certificates to farmers for requisitioned grain or cattle—but it was fixed at something more than forty-four million dollars. Hamilton proposed that this entire debt be funded, with the almost worthless old securities exchanged at face value for new bonds, which would be gradually retired through excise taxes. Hamilton further proposed that the Government assume some $21,500,000 in debts owed by the states. The financial community approved Hamilton's plan, but elsewhere there was intense opposition. Most of the certificates given to farmers and soldiers had long since passed into the hands of speculators for a few cents on the dollar. James Madison fought hard but unsuccessfully for a plan to make at least partial payment to the original bearers of certificates. There was even greater controversy over federal assumption of state debts. The southern states, except South Carolina, had already paid their war debts and had no desire to be taxed again to help New Englanders who had let their obligations drift.

In mid-May Washington became so ill with pneumonia that his doctors believed he was dying; then he passed a crisis and a week later was able to go out in his carriage for exercise. In mid-June, Congress was still wrangling over the money bill, and Washington was well enough to write to Dr. David Stuart, husband of the widow of Jack Custis. Stuart had complained that Virginia sentiment toward the new government had been soured by the actions of Congress, by its slowness, and because the members "it is said, sit only four hours a day, and like School-boys observe every Saturday as a Holy day." In his reply Washington defended the legislature.

> New York June 15. 1790.
> Your description of the public mind in Virginia gives me pain—It seems to be more irritable, sour, and discontented than (from the information I receive) it is in any other State in the union, except Massachusetts, which from the same causes, but on quite different principles is tempered like it.
>
> That Congress does not proceed with all that dispatch which people at a distance expect, and which, were they to hurry business they possibly might, is not to be denied. That measures have been agitated which are not pleasing to Virginia, and others, pleasing perhaps to her, but not so to some other States is equally unquestionable.

Can it well be otherwise in a Country so extensive, so diversified in its interests? And will not these different interests naturally produce in an Assembly of Representatives, who are to legislate for, and to assimilate, and reconcile them to the *general* welfare, long, warm, and animated debates? Most assuredly they will—and if there was the same propensity in mankind for investigating the motives, as there is for censuring the conduct of public characters, it would be found that the censure so freely bestowed is oftentimes unmerited and uncharitable—for instance, the condemnation of Congress for sitting only four hours in the day. The fact is, by the established rules of the House of Representatives, no Committee can sit whilst the House is sitting; and this is and has been for a considerable time, from ten o'clock in the forenoon until three, often later, in the afternoon; before and after which the business is going on in Committees. If this application is not as much as most constitutions are equal to, I am mistaken: Many other things which undergo malignant constructions, would be found, upon a candid examination to wear better faces than are given to them. The misfortune is, that the enemies to the Government, always more active than its friends— and always upon the watch to give it a stroke—neglect no opportunity to aim one. If they tell truth, it is not the whole truth, by which means one side only of the picture is exhibited; whereas if both sides were seen, it might and probably would, assume a different form in the opinion of just and candid men, who are disposed to measure matters on a continental scale. I do not mean, however, from what I have here said, to justify the conduct of Congress in all its movements; for some of these movements, in my opinion, have been injudicious, and others unseasonable; whilst the questions of assumption, residence, and other matters, have been agitated with a warmth and intemperence—with prolixity and threats, which it is to be feared has lessened the dignity of that body, and decreased that respect which was once entertained for it—and this misfortune is encreased by many Members, even among those who wish well to the Government ascribing in letters to their respective States when they are defeated in a favorite measure, the worst motives for the conduct of their Opponents; who, viewing matters through another medium, may,

Carriage built for George Washington during his first presidential term

and do, retort in their turn, by which means jealousies and distrusts are spread most impoliticly far and wide, and will it is to be feared, have a most unhappy tendency to injure our public affairs, which if wisely managed might make us (as we are now by Europeans thought to be) the happiest people upon Earth....

The question of assumption has occupied a great deal of time, and no wonder; for it is certainly a very important question; and, under *proper* restrictions, and scrutiny into accounts will be found, I conceive, to be a just one. The cause, in which the expenses of the war was incurred was a common cause. The States (in Congress) declared it so at the beginning, and pledged themselves to stand by each other; If then, some States were harder pressed than others, or from particular or local circumstances contracted heavier debts, it is but reasonable when this fact is clearly ascertained, though it is a sentiment which I have not communicated here, that an allowance ought to be made them. Had the invaded and hard pressed States believed the case would have been otherwise, opposition would very soon, I believe, have changed to submission in them, and given a different termination to the war.

In a letter of last year to the best of my recollection, I informed you of the motives, which *compelled* me to allot a day for the reception of idle and ceremonious visits (for it never has prevented those of sociability and friendship in the afternoon, or at any other time) but if I am mistaken in this, the history of this business is simply and shortly as follows. Before the custom was established, which now accommodates foreign characters, Strangers, and others who from motives of curiosity, respect, to the Chief Magistrate, or any other cause, are induced to call upon me I was unable to attend to any business *whatsoever*; for Gentlemen, consulting their own convenience rather than mine, were calling from the time I rose from breakfast—often before—until I sat down to dinner. This, as I resolved not to neglect my public duties, reduced me to the choice of one of these alternatives, either to refuse them *altogether*, or to appropriate a time for the reception of them. The first would, I well knew, be disgusting to many—The latter, I *expected*, would undergo animadversion, and blazoning from those who would find fault,

The large house in New York City to which the Washingtons moved in 1790

with, or *without* cause. To please every body was impossible—I therefore adopted that line of conduct which combined public advantage with private convenience, and which in my judgment was unexceptionable in itself. That I have not been able to make bows to the taste of poor Colonel Bland, (who by the by I believe never saw one of them) is to be regretted especially too as (upon those occasions) they were indiscriminately bestowed, and the best I was master of—would it not have been better to have thrown the veil of charity over them, ascribing their stiffness to the effects of age, or to the unskillfulness of my teacher, than to pride and dignity of office, which God knows has no charms for me? for I can truly say I had rather be at Mount Vernon with a friend or two about me, than to be attended at the 'Seat of Government by the Officers of State and the Representatives of every Power in Europe.

By and large, things were going well for the new nation. The Bill of Rights, or first ten amendments to the Constitution, had been submitted to the states for ratification and would become part of the fundamental law on December 15, 1791. Meanwhile Rhode Island, the last hold-out, ratified the Constitution in May, 1790 (North Carolina had done so the previous November). But Hamilton's plan for funding the debt seemed doomed; federal assumption of state debts had been voted down in the House committee sessions. Hamilton, in despair, went to Jefferson for help. The issue could split the nation, he said. New England might well secede if assumption were defeated. Jefferson recognized the gravity of the situation and agreed there was probably room for compromise. At a meeting with Hamilton and James Madison an agreement was worked out: in return for the Southerners' accepting assumption of debts, there would be northern support for locating the permanent capital of the country in the South, at a site to be selected by Washington on the banks of the Potomac River. As a sop to Pennsylvania politicians, the capital was to be moved to Philadelphia until the new city on the Potomac was ready. Within a few weeks the bills to move the capital and to approve the funding measures had been passed by Congress.

After Congress adjourned in August, Washington remained in New York only long enough to make his personal arrangements for moving. On August 30 he left for Philadelphia. Although the largest house in the city, that of Robert Morris, had been placed at his disposal, he found fault with it, and wrote to his secretary, Tobias Lear, about changes in the dwelling and arrangements for making it the Executive Mansion.

A 1790 cartoon depicting Robert Morris, led by the devil, removing the capital from New York City

Philadelphia, Septr. 5th. 1790.

After a pleasant Journey we arrived in this City about 2 Oclock on thursday last. Tomorrow we proceed (if Mrs. Washingtons health [allows?], for she has been much indisposed since she came here) towards Mount Vernon.

The House of Mr. R. Morris had, previous to my arrival, been taken by the Corporation for my residence. It is the best they could get. It is, I believe, the best *single House* in the City; yet, without additions it is inadequate to the *commodious* accomodation of my family. These, I believe, will be made.

The first floor contains only two public Rooms (except one for the *upper* Servants). The second floor will have two public (drawing) Rooms, & with the aid of one room with the partition in it in the back building will be Sufficient for the accomodation of Mrs. Washington & the Children, & their Maids—besides affording me a small place for a private Study & dressing Room. The third Story will furnish you & Mrs. Lear with a good lodging room—a public Office (for there is no place below for one) and two Rooms for the Gentlemen of the family. The Garret has four good Rooms which must serve Mr. and Mrs. Hyde (unless they should prefer the room over the wash House)—William—and such Servants as it may not be better to place in the addition (as proposed) to the Back Building. There is a room over the Stable (without a fire place, but by means of a Stove) may serve the Coachman & Postilions; and there is a Smoke House, which, possibly, may be more useful to me for the accomodation of Servants than for Smoking of meat. The intention of the addition to the Back building is to provide a Servants Hall, and one or two (as it will afford) lodging rooms for the Servants; especially those who are coupled. There is a very good Wash House adjoining to the Kitchen (under one of the rooms already mentioned). There are good Stables, but for 12 Horses only, and a Coach House which will hold all my Carriages....

PS. In a fortnight or 20 days from this time it is expected Mr. Morris will have removed out of the House. It is proposed to add Bow Windows to the two public rooms in the South front of the House—But as all the other apartments will be close & secure the sooner after that time you can be in the House with the furniture, the better, that you may be well fixed and see how matters go on during my absence.

From Philadelphia the President continued on to Mount Vernon, where he remained more than two months, conducting some official business by mail, happily writing letter after letter to Tobias Lear about arrangements for the new President's House, and thoroughly enjoying being home again. He returned to Philadelphia late in November, and on December 8, 1790, made his second annual address to Congress when that body met for the first time in the new capital. In his message the President reported that he found crops good, commerce flourishing, the national credit improving. A loan had been obtained from Holland; the Kentucky District of Virginia was applying for separate statehood; the threats of war between Europe's maritime powers should make the United States think of building up its own merchant marine. Washington also devoted a considerable part of his address to the Indians on the western frontier.

[Philadelphia, December 8, 1790]
It has been heretofore known to Congress, that frequent incursions have been made on our frontier settlemts. by certain banditti of Indians from the North West side of the Ohio. These with some of the tribes dwelling on and near the Wabash have of late been particularly active in their depridations; and being emboldened by the impunity of their crimes, and aided by such parts of the neighbouring tribes as could be seduced to join in their hostilities or afford them a retreat for their prisoners and plunder, they have, instead of listening to the

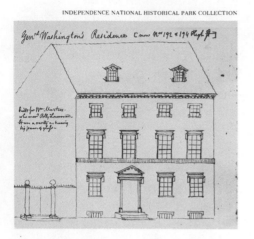

The Morris house in Philadelphia,
which became home to the
Washingtons after 1790

humane overtures made on the part of the United States, renewed their violences with fresh alacrity and greater effect. The lives of a number of valuable Citizens have thus been sacrificed, and some of them under circumstances peculiarily shocking; whilst others have been carried into a deplorable captivity.

These aggravated provocations rendered it essential to the safety of the Western Settlements that the aggressors should be made sensible that the Governmt. of the Union is not less capable of punishing their crimes, than it is disposed to respect their rights and reward their attachments. As this object could not be effected by defensive measures it became necessary to put in force the Act which empowers the President to call out the Militia for the protection of the frontiers. And I have accordingly authorized an expedition in which the regular troops in that quarter are combined with such drafts of Militia as were deemed sufficient. The event of the measure is yet unknown to me.

Indian matters had absorbed much of Washington's time almost from the day he took office and would do so until he retired. The frontier was always a sensitive area and the possibility of trouble ever-present. Although the Administration did what it could to protect the treaty rights of the Indians, settlers disregarded boundaries and treaties when they wanted to move onto Indian land. To aggravate the situation, both Spain and England turned the unrest of the red men to their own uses. The Spanish in Florida and Louisiana surreptitiously encouraged tribesmen in the southwestern United States to resist settlers from the southern states; in the Northwest the British at Detroit and other posts on American soil quietly aided the Indians north of the Ohio River. In his address, Washington was referring to certain tribes north of the Ohio who were warring with the encroaching settlers. The President, however, was not entirely candid in saying that he had no idea at that moment of the outcome of the military expedition sent against the Indians, for at least a week earlier he had had an unofficial report that the force, led by Brigadier General Josiah Harmar, had been defeated. When the official report arrived, it showed that 180 men had been lost. (Another expedition sent on the same mission a year later suffered much more grievously; six hundred of its nine hundred officers and men were killed or wounded.)

The subsequent session of Congress was concerned chiefly with two measures prepared by Hamilton to further strengthen the nation's credit. One was a revenue bill to place higher taxes on imported liquors and to levy excise taxes on those distilled in the United States. The excise tax bill would have eventful consequences before Washington left the Presidency. The other measure was a bill to create a national bank modeled after the Bank of England. Both bills were passed despite strong opposition, and Washington was then faced with deciding whether the bank bill was constitutional. Among his advisers, Randolph and Jefferson, both Republicans and literal interpreters of the Constitution, argued that the Constitution did not give Congress authority to create such a corporation as the bank. Hamilton, of course, had no doubts. Washington, convinced that the young nation must have a strong central government if it was to survive, accepted Hamilton's arguments and signed the bill into law. Congress adjourned on March 3, 1791, and later in the month Washington set out to tour the South, as he had New England a year and a half earlier.

Monday, 21st [March, 1791]. Left Philadelphia about 11 O'clock to make a tour through the Southern States. Reached Chester about 3 oclock — dined & lodged at Mr. Wythes. Roads exceedingly deep, heavy & cut in places by the Carriages which used them.

In this tour I was accompanied by Majr. Jackson. My equipage & attendance consisted of a Chariet & four horses drove in hand — a light baggage Waggon & two horses — four saddle horses besides a led one for myself — and five Servants — to wit — my Valet de Chambre, two footmen, Coachman & Postilion.

Tuesday, 22d.   At half past 6 Oclock we left Chester, & breakfasted at Wilmington. Finding the Roads very heavy — and receiving unfavourable Accts. of those between this place and Baltimore I determined to cross the Bay by the way of Rockhall and crossing Christiana Creek proceeded through Newcastle & by the Red Lyon to the Buck tavern 13 Miles from Newcastle and 19 from Wilmington where we dined and lodged. At the Red Lyon we gave the horses a bite of Hay — during their eating of which I discovered that one of those wch. drew the Baggage Waggon was lame and appd. otherwise much indisposed — had him bled and afterwards led to the Buck tavern.

This is a better house than the appearances indicate.

Wednesday, 23d.   ... The lame horse was brought on, and while on the Road appd. to move tolerably well, but as soon as he stopped, discovered a stiffness in all his limbs which indicated some painful disorder. I fear a Chest founder. My riding horse also appeared to be very

Columbian Magazine, NOVEMBER, 1787; NEW-YORK HISTORICAL SOCIETY

Christ Church in Philadelphia, where Washington had a pew

unwell, his appetite havg. entirely failed him.

The Winter grain along the Road appeared promising and abundant.

Thursday, 24th.   Left Chester town about 6 Oclock. Before nine I arrived at Rock-Hall where we breakfasted and immediately; after which we began to embark—The doing of which employed us (for want of contrivance) until near 3 Oclock—and then one of my Servants (Paris) & two horses were left, notwithstanding two Boats in aid of the two Ferry Boats were procured. Unluckily, embarking on board of a borrowed Boat because She was the largest, I was in imminent danger, from the unskillfulness of the hands, and the dulness of her sailing, added to the darkness and storminess of the night. For two hours after we hoisted Sail the Wind was light and a head—the next hour was a stark calm—after which the wind sprung up at So. Et. and encreased until it blew a gale—about which time, and after 8 Oclock P.M. we made the Mouth of Severn River (leading up to Annapolis) but the ignorance of the People on board, with respect to the navigation of it run us aground first on Greenbury point from whence with much exertion and difficulty we got off; & then, having no knowledge of the Channel and the Night being immensely dark with heavy and variable squals of wind—constant lightning & tremendous thunder. We soon grounded again on what is called Hornes point—where finding all efforts in vain, & not knowing where we were we remained, not knowing what might happen, 'till morning.

Friday, 25th.   Having lain all night in my Great Coat & Boots, in a birth not long enough for me by the head, & much cramped; we found ourselves in the Morning within about one mile of Annapolis & still fast aground. Whilst we were preparing our small Boat in order to land in it, a sailing Boat came of to our assistance in wch. with the Baggage I had on board I landed, & requested Mr. Man at whose Inn I intended lodging, to send off a Boat to take off two of my Horses & Chariet which I had left on board and with it my Coachman to see that it was properly done—but by mistake the latter not having notice of this order & attempting to get on board afterwards in a small Sailing Boat was overset and narrowly escaped drowning.

It is possible Washington overestimated the peril of crossing Chesapeake Bay; although brave in battle, he never had cared much for the water. He received a heartfelt welcome from the worried officials at Annapolis, the Maryland state capital, who had been waiting for hours for his overdue boat. Then he proceeded to Georgetown, on the site of the permanent national capital, where he met with the commissioners, discussed plans, examined the sketches of Pierre Charles L'Enfant, who was designing the city, and looked over the grounds. A paragraph from a later entry in his diary throws a very human and revealing light on Washington, whose innate courtesy so often made him suffer fools. Tired of having ridden all day in the midst of clouds of dust raised by escorts of local horsemen in southern Virginia, he resorted to a stratagem to obtain some relief the next morning.

> *Friday,* 15th [April, 1791].   Having suffered very much by the dust yesterday—and finding that parties of Horse, & a number of other Gentlemen were intendg. to attend me part of the way to day, I caused their enquiries respecting the time of my setting out, to be answered that, I should endeavor to do it before eight O'clock; but I did it a little after five, by which means I avoided the inconveniences above-mentioned.

L'Enfant's plan for Federal City

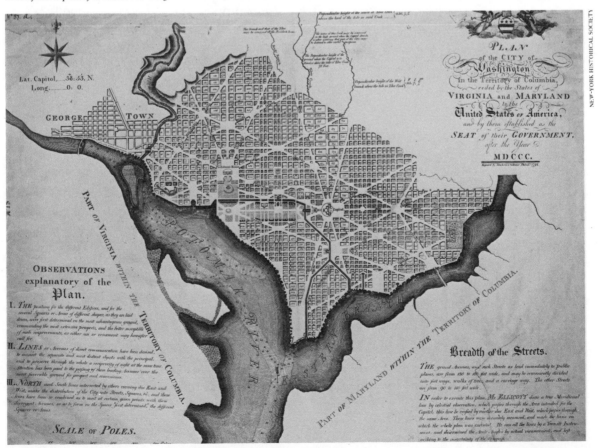

Washington found the South poorer, less populous, and much less developed than New England, with very little industry. His welcomes, however, were just as warm. Some typical excerpts from his diary follow.

Saturday, 16th [April, 1791]. Got into my Carriage a little after 5 Oclock, and travelled thro' a cloud of dust until I came within two or three miles of Hix' ford when it began to rain. Breakfasted at one Andrews' a small but decent House about a mile after passing the ford (or rather the bridge) over Meherrin River. Although raining moderately, but with appearances of breaking up, I continued my journey—induced to it by the crouds which were coming into a general Muster at the Court House of Greensville [Virginia], who would I presumed soon have made the Ho. I was in too noizy to be agreeable. I had not however rode two miles before it began to be stormy, & to rain violently which, with some intervals, it contind. to do the whole afternoon. The uncomfortableness of it, for Men & Horses, would have induced me to put up; but the only Inn short of Hallifax having no stables in wch. the horses could be comfortable, & no Rooms or beds which appeared tolerable, & every thing else having a dirty appearance, I was compelled to keep on to Hallifax [North Carolina]; 27 miles from Andrews—48 from Olivers—and 75 from Petersburgh. At this place (i.e. Hallifax) I arrived about Six Oclock, after crossing the Roanoke; on the South bank of which it stands....

Wednesday, 20*th.* Left Allans before breakfast, & under a misapprehension went to a Colo. Allans, supposing it to be a public house; where we were very kindly & well entertained without knowing it was at his expence, until it was too late to rectify the mistake. After breakfasting, & feeding our horses here, we proceeded on & crossing the River Nuse 11 miles further, arrived in Newbern [North Carolina] to dinner....

Thursday, 21st. Dined with the Citizens [of Newbern] at a public dinner given by them; & went to a dancing assembly in the evening—both of which was at what they call the Pallace—formerly the government House & a good brick building but now hastening to ruins. The Company at both was numerous—at the latter there were abt. 70 ladies....

Sunday, 24th. Breakfasted at an indifferent House about 13 miles from Sages—and three Miles further met a party of Light Horse from Wilmington [North Carolina]; and after them a Commee. & other Gentlemen of the Town; who came out to escort me into it, and at which I arrived under a federal salute at very good lodgings prepared for me, about two Oclock. At these I dined with the Commee. whose company I asked....

Wilmington is situated on the Cape Fear River, about 30 Miles *by water* from its mouth, but much less by land. It has some good houses pretty compactly built. The whole undr. a hill; which is formed entirely of Sand. The number of Souls in it amount by the enumeration to about 1000, but it is agreed on all hands that the Census in this State has been very inaccurately & shamefully taken by the Marshall's deputies; who, instead of going to Peoples houses, & there, on the spot, ascertaining the Nos.; have advertised a meeting of them at certain places, by which means those who did not attend (and it seems many purposely avoided doing it, some from an apprehension of its being introductory of a tax, & others from religious scruples) have gone, with their families, unnumbered. In other instances, it is said these deputies have taken their information from the Captains of Militia companies; not only as to the Men on their Muster Rolls, but of the souls in their respective families; which at best, must in a variety of cases, be mere conjecture whilst all those who are not on their lists—Widows and their families—&ca. pass unnoticed.

Charleston, South Carolina, in 1780

His years and the cares of office had not diminished Washington's lively interest in the ladies who turned out to meet him.

Tuesday, 3d [May, 1791]. Breakfasted with Mrs. Rutledge (the Lady of the Chief justice of the State who was on the Circuits) and dined with the Citizens at a public dinr. given by them at the Exchange.

Was visited about 2 Oclock, by a great number of the most respectable ladies of Charleston [South Carolina]—the first honor of the kind I had ever experienced and it was as flattering as it was singular.

Wednesday, 4th. Dined with the Members of the Cin-

Washington visited Sullivans Island (above) and Cowpens (below), scene of one of the battles of the Revolution. When he returned, he heard of the "Bloody Indian Battle" in Ohio, which the broadside opposite describes.

Pictorial Field-Book of the Revolution, LOSSING

cinnati, and in the evening went to a very elegant dancing Assembly at the Exchange—at which were 256 elegantly dressed and handsome ladies.

In the forenoon (indeed before breakfast to day) I visited and examined the lines of attack & defence of the City and was satisfied that the defence was noble & honorable altho the measure was undertaken upon wrong principles and impolitic.

Thursday, 5th. Visited the works of Fort Johnson on James's Island, and Fort Moultree on Sullivans Island; both of which are in ruins, and scarcely a trace of the latter left—the former quite fallen.

Dined with a very large Company at the Governors, & in the evening went to a Concert at the Exchange at wch. there were at least 400 lad[ie]s the number & appearance of wch. exceeded any thing of the kind I had ever seen.

Friday, 6th. Viewed the town on horseback by riding through most of the principal Streets.

Dined at Majr. Butlers, and went to a Ball in the evening at the Governors where there was a select company of ladies.

There were "about 100 well dressed and handsome ladies" at a "dancing Assembly" at Purysburg, South Carolina; "between 60 and 70 well dressed ladies" at an assembly in Augusta; at Columbia, South Carolina, there were "a number of Gentlemen and Ladies... to the amount of 150, of which 50 or 60 were of the latter." Washington also visited the scenes of most of the important Revolutionary battles that had been fought in the South. This was his first view of these battlefields; he inspected them with interest, occasionally giving a terse criticism.

The President stopped at Mount Vernon and was back in Philadelphia in early July after a trip he reckoned at 1,887 miles. Old problems waited. The British still refused to give up frontier posts within the northern United States, arguing, with some merit, that the United States had not honored some parts of the peace treaty. Spain controlled the mouth of the Mississippi, an essential outlet for the commerce of western settlers. In August, the ominous news came that the French King had been virtually imprisoned; the uprising that had produced constitutional government in 1789 was turning into revolution. And as 1791 drew to a close, word came that an expedition sent against the Indians north of the Ohio River had been disastrously routed, leaving some six hundred dead or wounded.

What distressed the President most was the increasing division of the Government and of the country into political parties. The terms Federalist and Antifederalist, which only recently had denoted those for and those against the Constitution, had come to mean something quite different. The Federalists, whose chief spokesman was Alexander Hamilton, now were those who supported a strong central government, favored encouragement of industry, commerce, and finance, and believed that government should be by an elite of the propertied class and that the mass of the people could not be trusted to govern themselves. In the Cabinet, Secretary of War Knox sided with Hamilton.

Thomas Jefferson dominated the Antifederalist, or Republican, faction. The Republican point of view was that the people should govern themselves democratically, that government should be decentralized, that the best nation was one of small farmers with few cities, little industry, and a minimum of bankers. There were among the Republicans many who ac-

cused Washington of an overfondness for pomp and circumstance and even a secret ambition to become a monarch. The criticism was muted at first because of Washington's tremendous popularity, but it would grow, and in time would produce a tide of hate and invective. Possibly the growing division into antagonistic parties was what caused Washington to hedge slightly when he asked James Madison to help him prepare a farewell address as election time neared.

Mount Vernon May 20th. 1792.

As there is a possibility if not a probability, that I shall not see you on your return home; or, if I should see you, that it may be on the road and under circumstances which will prevent my speaking to you on the subject we last conversed upon; I take the liberty of committing to paper the following thoughts, & requests.

I have not been unmindful of the sentiments expressed by you in the conversations just alluded to: on the contrary I have again, and again revolved them, with thoughtful anxiety; but without being able to dispose my mind to a longer continuation in the Office I have now the honor to hold. I therefore still look forward to the fulfilment of my fondest and most ardent wishes to spend the remainder of my days (which I can not expect will be many) in ease & tranquility.

Nothing short of conviction that my deriliction of the Chair of Government (if it should be the desire of the people to continue me in it) would involve the Country in serious disputes respecting the chief Magestrate, & the disagreeable consequences which might result therefrom in the floating, & divided opinions which seem to prevail at present, could, in any wise, induce me to relinquish the determination I have formed: and of this I do not see how any evidence can be obtained previous to the Election. My vanity, I am sure, is not of that cast as to allow me to view the subject in this light.

Under these impressions then, permit me to reiterate the request I made to you at our last meeting—namely— to think of the proper time, and the best mode of anouncing the intention; and that you would prepare the latter. In revolving this subject myself, my judgment has always been embarrassed. On the one hand, a previous declaration to retire, not only carries with it the appearance of vanity & self importance, but it may be construed into a manoeuvre to be invited to remain. And on the other hand, to say nothing, implys consent; or, at any rate,

A commemorative medal shows an Indian chief with a peace pipe after the signing of a peace treaty in 1792.

Washington's letter to Hamilton, trying to heal the split between him and Jefferson, admits "differences in political opinions are as unavoidable as, to a certain point they may, perhaps, be necessary."

would leave the matter in doubt, and to decline afterwards might be deemed as bad, & uncandid.

I would fain carry my request to you farther than is asked above, although I am sensible that your compliance with it must add to your trouble; but as the recess may afford you leizure, and I flatter myself you have dispositions to oblige me, I will, with out apology desire (if the measure in itself should strike you as proper, & likely to produce public good, or private honor) that you would turn your thoughts to a Valadictory address from me to the public; expressing in plain & modest terms—that having been honored with the Presidential Chair, and to the best of my abilities contributed to the Organization & Administration of the government—that having arrived at a period of life when the private Walks of it, in the shade of retirement, becomes necessary, and will be most pleasing to me; and the spirit of the government may render a rotation in the Elective Officers of it more congenial with their ideas of liberty & safety, that I take my leave of them as a public man; and in bidding them adieu (retaining no other concern than such as will arise from fervent wishes for the prosperity of my Country) I take the liberty at my departure from civil, as I formerly did at my military exit, to invoke a continuation of the blessings of Providence upon it—and upon all those who are the supporters of its interests, and the promoters of harmony, order & good government.

During the next months the feud between Hamilton and Jefferson turned from one of political philosophy to a bitter personal antagonism. Washington, deeply perturbed by the split between his close friends and advisers, cautiously wrote of the schism to his Secretary of State in a letter that otherwise dealt with Spanish Florida and western Indians.

Mount Vernon, August 23, 1792.
How unfortunate, & how much is it to be regretted then, that whilst we are encompassed on all sides with avowed enemies & insidious friends, that internal dissensions should be harrowing & tearing our vitals. The last, to me, is the most serious, the most alarming & the most afflicting of the two; and without more charity for the opinions & acts of one another in governmental matters; or some more infallible criterion by which the truth of speculative opinions, before they have undergone the

test of experience, are to be forejudged, than has yet fallen to the lot of fallibility, I believe it will be difficult, if not impracticable to manage the reins of Government, or to keep the parts of it together; for if, instead of laying our shoulders to the machine after measures are decided on, one pulls this way & another that, before the utility of the thing is fairly tried, it must inevitably be torn asunder: and, in my opinion, the fairest prospect of happiness & prosperity that ever was presented to man will be lost—perhaps, forever!

My earnest wish & my fondest hope, therefore is, that, instead of wounding suspicions & irritable charges, there may be liberal allowances, mutual forbearances & temporizing yieldings on *all sides.* Under the exercise of these, matters will go smoothly, and, if possible, more prosperously. Without them every thing must rub; the wheels of Government will clogg; our enemies will triumph, & by throwing their weight into the disaffected scale may accomplish the ruin of the goodly fabrick we have been erecting.

I do not mean to apply this advice, or these observations to any particular person or character. I have given them in the same general terms to other Officers of the Government; because the disagreements which have arisen from difference of opinions—and the attacks which have been made upon almost all the measures of Government, & most of its Executive Officers, have, for a long time past, filled me with painful sensations; and cannot fail, I think, of producing unhappy consequences at home and abroad.

A similar letter went to Hamilton three days later. Each man answered by defending his own position and claiming to be the injured party. Both gave rather unconvincing promises that they would try to compromise their differences. Hamilton and Jefferson did agree in one thing; they were both among the chorus of Washington's friends who urged the President to run for another term, as the only man who could hold the infant nation together in a time of troubles. The farewell address Washington had asked Madison to prepare went undelivered—for the time being, at least. When the electors met early in 1793, the only contest was between John Adams, who received seventy-seven votes for Vice President, and George Clinton, an avowed Republican, who got fifty. Washington once again was the unanimous choice for President.

A Picture Portfolio

First in Peace

"NO FASCINATING ALLUREMENTS FOR ME"

George Washington was unanimously elected the nation's first President on February 4, 1789, by members of the Electoral College from ten of the thirteen states whose seals ring the engraved portrait at left. On the probability that this honor might be bestowed on him, he had written earlier to his old friend and confidant the Marquis de Lafayette that "it has no enticing charms, and no fascinating allurements for me." His reluctance was very real. But he also knew all too well that "the first transactions of a nation, like those of an individual upon his first entrance into life, make the deepest impression, and...form the leading traits in its character...." After so many years of service to the infant country, he could never have refused the new call to leadership. He set off on horseback from Mount Vernon for the triumphal journey to his inauguration in New York, greeted everywhere by joyous throngs in gaily bedecked cities such as Trenton (below), the scene of one of his greatest military victories.

FIRST CAPITALS

"Long live George Washington, President of the United States!" cried Chancellor Robert Livingston of New York, after he administered the oath on the balcony of Federal Hall (below); and the crowds in the streets took up the cheer. Washington never lived in the elegant house in New York City (right) provided for him by a grateful citizenry, since the capital was soon moved to Philadelphia. There the Washingtons moved into the Robert Morris house (right, below).

SOCIETY LEADERS

The portraits of George and Martha Washington below were painted in 1790 by Edward Savage for Vice President John Adams, and they still hang, as they always have, above the sideboard in the Adams house in Quincy, Massachusetts. During the first year of his Presidency, the Washingtons rented a large house on Broadway in New York, and four days later held their first reception, like the one portrayed in the nineteenth-century painting at right. Mrs. Washington stands serenely on a dais (left), with Chief Justice John Jay, Vice President John Adams, and Secretary of the Treasury Alexander Hamilton on her right. Behind them are Mrs. Adams and Mrs. Hamilton. In describing these levees, Abigail Adams wrote that she was received with "great ease and politeness" by her hostess, and she waxed enthusiastic about Washington, in a black velvet suit (center), whom she found "affable without familiarity, distant without haughtiness, grave without austerity, modest, wise and good." Her acerbic husband, on the other hand, was not always as enchanted and once referred to Washington as "an old mutton head."

BURDENS OF OFFICE

During his terms as President, two of Washington's most crucial tests of leadership were in putting down the Whisky Rebellion of 1794 and in keeping peace between his Federalist Secretary of the Treasury Alexander Hamilton (below, far left) and his Antifederalist Secretary of State Thomas Jefferson (below, near left). When the federal excise tax on whiskey enraged western Pennsylvanians, Washington donned his old uniform, raised a force of twelve thousand men, rode to Fort Cumberland (left), and by so doing stopped the rebellion cold. He was not so lucky with Hamilton and Jefferson, who remained bitterly opposed to each other's policies. As he neared the end of his Presidency in 1796, Washington was again painted in uniform, this time with his family (below), as they gathered around a large map of the projected Federal City, the plan for a new national capital he had put into effect but did not live to see completed.

The Washington Family BY EDWARD SAVAGE, NATIONAL GALLERY OF ART, WASHINGTON, D.C., ANDREW MELLON COLLECTION

LADY
WASHINGTON'S
LAMENTATION FOR THE
DEATH OF HER HUSBAND.

WHEN Columbia's brave sons sought my hero to
    lead them,
To vanquish their foes and establish their freedom,
I rejoic'd at his honors, my fears I dissembled,
At the thought of his dangers my heart how it
    trembled,
    Oh, my Washington! O my Washington!!
    Oh, my washington! all was hazardous.

The contest decided, with foes to the nation,
My hero return'd 'midst loud acclamation,
Of men without number and praise without measure,
And my own heart exulted in transports of pleasure,
    Oh my Washington. Oh, &c. all was hazardous.

Our freedom with order by faction rejected,
A new constitution our country elected,
My hero was rais'd to preside our the union,
And his cares interrupted our bliss and communion,
    Oh, my happiness! &c. &c. how precarious.

Declining the trust of his dignified station,
With joy to the seat of his dear estimation,
Surrounded with honors he humbly retreated,
Sweet hope softly whisper'd my bliss was completed.
    Oh, my happiness! &c. &c. how precarious.

When the pangs of disease, had, ah! fatally seiz'd
    him,
My heart would have yielded its life to have eas'd
    him,
And I pray'd the Most High if for death he design'd
    him,
That he would not permit me to loiter behind him.
    Oh, my Washington! &c. &c. all was dubious.

When my hopes had all fled, and I saw him resign-
    ing
His soul to his God without fear or repining,

What, my heart, were thy feelings? lamenting, ad-
    miring,
To behold him so calmly, so nobly expiring,
    Oh, my Washington! &c. &c. has forsaken us.

When I follow'd his corpse with grief unconfined,
And saw to the tomb his dear relics consigned,
When I left him in darkness and silence surround-
    ed,
With what pangs of fresh anguish my bosom was
    wounded!
    Oh, my Washington! &c. &c. has forsaken us.

An aspect so noble pale grave clothes disfigure,
His conquering arm is despoil'd of its vigour,
On those limbs which dropt wisdom is silence im-
    posed,
And those kind beaming eyes now forever are
    closed,
    Oh, my Washington? &c. &c. has forsaken us.

When with tears of sweet musing I ponder the
    story,
Of his wars, of his labours, his virtues and glory,
I breathe out a pray'r with sad order of spirit,
Soon to join him in bliss and united inherit
    Endless Blessedness! &c. &c. oh, how glorious.

But why with my own single grief so confounded,
When my country's sad millions in sorrows are
    drowned,
Let me mingle the current that flows from my bosom,
With my country' vast ocean of tears while they
    lose them,
    Tho' my Washington, &c. &c. has forsaken us.

PRINTED AND SOLD BY NATHANIEL COVERLY, JR.
CORNER THEATRE-ALLEY, *Milk-Street*—BOSTON.

"WHY DOTH AMERICA WEEP!"

Washington did not intend "to quitt the theatre of this world until the new century had been rung in," Martha later wrote. But a ride on a chill and wet December day in 1799 brought his doctors to his bedside (above, near left), and he died on December 14, at the age of sixty-seven, just short of that joyous celebration. "Why doth America weep!" mourned the verses on the print above, far left, as the tributes and elegies poured forth from the presses of the grief-stricken nation. Thomas Birch drew one of the somber processions in commemoration of Washington's death as it passed the country marketplace on High Street in Philadelphia (left). Martha Washington survived her beloved husband by only three years. The poignant cry attributed to her in the lamentation on the broadside above was really the cry from millions of American hearts: "Oh, my Washington! Oh, my Washington! Oh, my Washington! has forsaken us."

Chapter 10

The Discords of Party

Washington had won another splendid victory. For a second time he had been elected President without a single dissenting vote, in an outpouring of confidence and affection such as is granted to very few men. He would not have been human if he had not been pleased, but at the same time he faced his second term with the reluctance he always felt about giving up his cherished private life at Mount Vernon to take on a public duty. He wrote of his feelings in a letter to his old and close friend Governor Henry Lee of Virginia.

> Philadelphia Jany. 20th. 1793.
> I have been favored with your letter of the 6th. instant congratulatory on my re-election to the Chair of Government. A mind must be insensible indeed, not to be gratefully impressed by so distinguished, & honorable a testimony of public approbation & confidence: and, as I suffered my name to be contemplated on this occasion, it is more than probable that I should, for a moment, have experienced chagreen if my re-election had not been by a pretty respectable vote. But to say I feel pleasure from the prospect of *commencing* another tour of duty, would be a departure from truth; for however it might savour of affectation in the opinion of the world (who by the bye can only guess at my sentimts. as it never has been troubled with them) my particular, & confidential friends well know, that it was after a long and painful conflict in my own breast, that I was withheld (by considerations which are not necessary to mention) from requesting, *in time,* that no vote might be thrown away upon me; it being my fixed determination to return to the walks of private life, at the end of my term.

Washington's averseness to a second term would have been greater could he have foreseen the troubles that would beset him during the next four years. Some of them were already taking form even as he wrote to Governor Lee. Congress had increasingly taken sides in the Hamilton-Jefferson dispute, until the split between Federalists and Republicans was so wide that no serious business was being conducted during the first months of 1793, and the legislators were engaged in purely partisan wrangles. Washington remained outside the conflict and did what he could to reconcile the warring factions.

The feud was carried on in the press as well. Although his Administration was violently attacked, especially by the fanatically Republican *National Gazette* edited by Philip Freneau, Washington himself had been spared. That period of grace ended when the nation observed the President's sixty-first birthday on February 22, 1793, and Freneau took advantage of the occasion to accuse Washington of ambitions to be a king: "The monarchical farce of the birthday was as usual kept.... Hitherto [the American people] have passed over the absurdities of *levees, & every species of royal pomp and parade*, because they were associated with the man of their affections, and perhaps, in hopes that they might serve as a new rattle, which would amuse during its novelty, and be thrown aside, when it was worn off...."

Political problems had not freed Washington from personal ones. His nephew, George Augustine Washington, who had managed Mount Vernon since the time of the Constitutional Convention, had been in steadily failing health for many months. A month before Freneau's attack, the President had sat down to that most difficult of tasks, writing a letter to someone very close who is dying, and who knows he is dying. George Augustine died a week after his uncle penned the following letter.

Philada. January 27. 1793.

I do not write to you often, because I have no business to write upon—because all the News I could communicate is contained in the papers which I forward every week—because I conceive it unnecessary to repeat the assurances of sincere regard & friendship I have always professed for you or the disposition I feel to render every service in my power to you & yours; and lastly, because I conceive the more undisturbed you are, the better it is for you.

It has given your friends much pain to find that change of air has not been productive of that favorable change in your health which was the wishes of them all. But the will of Heaven is not to be controverted or scrutinized by the children of this world. It therefore [becomes] the creatures of it to submit [with patience and resignation] to the will of the Creator, whether it be to prolong or to

Rare British caricature of George Washington, which was done in 1796

Washington's unanimous election to a second term was recorded (above) in the Senate Journal; broadside at right lists names and addresses of both Senators and Representatives.

shorten the number of our days—to bless them with health, or afflict them with pain.

My fervent wishes attend you, in which I am heartily joined by your Aunt, & these are extended with equal sincerity to Fanny & the Children. I am always Your affectionate Uncle.

The President had hired a new manager, Anthony Whiting, for Mount Vernon. Although Whiting was hard-working and capable, the affairs of the plantation were so complex and Washington was so exacting that long and detailed letters left the President's desk almost weekly. They advised, commanded, questioned, explained, sometimes scolded. The following letter is typical of scores of such dispatches he found time to write in the midst of his official duties.

Philadelphia Feby. 3d. 1793.

Mr. Whiting:

Your letter of the 25th. of Jany. came duly to hand; but the usual one, containing the Reports, is not yet arrived; detained, as is supposed with the Mail, by Ice in the Susquehanna.

Under cover with this letter you will receive some Lima Beans which Mrs. Washington desires may be given to the Gardener; also Panicum or Guinea Corn, from the Island of Jamaica, which may be planted merely to see the uses it can be applied to; & the white bent grass with the description of it by Mr. Hawkins (one of the Senators, who had it from Mr. Bassett of Delaware State, another of the Senate). If the acct. of it be just, it must be a valuable grass; I therefore desire it may be sowed in drills, & to the best advantage for the purpose of seed. *These things* which are intended for experiments, or to raise as much seed from, as can be; shd. never be put in fields, or meadows; for there, (if not forgot) they are neglected; or swallowed up in the fate of all things within the Inclosures that contain them. This has been the case of the Chicorium (from Mr. Young) & a grass which sold for two Guineas a quart in England and presented to me—and the same, or some other fate equally as bad has attended a great many curious seeds which have been given to, & sent home by me at different times but of which I have heard nothing more; either from the inattention which was given to them in the first instance; neglect in the cultivation; or not watching the period of their seeding, and gathering them without waste....

I will enquire if Orchard grass seed is to be had here & will send some; but I must entreat you to save me, as much as possible from the necessity of purchasing seeds; for the doing it is an intolerable expence. I once was in the habit of saving a great deal of this & other seeds annually; and this habit might easily have been continued, if measures had been taken in time for it.

I am sorry to hear that you have so sick a family. In all cases that require it, let the Doctor be sent for in time. As I do not know what boy (before I get home) would be best to send to the Mill, the measure may be suspended until I arrive. If the Miller would be attentive (in time) to the wants of the Mill, there is certainly intercourse enough between the Mansion house and it, to obtain supplies without special messengers; & I know no right he has to be sending my people on any other business.

I have no doubt, at all, of wheat and flours bearing a good price this Spring; the causes that occasioned the rise in these articles still exist, & in a greater degree; but, that

Fanny Bassett Washington, *wife of George Augustine, Washington's favorite nephew and manager of Mount Vernon until his death in 1793*

I may know when the price offered, comes up to my ideas, keep me regularly advised of the Alexandria rates; the prices here of Superfine flour is 42/. [42 shillings] & that of fine 39/. pr. Barrl. of 196 lbs.—wheat 8/6 [8 shillings, 6 pence] pr. Bushl.

It appears to me, that it is scarcely necessary to put Tom Davis to the saw so late in the season; the time is not far off when Brick laying—preparing the foundation—&ca. must necessarily take him from it. Therefore, as he is better acquainted with the business than any of my people I should conceive he had better employ the interval in finishing the painting, unless you think (house) Frank could do it equally well. In that case, as it will probably be the last of March before I shall be at home —for a few days—he might be as advantageously occupied in that business as in any other.

Speaking of laying bricks (by which I mean the foundation for the Barn at Dogue run) it reminds me of asking again if the Bricks at that place have been assorted & counted; that the deficiency of the wanted number, if any, might have had the earth thrown up, from the foundation of the building, in time to be ameliorated by the frosts of the winter. Directions will forever escape you, unless you keep a pocket Memorandum book to refresh the memory; and questions asked (in my letters) will often go unanswered unless, when you are about to

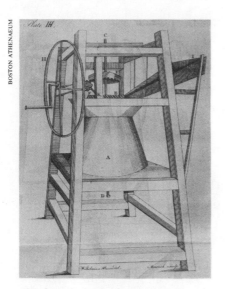

Washington's lifelong interest in all things agricultural is most in evidence among the many books on the subject in his personal library. The engraving above is from a book on farm implements. At right is the handsome certificate admitting him as a Foreign Honorary Member of the Board of Agriculture in London.

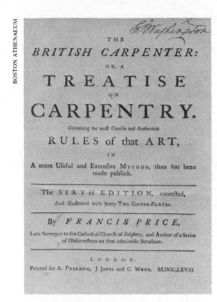

Book on carpentry, published in England, from Washington's library

write, the letter *is then,* not only read over, but all the parts, as you read on, is noted, either on a piece of waste paper, or a Slate which require to be touched upon in your answr.

I hope the delivery to and the application of Nails, by the Carpenters, will undergo a pretty strict comparative scrutiny, without expressing any suspicion, unless cause shall be given for it. I cannot conceive how it is possible that 6000 twelve penny Nails could be used in the Corn house at River Plantn. but of one thing I have no great doubt and that is—if they can be applied to other uses—or converted into cash, rum, or other things, there will be no scruple in doing it.

I can conceive no latch (sufficient to answer the purpose, & not always out of sorts) more simple or cheaper than those to the white gates, unornimented, which is unnecessary. A thin plate of Iron, kept in place by an old Iron hoop (of which I presume hundreds could be got in Alexandria for a mere song) & staple for it to catch in, is, in my opinion, as cheap as anything that (will not always be a plague) can be devised. The advantage of this latch is, that let the Gate swag as it may, it always catches. . . .

It would be proper, I conceive, as the house people are under the care of Mr. Butler, to entrust Will (Overseer as he is called) in preference to Davis, with the Command of the Boat, & such other out of sight jobs, as may occur, and require confidence; and, as they do not agree, to let them interfere as little as can be avoided, with each other. The latter is high spirited, and in the instance you mention was disobedient to the other whom he ought to have respected on two accts.—namely—being his uncle, & having been an Overseer. The former (Will) unless he feels hurt on being superseded in his Overseership, is entitled to more confidence; though, I believe, both of them will drink.

Sarah Flatfoot (you call her Lightfoot) has been accustomed to receive a pair of Shoes, Stockings, a Country cloth Petticoat, & an Oznabrig shift, all ready made, annually, & it is not meant to discontinue them: you will therefore furnish them to her.

As the matter has been mentioned to Mr. Chichester, I now wish you would see him yourself on the subject of Major Harrisons land; and find out, if you can from him, the circumstances under which it is—whether he seems to have any inclination to become the purchaser of it—At what price pr. Acre, or otherwise, it was offered to him; and for what he thinks it could be bought; Intimating what you conceive to be my motives for making it—if made at all by me.

If the Mail should arrive before this letter is closed, and I have time, I will acknowledge the receipt of it; if not, and nothing requires to be noticed sooner, I shall delay writing until this day week as usual.

There were no precedents for the time or manner of a change in presidential terms, so after discussion with his Cabinet, Washington directed that the ceremony be held on March 4 in the Senate chamber, with a justice of the Supreme Court administering the oath. The inaugural was a simple ceremony. Washington arrived at the Senate chamber about noon, was ushered inside, and after John Adams announced in a sentence that a justice of the Supreme Court was ready to administer the prescribed oath, Washington stood and read what probably remains the shortest inaugural address on record.

[Philadelphia,] March 4th. 1793.

Fellow-Citizens:

I am again called upon by the voice of my Country to execute the functions of its Chief Magistrate. When the occasion proper for it shall arrive, I shall endeavour to express the high sense I entertain of this distinguished honor, and of the confidence which has been reposed in me by the people of United America.

Previous to the execution of any official act of the President, the Constitution requires an Oath of Office. This Oath I am now about to take—and in your presence—that if it shall be found during my administration of the Government, I have in any instance violated willingly, or knowingly, the injunctions thereof, I may (besides incurring Constitutional punishmt.) be subject to the upbraidings of all who are now witnesses of the present solemn Ceremony.

Washington then repeated the oath, walked from the room, and returned to work. Soon news from abroad, always many weeks behind the event, brought increasingly ominous dispatches from France. That country was at war with Austria and Prussia, and Washington's close

*George Washington painted during
second term by Adolph Wertmuller*

friend Lafayette, commanding a French army, had been outlawed by the
radical government in Paris, had fled, and had been imprisoned in Austria.
The President, already working for the release of Lafayette, responded to
a direct appeal for help from Lafayette's wife, couching his letter in cautious
terms in case it was intercepted.

Philada. 16 March 1793.

Dear Madam:

I addressed a few lines to you on the 31st. of January,
in a state of entire uncertainty in what country or condition they might find you: as we had been sometimes told
you were in England, sometimes in Holland, & at sometimes in France. Your Letter of Octob: 8 — 1792, first relieved me from doubt, & gave me a hope that, being in
France: and on your own Estate, you are not as destitute
as I had feared, of the resources which that could furnish.
But I have still to sympathize with you on the deprivation
of the dearest of all your resources of happiness, in comparison with which, others vanish. I do it in all the sincerity of my friendship for him, & with ardent desires for
his relief; in which sentiment I know that my fellow-citizens participate. The measures you were pleased to intimate in your letter, are perhaps not exactly those which
I could pursue—perhaps indeed not the most likely, un-

der actual circumstances to obtain our object. But be assured, that I am not inattentive to his condition, nor contenting myself with inactive wishes for his liberation. My affection to his nation & to himself are unabated, & notwithstanding the line of separation which has been unfortunately drawn between them I am confident that both have been led on by a pure love of Liberty, & a desire to secure public happiness; and I shall deem that among the most consoling moments of my life which shall see them reunited in the end, as they were in the beginning, of their virtuous enterprise. Accept I pray you the same lively sentiments of interest & attachment to yourself & your dear children, from Dr. madm. Your most obt. & devoted servt.

Lafayette would eventually be released unharmed, but not for another four years. In mid-March came news that King Louis XVI had been guillotined and a Republic of France proclaimed. Despite rumors of general war in Europe, Washington went to Mount Vernon at the beginning of April. He had much to do at home. There was the burial of his nephew George Augustine Washington, a simple and private ceremony. He wanted to try to sell his land holdings in the Dismal Swamp and on the Kanawha River. There were long-overdue debts he hoped to try to collect. And many plantation problems demanded his attention. But he had been at Mount Vernon only a brief while when a letter from Alexander Hamilton confirmed that France, already at war with Austria, Prussia, and Sardinia, had declared war on England, Spain, and Holland.

The President cut his stay short and returned to Philadelphia. He was worried about the wild enthusiasm many Americans were showing for the new revolutionary government in France, and he was uncertain what course the United States should take toward the new republic. When France had recognized the independence of the Colonies in 1778 during the Revolution, the two nations signed a pair of treaties. One was simply a treaty of amity and commerce, to put trade on a mutually advantageous basis. The other was a treaty of alliance, to become operative in case recognition caused Britain to make war on France, as it did. It stipulated that neither country would make a separate peace, and that after the United States had become a free nation, France would guarantee American independence and boundaries, and the United States in its turn would guarantee France in possession of her islands in the West Indies.

Now, with France and England at war, the United States could be drawn into the conflict if France insisted that her ally adhere to the terms of the treaty. Many questions were raised. The treaty of alliance had been made with a French monarchy but now a revolutionary government was in power; was the treaty then any longer in effect? Republicans said an emphatic Yes, Federalists, No. And what of the envoy being sent by the revolutionary government, in what manner should he be received—or should he be received at all? Washington sent to each of his Cabinet members a list of questions to study before a meeting the next day.

Philada. 18 April 1793.

Question I.   Shall a proclamation issue for the purpose of preventing interferences of the Citizens of the United States in the War between France and Great Britain &ca.? Shall it contain a declaration of neutrality, or not? What shall it contain?

Quest. II.   Shall a Minister from the Republic of France be received?

Quest. III.   If received, shall it be absolutely, or with qualifications; & if with qualifications—of what kind?

Quest. IV.   Are the U.S. obliged, by good faith, to consider the treaties, heretofore made with France, as applying to the present situation of the parties? May they either renounce them, or hold them suspended 'till the Government of France shall be *established*?

Questn. V.   If they have the right, is it expedient to do either, and which?

Questn. VI.   If they have an option, would it be a breach of neutrality, to consider the treaties still in operation?

Quest. VII.   If the treaties are to be considered as now in operation, is the Guarantee in the treaty of alliance applicable to a defensive war only, or to war either offensive or defensive?

VIII.   Does the war, in which France is engaged, appear to be offensive, or defensive, on her part? or of a mixed & equivocal character?

IX.   If of a mixed & equivocal character, does the Guarantee in any event apply to such a war?

X.   What is the effect of a Guarantee, such as that to be found in the treaty of Alliance between the U.S. & France?

XI.   Does any article, in either of the treaties, prevent Ships of war, other than privateers, of the Powers opposed to France, from coming into the Ports of the United States, to act as convoys to their own Merchantment? or does it lay any other restraints upon them more than would apply to the Ships of war of France?

Contemporary engraving of the execution of King Louis XVI from La Revolution Française *by Berthault*

Quest. XII.   Should the future Regent of France send a Minister to the United States, ought he to be received?

XIII.   Is it necessary, or adviseable, to call together the two Houses of Congress, with a view to the present posture of European affairs? If it is, what should be the particular objects of such a call?

At its meeting the next day the Cabinet agreed to proclaim American neutrality. Jefferson, the one Nay vote, argued that a declaration of neutrality was nothing more than "a declaration that there should be no war," and that Congress alone had the power to decide a question of war or peace. It was agreed, then, that the word "neutrality" would not be contained in the proclamation. All four members were in accord that the minister of the French Republic, Edmond Genêt (Citizen Genêt), should be received, but there was intense disagreement on whether he should be received with or without qualification. Hamilton argued that to receive Genêt without qualification would be tantamount to announcing that the United States was continuing the treaties of alliance and commerce made with the French monarchy in 1778. We should wait, said Hamilton, until we see what form the French Republic finally takes before committing ourselves. Jefferson, the champion of republican France, violently disagreed, and the matter was temporarily resolved only by putting it aside for further study. Three days later Washington issued the Proclamation of Neutrality.

[Philadelphia, April 22, 1793]

Whereas it appears that a state of war exists between Austria, Prussia, Sardinia, Great-Britain, and the United Netherlands of the one part and France on the other, and the duty and interest of the United States require that they should with sincerity and good faith adopt and pursue a conduct friendly and impartial towards the belligerent powers:

I have therefore thought fit by these presents to declare the disposition of the United States to observe the conduct aforesaid towards those powers respectively, and to exhort and warn the citizens of the United States carefully to avoid all acts and proceedings whatsoever which may in any manner tend to contravene such disposition.

And I do hereby also make known that whosoever of the citizens of the United States shall render himself liable to punishment or forfeiture under the law of nations by committing, aiding, or abetting hostilities against any of the said powers, or by carrying to any of them those articles which are deemed contraband by the *modern* usage of nations, will not receive the protection of the United States against such punishment or forfeiture; and further, that I have given instructions to those officers to whom it belongs to cause prosecutions to be instituted against all persons who shall, within the cognizance of the courts of the United States, violate the law of nations with respect to the powers at war, or any of them.

Citizen Genêt had already landed in Charleston, South Carolina, where he remained long enough to commission four privateers to prey on British shipping. Then—already a hero to Republicans but a villain to Federalists—he journeyed to Philadelphia, being greeted with ovations along the way. On May 18, almost six weeks after his arrival in the United States, he presented his credentials to Washington, who received him with cool formality. On June 5 the President had Jefferson inform Genêt that his granting of commissions on American soil was an infringement of American sovereignty; furthermore, that the privateers already commissioned would. have to leave American waters. Genêt promised to comply but before long blandly ordered the arming of a British ship, the *Little Sarah,* which had been captured by a French vessel. Told not to send the vessel—refitted and renamed *La Petite Démocrate*—to sea, Genêt threatened to appeal to the American people over Washington's head. Washington, angered, asked his Secretary of State what action should be taken.

Philadelphia 11 July 1793

After I had read the papers (which were put into my hands by you) requiring "instant attention," & before a messenger could reach your Office, you had left town.

What is to be done in the case of the Little Sarah, now at Chester? Is the Minister of the French Republic to set the Acts of this Government at defiance, *with impunity?* and then threaten the Executive with an appeal to the people? What must the world think of such conduct & of the Government of the U. States in submitting to it?

These are serious questions. Circumstances press for decision and as you have had time to consider them (upon me they come unexpectedly) I wish to know your opinion upon them—even before tomorrow—for the Vessel may then be gone.

Two or three days after Washington wrote his note to Jefferson, Genêt did give the word that sent *Little Sarah* to sea. Even Jefferson felt that the French ambassador had gone too far. The President's

Proclamation of Neutrality came increasingly under intemperate attack both in the pro-French Republican press and by many private citizens. Washington usually bore such attacks stoically, but occasionally he unburdened himself in private to good friends, as in the following letter to Governor Henry Lee of Virginia.

Philadelphia July 21st. 1793.

I should have thanked you at an earlier period for your obliging letter of the 14th. ulto., had it not come to my hands a day or two only before I set out for Mount Vernon; and at a time when I was much hurried, and indeed very much perplexed with the disputes, Memorials and what not, with which the Government were pestered by one or other of the petulant representatives of the Powers at War—and because, since my return to this City (nine days ago) I have been more than ever overwhelmed with their complaints. In a word, the trouble they give is hardly to be described.

My journey to and from Mt. Vernon was sudden & rapid, and as short as I could make it. It was occasioned by the unexpected death of Mr. Whitting (my Manager) at a critical season for the business with which he was entrusted. Where to supply his place, I know not; of course my concerns at Mt. Vernon are left as a body without a head—but this bye the by.

The communications in your letter were pleasing and grateful. For, although I have done no public act with which my Mind upbraids me, yet, it is highly satisfactory to learn that the things which I do (of an interesting tendency to the peace & happiness of this Country) are generally approved by my fellow Citizens. But were the case otherwise, I should not be less inclined to know the sense of the People upon every matter of great public concern; for as I have no wish superior to that of promoting the happiness & welfare of this Country, so, consequently, it is only for me to know the means to accomplish the end, if it is within the compass of my Powers.

That there are in this, as in all other Countries, discontented characters, I well know; as also that these characters are actuated by very different views—Some good, from an opinion that the measures of the general Government are impure—Some bad, and (if I might be allowed to use so harsh an epithet) diabolical; inasmuch as they are not only meant to impede the measures of that Government generally, but more especially (as a great mean towards the accomplishment of it) to destroy the confidence, which it is necessary for the People to place (until they have unequivocal proof of demerit) in their public Servants; for in this light I consider myself, whilst I am an occupant of Office; and, if they were to go farther & call me there Slave, (during this period) I would not dispute the point. But in what will this abuse terminate? The result, as it respects myself, I care not; for I have a consolation within that no earthly efforts can deprive me of—and that is, that neither ambitious nor interested motives have influenced my conduct. The arrows of Malevolence therefore, however barbed & well pointed, never can reach the most valuable part of me; though, whilst I am *up* as a *mark,* they will be continually aimed. The publications in Freneau's and Beache's [Benjamin Franklin Bache, editor of the *Aurora* of Philadelphia] Papers are outrages on common decency; and they progress in that style in proportion as their pieces are treated with contempt, and are passed by in silence by those at whom they are aimed. The tendency of them, however, is too obvious to be mistaken by men of cool & dispassionate minds, and, in my opinion, ought to alarm them; because it is difficult to prescribe bounds to the effect.

The light in which you endeavored to place the views and conduct of this Country to Mr. G---t [Genêt]; and the sound policy thereof as it respected his own; was, unquestionably the true one, and such as a man of penetration, left to himself, would most certainly have viewed them in—but mum on this head. Time may unfold more, than prudence ought to disclose at present.

As we are told that you have exchanged the rugged & dangerous field of Mars, for the soft and pleasurable bed of Venus, I do in this as I shall in every thing you may pursue, like unto it good & laudable, wish you all imaginable success and happiness. . . .

Edmond Charles Genêt

The mischief-making of Genêt continued. He had spent much of his time in America with radical Republicans and became president of the pro-French "Friends of Liberty and Equality" in Philadelphia. Such societies, patterned after the Jacobin clubs of Paris, were set up in other cities, notably Charleston and New York, and became anathema to the Federalists—and to Washington, who was more and more taking the advice

351

of Hamilton. But whatever his support among hotheads, Genêt had gone too far. When the story of his machinations sifted through to the public, a small flood of messages came to Washington, expressions of support for their President, who had been insulted by the man from France. Genêt went into an eclipse, although he quietly continued to stir up trouble, including an intrigue to recruit Americans on the southwestern frontier to attack Spanish Louisiana. But at last the slow sailing ships brought word that the French Government had acted, and Washington was able to give a brief but unmistakably satisfied report to Congress.

> United States, Jany. 20 1794.
> Gentlemen of the Senate, and of the House of Representatives:
> Having already laid before you a letter of the 16. of August 1793. from the Secretary of State to our Minister at Paris; stating the conduct, and urging the recall of the Minister plenipotentiary of the Republic of France; I now communicate to you, that his conduct has been unequivocally disapproved; and that the strongest assurances have been given, that his recal should be expedited without delay.

When the new French minister, Joseph Fauchet, arrived in late February of 1794, he bore a request for the arrest and return to France of Genêt. The Girondist faction, which had sent Genêt, had been ousted by the even more radical Jacobins. Washington, knowing that return would mean death on the guillotine for Genêt, permitted the man who had acted so cavalierly toward him to remain in the United States. Genêt moved to Albany, eventually married the daughter of Governor George Clinton, and lived out his days as an obscure American citizen. Thus, one crisis had been survived; but others were ahead. The British still held the northwest frontier forts on American soil, had been confiscating American cargoes at sea, and were otherwise acting in ways that appalled even Federalists. War seemed probable. Washington sent a brief message to the Senate.

> United States 16 April 1794.
> Gentlemen of the Senate:
> The communications, which I have made to you during your present session, from the dispatches of our Minister in London, contain a serious aspect of our affairs with Great Britain. But as peace ought to be pursued with unremitted zeal, before the last resource, which has so often been the scourge of nations, and cannot fail to check the advanced prosperity of the United States, is contemplated; I have thought proper to nomi-

History of Philadelphia, BY SCHARF AND WESTCOTT, 1884

Both Genêt and Fauchet lived in this house, one of Philadelphia's finest.

nate, and do hereby nominate

John Jay, as Envoy extraordinary of the United States to his britannic majesty.

My confidence in our Minister plenipotentiary in London continues undiminished. But a mission, like this, while it corresponds with the solemnity of the occasion, will announce to the world a solicitude for a friendly adjustment of our complaints, and a reluctance to hostility. Going immediately from the United States, such an envoy will carry with him a full knowledge of the existing temper and sensibility of our Country; and will thus be taught to vindicate our rights with firmness, and to cultivate peace with sincerity.

Washington was sending John Jay, Chief Justice of the United States, on a delicate mission that involved more than frontier forts. The financial security of the country depended in large part on tariff revenues, and most of those revenues came from trade with Great Britain. If trade with Britain were cut off in retaliation for English acts, as the Republicans were clamoring that it be, it would wreck the American economy. Jay was to put things right, but instead his actions would, in coming months, bring down a torrent of abuse on Washington.

Changes had taken place in the tight circle around Washington. Tobias Lear, his secretary since 1786, had left him the previous June, first to go to Europe and then to set himself up in business in the Federal City, which was taking shape on the Potomac. Anthony Whiting, his manager at Mount Vernon, had died the same June, and Washington was now sending his letters about seeding, harvest, and the management of lazy slaves to a new manager, William Pearce. Of much greater import, not only to Washington but to the nation, was the loss of Thomas Jefferson, whose resignation as Secretary of State became effective at the end of 1793. He was replaced by Attorney General Edmund Randolph, whose office in turn was filled by William Bradford, a little-known lawyer and a veteran of the Revolution. Although the President had been veering away from Jefferson's philosophy and turning more and more toward Hamilton's Federalism, he did not forget old friends. Jefferson was no longer one of his official family, but he was nevertheless a fellow farmer. A personal letter went to him on a matter of mutual interest.

Phila. 24th. April 1794

The letter herewith enclosed, came under cover to me in a packet from Mr. Lear, accompanied with the following extract of a letter, dated—London February 12th. 1794.

"A Mr. Bartrand, a famous Agriculturalist belonging to Flanders, put into my hands a few days ago several papers for Mr. Jefferson on the Subject of Manuring & vegitation, requesting that I would forward them to him by some vessel going to America; being uncertain whether Mr. Jefferson is in Philada. or Virginia, I have taken the liberty of putting them under cover to you."

Nothing, is more wanting in this Country, than a thorough knowledge of the first; by which the usual, and inadequate modes practiced by us may be aided. Let me hope then, if any striking improvements are communicated by Mr. Bartrand on the above important Subjects that you will suffer your friends to participate in the knowledge which is to be derived from his instructions.

We are going on in the old way "Slow." I hope events will justify me in adding "and sure" that the proverb may be fulfilled—"Slow and Sure." With very great esteem etc.

One feature of Hamilton's controversial fiscal plan had been an excise tax on whiskey. It was a tax opposed by back-country Americans ever since it was passed in 1791, for the only way a western farmer could possibly take his grain to market across the mountains and make any profit was by first reducing it to whiskey. The democratic Westerners bitterly resented Hamilton's entire program as putting power in the hands of the upper classes, and the tax on whiskey was the most obvious target on which to vent their accumulated resentment. In July of 1794 a federal marshal was attacked while serving papers on a distiller in western Pennsylvania, and the home of the excise inspector in the same area was burned. There were other acts against authority, in what came to be known as the Whisky Rebellion. Washington, groping for a course of action, called on his Cabinet for advice. Hamilton held that the insurgents were in a state of treason, and that the insurrection should be quelled by force. There was cooler counsel. Secretary of State Randolph believed that force would only harden the resolve of the rebels to resist. It was decided to send federal commissioners to western Pennsylvania to offer amnesty to the rebels, while at the same time the recruiting of some thirteen thousand militia was to begin in case force became necessary. A proclamation of warning was issued by Washington the next day.

[Philadelphia, August 7, 1794]

Whereas combinations to defeat the execution of the

laws laying duties upon spirits distilled within the United States, and upon stills, have from the time of the commencement of those laws existed in some of the Western parts of Pennsylvania:

[Here follows a long series of whereases, detailing the unlawful acts of the Westerners, after which the point of the proclamation is reached.]

Wherefore, and in pursuance of the proviso above recited, I, GEORGE WASHINGTON, President of the United States, do hereby command all persons, being insurgents as aforesaid, and all others whom it may concern, on or before the first day of September next, to disperse and retire peaceably to their respective abodes. And I do moreover warn all persons whomsoever against aiding, abetting, or comforting the perpetrators of the aforesaid treasonable acts; and do require all officers and citizens, according to their respective duties and the laws of the land, to exert their utmost endeavors to prevent and suppress such dangerous proceedings.

While he waited for word from the peace commissioners, Washington wrote of the insurrection and what he considered its causes to his friend Governor Henry Lee of Virginia.

German Town Augt. 26th. 1794.

As the Insurgents in the western Counties of this State are resolved (as far as we have yet been able to learn from the Commissioners, who have been sent among them) to persevere in their rebellious conduct until what they call the excise Law is repealed, and acts of oblivion and amnesty are passed; it gives me sincere consolation amidst the regret with which I am filled, by such lawless & outrageous conduct, to find by your Letter above mentioned, that it is held in general detestation by the good people of Virginia; and that you are disposed to lend your *personal* aid to subdue this spirit, & to bring those people to a proper sense of their duty.

On this latter point I shall refer you to letters from the War office; and to a private one from Colo. Hamilton (who in the absence of the secretary of war, superintends the *military* duties of that Department) for my sentiments on this occasion.

It is with equal pride and satisfaction I add, that as far as my information extends, this insurrection is viewed with universal indignation; and abhorrence; except by those who have never missed an opportunity by side blows, or otherwise, to aim their shafts at the General Government; and even among these there is not a spirit hard enough, yet, *openly* to justify the daring infractions of Law and order; but by palliatives are attempting to suspend all proceedings against the insurgents until Congress shall have decided on the case, thereby intending to gain time, and if possible to make the evil more extensive—more formidable—and of course more difficult to counteract and subdue.

I consider this insurrection as the first *formidable* fruit of the Democratic Societies; brought forth I believe too prematurely for their own views, which may contribute to the annihilation of them.

That these Societies were instituted by the *artful* & *designing* members (many of their body I have no doubt mean well but know little of the real plan) primarily to sow the seeds of jealousy & distrust among the people, of the government, by destroying all Confidence in the administration of it; and that these doctrines have been budding & blowing ever since, is not new to any one who is acquainted with the characters of their leaders, and have been attentive to their manoeuvres. I early gave it as my opinion to the confidential characters around me, that if these Societies were not counteracted (not by prosecutions, the ready way to make them grow stronger) or did not fall into disesteem from the knowledge of their origin, and the views with which they had been instituted by their father, Genet, for purposes well known to the Government; that they would shake the government to its foundation. Time and circumstances have confirmed me in this opinion, and I deeply regret the probable consequences, not as they will affect me personally—(for I have not long to act on this theatre, and sure I am that not a man amongst them can be more anxious to put me aside, than I am to sink into the profoundest retirement) but because I see, under a display of popular and fascinating guises, the most diabolical attempts to destroy the best fabric of human government & happiness, that has ever been presented, for the acceptance of mankind.

During these weeks of marking time, the President received from Martha Washington's granddaughter Elizabeth Parke Custis a letter asking for his picture. It was one of the few softer and lighter moments of many months; he responded partly playfully, partly with a shower of the maxims he could not resist when writing to someone young.

German Town, Septr. 14th. 1794.

My dear Betcy:

Shall I, in answer to your letter of the 7th. instant say —when you are as near the *Pinnacle* of happiness as your sister Patcy conceives herself to be; or when your candour shines more conspicuously than it does in *that* letter, that I will *then*, comply with the request you have made, for my Picture?

No—I will grant it without either: for if the latter was to be a preliminary, it would be sometime I apprehend before *that* Picture would be found pendant *at* your breast; it not being within the bounds of probability that the contemplation of an inanimate thing, whatever might be the reflections arising from the possession of it, can be the *only* wish of your heart.

Respect may place it among the desirable objects of it, but there are emotions of a softer kind, to wch. the heart of a girl turned of eighteen, is susceptible, that must have generated much warmer ideas, although the fruition of them may, apparently, be more distant than those of your Sister's.

Having (by way of a hint) delivered a sentiment to Patty [Elizabeth's sister Martha Parke Custis, then engaged to be married], which may be useful to her (if it be remembered after the change that is contemplated, is consummated) I will suggest another, more applicable to yourself.

Do not then in your contemplation of the marriage state, look for perfect felicity before you consent to wed. Nor conceive, from the fine tales the Poets & lovers of old have told us, of the transports of mutual love, that heaven has taken its abode on earth: Nor do not deceive yourself in supposing, that the only mean by which these are to be obtained, is to drink deep of the cup, & revel in an ocean of love. Love is a mighty pretty thing; but like all other delicious things, it is cloying; and when the first transports of the passion begins to subside, which it assuredly will do, and yield —oftentimes too late—to more sober reflections, it

Elizabeth Parke Custis, a portrait by Robert Edge Pine painted in 1785

*During the Whisky Rebellion, a
federal tax collector was tarred and
feathered by a Pennsylvania mob.*

serves to evince, that love is too dainty a food to live upon *alone,* and ought not to be considered farther than as a necessary ingredient for that matrimonial happiness which results from a combination of causes; none of which are of greater importance, than that the object on whom it is placed, should possess good sense—good dispositions—and the means of supporting you in the way you have been brought up. Such qualifications cannot fail to attract (after marriage) your esteem & regard, into wch. or into disgust, sooner or later, love naturally resolves itself; and who at the sametime, has a claim to the respect, & esteem of the circle he moves in. Without these, whatever may be your first impressions of the man, they will end in disappointment; for be assured, and experience will convince you, that there is no truth more certain, than that all our enjoyments fall short of our expectations; and to none does it apply with more force, than to the gratification of the passions.

On September 24 word came from the commissioners that all attempts to reach an agreement with the insurgents had met with dead ends. The next day Washington issued a second proclamation, saying that he was calling out the militia of four states to suppress the Whisky Rebellion. In those simple, early days of the nation, Washington felt that as Commander in Chief he should accompany the militia, at least until the action was well launched. On the last day of September he left Philadelphia with his private secretary and Hamilton, who, in the temporary absence of Henry Knox, was acting Secretary of War as well as Treasury Secretary. Washington in his diary described the journey westward.

> Tuesday, 30th [September, 1794]. Having determined from the Report of the Commissioners, who were appointed to meet the Insurgents in the Western Counties in the State of Pennsylvania, and from other circumstances—to repair to the places appointed for the Rendezvous, of the Militia of New Jersey Pennsylvania Maryland & Virginia; I left the City of Philadelphia about half past ten oclock this forenoon accompanied by Colo. Hamilton (Secretary of the Treasury) & my private Secretary. Dined at Norris Town and lodged at a place called the Trap—the first 17, and the latter 25 Miles from Philadelphia.
>
> At Norris Town we passed a detachment of Militia who were preparing to March for the rendezvous at

Carlisle—and at the Trap, late in the evening, we were overtaken by Major Stagg principal Clerk in the Department of War with letters from Genl. Wayne & the Western Army containing official & pleasing accounts of his engagement with the Indians near the British Post at the Rapids of the Miami of the Lake and of his having destroyed all the Indian Settlements on that River in the vicinity of the said Post quite up to the grand Glaize —the quantity not less than 5000 acres—and the Stores &c. of Colo. McGee the British Agent of Indian Affairs a mile or two from the Garrison.

The news of Anthony Wayne's victory was welcome indeed. Twice during Washington's first Administration, expeditions sent against the same Indians had been badly defeated; now the area would be safe for settlers, and as a result of the treaty concessions that would inevitably be wrung from the natives, large tracts of land would be opened to settlement. It was not, however, the end of all Indian problems. During the months and years still left of his Presidency, Washington would often be turning his attention to the endless futility of treaty making or would be impotently railing at the invasion of Indian lands by white frontiersmen. After having spent the first part of October organizing various units of militia, the President—as his diary relates—met with two members of a committee from the rebellious Pennsylvania counties.

[October, 1794]. ... On the 9th. William Findley and David Redick—deputed by the Committee of safety (as it is disignated) which met on the 2d. of this month at Parkinson Ferry arrived in Camp with the Resolutions of the said Committee; and to give information of the State of things in the four Western Counties of Pennsylvania to wit—Washington Fayette Westd. [Westmoreland] & Alligany in order to see if it would prevent the March of the Army into them.

At 10 oclock I had a meeting with these persons in presence of Govr. Howell (of New Jersey) the Secretary of the Treasury, Colo. Hamilton, & Mr. Dandridge: Govr. Mifflin [of Pennsylvania] was invited to be present, but excused himself on acct. of business.

I told the Deputies that by one of the Resolutions it would appear that they were empowered to give information of the disposition & of the existing state of matters in the four Counties above men.; that I was ready to hear & would listen patiently, and with candour

Dramatic depiction of Wayne's fight with the Indians, from John Frost's Pictorial Life of Washington, *1853*

to what they had to say.

Mr. Findley began. He confined his information to such parts of the four Counties as he was best acquainted with; referring to Mr. Reddick for a recital of what fell within his knowledge, in the other parts of these Counties.

The substance of Mr. Findleys communications were as follows—viz.—That the People in the parts where he was best acquainted, had seen there folly; and he believed were disposed to submit to the Laws; that he thought, but could not undertake to be responsible, for the re-establishment of the public Offices for the Collection of the Taxes on distilled Spirits & Stills—intimating however, that it might be best *for the present,* & until the peoples minds were a little more tranquilized, to hold the Office of Inspection at Pitsburgh under the protection—or at least under the influence of the Garrison; That he thought the Distillers would either enter their stills or would put them down; That the Civilian authority was beginning to recover its tone; & enumerated some instances of it; That the ignorance, & general want of information among the people far exceeded any thing he had any conception of; That it was not merely the excise law their opposition was aimed at, but to *all* law, & Government; and to the Officers of Government; and that the situation in which he had been, & the life he had led for sometime, was such, that rather than go through it again, he would prefer quitting this scene altogether....

[Mr. Redick] added, that for a long time after the riots commenced, and until lately, the distrust of one another was such, that even friends were affraid to communicate their sentiments to each other; That by whispers this was brought about; and growing bolder as they became more communicative they found their strength, and that there was a general disposition not only to acquiesce under, but to support the Laws—and he gave some instances also of Magistrates enforcing them.

He said the People of those Counties believed that the opposition to the Excise law—or at least that their dereliction to it, in every other part of the U. States was similar to their own, and that no Troops could be got to march against them for the purpose of coercion; that every acct. until very lately, of Troops marching

William Findley, by Rembrandt Peale

against them was disbelieved; & supposed to be the fabricated tales of governmental men; That now they had got alarmed; That many were disposing of their property at an under rate, in order to leave the Country, and added (I think) that they wd. go to Detroit....

After hearing what both had to say, I briefly told them—That it had been the earnest wish of governmt. to bring the people of those counties to a sense of their duty, by mild, & lenient means; That for the purpose of representing to their sober reflection the fatal consequences of such conduct Commissioners had been sent amongst them that they might be warned, in time, of what must follow, if they persevered in their opposition to the laws; but that coercion wou'd not be resorted to except in the dernier resort: but, that the season of the year made it indispensible that preparation for it should keep pace with the propositions that had been made; That it was unnecessary for me to enumerate the transactions of those people (as they related to the proceedings of government) forasmuch as they knew them as well as I did; That the measure which they were now witness to the adoption of was not less painful than expensive— Was inconvenient, & distressing—in every point of view; but as I considered the support of the Laws as an object of the first magnitude, and the greatest part of the expence had already been incurred, that nothing Short of the most unequivocal *proofs* of absolute Submission should retard the March of the army into the Western counties, in order to convince them that the government could, & would enforce obedience to the laws—not suffering them to be insulted with impunity. Being asked again what proofs would be required, I answered, they knew as well as I did, what was due to justice & example. They understood my meaning—and asked if they might have another interview. I appointed five oclock in the Afternoon for it.

INCIDENTS

OF THE

INSURRECTION

IN THE

Weſtern Parts of Pennſylvania,

In the Year 1794.

By HUGH H. BRACKENRIDGE.

PHILADELPHIA:
Printed and ſold by JOHN M'CULLOCH, No. 1, North Third-ſtreet.——1795.

George Washington's own copy of a book describing the Whisky Rebellion

Washington talked with the two men the next day, but nothing further was accomplished. He could only promise that if the Westerners met the troops peaceably, there would be no bloodshed. Then, after he had put Governor Henry Lee of Virginia in command of the militia, Washington started back to Philadelphia to be there for the convening of Congress on November 3. During the following weeks Hamilton sent frequent reports of mass arrests and seizures of stills. By late November the Whisky Rebellion had been quelled without bloodshed. The military action had decisively established the ascendancy of the Federal Government and strengthened the power of Hamilton and the Federalists. In fact, there is some evidence that Hamilton had quietly caused the peacemaking efforts of the federal commissioners to fail so that there could be a military confrontation. Of the few dozen insurrectionists arrested, only two were convicted in trials, and Washington would pardon both.

Hamilton and Knox resigned from the Cabinet, leaving only Edmund Randolph of the original four. Knox was replaced by Postmaster General Timothy Pickering, a capable negotiator with the Indians, which was then probably the main qualification of a War Secretary. At the end of January, 1795, Comptroller of the Treasury Oliver Wolcott succeeded Hamilton.

No important matters were calling for the President's instant attention those first weeks of the new year, but the relative calm was broken on March 7 when there arrived a copy of the "Treaty of Amity, Commerce, and Navigation," the result of John Jay's long negotiations in England. Jay had written, "It must speak for itself.... To do more was not possible." Washington read the text of the treaty with some consternation. Jay had failed to achieve most of his objectives, although Britain did promise to move out of the frontier posts by June 1, 1796. Article XII opened the important British West Indies trade to American vessels, but only to those of seventy tons or less, and they could not carry cotton, sugar, or molasses, the main source of profit for American traders. Mixed commissions were to be set up to settle such things as disputed boundaries. The treaty ignored such matters as payment by the British for slaves removed during the war and impressment of American seamen. What Jay had not known was that his power to negotiate had been undermined from the beginning; Hamilton, fearful that something might happen to the British trade so important to his fiscal plans, had quietly let the British know in advance the limits of Jay's bargaining power.

The President continued, as always, to be plagued by cadgers and special pleaders. Charles Carter, a friend from Fredericksburg, Virginia, wrote to ask the President for a loan of one thousand pounds for his son's business and got a report on the state of Washington's finances instead.

> Philadelphia 10th. March 1795.
>
> Your favor of the 23d. Ulto. came duly to hand. I wish, sincerely it was in my power to comply with your request in behalf of your son, but it really is not, to the extent of it.
>
> My friends entertain a very erroneous idea of my pecuniary resources, when they set me down for a money lender, or one who (now) has a Command of it. You may believe me, when I assert that the bonds which were due to me before the Revolution, were

John Jay was hanged in effigy when the terms of his treaty became known.

discharged during the progress of it—with a few exceptions in depreciated paper (in some instances as low as a shilling in the pound). That such has been the management of my Estate, for many years past, especially since my absence from home, now six years, as scarcely to support itself. That my public allowance (whatever the world may think of it) is inadequate to the expence of living in this City; to such an extravagant height has the necessaries as well as the conveniencies of life arisen. And moreover, that to keep myself out of debt, I have found it expedient, now and then to sell Lands, or some thing else to effect this purpose.

These are facts I have no inclination to publish to the World, nor should I have disclosed them on this occasion, had it not been due to friendship, to give you some explanation of my inability to comply with your request. If, however by joining with nine others, the sum required can be obtained—notwithstanding my being under these circumstances—and notwithstanding the money will be to be withdrawn from another purpose—I will contribute one hundred pounds towards the accommodation of your sons wants, without any view to the reccipt of interest therefrom.

In the meantime, Washington and Secretary of State Randolph kept the terms of Jay's Treaty a tight secret until the Senate returned on June 8 and was given the treaty to consider. Even then secrecy was preserved, for the bitter debate was carried on behind closed doors. Washington's own attitude toward the treaty was that if it accomplished nothing else, it would prevent war with England, which would have been disastrous to the United States. The Republicans, opposed to any treaty that did not favor France, were outmaneuvered on all points except Article XII, the West Indies trade section, which even many Federalists found too bitter to swallow. On June 24 the Senate approved the treaty, except Article XII, for which Washington was to prepare a substitute; when the substitute was approved by the Senate, he could ratify the treaty and return it to Britain. Even while the Senate was still debating, a copy of the treaty had leaked out to the Republican press. John Jay was hanged in effigy. Mass meetings were held, some for, most against, the treaty. Addresses from a score of cities protesting the treaty came to the President. In New York City, when Alexander Hamilton tried to speak in defense of the treaty, he was stoned. Washington, in a letter to Hamilton, unburdened himself of some of his anger and frustration.

Mount Vernon, July 29, 1795.

As the measures of the government, respecting the treaty, were taken before I left Philadelphia, something more imperious than has yet appeared, must turn up to occasion a change. Still, it is very desirable to ascertain, if possible, after the paroxysm of the fever is a little abated, what the real temper of the people is, concerning it; for at present the cry against the Treaty is like that against a mad-dog; and every one, in a manner, seems engaged in running it down.

That it has received the most tortured interpretation, and that the writings agt. it (which are very industriously circulated) are pregnant of the most abominable misrepresentations, admits of no doubt; yet, there are to be found, so far as my information extends, many well disposed men who conceive, that in the settlement of *old* disputes, a proper regard to reciprocal justice does not appear in the Treaty; whilst others, also well enough affected to the government, are of opinion that to have had *no* commercial treaty would have been better, for this country, than the restricted one, agreed to; inasmuch, say they, the nature of our Exports, and imports (without any extra: or violent measures) would have forced, or led to a more adequate intercourse between the two nations; without any of those shackles which the treaty has imposed. In a word, that as our *exports* consist chiefly of *provisions* and *raw materials,* which to the manufacturers in G. Britain, and to their Islands in the West Indies, affords employment and food; they must have had them on *our* terms, if they were not to be obtained on their *own;* whilst the *imports* of this country, offers the best mart for their fabricks; and, of course, is the principal support of their manufacturers: But the string which is most played on, because it strikes with most force the popular ear, is the violation, as they term it, of our engagements with France; or in other words, the prediliction shown by that instrument to G. Britain at the expence of the French nation.

The consequences of which are more to be apprehended than any, which are likely to flow from other causes, as ground of opposition; because, whether the fact is, in *any* degree true, or not, it is the interest of the French (whilst the animosity, or jealousies betwn. the two nations exist) to avail themselves of such a spirit, to

The American copy (above) of Jay's "Treaty of Amity, Commerce, and Navigation" and the version issued in Great Britain (opposite)

keep *us* and *G. Britain* at variance; and they will, in my opinion, accordingly do it. To what *length* their policy may induce them to carry matters, is too much in embryo at this moment to decide: but I predict much embarrassment to the government therefrom, and in my opinion, too much pains cannot be taken by those who speak, or write, in favor of the treaty, to place this matter in its true light.

I have seen with pleasure, that a writer in one of the New York papers under the Signature of Camillus, has promised to answer, or rather to defend the treaty, which has been made with G. Britain. To judge of this work from the first number, which I have seen, I auger well of the performance; and shall expect to see the subject handled in a clear, distinct and satisfactory manner: but if measures are not adopted for its dissimination a few only will derive lights from the knowledge, or labour of the author; whilst the opposition pieces will spread their poison in all directions; and Congress, more than probable, will assemble with the unfavorable impressions of their constituents. The difference of conduct between the friends, and foes of order, and good government, is in nothg. more striking than that, the latter are always working, like bees, to distil their poison; whilst the former, depending, often times *too much,* and *too long,* upon the sense, and good dispositions of the people to work conviction, neglect the means of effecting it.

Washington had gone to Mount Vernon for a brief rest, but his stay there was cut short by a mysterious note from Secretary of War Timothy Pickering, saying there was a "special reason" for the President to hurry back, "which can be communicated to you only in person." On his return Washington was shocked to be told by Pickering that during his absence the British had delivered an intercepted letter, written a year earlier by French Ambassador Joseph Fauchet to his superiors in Paris. In it Fauchet implied that Randolph had come to him proposing that for a suitable bribe he, Randolph, could bring about a peaceable end to the Whisky Rebellion and so prevent the crushing of the pro-French Westerners. Washington said nothing for eight days, until Randolph had readied Jay's Treaty and an accompanying memorial to the British ambassador. Then, on the morning of August 19, in the presence of Pickering and Secretary of the Treasury Wolcott, Washington handed a translation of the incriminating

365

letter to Randolph. After trying to explain the apparently damning evidence against him, Randolph, Washington's friend of twenty years, his closest adviser, resigned in a letter expressing his resentment over the humiliating way he had been treated. He asked for a copy of the original of the letter and of dispatch No. 6, referred to in Fauchet's letter. Washington replied with chilly formality.

Philadelphia 20 Aug. 1795.

Sir:

Your resignation of the office of State, is received.

Candor induces me to give you in a few words, the following narrative of facts.

The Letter from Mr. Fauchet, with the contents of which you were made acquainted yesterday, was, as you supposed, an intercepted one. It was sent by lord Grenville to Mr. Hammond—by him put into the hands of the secretary of the Treasury; by him shewn to the Secy. of War & the Attorney General; and a translation thereof was made by the former for me.

At the time Mr. Hammond delivered the letter, he requested of Mr. Wolcott an attested copy; which was accordingly made by Mr. Thornton his late secretary, and which is understood to remain at present with Mr. Bond. Whether it is known to others I am unable to decide. Whilst you are in pursuit of means to remove the strong suspicions arising from this letter, no disclosure of its contents will be made by me; and I will enjoin the same on the public officers (who are acquainted with the purport of it) unless something shall appear to render an explanation necessary on the part of Government—& of which I will be the Judge.

A Copy of Mr. Fauchets' letter shall be sent to you— No. 6 referred to therein, I have never seen.

Oliver Wolcott, by Trumbull

It has appeared with the passage of time that Randolph was probably innocent. Ambassador Fauchet denied that Randolph had proposed a bribe; when dispatch No. 6 appeared, it further weakened the case against Randolph. The culprits were apparently Wolcott and Pickering, who, even if they believed Randolph guilty, connived to convict him without a trial. As staunch Federalists, the two men must have feared that Randolph might be standing in the way of swift ratification of the treaty and wished to discredit him with Washington. But if Washington ever felt he had made a mistake, there is no evidence of it. There was a continuing torrent of abuse over Jay's Treaty in the Republican press during the following months, and protests came to the President from a number of cities. Except for one or two that he considered too abusive to deserve a reply, he answered the protests formally but politely.

Edmund Randolph

Philada. 31st. Augt. 1795.

I have received your Letter of the 6th. inst. inclosing the proceedings of the meeting at Norfolk on the 5th. relative to the Treaty lately negociated between the United States and Great Britain.

On subjects of so complex *and relative* a nature as those embraced by the Treaty a diversity of opinion was to have been expected. My determination which is known to have been in affirmance of the Treaty as advised and consented to by the Senate, was formed after the most mature deliberation and with a sincere regard to the public good.

Though it cannot be uninteresting to me to know that the wishes of a part of my fellow Citizens have been contravened by this decision, yet if the purity of my intentions will entitle me to their approbation, it has not been forfeited on the present important occasion.

The national political climate was such that the President trod gingerly in whatever he did. When in late September he received a letter from George Washington Lafayette, son of the Marquis de Lafayette and newly arrived in Boston from France, his instinct must have been to invite the youth to Philadelphia at once. Instead, he had to stop and consider what effect taking him into his home might have on relations with republican France, and even more so, how it could exacerbate the antagonisms between Federalists and Republicans at home. As a result, he wrote to George Cabot, Federalist Senator from Massachusetts, asking Cabot to act in his stead for a time. As a matter of fact, Washington did not see young Lafayette in Philadelphia until the following April, after Congress had formally taken note of the youth's presence in the United States.

Philadelphia, September 7, 1795.

The enclosed letters (which after reading, be so good as to return to me) will be the best appology I can offer for the liberty I am about to take and for the trouble, if you comply with my request, it must necessarily give.

To express all the sensibility wch. has been excited in my breast by the receipt of young Fayettes letter, from the recollection of his fathers merits, services and sufferings, from my friendship for him, and from my wishes to become a *friend* and *father* to his Son; are unnecessary.

Washington's namesake, George Washington Lafayette, son of the General's wartime friend and ally

Let me in a few words, declare that I *will be his friend;* but the manner of becomg. so considering the obnoxious light in which his father is viewed by the French government, and my own situation, as the Executive of the U. States, requires more time to consider in all its relations, than I can bestow on it at present; the letters not having been in my hands more than an hour, and I myself on the point of setting out for Virginia to fetch my family back whom I left there about the first of August.

The mode which, at the first view strikes me as the most eligable to answer his purposes and to save appears. is, I. to administer all the consolation to young Gentleman that he can derive from the most unequivocal assurances of my standing in the place of and becoming to him, a *Father, friend, protector,* and *supporter.* but 2dly. for prudential motives, as they may relate to himself; his mother and friends, whom he has left behind; and to my *official* character it would be best not to make these sentiments public; of course, that it would be ineligable, that he should come to the Seat of the genl. government where all the foreign characters (particularly that of his own nation) are residents, until it is seen what opinions will be excited by his arrival; especially too as I shall be necessarily absent five or Six weeks from it, on business, in several places. 3. considering how important it is to avoid idleness and dissipation; to improve his mind; and to give him all the advantages which education can bestow; my opinion, and my advice to him is, (if he is qualified for admission) that he should enter as a student at the University in Cambridge [Harvard] altho' it shd. be for a short time *only.* The expence of which, as also of every other mean for his support, I will pay; and now do authorise you, my dear Sir, to draw upon me accordingly; and if it is in any degree *necessary,* or *desired,* that Mr. Frestel his Tutor should accompany him to the University in that character; any arrangements which you shall make for the purpose, and any expence thereby incurred for the same, shall be borne by me in like manner.

One thing more, and I will conclude: Let me pray you my dear Sir to impress upon young Fayette's mind, and indeed upon that of his tutors that the reasons why I do not urge him to come to me, have been frankly related, and that their prudence must appreciate them with caution. My friendship for his father so far from being diminshd. has encreased in the ratio of his misfortunes; and my inclination to serve the son will be evidenced by my conduct; reasons wch. will readily occur to *you*, and wch. can easily be explained to him, will acct. for my not acknowledging the receipt of his, or Mr. Frestal's Letter. With sincere esteem &c.

PS. You will perceive that young Lafayette has taken the name of Motier. Whether it is best he should retain it and aim at perfect concealment, or not, depends upon a better knowledge of circumstances than I am possessed of, and therefore I leave this matter to your own judgment after a consultation with the parties.

As 1795 drew to a close, Alexander Hamilton had become the constant though unofficial adviser to the President; Washington wrote to his former Secretary of the Treasury for counsel frequently and on a wide variety of matters. Letters to James Madison, his most trusted adviser of his first years as President, and to Jefferson, on whom he had also once leaned so heavily, were now few and far between and never on matters of national policy; his infrequent correspondence with the two Republicans was on such subjects as crops and fertilizers and plans for a national university. At year's end the Cabinet was solidly Federalist, four good disciples of Hamilton. Although Washington spoke often about the evils of party division, he found the conservatism of Federalism much more congenial than the tenets of the Republican party. The concerns of government, however, did not distract Washington from his long-time preoccupation with the affairs of Mount Vernon. Early in 1796 an advertisement appeared in a number of American newspapers and in England as well.

Philadelphia, February 1, 1796.

TO BE LET

AND POSSESSION GIVEN IN AUTUMN

The Farms appertaining to the Mount Vernon Estate, in Virginia; four in number; adjoining the Mansion House Farm. Leases will be given for the term of fourteen years to *real* farmers of *good* reputation, and none others need apply.

The largest of these, called River Farm, contains 1207 acres of ploughable land; 879 of which, are in seven fields, nearly of a size, and under good fences; 212 acres (in one enclosure) are, generally in a common grass pasture; and 116 acres more, are in *five* grass lots, and an orchard (of the best grafted fruit) all of them contiguous to the dwelling house and barn. On the premises, are a comfortable dwelling house (in which the Overlooker resides) having three rooms below, and one or two above; an old barn (now in use) and a brick one building 60 by 30 feet; besides ends and wings, sufficient for stabling 20 working horses, and as many oxen; and an excellent brick dairy, with a fine

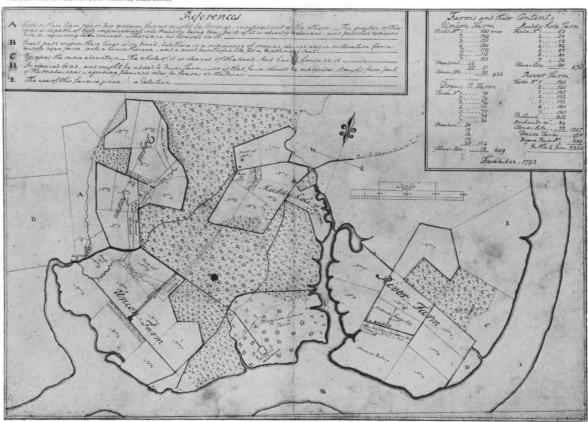

Drawn from field notes, this map by Washington, made in December, 1793, shows the four farms surrounding the Mount Vernon mansion house and estate.

spring in the middle of it. Thirty black labourers (men and women) being the usual number which have been employed on this farm, are, with their children, warmly lodged chiefly in houses of their own building. The soil is a loam, more inclined to clay than sand, and with slight dressings yields grain well, particularly wheat. Encompassed on two sides by the river Potomack, and on a third by a navigable creek, the inlet therefrom, in a variety of places, afford an inexhaustible fund of rich mud for manure or compost. The water abounds in a variety of fish and wild fowl; and one or more shad and herring fisheries might be established thereon.

The advertisement described in similar fashion the other three dependent farms of Mount Vernon, with the terms on which they could be rented. Washington, after he had assembled over the years, often field by field, thousands of Mount Vernon's acres, looked down the short road of his remaining years and decided that there was too much plantation for an aging man. He did not mean to give any of it up, only to rent it, but for a man who knew and loved every foot of its great expanse, even the thought of familiar fields in the hands of tenant farmers must have been a wrench. None of it, though, would ever be farmed by a tenant while Washington lived, for he would never find a prospective renter who satisfied him. Near the end of February, Washington sent a brief but important message to the Senate.

United States Feby. 26th. 1796

Gentlemen of the Senate:

I send herewith the Treaty concluded on the 27th. of October last between the United States and Spain by their respective Plenipotentiaries.

The Communications to the Senate referred to in my message of the 16th. of December 1793 contain the instructions to the Commissioners of the United States, Messrs. Carmichael and Short, and various details relative to the negociations with Spain. Herewith I transmit Copies of the documents authorizing Mr. Pinckney the Envoy extraordinary from the United States to the Court of Spain, to conclude the negociation, agreeably to the original instructions above mentioned; and to adjust the Claims of the United States for the Spoliations committed by the Armed Vessels of his Catholic Majesty on the Commerce of our Citizens.

The numerous papers exhibiting the progress of the negociation under the conduct of Mr. Pinckney, being in the French and Spanish languages, will be communicated to the Senate as soon as the translations which appear necessary shall be completed.

Stripped of its eighteenth-century official phraseology, Washington's message to the Senate meant that after a dozen years of frustrating negotiations, agreement had at last been reached with Spain on navigation of the Mississippi River and on the southern boundary of the United States. The pact, signed in October of 1795, was the Treaty of San Lorenzo, or more familiarly, Pinckney's Treaty—for Thomas Pinckney, who, as special envoy, had helped conclude the negotiations. By the agreement, Spain granted American citizens free use of the Mississippi, whose lower reaches ran through Spanish territory. Also granted was the right of deposit at New Orleans of American freight brought down the river for transshipment by sea. Spain accepted the thirty-first parallel of latitude as the southwestern boundary of the United States (previously she had claimed a line about ninety miles farther north), and she promised to curb Indian incursions into American territory. And finally, the Spanish agreed to settle claims arising from their seizure of American ships. These sweeping concessions very probably were the result of Spanish fear that Jay's Treaty secretly provided for an Anglo-American alliance that could be a threat to Spain. In any event, the effect of the treaty was to ease the difficulties of western settlers and to remove the possibility that in frustration they might attempt to form a separate nation. For Washington, the agreement removed several problems that had vexed him from the beginning of his Presidency.

As the months of 1796 passed away, the President prepared a farewell address with Hamilton's help. The lengthy document was never actually delivered but was published widely, first in Philadelphia in the *American Daily Advertiser* of September 19, 1796. The Address was a notable message. In four basic sections, it gave Washington's reasons for refusing a third term; it inveighed against party divisions, especially along sectional lines; it counseled that the nation's credit must always be cherished and protected; and it warned against permanent foreign alliances. The caution against permanent alliances remained a keystone of American foreign policy until less than a generation ago; a thousand spread-eagle orators since have misquoted Washington as warning against "entangling alliances"—that phrase was to be Jefferson's. The core of what George Washington wrote follows.

> The great rule of conduct for us, in regard to foreign Nations, is in extending our commercial relations, to have with them as little *political* connection as possible. So far as we have already formed engagements let them be fulfilled with perfect good faith. Here let us stop.
>
> Europe has a set of primary interests, which to us have none, or a very remote relation. Hence she must be engaged in frequent controversies, the causes of which are essentially foreign to our concerns. Hence, therefore, it must be unwise in us to implicate ourselves, by artificial ties, in the ordinary vicissitudes of her politicks, or the ordinary combinations and collisions of her friendships, or enmities.
>
> Our detached and distant situation invites and enables us to pursue a different course. If we remain one People, under an efficient government, the period is not far off, when we may defy material injury from external annoyance; when we may take such an attitude as will cause

the neutrality, we may at any time resolve upon, to be scrupulously respected; when belligerent nations, under the impossibility of making acquisitions upon us, will not lightly hazard the giving us provocation; when we may choose peace or war, as our interest, guided by justice, shall counsel.

Why forego the advantages of so peculiar a situation? Why quit our own to stand upon foreign ground? Why, by interweaving our destiny with that of any part of Europe, entangle our peace and prosperity in the toils of European ambition, rivalship, interest, humour or caprice?

'Tis our true policy to steer clear of permanent alliances, with any portion of the foreign world; so far, I mean, as we are now at liberty to do it; for let me not be understood as capable of patronising infidility to existing engagements. I hold the maxim, no less applicable to public than to private affairs, that honesty is always the best policy. I repeat it, therefore, let those engagements be observed in their genuine sense. But in my opinion, it is unnecessary and would be unwise to extend them.

Taking care always to keep ourselves, by suitable establishments, on a respectable defensive posture,

The first page of Hamilton's draft
of Washington's farewell address

we may safely trust to temporary alliances for extra-ordinary emergencies.

[The President closed with a typical Washingtonian note of apology for his inadequacies, and of his pleasure at anticipating the joys of retirement.]

Though in reviewing the incidents of my administration, I am unconscious of intentional error: I am nevertheless too sensible of my defects not to think it probable that I may have committed many errors. Whatever they may be I fervently beseech the Almighty to avert or mitigate the evils to which they may tend. I shall also carry with me the hope that my Country will never cease to view them with indulgence; and that after forty five years of my life dedicated to its service, with an upright zeal, the faults of incompetent abilities will be consigned to oblivion, as myself must soon be to the mansions of rest.

Relying on its kindness in this as in other things, and actuated by that fervent love towards it, which is so natural to a man, who views in it the native soil of himself, and his progenitors for several generations; I anticipate with pleasing expectation that retreat, in which I promise myself to realize, without alloy, the sweet enjoyment of partaking, in the midst of my fellow Citizens, the benign influence of good laws under a free government — the ever favourite object of my heart, and the happy reward, as I trust, of our mutual cares, labours and dangers.

BOSTON ATHENAEUM

In July, 1796, a book was published in Boston containing Washington's speeches to Congress and other of his official pronouncements. This is the title page from his own copy.

By January, 1797, the results of the presidential election were known, and the growing strength of the Republicans was obvious. Although Federalist John Adams won, he barely edged out — 71 votes to 68 — Thomas Jefferson, who thereby became Vice President. Thomas Pinckney, Federalist, received 59 votes; Aaron Burr, Republican, 30.

The last three months of Washington's Administration spun to an end. He would not leave a secure and tranquil nation; both British and French warships were stopping American merchant vessels and removing goods bound for the other country; American citizens were bitterly divided as they took sides in the European conflict. But for the moment the United States appeared safe from war; Washington had started the country on its way and had given it a breathing spell. On March 3, 1797, he signed a pardon for ten men convicted of treason in connection with the Whisky Rebellion and remitted a fine imposed on a smuggler. These appear to be his last two official acts as President. That same day he gave a farewell dinner "to take my leave of the President elect, of the foreign characters, the heads of departments, &c." The next day he went alone to Congress Hall to witness the swearing in of John Adams as second President of the United States. The ceremony was brief, and in a few minutes Washington walked forth a private citizen. Of his two last days in office he left little record in his diary.

> 3 [March, 1797]. Mercury at 34. Morning very lowering & threatning but clear & pleasant afterwards— Wind fresh from the So. Wt.
>
> 4. Much such a day as yesterday in all respects— Mercury at 41.

When Washington was inaugurated in 1789, the Presidency of the United States was no more than a concept, words in the untried Constitution. In eight years he had created an office that was established and workable, flesh and blood. It is safe to say that no other man of his time could have done the same thing, such were his unique talents and the great trust the people reposed in him.

His Administration was not a flamboyant one, but like the man himself it was marked by caution, sober assessment of the prevailing situation, and careful planning. Perhaps the greatest of his achievements was to hold a number of self-willed states together until their people had acquired a sense of themselves as a nation. He kept the country at peace, divorcing America from the quarrels of Europe in spite of clamor around him for involvement, for he knew that war then could wreck the infant republic. He assumed the Presidency of a country submerged in debt and left it well on its way to fiscal soundness, a tribute not to his financial acumen but to his ability to choose able advisers and then to support the programs they recommended. He gave to the Presidency not only dignity but established it as a coequal arm with Congress; a lesser man might well have let the office become ceremonial and subservient to the legislature.

In one thing he failed. He had wanted to keep the new nation free of the divisiveness of party politics. It was a vain hope, for party divisions, Federalists against Republicans, were only the surface indications of deep economic and philosophical rifts, of bankers and merchants against farmers, of the wealthy few against the many poor. Washington for a long time attempted a nonpartisan stance, dividing his Cabinet equally between Federalists and Republicans, but his own instincts were conservative, and during his last years in office his Cabinet was composed entirely of Federalists, who shared his belief in a strong central government. It detracts little from Washington's greatness as a President to observe that he was basically a Federalist when he turned the Presidency over to John Adams.

Chapter 11

To Rest by the Potomac

Washington tarried a few days in Philadelphia, paying his respects to the new President, being honored at a dinner by the people of Philadelphia, breaking up his household. Happily, his dependable secretary of former years, Tobias Lear, was in the capital and could take over a big part of the chore of moving, including the packing of some two hundred boxes, trunks, casks, and other items belonging to Washington for shipment by water to Mount Vernon, and then cleaning and making the President's House ready for John Adams. Washington left for home the morning of March 9, 1797. In his party, besides Martha, were Martha's eighteen-year-old granddaughter Eleanor (Nelly), George Washington Lafayette, and Lafayette's tutor. As always, cities along the way paid honor to Washington as he passed through, not only Baltimore, Georgetown, and Alexandria, but also the still unfinished city of Washington—which the former President still modestly referred to as the Federal City. There an artillery escort turned out and gave him a sixteen-gun salute.

There was much to be done at Mount Vernon. As of the first of the year, still another manager, James Anderson, had taken over from rheumatic William Pearce, and although he was proving diligent and capable, he had much to learn that only Washington could teach him. Washington put painters to work freshening up the mansion house, only to discover that other things should have been taken care of first: a marble mantel was almost falling out, the main beam under one room was so badly decayed that it would have collapsed if the room had been filled with people, there was other deterioration in the outer buildings as well as in the mansion house. The owner spoke of his problems in a letter to Tobias Lear.

> Mount Vernon 25th. March 1797.
> Your letter of the 20th. instt., with the Bill of lading for the Goods in the Sloop Salem, and another letter of the 15th. are both received; and I hope this will find you

safely arrived in the Federal City.

I have got Painters at work in order to prepare my rooms for the furniture which is expected; but I find I have begun at the wrong end, for some joiners work (of the deficiency of which I was ignorant before it was examined) ought to have preceeded theirs, as the fixing of the chimney pieces ought also to do. The first I have engaged, but cannot, on enquiry, find that a skilful hand is to be had in Alexandria to execute the latter. I would thank you therefore for engaging one, if to be had in the Federal City or George town, to be here on Monday or tuesday at farthest as my work will be at a stand without. To prevent imposition, and to avoid disputes, I would prefer employing the artisan by the day. The work *immediately* foreseen, and which must be done without delay, is, to refix the Marble chimney piece in the Parlour which is almost falling out; to fix the New one (expected from Philadelphia) in the small dining room; to remove the one *now* there into what is called the School room; to fix the Grate which is coming round in the large dining room; and to give some repairs to the steps; which (like most things else I have looked into since I have been at home) are sadly out of repair.

Mount Vernon. LOSSING

The summer house at Mount Vernon

Washington received news of the death of his only sister, Betty Washington Lewis, in a letter from her son, George Lewis. The squire of Mount Vernon replied with a letter of condolence that reads very strangely, since it seems less concerned with their loss than with his building problems.

Mount Vernon, April 9, 1797.
Your letter of the 31st. Ult. from Culpeper County, came to my hands late at night on the 5th. inst., and the enclosure for your brother Fielding was sent to him early next morning.

The melancholy of your writing has filled me with inexpressable concern. The debt of nature however sooner or later, must be paid by us all, and although the separation from our nearest relatives is a heart rending circumstance, reason, religeon and philosophy, teach us to bear it with resignation, while time alone can ameliorate, and soften the pangs we experience at parting.

Washington's sister, Betty Lewis

It must have been a consoling circumstance to my deceased Sister, that so many of her friends were about her. I find myself almost in the Situation of a new beginner, so much does my houses, and every thing about them, stand in need of repairs. What with Joiners, Painters, Glasiers, etc. etc. I have scarcely a room to go into at present, that is free from one, or other of them. But the inside will soon be done, tho' it will require a good deal of time to make good the decays which I am every day discerning in the out buildings and Inclosures.

This leads me to ask if you know of a good House Joiner (white or black) that could be hired by the year, or month, and on what terms. I want one who is capable of making a rich finished pannel Door, Sash, and wainscot; and who could be relied on for his sobriety and diligence.

At any time, and at all times, we should be very glad to see you and Mrs. Lewis at this place; and with best regard to you both, in which your Aunt joins, I am, etc.

Washington was soon back in the familiar rhythm of a farmer's life, one regulated by the sun and the seasons. He also found himself caught up again in the demands of Virginia hospitality, as he had been before he became President; there was always someone eating at his table, asking to stay overnight, or begging other favors of him. He wrote to Secretary of War James McHenry, describing his life in retirement.

Mount Vernon 29th. May 1797.

I am indebted to you for several unacknowledged letters, but n'er mind that—go on as if you had them. You are at the source of information & can find many things to relate, while I have nothing to say that could either inform, or amuse a Secretary of War in Philadelphia.

To tell him that I begin my diurnal Course with the sun,—that if my Hirelings are not in their places at that time; I send them messages expressive of my sorrow for their indisposition, then having put these wheels in motion, I examine the state of things further; and the more they are probed the deeper I find the wounds are which my buildings have sustained by an absence & neglect of Eight Years. By the time I have accomplished these matters breakfast (a little after seven O'clock about the time I presume you are taking leave of Mrs. McHenry) is ready. This over I mount my horse and ride round my farms, which employs me until it is time to dress for dinner at which I rarely miss seeing strange faces, come as they say out of respect for me—Pray would not the word curiosity answer as Well? And how different this from having a few social friends at a chearful board? The usual time of Sitting at Table—a walk—and Tea, brings me within the dawn of candle light; previous to which if not prevented by company, I resolve that as soon as the glimmering taper supplies the place of the great luminary, I will retire to my writing table, & acknowledge the letters I have received but when the lights are brought I feel tired & disinclined to engage in this work, conceiving that the next night will do as well: the next comes & with it the same causes for postponement & effect & so on.

This will account for *your* letters remaining so long unacknowledged—and having given you the History of a day, it will serve for a year; and I am persuaded you will not require a second edition of it: but it may strike you that in this detail no mention is made of any portion of time allotted for reading; The remark would be just—for I have not looked into a Book since I came home, nor shall I be able to do it until I have discharged my Workmen, probably not before the nights grow longer, when possibly I may be looking in doomsday book.

China bearing motif of Society of the Cincinnati, purchased by Washington

Mount Vernon, LOSSING

Washington's complaint about visitors who came to Mount Vernon out of mere curiosity went back many years, but his innate hospitality made it impossible for him to close his gates to strangers. He sent a brief note on July 1 to Tobias Lear, who was still in business in the city of Washington: "I am alone *at present*, and shall be glad to see you this evening. Unless someone pops in, unexpectedly—Mrs. Washington and myself will do what I believe has not been done within the last twenty years by us—that is to set down to dinner by ourselves."

Despite what Washington had told McHenry about his simple daily routine, the truth was that much of his heart and mind remained with the affairs of the nation. He was kept informed of developments by the Secretaries of War and State, and the information was not always cheerful. Before he retired, Washington had appointed Charles Cotesworth Pinckney Minister to France to replace James Monroe. Previously Washington had offered Pinckney, at one time or another, command of the Army, a seat on the Supreme Court, and the secretaryships of War and State, and as a result he considered it not only an insult to the United States but a personal affront when the French Government—the Directory—refused to accept Pinckney's credentials. It sent relations with France from bad to worse. The United States was no more prepared for war with France than it had been to fight with England at the time of Jay's Treaty. President Adams sent John Marshall (later Chief Justice) and Elbridge Gerry (a Republican, to give the group a bipartisan image) to join Pinckney in dealing with the Government in Paris. About the first of December, Washington received letters from Pinckney and Marshall, written from Holland in September. His responses to both men were similar in tone; following is his letter to Pinckney.

> Mount Vernon 4 Decr. 1797.
>
> With much pleasure I received your letter of the 19th. of Septr. from Rotterdam; and that pleasure proceeded in a great measure from the congeniality of sentiments which prevail between you and Genl. Marshall, as I had taken the liberty of introducing him to you, as a Gentleman in whom you might place entire confidence.
>
> What has been the reception of the embassy by the French Directory, is, to me, unknown; and what will be the result of it, is not for me to predict. The change however which took place at Paris on the 4th. of Septr. [a coup d'état against the Directory] adds nothing to my hope of a favorable issue. In this I *may* be mistaken; but of another thing I am certain I shall not and that is, that the failure (if such be the case) cannot be attributed to the want of justice on the part of the United States or from the want of an able representation of it, on the part of their Negociators. Of course the issue must be favorable, or conviction will be produced in all Except those who do not want to be convinced, that we have nothing to expect from the [justice of the] Nation with whom we are treating. In either case we shall ascertain our ground.
>
> That the Government of France views us as a divided people I have little doubt, and that they have been led to entertain that opinion, from representations and the conduct of many of our own citizens, is still less doubtful, but I shall be very much mistaken in deed in the Mass of the people of the United States, if an occasion should call for an unequivocal expression of the public voice, if the first would not find themselves very much deceived—and the latter (their leaders excepted) to change their notes. I pray devoutly that the Directory may not bring the matter to trial....
>
> ...The enclosed for young Lafayette I must request

your care of. Having received premature advice (from some of his correspondants in Hamburg) of the liberation of his father and friends his eagerness to embrace them in the first moments of it could not be restrained, although I endeavoured to convince him that it would be more prudent to await the confirmation from *themselves,* and among other things observed to him, that although it was not *probable,* still it was *possible* that his parents might be on their voyage to America whilst he was seeking them in Europe. Should this prove to be the case (as appears not unlikely from the injunction of the Emperor) it will be a matter of sore regret to both. The confidence however which he placed in his information; the advancement of the Season & fear of a Winters passage; gave the preponderancy to his inclination over my opinion. He is a sensible & well disposed young man, full of filial affection & every sentiment to render him estimable.

Information with respect to public matters will go to you from a more direct and purer fountain than mine— (I mean the Department of State)—and things which more immediately concerns myself is too unimportant to trouble you with, further than to assure you, which I can do with much truth that in your public [mission] and in your private capacity—I wish you all the success and prosperity that your heart can desire;...

Silhouettes of George and Martha Washington in their later years

It was the last chance Washington would have to give either Pinckney or Marshall news and advice; there would be no further reports from any of the three envoys for many weeks. Meanwhile, Washington was facing problems with his grandson George Washington Parke Custis very reminiscent of those he had had a generation earlier with his stepson, the boy's father, Jack Custis. Like his father, young Custis was lazy, without ambition, had the same predilection for sporting companions, and possessed the same ability to soft-talk the squire of Mount Vernon into believing that no matter what transgressions or failures there had been in the past, a new leaf had just been turned. As Jack had dropped out of King's College after a desultory try, so had his son left the College of New Jersey (later Princeton) after a poor showing and returned to Mount Vernon. Washington, ever hopeful, sent the young man a memorandum outlining what was expected of him at Mount Vernon.

[Mount Vernon, January 7, 1798]

System in all things should be aimed at; for in execution, it renders every thing more easy.

If now and then, of a morning before breakfast, you are inclined, by way of change, to go out with a Gun, I shall not object to it; provided you return by the hour we usually set down to that meal.

From breakfast, until about an hour before Dinner (allowed for dressing, & preparing for it, that you may appear decent) I shall expect you will confine yourself to your studies; and diligently attend to them; endeavouring to make yourself master of whatever is recommended to, or required of you.

While the afternoons are short, and but little interval between rising from dinner and assembling for Tea, you may employ that time in walking, or any other recreation.

After Tea, if the Studies you are engaged in require it, you will, no doubt perceive the propriety & advantage of returning to them, until the hour of rest.

Rise early, that by habit it may become familiar—agreeable—healthy—and profitable. It may for a while, be irksome to do this; but that will wear off; and the practise will produce a rich harvest forever thereafter; whether in public, or private walks of Life.

Make it an invariable rule to be in place (unless extraordinary circumstances prevent it) at usual breakfasting, dining, and tea hours. It is [not] only disagreeable, but it is also very inconvenient, for servants to be running here, & there, and they know not where, to summon you to them, when their duties, and attendance, on the company who are seated, render it improper.

Saturday may be appropriated to riding to your Gun, or other proper amusements.

Time disposed of in this manner, makes ample provision for exercise & every useful, or necessary recreation; at the sametime that the hours allotted for study, *if really applied to it,* instead of running up & down stairs, & wasted in conversation with any one who will talk with you, will enable you to make considerable progress in whatsoever line is marked out for you: and that you may do it, is my sincere wish.

Washington realized that advice and rules of conduct were not going to be enough for the youth. Two weeks after having sent the letter above to young Custis, he wrote to the boy's stepfather, David Stuart, for advice. There was a note almost of resignation in his letter, as though he knew that the youth's character was already set, and that little could be done to change it.

Mount Vernon, January 22, 1798.
Washington leaves this today, on a visit to Hope Park, which will. afford you an opportunity to examine the progress he has made in the studies he was directed to pursue.

I can, and I believe do, keep him in his room a certain portion of the 24 hours, but it will be impossible for me to make him attend to his Books, if inclination, on his part, is wanting; nor while I am out, if he chuses to be so too, is it in my power to prevent it. I will not say this is the case, nor will I run the hazard of doing him injustice by saying he does not apply, as he ought, to what has been prescribed; but no risk will be run, and candour requires I declare it as my opinion, that he will not derive much benefit in any course which can be marked out for him at this place, without an *able* Preceptor always with him, nor then, for reasons, which do not require to be detailed.

What is best to be done with him, I know not. My opinion always has been that the University in Massachusetts [Harvard] would have been the most eligable Seminary to have sent him to, 1st., because it is on a larger Scale than any other; and 2nd., because I believe that the habits of the youth there, whether from the

Saint-Memin in Virginia: Portraits and Biographies
BY FILLMORE NORFLEET, 1942

George Washington Parke Custis

discipline of the School or from the greater attention of the People, generally, to morals and a more regular course of life, are less prone to dissipation and debauchery than they are at the Colleges South of it. It may be asked, if this was my opinion, why did I not send him there? The answer is as short, as to me it was weighty; being the only male of his family and knowing (although it would have been submitted to) that it would have proved a heart rending stroke to have him at that distance I was disposed to try a nearer Seminary, of good repute; which from some cause, or combinations of causes, has not, after the experiment of a year, been found to answer the end that was contemplated. Whether to send him there *now*, or indeed to any other public School, is at least problematical, and to suffer him to mispend his time at this place, will be disgraceful to himself and me.

If I was to propose to him, to go to the University at Cambridge (in Massachusetts) he might, as has been usual for him on like occasions, say he would go whereever I chose to send him; but if he should go contrary to his inclination, and without a disposition to apply his time properly, an expense without any benefit would result from the measure. Knowing how much I have been disappointed, and my mind disturbed by his conduct, he would not, I am sure, make a candid disclosure of his sentiments to me on this or any other plan I might propose for the completion of his education; for which reason I would pray that you (or perhaps Mrs. Stuart cd. succeed better than any other) would draw [mutilated] and explicit disclosure [mutilated] wishes and views are: for if they are absolutely fixed, an attempt to counteract them by absolute controul would be as idle as the endeavour to stop a rivulet that is constantly running. Its progress while mound upon mound is erected, may be arrested; but this must have an end, and everything would be swept with the torrent.

The more I think of his entering at William and Mary, (unless he could be placed in the Bishop's family) the more doubtful I am of its utility, on many accounts; which had better be the subject of oral communications than by letter. I shall wish to hear from you on the subject of this letter. On occasion of severe reprimand, I found it necessary to give Washington sometime ago, I received the enclosed from him. I have little doubt of his meaning well, but he has not resolution, or exertion enough to act well.

Consultations with Stuart brought a decision to send young Custis to St. John's College at Annapolis, Maryland, and the youth was sent off at the beginning of March. For a period he wrote his usual letters promising to work hard, and Washington responded with advice and encouragement. But when at the end of the school year the youth asked whether it might not be a good idea for him to leave St. John's, he drew a short and indignant reply from Washington.

Mount Vernon, 24th. July, 1798.
Your letter of the 21st. was received last night. The question, "I would thank you to inform me whether I leave it entirely, or not, so that I may pack up accordingly," really astonishes me! for it would seem as if *nothing* I could say to you made more than a *momentary* impression. Did I not, before you went to that seminary, and since by letter, endeavor to fix indelibly on your mind, that the object for which you were sent there was to finish a course of education which you yourself were to derive the benefit of hereafter, and for pressing which upon you, you would be the first to thank your friends so soon as reason has its proper sway in the direction of your thoughts?

As there is a regular stage between Annapolis and the federal city, embrace that as the easiest and most convenient way of getting to the latter, from whence Mr. Law or Mr. Peter will, I have no doubt, send you hither; or a horse might meet you there, or at Alexandria, at an appointed time.

French Foreign Minister Talleyrand

Long before Washington had written the last of the foregoing letters to his grandson, affairs with France had worsened. In early March of 1798 a report from the three envoys in France arrived at last. It detailed a long list of indignities. The ambassadors had been received only coldly and informally by French Foreign Minister Talleyrand, who thereafter declined to see them. Instead they were visited in turn by his underlings, who suggested that a bribe of $250,000 to Talleyrand, a loan of ten million dollars to France, and the withdrawal by President Adams of some "insults" to France made in a speech to Congress, would open the way to fruitful negotiations. All attempts by the Americans to get at the basic issues were met with veiled threats of French military strength and a constant return to the theme of money, until the exasperated Pinckney exclaimed, "No, no! Not a sixpence," a remark that was later transmuted and has gone down in history as "Millions for defense but not one cent for tribute." Pinckney and Marshall, considering any further attempts to negotiate useless, came home; Gerry naïvely believed that his continued presence in Paris would prevent war and remained a while longer. The envoys, in their report, referred to the French agents as X, Y, and Z, and after the report was made public the episode became popularly known as the XYZ Affair. When Talleyrand's duplicity became known, France's popularity in the United States plummeted. Washington's reaction was remarkably restrained. To Senator James Lloyd of Maryland, who sent him a copy of the XYZ papers, he replied with only a few sentences.

> Mount Vernon 15th. April 1798.
>
> For your kindness in forwarding a copy of the dispatches from our Envoys in France to the Government here, I pray you to accept my best thanks.
>
> What a scene of corruption and profligacy has these communications disclosed in the Directors of a People with whom the United States have endeavoured to Treat upon fair just & honorable ground.
>
> If they should be attended with the effect of "Speedily uniting our fellow Citizens with a firm determination to support our Government & preserve our Independence" as you seem to expect, it would indeed be cause for much congratulation, and no one wd. rejoice more at such an event than I should—But I wish it may be so.

A letter to Secretary of State Pickering a day later was equally brief. Washington was pessimistic that the experience of the three envoys would change the views of the most rabidly Francophile Republicans.

> Mount Vernon 16th. April 1798.
>
> Your obliging favor of the 11th. Inst. enclosing copies of the instructions to, & Dispatches from the Envoys of the United States at Paris was received with thankfulness by the last Post.
>
> One would think that the measure of infamy was filled, and the profligacy of, and corruption in the System pursued by the French Directory required no further disclosure of the principles by which it is actuated, than what is contained in the above Dispatches; to open the Eyes of the blindest; and yet, I am persuaded

that those Communications will produce no change in the *leaders* of the Opposition, unless there shoud appear a manifest desertion of the followers. There is a sufficient evidence already, in the *Aurora* of the turn they intend to give the business, and of the ground they mean to occupy—but I do not believe they will be able to maintain *that*—or any *other* much longer.

Then for well over a month, Washington's correspondence did not mention war or foreign affairs, except for a letter to the Secretary of War urging that the arsenal at the mouth of the Shenandoah (Harpers Ferry) be finished and activated as a piece of urgent business. Possibly so many years of contending with the problems of the nation, as well as advancing age, had wearied him to such a point that he was willing to let others cope with some of the affairs of the day. And very possibly, in such a mood of disenchantment with the present he had let his mind run back to a more carefree day, for he sat down to write a letter to Sally Fairfax, the love of his youth. He had not seen Sally since she and her husband had left for England in 1773, twenty-five years before, and he had never corresponded with her, although he had exchanged a few letters with her husband. Sally was long since a widow. Washington's letter was largely a catching up on the news of many years, but the fact that he wrote at all strongly suggests that he had never quite gotten over his first real love.

Mount Vernon May 16, 1798.

My dear madam:

Five and twenty Years have nearly passed away since I have considered myself as the permanent resident of this place; or have been in a situation to indulge myself in familiar intercourse with my friends by letter or otherwise.

During this period so many important events have occurred & such changes in man & things have taken place, as the compass of a letter wou'd give you but an inadequate idea of. None of which events however nor all of them together have been able to eradicate from my mind the recollection of those happy moments, the happiest of my life which I have enjoyed in your company.

Worn out in a manner by the toils of my past labour, I am again seated under my vine and Fig Tree, and wish I could add that there were none to make us affraid; but those whom we have been accustomed to call our good friends and allies are endeavouring if not to make

*Engraving of Mount Vernon made in
1798 by John Stockdale of London*

us affraid, yet to dispoil us of our property; and are provoking us to act of self defence which may lead to war. What will be the result of such measures, time that faithful expositor of all things must disclose. My wish is to spend the remainder of my days (which cannot be many) in rural amusements—free from the cares [from] which public responsibility is never exempt.

Before the war and even while it existed although I was eight years from home at one stretch (except the *en passant visits* made to it on my marchs to and from the siege of York Town) I made considerable additions to my dwelling houses and alterations in my Offices & Gardens, but the dilapidation occasioned by time & those neglects which are coextensive with the absence of proprietors have occupied as much of my time within the last twelve months in repairing them, as at any former period in the same space—and it is matter of sore regret when I cast my eyes towards Belvoir wch. I often do to reflect the former Inhabitants of it, with whom we lived in such harmony and friendship—no longer reside there—and that the ruins can only be viewed as the memento of former pleasures; permit me to add that I have wondered often (your nearest relations being in this country) that you should not prefer spending the Evening of your life among them rather than close the sublunary [scene] in a foreign Country, numerous as your acquaintances may be and sincere the friendships you may have formed.

A Century hence if this Country keeps United (& It is surely its policy and Interest to do so) will produce a City, though not as large as London yet of a magnitude inferior to few others in Europe, on the Banks of the Potomack; where one is now establishing for the permanent seat of the Government of the United States (between Alexandria and George Town, on the Maryland side of the River). A situation not excelled for commanding prospect, good water, salubrious air, and safe harbour, by any in the world; and where elegant buildings are erecting & in forwardness for the reception of Congress in the year 1800.

Alexandria within the last seven Years, since the establishment of the Genl. Government has increased in buildings, in population, in the improvement of its Streets, by well executed pavements, and in the extension of its wharves in a manner of which you can have very little idea. This shew of prosperity you will readily conceive is owing to its commerce. The extension of that Trade is occasioned in a great degree by opening of the Inland navigation of Potomack River now cleared to Fort Cumberland upwards of 200 miles and by a similar attempt to accomplish the like up the Shannandoah 150 miles more—in a word if this Country can stear clear of European Politics, stand firm on its bottom & be wise and temperate in its government, it bids fair to be one of the greatest & happiest nations in the world.

In the latter part of May a letter from Alexander Hamilton contained a disturbing thought: "In the event of an open rupture with France, the public voice will again call you to command the armies of your Country." Hamilton was also dubious that the XYZ Affair had united the country as much as was commonly believed. He felt that Washington could oppose French sympathizers in Virginia and North Carolina by making a tour of those states "under some pretence of health &c. This would call forth addresses public dinners &c. which would give you an opportunity of expressing sentiments in Answering Toasts &c. which would throw the weight of your character into the scale of Government and revive an enthusiasm for your person that may be turned into the right channel." Only a little more than a year out of the Presidency, Washington must have read with misgivings this first suggestion that he might be called upon to serve his country yet another time. He threw cold water on Hamilton's idea that he should make a tour, and also minimized the probability that there would be a war in which his leadership would be needed.

Mount Vernon 27th. May 1798.

Yesterday brought me your letter of the 19th. Instant.

You may be assured that my mind is deeply impressed with the present situation of our public affairs and not a little agitated by the outrageous conduct of France towards the United States and at the [inimical] conduct of its partisans who aid and abet their measures: You may believe further from assurances equally sincere that if there was any thing in my power which could be done with consistency to avert or lessen the danger of the crisis, it should be rendered with hand and heart.

The expedient however which has been suggested by you, would not in my Opinion answer the end which is proposed. The object of such a tour could not be vailed by the [ostensible] cover to be given to it; because it would not apply to the State of my health which never was better: and as the measure would be susceptible of two interpretations the enemies to it — always more active and industrious than friends wou'd endeavour, as much as in them lay, to turn it to their own advantage by malicious insinuations; unless that they should discover that the current against themselves was setting too strong, and of too serious a nature for them to stem — in which case the journey would be unnecessary, and in either case the reception might not be such as you have Supposed.

But my dear Sir dark as matters appear at present, and expedient as it is to be prepared at *all* points for the worst that can happen; (and no one is more disposed to this measure than I am) I can not make up my mind *yet,* for the expectation of *open War* or in other words for a formidable Invasion by France. I cannot believe although I think them capable [of] *any thing bad* that they will attempt to do more than they have done, that when they perceive the spirit & policy of this Country rising into resistance and that they have falsely calculated upon support from a large part of the *people* thereof — to promote their views and influence in it, that they will desist, *even from those practices;* unless unexpected events in Europe, or their possession of

Louisiana & the Floridas should induce them to continue the measure. And I believe further that although the *leaders* of their party, in this country will not change their sentiments, that they will be obliged nevertheless to change their plan, or the mode of carrying it on; from the effervescenc[e] which is appearing in all quarters & from the desertion of their followers, which must frown them into silence—at least for awhile.

If I did not view things in this light, my mind would be infinitely more disquieted than it is; for if a crisis should arrive when a sense of duty, or a call from my Country should become so imperious as to leave me no Choice I should prepare for the relinquishment & go with as much reluctance from my present peaceful abode, as I should do to the tombs of my ancestors.

The call to put on uniform again was not as remote a possibility as Washington liked to think. In early July he received two letters on the same day. One, from Secretary of War McHenry, asked, "May we flatter ourselves, that, in a crisis so awful and important, you will accept the command of all our armies?" The other, from President Adams, asked much the same thing, but in less specific terms. To McHenry, Washington replied at great length, opening his letter with an admission that he could not ignore a call to serve his country if he were really needed.

Secretary of War James McHenry in a portrait attributed to Sharples

Mount Vernon 4 July 1798.

Your letter of the 26th. Ulto. propounds a very serious, interesting & important question to me; a question that might have been answered with less delay if I had been as much in the habit since, as before I became a private Citizen, of sending regularly to the Post Office on Post days for letters.

The sentiments which I mean to express to you in this letter on the subject of yours, shall be frank, undisguised & explicit; for I see, as you do, that clouds are gathering and that a Storm may ensue. And I find too, from a variety of hints, that my quiet under these circumstances does not promise to be of long continuance.

It cannot be necessary for me to premise to you, or to others who know my Sentiments as well, that to quit the tranquil walks of retirement, and enter the boundless field of responsibility and trouble, would be productive of sensations which a better pen than I possess would find it difficult to describe. Nevertheless, the principle by which my conduct has been actuated through life, would not suffer me, in any great emergency, to withhold any services I could render, required by my Country—especially in a case where its dearest rights are assailed by lawless ambition, and intoxicated power, contrary to every principle of justice & in violation of solemn compact, and Laws which govern all Civilized Nations. And this too with obvious intent to sow thick the Seeds of disunion for the purpose of subjugating the Government and destroying our Independence & happiness.

Under circumstances like these accompanied by an actual Invasion of our territorial rights, it would be difficult for me, at any time, to remain an idle spectator under the plea of Age or Retirement. With sorrow, it is true, I should quit the shades of my peaceful abode and the ease & happiness I now enjoy to encounter a new the turmoils of War to which, possibly, my strength

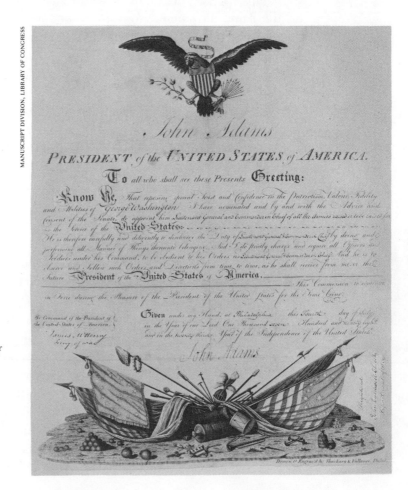

Washington's commission of July 4, 1798, appointing him "Lieutenant General and Commander in Chief of all the Armies," signed by Adams

and powers might be found incompetent. These, however, should not be stumbling blocks in my *own* way;
but there are other things highly important for me to
ascertain, and settle, before I could give a decided answer
to your question.

In the rest of his letter, Washington went on to discuss
such things as the qualifications of officers, his need to have people he
could trust about him if he were to command, and how important it was that
his age not be held against him. To the President he was briefer: if worse
came to worst he could not refuse the call of his country. But Adams, even
before he received Washington's letter, sent McHenry to Mount Vernon to
personally deliver a message. Two days later Washington gave his reply to
the President. He would, of course, serve.

Mount Vernon July 13th. 1798.
I had the honor on the evening of the 11th. instant, to
receive, by the hands of the Secretary of War, your favour
of the 7th., announcing, that you had, with the advice
and consent of the Senate, appointed me "Lieutenant
General and Commander in Chief of all the Armies
raised, or to be raised for the Service of the U.S."

I cannot express how greatly affected I am at this new
proof of public confidence, and the highly flattering
manner in which you have been pleased to make the
communication; at the same time I must not conceal
from you my earnest wish, that the Choice had fallen
upon a man less declined in years, and better qualified
to encounter the usual vicissitudes of War.

You know, Sir, what calculations I had made relative
to the probable [course] of events, on my retireing from
Office, and the determination I had consoled myself
with, of closing the remnant of my days in my present
peaceful abode; You will, therefore, be at no loss to
conceive and appreciate, the sensations I must have
experienced, to bring my mind to any conclusion, that
would pledge me, at so late a period of life, to leave
Scenes I sincerely love, to enter again upon the boundless field of public action—incessant trouble—and high
responsibility.

It was not possible for me to remain ignorant of,
or indifferent to recent transactions. The conduct of
the Directory of France towards our Country; their
insiduous hostility to its Government; their various

practices to withdraw the affection of the people from it; the evident tendency of their Arts, and those of their Agents to countenance and invigorate opposition; their disregard of solemn Treaties and the laws of Nations; their war upon our defenceless commerce; their treatment of our Ministers of Peace, and their demands, amounting to Tribute, could not fail to excite in me corresponding Sentiments with those my Countrymen have so generally expressed in their affectionate addresses to you. Believe me, Sir, no one can more cordially approve of the wise and prudent measures of your Administration. They ought to inspire universal confidence, and will, no doubt, combined with the state of things, call from Congress such laws and means as will enable you to meet the full force and extent of the Crisis.

Satisfied, therefore, that you have sincerely wished and endeavoured to avert war, and exhausted to the last drop the cup of reconciliation, we can with pure hearts appeal to Heaven for the justice of our Cause, and may confidently trust the final result to that kind Providence who has heretofore, and so often, signally favoured the people of the United States.

Thinking in this manner, and feeling how incumbent it is upon every person, of every description, to contribute at all times to his Country's welfare, and especially in a moment like the present, when everything we hold dear and sacred so seriously threatned, I have finally determined to accept the Commission of Commander in Chief of the Armies of the United States, with the reserve only, that I shall not be called into the field until the Army is in a situation to require my presence, or it becomes indispensable by the urgency of circumstances.

In making this reservation, I beg to be understood that I do not mean to withhold any assistance to arrange or organize the Army, which you may think I can afford. I take the liberty also to mention, that I must decline having my acceptance considered as drawing after it any immediate charge upon the Public, or that I can receive any emoluments annexed to the appointment, before entering into a situation to incur expence.

The Secretary of War being anxious to return to the Seat of Government, I have detained him no longer than is necessary to a full communication on the several points he had in charge.

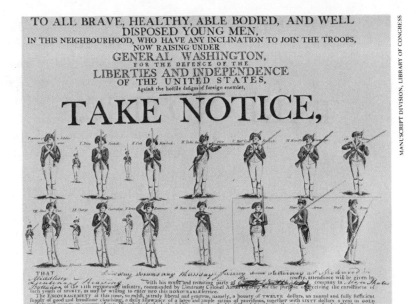

A 1798 recruiting poster used during the quasi war with France

Congress authorized increasing the size of the Army, which had shrunk to thirty-five hundred men, by another ten thousand. In addition, a "Provisional Army" of fifty thousand men and officers was to be recruited for the duration of the emergency. Washington's first problem was to select the three men who, as major generals, would be his immediate subordinates. For the senior of the three he wanted Alexander Hamilton. In that position Hamilton would rank second only to Washington and would ordinarily be in actual command, for Washington had stipulated that he should not be called to active duty until French invasion or other emergency required his presence in the field. Next, Washington nominated Charles Cotesworth Pinckney, although Pinckney's wartime rank of brigadier general outranked the lieutenant colonelcy of Hamilton. And third, Washington placed Henry Knox, a major general during the war, his dependable chief of artillery, his close friend, and his Secretary of War when he was President. Washington wrote to his old friend to explain his decision.

Mount Vernon 16th. July 1798.

Little did I imagine when I retired from the theatre of public life, that it was probable, or even possible, that any event would arise *in my day*, that could induce me to entertain, *for a moment*, an idea of relinquishing the tranquil walks, and refreshing shades, with which I am surrounded. But it is in vain, I perceive, to look for ease & happiness in a world of troubles.

The call of my Country, and the urgency of my friends to comply with it, have produced a letter from me to the

395

President of the United States, which, probably, will be given to the public; but if it should not, the principal feature thereof, is, that with the reservation of not being called into the Field until the Army is in a situation to require my presence, or it becomes indispensable by the urgency of circumstances, that I will accept the Commission with which the Secretary of War came charged. Desiring, however, that it might be understood, that my Coadjutors, in the first grades, and principal staff of the Army, must be men in whom I could place entire confidence; for that, it was not to be expected, at my time of life, that I would forsake the ease & comforts which are essential in old age—encounter the toils & vicissitudes of War, with all its concomitants—and jeopardize the reputation which the partiality of the World has been pleased to bestow on me (when the hazard of diminishing, is at least equal to the prospect of increasing it,) without securing such assistance as would enable me to go with confidence into such a field of responsibility.

After this exordium, it is almost unnecessary to add, that I have placed you among those characters on whom I wish to lean, for support. But my dear Sir, as you always have found, and I trust ever will find, candour a prominent trait of my character, I must add, that causes—which would exceed the limits of an ordinary letter to explain, are in the way of such an arrangement as might render your situation perfectly agreeable; but I fondly hope that, the difficulty will not be insurmountable, in your decision.

For the present, and augmented force, three Major Generals, and four Brigadiers are allowed by the Act establishing the latter; and in a consultation with the Secretary of War, the characters proposed for the former are Colo. Hamilton, Genl. Chas. Cotesworth Pinckney and yourself. The first of these, in the public estimation, as declared to me, is designated to be second in command; with some fears, I confess, of the consequences; although I must acknowledge at the sametime that I know not where a more competent choice could be made. General Pinckney's character as an active, spirited and intelligent Officer you are acquainted with, and know that it stands very high in the Southern Hemisphere—it being understood *there*, that he made Tactics as much, if not more his study, than any Officer in the American army during the last War. His character in other respects, in

Ice house at Mount Vernon
BOTH: *Mount Vernon*, LOSSING

that quarter before his late Embassy, was also high; and throughout the Union it has acquired celebrity by his conduct as Minister & Envoy. His connexions are numerous—their influence extensive; but most of all, with me, when to these considerations I add, as my *decided* opinion (for reasons unnecessary to enumerate) that if the French intend an Invasion of this Country *in force*, their operations will commence South of Maryland; & probably of Virginia; you will see at once the importance of embarking this Gentleman and all his connexions *heartily* in the active scenes that would follow, instead of damping their ardour, and thereby giving more activity to the leaven that is working in others, where unity of sentiment would be most desirable.

Viewing things in this light, I would fain hope, as we are forming an Army *A New*, which Army, if needful *at all*, is to fight for every thing that ought to be dear and sacred to freemen, that former rank will be forgot; and among the fit & chosen characters, the only contention will be, who shall be foremost in zeal, at this crisis, to serve his Country in whatever situation circumstances may place him. Most of those, who are best qualified to oppose the enemy, will have Sacrifices of ease—Interest—or Inclination to make; but what are these, when put in competition with the loss of our Independence or the Subjugation of our Government? both of which are evidently struck at, by an intoxicated, ambitious and domineering Foe.

The arrangement made with the Secretary of War is on a seperate Sheet of paper, and meant for your perusal *only*, until the decision of the President relative to it, is announced.

With that esteem & regard which you know I feel for you, I remain your sincere friend and Affectionate Servant.

P.S. From the best recollection I have of them, the Secretary of War is furnished with a list of Field & other Officers of the late Army of most celebrity, from whence to draw the Field Officers for the Corps to be raised. If you would afford your aid also it wd. be obliging.

Century plant sent to Washington from Puerto Rico (left) and a large lemon tree imported from West Indies

Knox's response was bitter and expressed his hurt at having his long devotion to Washington answered by seeing others "greatly my juniors in rank... preferred before me." Even more humiliating, said Knox, was that he had not been consulted in advance. Washington, deeply disturbed, tried to mollify Knox, and succeeded so well that Knox asked to serve as Washington's aide-de-camp if there was any fighting. Knox, however, refused the commission as Major General. Although he failed to gain the services of Knox, Washington did enlist another valuable associate of earlier days, his former secretary Tobias Lear. Lear had served him so well from 1785 until the end of his first Administration that he had become Washington's valued confidant and virtually a member of the family. Lear agreed to give up his business in the city of Washington and to take up his old duties as secretary once more. He would serve Washington for what remained of the latter's life.

> [Mount Vernon]
> Thursday night, August 30, 1798.
> I have, at length, received the President's answer (through the Secretary of War) to my request to be allowed a Secretary, who gives it as his opinion that I have an undoubted right to one, or all of my military family, if I find it convenient, and that their pay &c. will be allowed.
>
> And the Secretary having thrown a *mass* of Papers upon me which I have not looked into (being this moment arrived) I should be glad if you would now come & take your station.

Washington went to Philadelphia on November 10, to spend more than a month with Major Generals Hamilton and Pinckney discussing the Provisional Army, drawing up tables of organization, making plans for recruitment, compiling lists of prospective officers for the proposed twelve regiments, taking care of the countless other details involved. In addition, there were numerous dinners and receptions to consume Washington's time and energy. And there was at least one personal item to take care of. Washington had all his life been cursed with bad teeth and had lost them one by one, until after middle age they were all false. While in Philadelphia, Washington wrote to John Greenwood of New York, who had been his dentist for some time and in whom he had much confidence.

> Philadelphia 12th. Decr. 1798.
> Your letter of the 8th. came safe—and as I am hurrying, in order to leave this City tomorrow, I must be short.
>
> The principal thing you will have to attend to, in the alteration you are about to make, is to let the upper bar fall back from the lower one thus ❳ ; whether the teeth are quite straight, or inclining a little in thus, ❳ or a little rounding outwards thus ❱ is immaterial, for I find

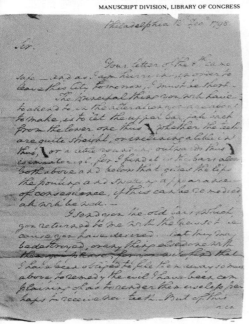

Washington's letter to his dentist

it is the bars alone both above and below that gives the lips the pouting and swelling appearance — of consequence, if this can be remedied, all will be well.

I send you the old bars, which you returned to me with the new set, because you have desired. But they may be destroyed, or any thing else done with them you please, for you will find that I have been obliged to file them away so much above, to remedy the evil I have been complaining of as to render them useless perhaps to receive new teeth. But of this you are better able to judge than I am. If you can fix the teeth (now on the new bars which you have) on the old bars which you will receive with this letter I should prefer it, because the latter are easy in the Mouth. And you will perceive moreover that when the edges of the upper and lower teeth are put together that the upper falls back into the mouth, which they ought to do, or it will have the effect of forcing the lip out just under the nose.

I shall only repeat again, that I feel much obliged by your extreme willingness, and readiness to accomodate me and that I am, etc.

On returning home, Washington became the Virginia farmer again, but never quite completely, for there was always a stream of letters about Army business passing to and fro. Occasionally personal and military business became intermixed, as in the matter of his grandson George Washington Parke Custis. The previous September Washington had decided that it would be a waste of time to send the young man off to college; now he wrote to David Stuart, young Custis's stepfather, to propose the Army as a place where the lackadaisical youth might find some purpose in life.

Mount Vernon 30th. Decr. 1798.

Company, ever since my return home, has prevented my mentioning a matter before, which will be the subject of this letter now.

When the applications for Military appointments come to be examined at Philadelphia, it was pleasing to find among them, so many Gentlemen of family, fortune & high expectations, soliciting Commissions; & not in the high grades.

This, and a thorough conviction that it was a vain attempt to keep Washington Custis to any literary pursuits, either in a public Siminary, or at home under the direction of any one, gave me the first idea of bringing him forward as a Cornet of Horse. To this measure too I was induced by a conviction paramount in my breast, that if real danger threatened the Country, no young Man ought to be an idle Spectator of its defence; and that, if a state of preparation would avert the evil of an Invasion, he would be entitled to the merit of proffered service, without encountering the dangers of War: and besides, that it might divert his attention from a matrimonial pursuit (for a while at least) to which his constitution seems to be too prone.

But, though actuated by these ideas, I intended to proceed no farther in the business than to provide a vacancy in one of the Troops of light Dragoons, & to consult Mrs. Stuart & his Grandmother as to their inclinations respecting his filling it, before any intimation of it should be given to him: But, Mr. Lear hearing the matter talked of, and not knowing that this was the ground on which I meant to place the appointment (if the arrangement met the Presidents approbation) wrote to Washington on the Subject, in order to know if it would be agreeable to him, or not, to receive it.

Under these circumstances (and his appearing highly delighted) concealment—I mean an attempt at it—would have proved nugatory. He stands arranged therefore a Cornet in the Troop to be Commanded by Lawrence Lewis [Washington's nephew] (who I intended as his Mentor)—Lawrence Washington junr. (of Chotanck) is the Lieutenant of the Troop. But all this it will be remembered is to be approved—first by the President, & consented to by the Senate to make it a valid act; & therefore, the less it is *publicly* talked of the better.

Mrs. Washington does not seem to have the least objection to his acceptance of the Commission; but it rests with Mrs. Stuart to express her Sentiments thereon, and soon; as I requested the Secretary of War to forward the Commissions for *this* Troop of Light Dragoons, under cover to me.

The only hesitation I had, to induce the caution before mentioned, arose from his being an only Son; indeed the only male of his Great great Grandfathers family; but the same Providence that wd. watch over & protect him in domestic walks, can extend the same protection to him in a Camp, or the field of battle, if he should ever be in one.

Washington's watch, seal, and key, with close-up impression of the seal

Although Washington was in constant correspondence with Hamilton and Secretary of War James McHenry about organizing the Provisional Army, weeks and months passed, and the patriotic zeal of Americans dwindled when there was no actual recruitment. Washington and Hamilton decided between them that the fault lay with McHenry, who fussed endlessly with details, was unable to delegate authority, and never made a firm decision. At last Washington took the problem to McHenry himself.

Mount Vernon 25th. March 1799.

You will not only consider this letter as a *private one*, but as a *friendly one*, from G.W. to J.M. And if the sentiments which you will find in it, are delivered with more freedom and candour than are agreeable, say so; not by implication only, but in explicit language; and I will promise to offend no more by such conduct; but confine myself (if occasion should require it) to an Official Correspondence.

Thus premising, let me, in the name and behalf of the Officers who have been appointed, and of the army intended to be raised, ask what keeps back the Commissions; and arrests the Recruiting Service?

Be assured that *both*, among the friends of Government, excite astonishment and discontent. Blame is in every Mind, but it is not known where to fix it. Some attach it to the P. [President]—some to the S. of W. [Secretary of War]—and some, *fertile in invention*, seek for other causes. Many of the appointed Officers have quitd. their former occupations, that they might be in perfect readiness to proceed in their Military duties the moment they should receive their Commissions & Recruiting Instructions. Others, who were about to enter into business, and plans of future life, stand suspended. Many are highly disgusted; some talk of giving up the idea of becoming Officers, unable to remain longer in the aukward situation they are involved; and *all* are complaining. Applications are made by numbers to me, to know what the cause of the delay is, what they are to expect, and what they ought to do. What could I say? Am I not kept in as much ignorance as they are themselves? Am I advised of any new appointments? any changes which have taken place? any of the views or designs of Government relatively to the Army? It is not unreasonable to suppose, that if there be reasons of State, operating the policy of these delays, that I was entitled to sufficient confidence to be let into the secret; or, if they proceeded from uncontroulable causes, *I*, still more than

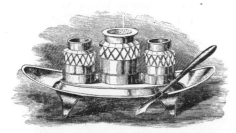

Inkstand used by Washington for his always voluminous correspondence
BOTH: *Mount Vernon*, LOSSING, 1883

the *Public*, ought not to have been left in the field of Conjecture, without a guide to direct me to the knowledge of them....

... The zeal, enthusiasm, and indeed resentments, which warmed the breasts of the American youth, and would have induced the sons of the respectable Yeomanry (in all parts of the United States) to have enlisted as non-commissioned officers & Privates, is now no more; they are evaporated, & a listlessness has supplied its place. The next, most favourable opportunity—namely—the idle, & dreary scenes of winter which bring on dissipation & want, from the cessation of labour, has also passed away! The enlivening prospect of Spring, the calls of the Husbandman, indeed of every avocation, for labourers in the approaching busy season, hath supplanted all thoughts of becoming Soldiers; and *now*, many young Gentlemen who had (conditionally) last Summer & Autumn, engaged their Companies, will find it difficult to enlist a *single man* of those so engaged—The latter Pretending, that having waited a considerable time to see if their services would be wanted in the Field, and no overtures for them made it became necessary for them to seek some other employment.

What is the natural consequence of all this? Why, that we must take the Rif-raf of the populous Cities; Convicts; & foreigners: or, have Officers without men. But even this is not the worst of it. The Augmented Corps (if I have conceived the matter rightly) must have been intended as a well organized, and well disciplined body of Men, for others (in case of need) to resort to, & take example from. Will this be the case if the enemy should invade this Country? Far from it! What better, in the first instance, are Regiments so composed than Militia? And what prospect have those who Command them, of rendering Service to their Country, or doing honor to themselves in the Field, opposed to Veteran Troops, practiced in Tactics, and unaccustomed to defeat? These, my dear McHenry, are serious considerations to a Man who has nothing to gain, and is putting every thing to a hazard....

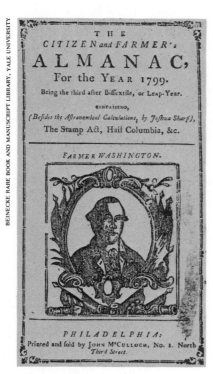

In the year of Washington's death he was labeled "Farmer Washington" on the cover of a farmer's almanac

Washington continued at length. He complained of the unfairness of the system of appointing officers, citing the case of one man strongly recommended by four generals and with a record of excellent service throughout the Revolution whose application for a commission was denied by "the Veto of a Member of Congress." Conversely, he told of an officer scarcely more than a boy who had been promoted over men older and better qualified. Washington's stance of objectivity and his indignation over outside influences in officer selection were forgotten briefly as he inquired, "... may I ask if there would be any impropriety in letting Mr. Custis step from a Cornetcy into the rank of Lieutenant? ... If ample fortune, good Education, more than common abilities, and good dispositions, free from Vice of any kind, give him a title, in the 19th. year of age, his pretensions thereto (though not to the injury of another) are good." Could this young paragon be the same grandson of whose indolence and lack of purpose Washington had often complained, the same who was taken out of college because he was learning nothing? But at last Washington reached the most delicate part of his letter. Although he tried to be gentle, it was not easy to tell a man that he was badly mishandling his job.

> ... There is one matter more, which I was in doubt whether to mention to you, or not, because it is of a more delicate nature than any I have touched upon; but finally, friendship have got the better of my scruples.
>
> It respects yourself *personally*. Whilst I was in Philadelphia—and after the Members of Congress had begun to Assemble, it was hinted to me, in pretty *strong terms* by more than one of them, that the Department of War would not—nay could not—be conducted to advantage (if War should ensue) under your auspices; for instead of attending to the *great* out lines, and *principles* of your office, & keeping the subordinate Officers of the Department rigidly to their respective duties, *they*, were inattentive, while *you*, were bewildered with trifles. You will recollect, I dare say, that more than once, I expressed to you my opinion of the expediency of committing the *Details* of the Department to the execution of others; and to bestow your thoughts and attention to the more important Duties of it; which, in the scenes we were contemplating, were alone sufficient to occupy the time, and all the consideration of the Secretary. I went no farther *then*, nor should I have renewed the subject *now*, had not the delay in issuing of the Commissions, and commencing the Recruiting service, excited general reprobation, and blame, though, as I have observed before, no one knows where, with precision, to fix it. Generally however, it is attributed to the want of System, & exertion in the Department of War. To apprise you of this, is my motive for this communication.

I prefaced the sentiments of this letter with a request, that they might be considered as proceeding from a private man to his friend. No one would be struck more forcibly than myself, with the impropriety of such a letter from the Commander in Chief of the Army of the U. States to the Secretary of War. If they are received in good part, the end is obtained. If otherwise, my motives, & the purity of my intentions, is the best apology I can offer for the liberty I have taken. In either case however, be assured of this truth, that with very great esteem and regard, I remain &c.

Washington's letter infused no new energy into McHenry. Recruiting continued to lag; the public had lost most of its patriotic ardor—and besides, the superiority of the British fleet made it extremely unlikely that any French armies would invade the United States. Only three thousand men were enlisted in the Regular Army, and the fifty-thousand-man Provisional Army never got beyond the paper stage. At sea the picture was considerably different. In the spring and early summer of 1798, Congress had created a Navy Department, authorized enlargement of the tiny three-frigate Navy, commissioned privateers, and ordered the Navy to capture all armed French vessels—virtually all merchant ships were armed. In the quasi war that followed, most action was by privateers, for the French navy was too busy in Europe to spare more than a few warships for American waters. American vessels were overwhelmingly successful, both in privateering enterprises and in the few encounters between naval vessels. American ships captured some ninety French vessels, the French took one American. The undeclared war ended somewhat inconclusively in the autumn of 1800.

Much of that, however, still lay in the future. At Mount Vernon, Washington continued to spend hours in the saddle checking on the affairs of the several farms of the plantation. His plan to rent out the dependent farms to tenants had come to nothing: no one he had considered qualified had applied. As always, he was surrounded by a sea of troubles. A duplex house he was building for rental in the city of Washington was costing more and taking longer than it should have. He was having difficulty re-establishing one of his boundary lines and was certain an effort was being made to cheat him out of a good many acres rightfully his. He attempted to collect debts long overdue, and his shortage of money became so acute that for the first time in his life he made a loan from a bank—and had to ask how to go about it. And he was upset at learning that President Adams was sending another envoy to France on reports that the French Government might at last be inclined to make peace.

Yet the entries in his diary, brief as they were, indicate that the spirit of Mount Vernon had not changed; it was a house always open to people, always ready to welcome guests, whether old friends or virtual strangers. November, 1799, was the last full month in the diary.

1 [November, 1799]. ... Mr. Craik went away after Breakfast....

2. ... Mr. Jno. Fairfax (formerly an overseer of mine) came here before dinner and stayed all Night.

3. ... Mr. Valangin came to dinner.

4. ... A Mr. Teakle from Accomack County dined here & returned as did Doctr. Craik. Mr. Lear returned from Berkeley....

5. ... Set out on a trip to Difficult-run to view some Land I had there & some belonging to Mr. Jno. Gill who had offered it to me in discharge of Rent which he was owing me. Dined at Mr. Nicholas Fitzhughs and lodged at Mr. Corbin Washingtons.

6. Set out from thence after 8 Oclk. being detained by sprinkling Rain, & much appearance of it until that hour. Reached Wiley's Tavern near Difficult Bridge to Breakfast and then proceeded to Survey my own Land—the day clearing & the weather becoming pleasant.

7. Weather remarkably fine. Finished Surveying my own Tract & the Land belonging to Gill—returning, as the Night before to Wileys Tavern.

8. Morning very heavy and about 9 oclock it commenced Raining which it continued to do steadily through the day—notwithstanding which I proceed[ed] to ascertain by actual measurement the qualities. This being finished betwn. 12 & 1 oclock I returned to Wiley's Tavern and stayed there the remainder of the day.

9. Morning & the whole day clear warm & pleasant. Set out a little after 8 Oclock. Viewed my building in the Fedl. City. Dined at Mr. Laws & lodged at Mr. Thos. Peter's.

10. ... Returned home about Noon. Mr. Law, Mr. Barry Mr. White & Doctr. Thornton came to Dinner & stayed all Night....

11. ... The Gentlemen above mentioned went away after breakft....

14. ... Mr. Valangen came to dinner & stayed all night.

15. ... Rode to visit Mr. now Lord Fairfax who was just got home from a Trip to England. Retd. to dinner.

16. ... Doctr. Craik came here in the afternoon on a

A check payable to William Thornton, the architect of the Capitol, was signed by Washington less than a month before his death.

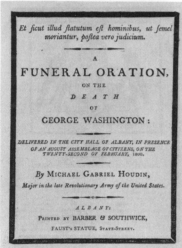

Et ficut illud ftatutum eft hominibus, ut femel moriantur, poftea vero judicium.

A

FUNERAL ORATION,

ON THE

D E A T H

OF

GEORGE WASHINGTON:

DELIVERED IN THE CITY HALL OF ALBANY, IN PRESENCE OF AN AUGUST ASSEMBLAGE OF CITIZENS, ON THE TWENTY-SECOND OF FEBRUARY, 1800.

BY MICHAEL GABRIEL HOUDIN,

Major in the late Revolutionary Army of the United States.

ALBANY:

PRINTED BY BARBER & SOUTHWICK,

FAUST'S STATUE, STATE-STREET.

visit to sick people.

17. ... Went to Church in Alexandria & dined with Mr. Fitzhugh. On my return fd. young Mr. McCarty here on his way back from the Federal City. Young McCarty came to Dinr. ...

20. ... Mr. McCarty went away after breakfast and Mrs. Summers—Midwife for Mrs. Lewis [Martha's grand-daughter Eleanor (Nelly) had married Washington's nephew Laurence Lewis] came here abt. 3 oclk.

21. ... Mrs. Stuart and the two eldest Miss Stuarts came here to dinner.

22. ... Colo. Carrington & Lady came in the afternn.

23. ... Colo. Carrington & Lady went away after Break-fast. Doctr. Craik came to dinner & Doctr. Stuart at Night. ...

25. ... Doctr. Craik & Doctr. Stuart both went away after Breakfast. ...

27. ... Doctr. Craik who was sent for to Mrs. Lewis (& who was delivered of a daughter abt. [ ] oclock in the forenoon) came to Breakfast & stayed [to] dinner. Mr. Dublois dined here, and both went away afterwards.

28. ... Colo. & Mrs. Carrington came to Dinner.

29. ... Young D. McCarty came to dinner and Mr. Howell Lewis & wife after dinner.

30. ... Colo. & Mrs. Carrington went away after B[reakfas]t.

Washington's diary continued only through December 13. On December 12 he recorded that snow began to fall about ten o'clock in the morning, soon changing to hail, and then settling down to a cold rain. The next day there was about three inches of snow on the ground; the snow ended early in the afternoon, the sky cleared, and by night the mercury was at 28 degrees. These were probably the last words Washington ever wrote.

On December 12 Washington made his usual horseback ride around the plantation. Before he returned he had been exposed for five hours to the snow, hail, and rain that he had recorded in his diary. When he returned home, Tobias Lear mentioned that his hair and neck were wet, but Washington answered that his great coat had kept him otherwise dry. The next day a sore throat and the falling snow made him decide to remain indoors, and as the day progressed he became somewhat hoarse, although not enough to prevent him from reading aloud from the newspapers in the evening. Sometime after midnight he woke Martha to tell her he was ill, with a throat so excruciatingly sore he could hardly speak and breathed with difficulty, but he would not let her get up in the cold room. At sunrise a servant was sent to call Tobias Lear and an overseer, who Washington wished should bleed him at once.

As soon as the overseer arrived, Washington insisted that he open a vein, and about half a pint of blood was taken. About nine o'clock James Craik, the family doctor, arrived, and after diagnosing the ailment as inflammatory quinsy, bled the patient again and tried various remedies, including blistering his throat to draw the inflammation to the surface. When none of these measures appeared to help, Craik did yet another bleeding, and when the first of two doctors who had been called for consultation arrived, he and Craik opened a vein for the fourth time. Through it all, Washington did not once complain, although he was in constant pain. In the afternoon he spoke to the doctors, thanking them for their attention, and saying that they had better not trouble themselves "but let me go off quietly; I cannot last long."

There were still a few hours left to him that day, December 14, and through them Washington remained completely clear of mind. About ten o'clock at night Lear saw that Washington wanted to speak, and leaned close to hear the low voice. "I am just going. Have me decently buried, and do not let my body be put into the vault in less than two days after I am dead." Lear nodded, but Washington, insistent, asked, "Do you understand me?" "Yes, sir," said Lear. "'Tis well," said Washington. Lear remained holding Washington's hand, but not many minutes later the hand was suddenly withdrawn, and there was a change in the face on the pillow. Lear called to Dr. Craik, who stepped to the bedside and saw in a moment that the last campaign was over.

A rare engraving of Washington appeared as the frontispiece to a funeral oration by a French army officer (opposite); later he was apotheosized in paintings such as the highly romantic version done on glass at left and in innumerable mourning prints (above).

407

Selected Bibliography

Alden, John R. *The American Revolution, 1775–1783.* New York: Harper & Row, 1962.

Bowers, Claude G. *Jefferson and Hamilton: The Struggle for Democracy in America.* Boston: Houghton Mifflin, 1925.

Bryan, William A. *George Washington in American Literature, 1775–1865.* New York: Columbia University Press, 1952.

Cook, Roy Bird. *Washington's Western Lands.* Strassburg, Va.: Shenandoah, 1930.

Cunliffe, Marcus. *George Washington, Man and Monument.* Boston: Little, Brown, 1958.

De Conde, Alexander. *Entangling Alliance: Politics and Diplomacy under George Washington.* Durham: Duke University Press, 1958.

Fitzpatrick, John C. *George Washington, Colonial Traveller, 1732–1775.* Indianapolis: Bobbs-Merrill, 1927.

Flexner, James Thomas. *George Washington: The Forge of Experience, 1732–1775.* Boston: Little, Brown, 1965.

————. *George Washington in the American Revolution, 1775–1783.* Boston: Little, Brown, 1968.

————. *George Washington and the New Nation, 1783–1793.* Boston: Little, Brown, 1970.

————. *George Washington: Anguish and Farewell, 1793–1799.* Boston: Little, Brown, 1972.

Ford, Paul Leicester. *George Washington.* Philadelphia: Lippincott, 1924.

Freeman, Douglas Southall. *George Washington.* 7 vols. New York: Charles Scribner's Sons, 1948–57. (Vol. 7 by John A. Carroll and Mary W. Ashworth.)

Irving, Washington. *Life of George Washington.* 5 vols. New York: G. P. Putnam, 1855–59.

Isely, Bliss. *The Horseman of the Shenandoah: A Biographical Account of the Early Days of George Washington.* Milwaukee: Bruce, 1962.

Knollenberg, Bernhard. *George Washington, the Virginia Period, 1732–1775.* Durham: Duke University Press, 1964.

————. *Washington and the Revolution, a Reappraisal: Gates, Conway, and the Continental Congress.* New York: Macmillan, 1940.

Marshall, John. *The Life of George Washington.* 5 vols. Philadelphia: C. P. Wayne, 1804–7.

Nettels, Curtis P. *George Washington and American Independence.* Boston: Little, Brown, 1951.

Rossiter, Clinton L. *1787: The Grand Convention.* New York: Macmillan, 1966.

Sears, Louis M. *George Washington and the French Revolution.* Detroit: Wayne State University Press, 1960.

Stetson, Charles W. *Washington and His Neighbors.* Richmond: Garrett and Massie, 1956.

Tebbel, John W. *George Washington's America.* New York: E. P. Dutton, 1954.

Thane, Elswyth. *Potomac Squire.* New York: Duell, Sloan and Pearce, 1963.

Washington, George. *Diaries, 1748–1799.* Edited by John C. Fitzpatrick. 4 vols. Boston: Houghton Mifflin, 1925.

————. *The Writings of George Washington.* Edited by Jared Sparks. 12 vols. Boston: American Stationers' Co.: 1834–37.

———— *The Writings of George Washington from the Original Manuscript Sources, 1745–1799.* Edited by John C. Fitzpatrick. 39 vols. Washington: U.S. Government Printing Office, 1931–44.

White, Leonard D. *The Federalists: A Study in Administrative History.* New York: Macmillan, 1948.

Whiteley, Emily Stone. *Washington and his Aides-de-Camp.* New York: Macmillan, 1936.

Wilson, Woodrow. *George Washington.* New York: Harper, 1896.

Acknowledgments

Unless otherwise specifically credited below, all documents reproduced in this volume are from George Washington Papers, Library of Congress, Washington, D.C., the greatest collection of Washington documents in existence. In addition the Editors would like to thank the following individuals and institutions for permission to reprint documents in their possession:

Alexander Hamilton Papers, Library of Congress, Washington, D.C., page 284
Detroit Public Library, Detroit, Mich., pages 304-09
Free Public Library, Trenton, N.J., page 298 (top)
Harvard University, Cambridge, Mass., pages 66-67
Henry E. Huntington Library and Art Gallery, San Marino, Calif., pages 169 (center), 314-15 (top), and 376-77 (top)
Historical Society of Pennsylvania, Philadelphia, pages 76 (bottom)-77 (top), and 79 (bottom)-80 (top)
John Carter Brown Library, Brown University, Providence, R.I., pages 118 (bottom)-119, and 120-21 (top)
Massachusetts Historical Society, Boston, pages 118 (top) and 293 (top)
Mount Vernon Ladies' Association of the Union, Mount Vernon, Va., pages 69 (top), 105 (bottom), 186 (top), 375, and 399 (bottom)-400
National Archives, Washington, D.C.
  Miscellaneous Papers, pages 338, 349, and 350-51
  Papers of the Continental Congress, pages 101 (bottom)-102 (top), 116 (bottom)-117, 121 (bottom)-122 (top), 148 (center), 149 (bottom)-150, 154-56 (top), 156 (bottom)-158 (top), 158 (bottom)-159 (top), 170 (bottom)-172, 173 (bottom)-174 (top), 175 (bottom)-176, 189 (bottom)-190 (top), and 204 (bottom)-205 (top)
New York Public Library, New York, N.Y., pages 393 (bottom)-394
Old South Association in Boston, Boston, Mass., pages 398 (bottom)-399 (top)
Pierpont Morgan Library, New York, N.Y., pages 324-25 (top) and 357-58 (top)
Thomas Jefferson Papers, Library of Congress, Washington, D.C., pages 353 (bottom)-354 (top)
University of Virginia, Charlottesville, page 28 (bottom)
Virginia Historical Society, Richmond, pages 43 (bottom)-46 (top), 60 (bottom)-62 (top), 317-18, 319, 320-21 (top), and 321 (bottom)-322
Wadsworth Atheneum, Hartford, Conn., page 126

The Editors also make grateful acknowledgment for the use of documents from the following works:

Custis, George Washington Parke. *Recollections and Private Memoirs of Washington by his Adopted Son.* New York, 1860. Page 385 (center)
Fitzpatrick, John C., ed. *The Writings of George Washington.* Washington, D.C., 1931-44. Pages 41 (bottom)-43 (top), 46 (center)-48 (top), 49-50 (top), 114 (bottom)-115 (top), 168 (bottom)-169 (top), 209-10 (top), 259, 364-65, 367 (bottom)-369 (top), 369 (bottom)-370, 377 (bottom)-378 (top), and 383 (bottom)-385 (top)
Ford, Worthington Chauncey, ed. *The Writings of George Washington.* New York, 1889. Pages 80 (bottom)-81 (top) and 97 (bottom)-98 (top)
Freeman, Douglas Southall. *George Washington,* vol. III. New York, 1948-57. Pages 102 (bottom)-104 (top)
*Letters and Recollections of George Washington...*London, 1906. Page 398 (top)
National Intelligencer. 22 October 1862. Pages 159 (bottom)-162 (top) and 166 (bottom)-168 (top)
Reed, William B. *Life and Correspondence of Joseph Reed.* Philadelphia, 1847. Pages 122 (bottom)-124 (top)
Richardson, James D., ed. *A Compilation of the Messages and Papers of the Presidents.* vol. I Washington, 1913. Pages 348 (bottom)-349 (top)

Sparks, Jared, ed. *Writings of George Washington*. Boston, 1836. Page 295 (top)
The Debates and Proceedings in the Congress of the United States; with an Appendix, Containing Important State Papers and Public Documents, and All the Laws of a Public Nature. Washington, 1849. Pages 354 (bottom)-355 (top)
The Journal of Major George Washington, Sent by the Hon. Robert Dinwiddie, Esq.: His Majesty's Lieutenant Governor, and Commander in Chief of Virginia to the Commandant of the French Forces on Ohio . . . Williamsburg, 1754. Pages 30-40

The Editors also wish to express their appreciation of the many institutions and individuals who made available their pictorial material for use in this volume. In particular the Editors are grateful to:

Mount Vernon Ladies' Association of the Union—Charles C. Wall, Resident Director; Christine Meadows, John Castellani
The Papers of George Washington, University of Virginia, Charlottesville—Donald Jackson, Editor; Dorothy Twohig
Beinecke Rare Book and Manuscript Library, Yale University, New Haven, Conn.
Boston Athenaeum, Boston, Mass.
Anne S. K. Brown Military Collection, Brown University, Providence, R.I.
Richard Storrs Childs, Norfolk, Conn.
Connecticut Historical Society, Hartford
Historical Society of Pennsylvania, Philadelphia
Independence National Historical Park Collection, Philadelphia, Pa.
Lewis Walpole Library, Farmington, Conn.
Library of Congress, Washington, D.C.—Mrs. Carolyn H. Sung
Metropolitan Museum of Art, New York, N.Y.
Museum of Fine Arts, Boston, Mass.
National Broadcasting Company, New York, N.Y.—Daniel W. Jones, Jr.
National Gallery of Art, Washington, D.C.
New Haven Colony Historical Society, New Haven, Conn.
New-York Historical Society, New York, N.Y.
New York Public Library, New York, N.Y.
Valley Forge Historical Society, Valley Forge, Pa.
Washington and Lee University, Lexington, Va.
Henry Francis du Pont Winterthur Museum, Wilmington, Dela.
Yale University Art Gallery, New Haven, Conn.

Finally the Editors thank Susan Storer in New York for assistance in obtaining pictorial material; Sylvia J. Abrams in Washington for copyediting and proofreading; and Mary-Jo Kline in New York for compiling the chronology and bibliography.

Index

Boldface indicates pages on which illustrations appear.

When
leizure (if th
will give you
of this quarte
my view & rec
I shall certain
of you, that
join very since
your health,
—and that Ia
ticrote esteem
&

Colo Humphrey,